this is POP

In Search of the Elusive at Experience Music Project

EDITED BY ERIC WEISBARD

Harvard University Press
Cambridge, Massachusetts
London, England
2004

Printed in the United States of America

LIBRARY OF CONGRESS CATALOGING-IN-PUBLICATION DATA

This is pop : in search of the elusive at Experience Music Project / edited by
Eric Weisbard.
   p. cm.
   Includes bibliographical references and index.
   ISBN 0-674-01321-2 (cloth : alk. paper)
   ISBN 0-674-01344-1 (pbk. : alk. paper)
   1. Popular music—History and criticism.
   I. Weisbard, Eric.   II. Experience Music Project.
ML3470.T48 2004
781.64—dc22   2003068816

Contents

II. Authorship

III. Values

Introduction: Who'll Write the Book of Love? Pop Music and Pop Prose

ERIC WEISBARD

This book first took shape in Seattle at Experience Music Project's in-augural Pop Conference, held in April 2002. As a popular music museum, a relatively new but growing category, Experience Music Project (EMP) is a hybrid institution: a tourist attraction with scholarly ambitions; a site for both artifact collections and performances by contemporary bands; an avant-garde building meant to encourage the musical participation of visitors who have no prior expertise.[1] Any conference held at EMP needed to be equally polyglot. Our hope was to build on earlier meldings of the academic, critical, musical, and literary, but to make such professional border crossings a regular event—and a way to promote work that combined the best aspects of scholarship, criticism, and pop's inherent unruliness.[2]

Also, the time felt right to revisit the terms and assumptions of pop music writing. The music itself has never seemed so impressively diverse and frustratingly hard to encompass: a dizzying range of genres, rooted in local impulses but reaching global audiences. Undergrounds flourish in number, if not in impact. Rock has ceded its throne, and arguably only hip-hop retains the ideological fanship that produced, for example, the "disco sucks" backlash. Popular music remains commercial culture's most egalitarian art form, open to aspirants and fans from every conceivable background.

How does one approach such a vast matrix? Increasing numbers of academics are trying, and they fall into genres too: musicologists and ethnomusicologists, sociologists and cultural studies types, literature scholars and historians. Critics and journalists work on different terms: often accused of overvaluing lyrics, they mostly respond to the music's evolving nature piece by piece, trying to semiologically decipher the tale as it unfolds. When musicians—or writers with literary backgrounds—dip in, the results can be startling for their immunity to established discourse. Rather than sift fields, or suggest a synthesis, this book is intended to suggest the breadth of an ongoing inquiry whose practitioners often seem barely aware of each other.

So: no one big story but a myriad of knots to untangle. Consider, for example, a band as relatively obscure and enigmatic as Book of Love. When their first album came out, in 1986, they were new wavers arrived late and on the wrong side of the Atlantic, a quartet of three women and one man, all just out of art school and quickly aligned with the postdisco, postpunk New York club scene. They had a minor hit called "Boy," about a woman not allowed into an all-male gay disco. I once saw them play in San Francisco, unflappably batting around a beach ball as the machines did all the work. After four albums of music that ranged from a cover of the Swiss punks Liliput to "Tubular Bells," Mike Oldfield's prog-rock antithesis of punk, they broke up in 1993, synth-poppers with an expansive aesthetic out of place in a rock moment fixated on grunge and a house and techno dance scene.

There's a Book of Love best-of, *I Touch Roses,* put out by Reprise in 2001 to virtually no public notice, though a remix of "Boy" topped the *Billboard* dance charts. Singer Susan Ottaviano and songwriter Ted Ottaviano, it was now stated publicly, were gay. With hopes of reforming, Book of Love remained stuck for a category to shelter under: not as transgressive as the Pet Shop Boys; neither disco nor doomy enough to catch on with a subculture; studio auteurs enchanted by beautiful artificiality, driven to live on the barbed edge of lyrical cliché. Good luck. Still, Book of Love's music hasn't dated a bit. When critic Sasha Frere-Jones recently sent me an eighteen-CD overview (!) of the sounds of 2002, "Boy" was on a disc of older songs that had become newly relevant, no doubt because a scene of synthy bands had lately sprung up calling themselves "electroclash."

What would it mean to look at pop from the perspective of a Book of Love? To a critic, they're one more interesting band among the thousands that have sprung up over the years. It is a job and a pleasure to absorb the quirks of each of them. But the process makes it very hard to generalize about pop at all. One can always think of an exception, to the point that escaping categories starts to seem like the music's most compelling feat—and any attempt to structure an interpretation the work of humorless pedants. Musicians make fun of critics; critics make fun of academics; academics raise an eyebrow in a discreet footnote at everybody else's pretensions to "authenticity." Quite the muddle.

Book of Love didn't seem to sweat their authenticity; we might start there. They aligned themselves with synthesizers against guitars, with a new wave whose commercialized production came off, to those who could decipher it, as a stylized rejoinder to punk's equally stylized belligerence or to blue-collar rock. The vibe of this period is probably caught best in Paul Morley's *Ask: The Chatter of Pop,* also released in 1986, a strange book of ersatz interviews with new wave, punk, and rock figures. Morley, a British journalist who'd gone on to be the impresario behind Frankie Goes to Hollywood, saw pop as Andy Warhol or a U.K. art school graduate might have: undergrounds and overgrounds blurring in a dandyish haze. His tone is fin de siècle, years too soon: "I go to America with my head pricking and crackling with the pop of Japan, ABC, Human League (pricking and cracking me as much as, oh, Rauschenberg, Tom Lehrer, Steve

Lacey and Dennis Potter). I come back with my head loaded with the rolling rocks of Tom Petty, Bruce Springsteen, Foreigner, Styx and Meatloaf. The bubbly pop tickles noses, colors tongues, shifts values and values shifts: the rolling rocks literally demolish or dictate people's lives. Rock and roll American reality has reached hysteria. All it's faced with is the CRASH!"[3] Even so, it seems now that Morley correctly sensed the end approaching for a kind of Anglo-American pop-rock alliance that had stretched from the Beatles to Wham.

Academics in 1986 hardly read Morley, I suspect; they "read" Madonna, who had already begun putting forth a vision of pop that didn't worry about Warhol, the Velvet Underground, Bowie, or Dylan—disco, queerness, MTV, and fashion photography were inspirations enough. Book of Love had been signed to Sire by Seymour Stein, the man who signed Madonna, and they shared her sense of dance music as Catholic ritual. Yet their identities were ultimately so different, the global icon and the subcultural worshippers of icons, that they seemed to exist in wholly different musical categories. Are sounds the essence of pop, or is it simply being played on the radio that gets you there? What role can exist within the music for art movement–style theorizing, or for work whose impact registers one person at a time, rather than in any truly social way?

There are many different definitions of pop. Stuff that moves units. Stuff that's catchy. Shorthand for anything within popular music now that rock or even rock and roll feels like too restrictive an umbrella category. I'd start with a different emphasis. Pop, it can be argued, is music that crosses over, that has qualities that reach beyond the context in which the sounds originated. When downtown classicists Kronos Quartet or Bang on a Can embrace rock, it registers as a pop move. When a Top 40 band of no particular distinction are taken into fans' hearts, their songs or image transformed in ways only partially in the music, that's a pop process. Book of Love sold precious few records. But the ambiguities surrounding who they were and what they intended are quintessentially pop.[4]

In calling the gathering held at Experience Music Project a Pop

Conference, we wanted to urge a crossover of a different kind. In recent years, academics have begun studying popular music in ever-increasing numbers. To frame my Book of Love questions, I might read Paul Theberge's confident study *Any Sound You Can Imagine: Making Music / Consuming Technology*, a cultural-studies look at the synthesizer, or philosophy professor Bernard Gendron's *Between Montmartre and the Mudd Club: Popular Music and the Avant-Garde*, its subject how the gap between popular music and high art was narrowed by bohemia, dissolving in spaces like New York's new wave Mudd Club, which "institutionalized borderline aesthetics."[5] (Ted Ottaviano played there as a School of Visual Arts student, with his first band, Head Cheese.) I could have attended a 2003 conference, organized by grad students at New York University, devoted exclusively to 1980s pop.

Yet it's still doubtful that many academics are reading Paul Morley or finding ways of incorporating a response to bands like Book of Love into their work. While the International Association for the Study of Popular Music (IASPM) was founded in the new wave early '80s with the intent of including nonacademics, over time that mandate has faded, leaving no place for rock critics, *Granta* essayists, autodidacts, and musicians as literate as Brian Eno or Nile Rodgers. Inevitably, as a price of this exclusion, few outside of the academy, including music writers passionate about keeping up with everything under the sun, have noticed the last decade's explosion in popular music literature.

This book illustrates what happens when you design the doors to revolve. Within these pages you can read Robert Christgau and Gary Giddins, pivotal critics, alongside Frith and Robert Walser, pioneers in the sociological and musicological study of popular music. Luc Sante and Geoffrey O'Brien write about sound with the same prose elegance they apply to noir or New York street life. Musicians Carrie Brownstein and Sarah Dougher, both active in the riot grrrl and rock scenes of the Pacific Northwest, examine as working artists how different audiences respond and how that affects their craft and calling. John Darnielle, of the Mountain Goats and the idiosyncratic zine *Last Plane to Jakarta*, allots much of his space to the Web postings of hair metal fans, trying to bring his sensibility to bear on theirs.

This range of perspectives is vital because the sphere of meanings that "pop" can occupy has grown vastly larger over the past two decades. Book of Love began releasing albums in 1986, at the onset of an era that saw the pop sphere defined by Anglo-American rock begin to dissolve. CDs replaced vinyl on the way to downloadable MP3s, upending the central rituals of consumption. Hip-hop, "new country," teen pop, Latin music, electronica, and a host of other genres jostled with rock, itself fragmented into alternative, metal, AAA (adult album alternative), and so on. It became impossible for a so-called Top 40 station to play all the types of hits, let alone for an outside observer to define just one as the essence of commercially popular music. Reissues kept the music of the past eternally present. Indie labels produced tens of thousands of albums each year. It seems old-fashioned now to think in baby boomer terms of a counterculture, or even in punk terms of subcultures and movements. At this point, all pop is what academics are fond of calling "glocal": a globally connected range of competing styles and icons filtered through localized experience and personal proclivity.

The globalization of pop, the destruction of the boomer rock and roll mythic narrative into a thousand shards—these are developments that academics have conceptualized and responded to far more capably than music journalists. This makes sense, given the networks that academics have to draw on: journals that publish an international collection of writers, conferences like IASPM's biennial convocation. The collection *Global Noise*, edited by Australian Tony Mitchell, traces rap scenes across multiple continents.[6] The catch-all anthology *Popular Music Studies*, meant to sum up the surging state of the academic field, culminates with a fine essay by Israeli sociologist Motti Regev, "The 'Pop-Rockization' of Popular Music." Regev looks at the hybrid form he calls "pop/rock" as a product of modernity, springing from the last half-century's "constant growth in the number and sophistication of actors in the market of collective identities."[7] Himself included.

Music critics, by contrast, cultivate their record collections the way academics do their bibliographies. Here too there are structural reasons: promo copies and the duty of reviewing. Recall my writer friend Sasha's eighteen-CD collection of 2002's music. His idea of "pop songs" includes MTV fodder, college rock, *rock en español*, Brazilian tropicalia, singer-songwriters, and a bit of country, plus two CDs of instrumental electronica and five CDs of hip-hop. The year's biggest trend, appropriately, was "mashups": two songs, usually from different genres, shoved together illegally by a home remixer and released on the Internet—the flagship statement of pop hybridity. It all adds up to about twenty-four hours of music, or 365 tracks, a golden day assembled one song du jour at a time that throws down the gauntlet for anyone tempted to generalize about pop.

Is it a worthier project to sketch out the broad flow of music or to train oneself to hear as much as possible within its echoes and permutations? The Pop Conference's double keynote featured Simon Frith and Robert Christgau speaking on the subject of American exceptionalism in music. Though Frith is a great critic when he chooses to be, and Christgau reads academic studies as much as any working journalist, their approaches suggest a typical academic / critic dichotomy. Frith's essay riffs precisely on the structural nature of music past and present, asserting with some glee that American pop is no longer globally dominant. Christgau contentiously flips on his stereo. If that's so, he wants to know, why does hip-hop from outside the U.S. have such derivative beats? Why is there nothing elsewhere like the uber-indie rock band Pavement? And for that matter, why do academics have no time for music as pleasureful and intellectually provocative as Pavement's, or for matters of taste altogether?

It's a division that cuts deeply through this book. Robert Walser, Deena Weinstein, Gayle Wald, David Sanjek, and Jason Toynbee, writing from an academic perspective, want to debunk standing assumptions about the essential nature of rock and pop. They're drawn to putting underappreciated figures like Sister Rosetta Tharpe and Earth, Wind & Fire on the pedestal, while questioning the values that have canonized Bob Marley, that assume that a song concocted for the studio by Merle Travis is as old as the hills, or that blindly hail the rock band as a model of musical populism. In contrast, Simon Reynolds, RJ Smith, Kelefa Sanneh, Chuck Klosterman, and Ann Powers write as critics, itemizing and marveling at, gut response by gut response, the mysteries of pop. Record collecting, the oft-covered R&B ditty "Open the Door, Richard," rap braggadocio, rock hype, and pop mediocrity: all are held up to the light, one example at a time, their pleasures and meaning open questions.

Regardless of approach, those writing at the turn of the twenty-first century confront a fin de siècle more complicated than Paul Morley imagined: mountains of recordings, streams of Web arcana, and forests of period statements about how this or that movement was changing music decisively. Consequently, a sense of breathlessness has gone out of music prose. Gary Giddins here sardonically examines jazz's ever-tormented popular status. Luc Sante's essay on the differing legacies of Mississippi blues for rock and Texas blues for soul, and Geoffrey O'Brien's memoiristic account of how the movie soundtrack quickened over the generations, derive much of their force from how baroquely rich the story has become. There are no unifying theories of pop anymore. Instead, as Julian Dibbell's preliminary stab at an ethos of downloading, Reynolds's record collectors, and Darnielle's take on hair metal fans conclude in different ways, taking possession of a personalized narrative of music history may be emerging as a critical element of listener participation.

What do musicians make of all this? If Dougher, Brownstein, and Tim Quirk's essays are any indication, performers are still likely to be focused on the question of what becomes of their voice and their sense of commitment, given the range of contemporary options. For Brownstein, guitarist in the acclaimed and revered band Sleater-Kinney, playing live affords a chance to escape from the contradictions that come with being a public figure. For Dougher, one of many musicians with ties to academia, finding an authoritative presence in either realm is equally problematic. And for Quirk, who moved from the ultracollegiate major-label band Too Much Joy to the equally sales-challenged Internet economy, crossing over means questioning whether his passion for music has led him to resemble the woman who flashes AC/DC on camera at the big arena show. Somehow, they're both part of the circus.

As these pieces indicate, a key change connected to the swelling ranks of the pop army is that musicians are now often more likely to interact with writers as peers, or co-conspirators, than to be seen as exotic and distant figures. Stephen Burt captures this shift in his essay on recent poetry about rock, which unlike earlier work tends to see musicians as fellow literateurs rather than as pagan gods of mass culture. In contrast, Joshua Clover, one of the poets that Burt cites, writes here from an opposing perspective, prizing above all else the Top 40 as a creature unto itself that captures in toto the ephemera and shifts of modernity. But ultimately Clover's fantasy may be that cultural commentators start to feel the same kinship with the ebbs and flows of commercial pop that they've long since learned to bring to indie rockers who went to the same colleges they did. Daphne Brooks's essay aligns her, despite significant reservations, with post–Civil Rights, post-soul African American artists like Mos Def and Chris Rock, who function as public intellectuals of a kind, satirizing rock's underpinnings on the border of the underground and commerciality.

Pop these days moves in all directions. Crossroads have become its very essence. Can writing about pop capture the same interplay? People who interpret music professionally, either as journalists or academics, are constantly urged to know their place. After questioning one conference participant about why his work on the literature of hip-hop included little of great critics like Greg Tate and Nelson George, I received this e-mailed response:

> There is a tension between popular criticism and academic critical writing that has to do with legitimacy in the eyes of the university and an assumed rigor. When we, from various disciplines, are trying to do academic work in hip-hop while under the skeptical gaze of some of our more traditional colleagues (who may have a say in our tenure progress) there is a sense that we must use "scholarly" articles and arguments as the core of the

syllabus . . . journalism is there for sure, but it has to be brought
in under a rather different context it seems.

I'm sure that if I asked a magazine editor about trying to work with
academics or incorporate their insights, I'd receive an equally dismissive reply, though the explanation might be that the work is inherently uninteresting. ("Do I get two credits for reading it?") The
irony is, to the outside world the notion that either group brings expertise to bear on pop or rock still seems a tad ridiculous. After all,
expertise isn't in the spirit of the music, right? Just look at what you
see on television!

My argument, to academics whose insecurities lead them to
drape themselves in a bland "professionalism" of one kind, and to
journalists cloaked in a slick "professionalism" of another, would actually share something with that of the scoffers. Pop *is* a hybrid, a
category fouler. Its study *should* make university departments and
genteel publications a bit uncomfortable. The thrust should not
only be interdisciplinary but also extradisciplinary and quite possibly antidisciplinary. Pop inquiry's place is not with the expansion of
the professions that produced liberal arts departments and philhar-
monics but with the permeation of youth culture, adult bohemia,
and a notion of the arts that rejects hierarchy and sacralization. This
accounts for its crossover appeal, for why even as university departments hold back on creating tenured jobs, university presses rush to
start popular music series and young writers wear as many work hats
at the same time as they possibly can.

There's a difference between embracing a vision of pop as crossover culture and rock's legacy of a particular kind of wildness. The
story is bigger than that. Popular music's ability to trade on a mixture
of training and amateurism, to reflect and anticipate every wrinkle in
the social fabric, to interject literacy and spectacle in unexpected
places, to wage identity against modernity: these are the great topics
that drew us to it in the first place. The challenge for interpreters,
sensitive to the requirements of teaching students or reaching a general audience, is to draw on a body of writing nearly as ungainly in its

ambitions and style as the music itself. The glory of pop is that the answers to these ongoing questions remain so complicated.

The glory of pop? Can one still write that way? As the mythos of rock and jazz has grown threadbare, it has become common to hear critiques of an impulse toward "authenticity"—or of seeing in music a reflection of our best self. But disengaged attitudes are little help in reckoning with a field that often produces sublime work from suspect beliefs. Arguably, this book's contents indicate an intent to take the next step and remember the power of that mystification. Ideologies of self-expression and communal expression, vying with forces of commodification and homogenization, fuel the passions of musicians and listeners alike. Holding up a mirror to a mirror, these essays relish the contradictions out of which the music takes shape, aiming to capture its messiness rather than clean it up into idealized categories, to be fellow travelers in a realm of fantasy, legend, and recrimination.

Let's return one last time to Book of Love and think about all the work still to be done. An essay by one of the band members might give us an all-too-rare clue to their own sense of mission. Reporting might shed light on the band's liminal commercial position; such investigations are also unusual, save to promote product—Douglas Wolk's chapter here on sound compression shows what's possible. An extended creative analysis of the sort Robert Polito in this book offers on Ray Davies of the Kinks is usually relegated to liner notes. Minor artists like Book of Love virtually never rate.[8] Finally, one could dissect the balance of minimalist affect and lush effect in their gnomic grooves; as Walser and Toynbee show here, academics have taken great steps in adding this kind of analysis to the literature.

But in the absence of any attempt to reckon with the aesthetics, or, if that's too dry a word, the *rapture* of new wave, what would be the driving spirit behind such an inquiry? What touches me the most about Book of Love is that, for all their resistance to blustering rock notions of realism, theirs is still such a music of pop faith. The legacy of music criticism, invested in but also distinct from the energies of any given pop moment, is vital to capturing the paradoxical impact of the music that obsesses us. Listen to Hobey Echlin, sampled from the kind of off-the-cuff writing that critics do all the time, cinching in one stuffed sentence the contemporary case for the band I've been pimping: "And now that in our age of overstimulated, posteverything refinement, we need the '80s to remind us of a time as awkward and innocent and over-the-top as we were, no band was more of all three than Book of Love."[9]

Lawrence Grossberg has recently complained that popular music studies lacks shared theoretical paradigms, a common vocabulary, and political commitment.[10] This book may well make things worse. But bringing the cultural studies of the academy into dialogue with journalism and other writing feels like a cause unto itself—even if the results are as much karaoke contest as town hall meeting. At a moment when pop's crossover identities have never been more complicated, those who think about music could use to summon a heaping dose of what Bob Dylan, recording his first rock and roll single years before anyone knew he'd "gone electric," called "Mixed-Up Confusion." Let the exceptions be seen as the norm. And as Book of Love put it, touch roses.

I.

Narratives

chapter 1

"And I Guess It Doesn't Matter Any More": European Thoughts on American Music

SIMON FRITH

On February 9, 2002, the British trade paper *Music Week* reported that industry-funded consultants had recommended the creation of a U.K. Music Office in New York City.[1] The move was supported by all the industry's lobby groups: the British Phonographic Industry, the Association of Independent Music, the Music Managers Forum, and the Music Publishers Association. The Departments of Culture, Media and Sport, and Trade and Industry were supportive of the idea in principle. Negotiations were under way for state funding to get the UKMO up and running. As *Music Week* reported, the difficulties of selling British acts in the U.S. market could no longer be ignored. In 1984, 28 percent of the best-selling albums in the United States were British. In 1999 the figure was 0.2 percent, and by the end of April the press was reporting, rather gleefully, that "for the first time since October 1963, there is not one British artist in the American Top 100 singles chart."[2]

This story interests me for three reasons. First, it lays to rest the idea of an Anglo-American rock and pop axis. The U.K., it turns out, is just another European music producer. Rather than having a special relationship with American consumers, British record companies are looking to long-mocked countries like France and Finland for the state-funded music office model. Second, it suggests not just that the American music market is important—for its size—but that it is peculiar. British companies that have been highly successful in selling their acts domestically and in Europe and Japan need special help, native experts, to explain the U.S. sales process. And, third, it shows that the British music business, like the European music business generally, is less concerned these days with protecting its market from American imports (the general line before the Beatles) than in getting support for its export trade.[3] The American market may be peculiar, but it is no longer assumed that American music is exceptional. The International Federation of Phonogram Industries (IFPI) notes that sales figures for the year 2000 "saw the continuation of one of the recording industry's major global trends of the decade—the rising popularity and sales of music from local artists and record labels." In nearly every national music market, the sales percentage of domestic repertoire steadily increased in the 1990s; the sales percentage of international (i.e., American) repertoire steadily declined.

Before reflecting on what these figures might mean in terms of the global significance of American popular music now, I need to

Average repertoire origin (% of value)

Year	Domestic	International
1991	58.3	35.6 (+ 6.1% classical)
1995	62.3	32.8 (+ 4.9%)
2000	68.2	27.5 (+ 4.3%)

Source: IFPI, *2001: The Recording Industry in Numbers* (London, 2001), p. 16.

make some remarks on why it became so important in the first place. My starting point is agreement with Robert Christgau. Rock 'n' roll was an essentially American form of music, and its global impact has to be understood in terms of what makes the USA exceptional. Indeed, what is now meant by "popular music" in almost every country in the world can be understood only by reference to American ways of making and marketing music, and again I agree with Christgau: rock 'n' roll is an important strand of American culture, but the special global importance of American popular music is rooted in a much longer history. To understand this we need to go back to the latter half of the nineteenth century. My second assumption here is that the remarkable international impact of American music cannot be explained in terms of cultural imperialism, by reference to particular uses of cultural or corporate power. Clearly there have been imperialistic institutions that have helped export American sounds— Hollywood most obviously, but also American soldiers and American missionaries. For many Europeans the first radio exposure to rock 'n' roll and R&B was on the American Armed Forces Network, the first live exposure on local U.S. air bases, while for many people in the rest of the world the most significant foreign music was the evangelical hymn. But even here the impact of the music is of a quite different order than as an aspect of conquest or conversion.

I can clarify my point by noting the central importance of African American sounds, styles, and performers to the global spread of American music. If the influence of African American music on popular music in Europe has been remarkable since the 1850s, it has also been remarkably odd, given the ongoing levels of popular racism in Europe (still reflected in the political debate about immigration and asylum seekers) and the deep-rooted institutional racism in cultural, media, and state organizations.[4] At the same time, the U.S.A.'s most successful cultural industries in export terms (Disney, for example) have been distinctly white. It is certainly arguable that American popular music had a global impact despite and not because of cultural institutions. To explain this impact we have to look to the qualities of the music itself rather than to the machinations of the American music industry.

Here, then, is a crude and schematic sketch of what, from the mid-nineteenth century, made American popular music distinctive.

Hybridity

American popular music exemplified hybridity, music made out of cultural intermingling, the uprooting and rerooting of people. It was the label for a process of musical change (and can be contrasted with the nineteenth-century European construction of "folk" music in terms of tradition and nationalism).

Sentimentality

American popular music involved the articulation of strong feelings, and in particular of strong negative feelings—sadness, loss, longing, frustration. The European popularity of the blues was prefigured by the success of minstrelsy, spirituals, and plantation songs. The appreciation of American music meant empathy, a feeling of sympathy and even identity with the performer, and a kind of religiosity, a sense of collective uplift. In Britain, at least, the sentimental song (and hymn) had been an important part of middle-class culture in the early decades of the nineteenth century, but bourgeois ideology disdained the public display of emotion as vulgar.[5] The emotional uplift of classical music was taken to be entirely mental, as concert audiences sat through romantic symphonies in silence, and the parlor song was, by its nature, formally staid—parlor singers didn't expect to make their listeners cry. It was American popular music—with first its African American and then its Jewish inflections—that in its very foreignness provided an acceptable musical way to be emotionally vulgar.

Primitivism

American popular music and in particular African American popular music was heard by Europeans as having a kind of natural human expressivity, a direct articulation of biological forces (sexuality, hunger). This perception was a crucial strand of a romanticism that regretted the rational underpinnings of industrial capitalism and the nation-state. The arts in general, music in particular, were valued as releasing us from the constraints of civilization. The more "primitive" the music, the more heady the release.

Realism

American popular music was (and is) taken to be directly expressive of its conditions of production, to involve people singing about their own lives (and contrasted to the artifice or schooling involved in European song). Notions of truth and sincerity thus became crucial to the popular music aesthetic (hence rock ideology and its investment in "authenticity") in ways that often reflected a profound ignorance of how the music was actually produced. American popular music could thus be treated as a documentary form in a way in which music hall was not, with the curious consequence that music that later reached Europe as a mass-mediated commodity, the record, was heard as an unmediated performance (this is most evident in European approaches to jazz).[6]

Modernity

American popular music was taken both to pioneer the use of new technologies (and industrial processes—this was one of Adorno's arguments) and to reflect modern living. It was, in Charlie Gillett's later words, the sound of the city. One of the ironies here is that because African American music like jazz was heard to be contemporary, Hollywood studios in the 1930s drew for their scores on the "timeless" emotional codes of nineteenth-century European orchestral music.

If European listeners at the turn of the nineteenth century responded directly to specific sounds, to particular vocal qualities and rhythmic shapes, they also interpreted what they heard. American popular music was evaluated ideologically, as it were. Twentieth-century European-American musical relations were tied up with class divisions and transatlantic distinctions between high and low art. While American popular music made its way round the world in one direction, European concert music was making its global impact in another. If "low" music was everywhere Americanized, "high" music was everywhere Europeanized. This is the context in which American popular music came to represent the vernacular, European concert music the sacred. And ultimately it was as the source of a vernacular musical language that American popular music became global. The pop music experience became the heightening of the everyday (rather than its transcendence) through commercial entertainment.

There are two final observations I need to make about this. First, I have no doubt that one important reason for the global impact of American popular music was its articulation of a certain kind of nostalgia. Again the driving force here was African American music, which for much of the twentieth century stood for both the urban and the pastoral and was heard to celebrate and regret modernity simultaneously, thus giving voice first to American, then to European, and then to much of the rest of the world's experience. This underlay the formal ways in which to European ears African American music, whether spirituals, ragtime, or jazz, blues or R&B or soul, seemed at once familiar and strange. And this leads to my second point, which might seem more trivial. From a historical perspective, it is clear that knowledge of American and particularly African American music has been a significant source of intellectual cultural capital in Europe. Music that is valued for its directness, its banality, its artlessness, and its strength of feeling has not just been consumed but treasured as an object for the connoisseur and the scholar, for a decidedly unpopular and, indeed, rather un-American kind of pleasure.

One concern of these intellectuals, of course, has been to relate the exceptional qualities of American music to the exceptional qualities of the U.S.A., not simply to the peculiar institution of slavery but also to the other cultural consequences of North American history: high social and geographical mobility coupled with a strong sense of place; the equal importance of ethnic and national identities; strongly developed market forces and a culturally inactive state.

But my concern here is different. What happens when American popular music becomes everyday listening in other countries? How is it adapted to other social circumstances?

As my schema above suggests, the pleasures of American popular music are in practice varied and contradictory. The music reaches different audiences in different ways and reemerges in a great mélange of local sounds that draw on the same American sources but have to be understood in terms of their own specific histories. Japanese and French rappers, for example, may have begun by listening to Public Enemy or Run-D.M.C. but they don't sound much like them or each other. That said, the very process of music made by adaptation does involve some shared characteristics. It is always going to have elements of imitation and pastiche (from minstrelsy to Mick Jagger); it is always going to involve the use of performing gestures, gestures (often ironic) that acknowledge that there is behind this sound something more authentic across the sea. Local adaptations of American music, whether jazz or Broadway tunes, blues or country music, rock 'n' roll or rap, are not *just* local. They echo back across the Atlantic and take their own place in the crossnational circulation of sounds.

This was most obvious in the global construction of rock music in the period from 1963 to 1980. Rock, as against rock 'n' roll, can be described as an Anglo-American form. If Swedish jazz or Italian hip-hop are labels for locally distinct versions of American music, to use the phrase "British rock" was to use a redundant adjective—rock was essentially British as well as American and, for this brief period, the flow of sounds (and dollars) back and forth across the sea was equally strong in each direction. There is much academic writing on rock that tries to explain this, to examine the historical conjuncture of art schools, youth subcultures, media institutions (like the BBC), and state policies (on education and welfare) that produced the Beatles, Stones, and so on.[7] And the point I want to stress is that any explanations do have to be historical. The global success of British music was, in the long view, an accident, the result of a momentary confluence of factors.

British politicians still proclaim that Britain has a unique musical "talent pool," that it is the "market leader" in terms of new musical trends and tastes.[8] But they are wrong. The most successful international British acts in the twenty-first century are still the old rock groups, the Beatles, Stones, etc., and, in North American sales terms, Irish acts (from U2 to Enya) are nowadays rather more successful than British musicians. Why else would the industry so desperately want government funds for a U.K. Music Office? It is a long time since a new British hit group—the Spice Girls!—had anything like commensurate U.S. success. This is not to say that a British band won't again become globally significant (Coldplay are presently being touted for such success) but, rather, that shared transatlantic tastes can no longer be taken for granted. British music now in effect occupies a U.S. niche, a cult place on Hollywood youth film soundtracks, in certain suburban clubs and college indie scenes. It no longer commands any sort of grand commercial influence. The American success of Radiohead, for example, is of a quite different order than that of Led Zeppelin or Pink Floyd.

Lying behind the campaign for a U.K. Music Office in New York is the rather desperate belief that if only they were marketed properly new British acts would command solid American sales. I doubt this. The history of American popular music suggests that what's at stake here is not marketing skills but what I would call cultural resonance. It is certainly interesting to trace the commercial route that led Little Richard's "Tutti Frutti" into my bedroom in a small town in North Yorkshire in 1956, but it is even more interesting—and rather more difficult—to explain why it instantly felt like music that made my life different. The question here, in other words, is not just about British music and American taste but about American music and British taste. Does American popular music still have transforming power? Although it is nowhere stated, one assumption of the UKMO campaign is that British music is, post-Beatles, just as good as American music. This assumption obviously reflects not what is happening in the United States but what is happening in Europe, where it is no longer obvious that local product is inferior. French rappers easily outsell U.S. rappers; European dance music producers dominate the club music market. Indeed, it could be argued that the most interest-

ing American rock music nowadays (Americana, as it is labeled by re-
tailers) occupies the same sort of niche market here as the most interesting British rock music occupies in the U.S.A.

The question I want to raise here, then, is this. If British popular
music was exceptional only for a limited historical period, for specific historical reasons, could the same argument be true of American popular music? Is its "exceptionalism" also a matter of history?
To answer this I need to summarize my argument so far. Popular
music, I suggest, is now organized globally according to a model of
music as a social and commercial practice that was constructed in
the U.S.A. between 1850 and 1960. Such popular music is not just a
set of technical institutions (record companies, music radio, retail-
ers, promoters, domestic listeners, and so on) but also a set of expectations about pop's value and purpose. Within this broad cultural
framework there is a host of music that draws on, addresses, and reflects immediate cultural conditions and histories. Such music can
be both determinedly local *and* attractive to people elsewhere precisely because of the underlying consensus about music as a social
practice. The global spread of American popular music, in other
words, was necessary to create the conditions for what is now called
world music (and European intellectuals and connoisseurs have duly
switched their attention from the U.S.A. to Jamaica and Senegal, to
Bulgaria and Bolivia).

This points to a paradoxical conclusion. In the context of world
music, sounds from the U.S.A. continue to reflect a specific cultural
history and to have potential global appeal, but in this *they are no
longer exceptional*. Is there really any reason to think that in the
twenty-first century popular music from the U.S.A. will continue to
be more significant than popular music from elsewhere, that what is
local to the U.S.A. will inevitably become global for everyone else?

My own answer to these questions is no. This is partly a matter
of taste—I no longer hear American records as distinctive. And partly
a matter of commercial logic. The Americanization of the world
means that everyone speaks a global language, and the major music
corporations are just as interested in the global market for Hollywood film stars as for Midwest metal bands. This is the implication

of those sales statistics showing the increasing importance of domestic repertoire. They don't indicate the rise of local independent record companies at the expense of the global majors. Rather, they mean that the global majors are now geared to gather up all music rights for exploitation in all music markets. They no longer seek to restrict musical movement to one direction on their own freeways but, rather, hope to levy a toll on all movement along all geographical and taste and digital networks, however big or small.

The globalization of cultural industries (of which the music industry is just an example) is usually discussed by academics in terms of postmodernism, but what interests me is the effect of such changes on American exceptionalism. On the one hand, it could be argued that in the new communicative order the U.S.A. has become just another country dependent on (and resistant to) the movement of global capital. And, certainly, the politics of music in the United States seems to be much closer to the politics of music in Europe than it used to be. This was apparent at the Pop Conference, for example, in the reiterated complaints about Clear Channel and in discussions of the Recording Industry Association of America's copyright campaigns. It's as if, since the success of Nirvana, the distinction between global music and American music has become absolute. Today's global superstars, Celine Dion, Backstreet Boys, U2, Moby, the Corrs, follow the multimedia sales strategies developed by Madonna and Michael Jackson, but they are essentially stateless; only Eminem sells records on the back of a distinctive American sensibility. In Seattle I got the impression that it was just as difficult for new American music to make a commercial impact in the U.S.A. as for new British music.

On the other hand, it could equally be argued that world musicians are more likely than American musicians these days to articulate the day-to-day experience of twenty-first-century globalization, the restless movement of labor back and forth, the problems of never-settled cultural histories and identities, the pleasure and defiance of do-it-yourself mobile, temporary, hybrid musical communities. Maybe, though, this argument—that the American experience no longer stands for world history—should be read in a different way.

With the end of the cold war, the U.S.A. has become so exceptional (as the only world power) as to be increasingly seen as a symbol of anxiety (and threat) rather than liberty (and hope), and this has its own musical consequences. Culturally, the U.S. response to the events of September 11 seems from a European perspective both very American and very provincial. Listen, for example, to Alan Jackson's "Where Were You (When the World Stopped Turning)." It describes a state of feeling that is not so much foreign as dulled; it marks a kind of baffled retreat into supposed historical certainties rather than any reflection on how the world is changing. The Terrorist becomes as inhuman, as alien, as the Communist in the 1950s or, indeed, the Red Indian in the 1850s.

Academically, it has always been difficult to establish any clear relationship between the state of a nation and the shape of its music, but I don't think there can be any doubt that in the twentieth century there was some kind of connection between the dynamism of U.S. culture and economy and the dynamism of its music, which is why Robert Christgau can root American musical exceptionalism in its sense of rhythm. Now, though, listening to U.S. music I begin to feel that it is moving to a different, less expansive, more introspective and oppressive beat.

chapter 2

U.S. and Them: Are American Pop (and Semi-Pop) Still Exceptional? And By the Way, Does That Make Them Better?

ROBERT CHRISTGAU

American exceptionalism got large as part of the anti-Soviet ideology of the nascent American studies movement in the early 1950s. Its central assumption, to quote two skeptical scholars, is what contemporary reception theorist Janice Radway derogates as "American culture conceived as a unified whole," or what radical historian Gene Wise summed up in the '70s as "a homogeneous American mind."[1] But in fact American studies goes back to the '30s—to the half-forgotten popular culture historian Constance Rourke, the pioneering racial analysts Carey McWilliams and Oliver Cox—and the phrase "American exceptionalism" originated with American leftists. What was it about America, they wanted to know, that inhibited the rise of the working-class movements thriving in Europe? All the answers that became standard—the frontier, prosperity, ethnic division—have their truth value. But I confess I'm also taken with one Michael Denning unearths in the totally forgotten socialist Leon Samson, who believed that Americanism as a belief system preempted socialism, because its shibboleths–namely, "democracy, liberty, opportunity"–functioned as what he called a "substitutive counter-concept." No wonder, he concluded, that "the socialist argument falls so fruitlessly on the American ear."[2]

And no wonder either that during the cold war both American exceptionalism and American studies, like such excellent American ideas as pluralism and pragmatism, were co-opted by capitalist frontmen doing business as antitotalitarian freedom fighters. As rock critics know well, capitalism can co-opt damn near anything– this stuff was a gimme. But though I'm sure American studies was a CIA plot, the plot worked because the idea filled a hole. To cite an example I took to heart, the honors program designed to prepare me for the literary priesthood at Dartmouth, an elite institution that in 1958 proffered me "democracy, liberty, opportunity" in the palpable form of a full-tuition scholarship, surveyed the English classics from Chaucer to Hardy while requiring not a single course in American literature.

I don't want to overstate. Dartmouth's comprehensive reading list included American authors, and from abstract expressionism to the belatedly canonized *Moby Dick*, native art got serious respect from the '50s intelligentsia. But American cultural life in that era had been enriched and to a remarkable extent transformed by an influx of European refugees all too aware of how relentlessly Hitler exploited a radio medium they blamed on a "culture industry" they blamed on the United States. Traumatically uprooted, most of them were overwhelmed and offended by America, though not even T. W. Adorno put it as baldly as his respected right-wing coequal Ernest van den Haag, who in 1957 posed the question: "Why is Brooklyn, so much bigger and richer, so much more literate and educated–and with more leisure–so much less productive culturally than was Florence?"[3] And if only because the battle against gentility is never ending, Anglophilia still pervaded literary studies, where too many elitists fretted along with the *Partisan Review*'s Philip Rahv, who in a famous 1938 essay divided American novelists into two camps, each incapable of "that mature control which permits the balance of impulse with sensitiveness, of natural power with philosophical depth": "palefaces" for depth and sensitiveness, naturally, and, specializing in impulse and natural power, "redskins."[4]

A striking choice of metaphor. Maybe Rahv was scared of Hollywood. Or maybe he was sidestepping what's always made America most exceptional of all, to its incalculable benefit and disgrace. As Leslie Fiedler would point out, *Moby Dick* turns on two interracial relationships, Ishmael and Queequeg and Ahab and Fedallah, and *Huckleberry Finn* is about one. Michael Rogin would later remind Hollywood watchers that a black-white polarity powered its three early great leaps forward: *Birth of a Nation, The Jazz Singer,* and *Gone with the Wind.* And of course, black and white has been the story line of American music since minstrelsy if not before—assuming, that is, you grant white people a share of the agency.

After careful consideration, I do. American music was polyglot, and that's big—British folk and English genteel, Irish and Italian and German and last but not least Jewish, plus Spanish slash Latin slash Caribbean. It was democratic, too—by the 1850s "music for the millions," designating a melodically and emotionally direct product that had thrived since at least the 1820s, was a catchphrase.[5] And however much this music trafficked in loneliness, morbid sentimentality, and home sweet home, it also radiated an optimism born of "democracy, liberty, opportunity"—which must have been a white optimism, since for black Americans its preconditions didn't exist.

But already we're on shaky ground. For starters, of course, the democracy, liberty, and opportunity of white Americans were being underwritten by chattel slavery even as the few blacks who'd managed to manumit themselves made what they could of them. And obliterating these contradictions is an even bigger contradiction, which is that as far as most admirers are concerned, the optimism of American music isn't about the frontier or prosperity or the permeability of the American class system—it's about black people. Maybe "Oh! Susannah" was literally stolen from some plantation, maybe it was a polkafied gloss on William Dempster's "The May Queen," or maybe, as I prefer, it was the impure, multidetermined product of

Stephen Foster's conflicted imagination. Don't matter, because it was understood, perhaps even by the many blacks who sang it, as an expression of the African American capacity for the transcendence we call fun. And while this was clearly a racist construction in the 1840s minstrel show, where faux darkies doing the walkaround were inventing American show business, by the 1890s at the latest it was a conscious African American aesthetic. As Albert Murray describes it: "The sense of well being that always goes with swinging the blues is generated, as anyone familiar with the Negro dance halls knows, not by obscuring or denying the existence of the ugly dimensions of human nature, circumstances, and conduct, but rather through the full, sharp, and inescapable awareness of them."[6]

Murray often cites Constance Rourke's conceit that the American was one-third Yankee, one-third backwoodsman or Indian ("redskin"), and one-third Negro, just as his disciple Stanley Crouch often cites Carl Jung's observation that "white Americans walked, talked, and laughed like Negroes, while Africans usually think of Negro Americans as dark-skinned white people."[7] Both are passionate about a proposition Murray goes so far as to italicize: "American culture, even in its most rigidly segregated precincts, is patently and irrevocably composite. It is, regardless of all the hysterical protestations of those who would have it otherwise, incontestably mulatto."[8] And then, having posited the primacy of the Afro-European, both these crucial African American critics devote their considerable musical insight and rhetorical force to a jazz they're reluctant to extend beyond bebop—a limited canon with room for very few white people.

Some would say that this means they're too conservative and/or racebound to be trusted, and let's not mention essentialism, that bad word. But critics don't have to be right to do right—they just have to make us think. Murray's sense of blues and conception of the African American as omni-American are ideas that become more resonant with the rise of the rock and roll Murray looks down on. As for his mulatto idea, well, a prog in a bad mood could slot that foreshadowing of multiculturalism as an all-too-patriotic Africanization of the melting pot myth—everybody one heartwarming shade of high yalla. But Murray has always been a propagandist for difference not just in America but in Afro-America—difference in hairstyle, skin tone, mind-set. Not all strains of American exceptionalism are coextensive with simplistic notions of an "American culture conceived as a unified whole" or a "homogeneous American mind."

The melting pot metaphor refers to the process in which different metals liquefy and combine to form a new and implicitly stronger alloy. For most of us here, that metaphor is over. A replacement beloved of rock critics is the African American gumbo, that Caribbean-inflected creation of blended flavors and complex texture that leaves larger constituents recognizably whole, but others might prefer the Gallic chicken stew called the gallimaufry, now a synonym for hodgepodge, or the olio, which is what minstrels called the segment where one variety act followed another willy-nilly. CIA or no CIA, some sort of gumbo or olio is what became of American studies, which is now a stronghold, albeit an embattled one, of articulated difference and identity politics. A similar fate has befallen the oldest rock and roll creation myth—the blues-and-country-had-a-baby theory. It was always partial, always about the adoration of rockabilly, about Elvis and Buddy Holly and just for luck Chuck Berry but not Little Richard or Bo Diddley or the Coasters or your favorite doo wop group, and pretty soon not Frankie Avalon, or the Beach Boys, or the Byrds. These days, it's cited uncritically only by musical neoconservatives who deploy the so-called roots genres against the beat-based, the arty, the newfangled, the young, and actually existing black people; or, even worse, by those committed to a "rock" that, after a bracing immersion in the tar pit, redounds almost exclusively to bands of white youths bearing guitars and proud of themselves for liking Jimi Hendrix.

Obviously, the great virtue of blues-and-country-had-a-baby is that it's mulatto. Although it's as American exceptionalist as can be, claiming the American South as the cradle of world popular music, it's also a reproof to all the overviews of the national character whose default American was white—until the civil rights movement forced the paradigm shift that, among many other things, made blues-and-country-had-a-baby inevitable. The theory's drawbacks are (a) that its biracialism is too bi, ceding whites a dubious parity, and (b) that it ignores two other white precincts, both more important in the end: the music business rock and roll rebelled against but didn't defeat or reject, and the bohemia that by 1960 would spark a very different paradigm shift that soon had American folkies following the lead of such English art students as John Lennon, Keith Richards, Pete Townshend, and Eric Burdon.

As I shade the rock and roll foundation myth toward my own polemical purposes, I have no intention of minimizing American music's black-and-white story line. But I do want to emphasize what in the '60s me and my contemporaries didn't really know or want to know, which is that it didn't begin with Elvis and Chuck. It goes back to young white dancers caught jigging to slave fiddlers in 1690, to minstrelsy and Foster and the integrated Five Points music joint Dickens described in *American Notes*, to Vernon and Irene Castle taking distribution on James Reese Europe's fox-trot, to the many visionary and/or compromised and/or exploitative racial interactions of the so-called Jazz Age and Swing Era. Rock and roll was merely a major stage in a vexed process that has never progressed in a straight line toward utopia.

In a way, that's also true of the closely related factor I want to emphasize instead, rhythm, although rhythm's progress has been more inexorable. Rhythm isn't exclusively African, obviously. But that doesn't mean "Oh! Susannah" didn't lilt more infectiously than the "Cellarius Polka Quadrille," a big hit in Paris at around the same time, and throughout the twentieth century African American rhythms continually gained crossover play even while gathering internal complexity and power. In rock and roll the crucial change is a matter of foregrounding. 'Tis oft said that rock and roll worked the upbeat, which it did. But there are many rock and roll beats, and the reason Alan Freed called all of them "the big beat" wasn't that Fats Domino's "The Big Beat" drove harder than Count Basie's "One O'Clock Jump," which it didn't, but that the beat looms so large within early rock and roll's individual compositions, arrangements, recordings, whatever. There's less there to distract from the body-work at hand—less harmony, less melody, less virtuosity, less content.

Few doubt that rhythm's pop primacy has African origins, but many would deny that they need be African American—especially U.S. African American—because the great exception to musical American exceptionalism is the Caribbean. The music of New Orleans, symbolic birthplace of jazz and maybe funk too, is steeped in Haiti and especially Cuba—what Jelly Roll Morton called "the Spanish tinge." Cuba had at least as drastic an effect on African pop as American R&B. Jamaica jump-started hip-hop in the Bronx shortly before Bob Marley turned reggae into the music of the world's downpressed. And so forth.

Nevertheless, the special history of blacks in the United States has been good for some formal advantages. Start with Peter van der Merwe's unorthodox argument that structural congruences between African and British folk musics are the great melodic resource of blues, which he believes thrived as much on tune as beat—to which I'd add my own guess that it was American democracy, personified by a poor white population much denser in the American South than in any Caribbean place, that gave those congruences a fair chance to come together. Moreover, as African American bluesmen fabricated a cultural identity from memory and oppression, omni-American songsters, minstrels, and composers for hire accessed the melodic resources of what, even without them, would have been the most multicultural music in history—and the industry developed to diffuse it. Nor did it hurt that American blacks spoke English, an international language. Finally, utterly fucked over though they were, African Americans were the world's most affluent black population per capita, with unparalleled access, comparatively speaking, to technology, education, and—comparatively speaking—prosperity.

Two other factors also flourished here. Late-nineteenth-century Britain had its professional songwriters, as well as a music hall circuit as lively as vaudeville. But even before the ragtime boom of 1912, British songs never traveled as well as their hard-hitting, hard-sold Tin Pan Alley counterparts, and then it was time for Kern and Berlin and Gershwin and Porter and beyond—a beyond that continues into the rock and roll era with the Brill Building and its outposts in L.A., Nashville, and, lately, Atlanta, the commercial hub of contemporary R&B. Similarly, authenticity has been an animating myth in Europe since folk songs were called popular ballads. But it's always had extra kick in America. In the form of a marketable sincerity that was pop's stock in trade by the 1840s, it was less about where you came from than where you brought it—less about origins than about unmediated expressive outreach. And when we grew a folk music movement of our own, sincerity continued to get confused with authenticity as an aesthetic value, with dire effects corrected by British example—by the reflexive irony of pop bohemians who never kidded themselves that they could become American, much less African American, and invented their own style of fun pretending to try.

Why should the music I've just abstracted for purposes of argument—altogether omitting such matters as youth, rock and roll's prime identity marker—sweep the world? Obviously there are sociological and economic factors, and I don't dismiss either. But just for fun, let me throw out a more radical suggestion. Let me pretend that it swept the world because it sounded so good.

In this matter of taste, I feel obliged to call in a food theorist—a pioneer, Sidney W. Mintz. In his 1985 *Sweetness and Power: The Place of Sugar in Modern History,* Mintz emphasizes what is clearly true—that refined sugar didn't sweep the world merely because (a) people liked sweet, and (b) white sugar was the most effective sweet ever devised. But he does recognize "an underlying hominid predisposition toward sweetness," and not only that, he's so appalled by the political, economic, nutritional, and gastronomic consequences of that predisposition in England that he momentarily abandons the anthropological open-mindedness he lives by: "The less conspicuous roles of sugar in French and Chinese cuisines," he writes, "may have something to do with their excellence. It is not necessarily a mischievous question to ask whether sugar damaged English cooking, or whether English cooking in the seventeenth century had more *need* of sugar than French."[9]

I know of no metaphor system that can change rock and roll into strawberry trifle or boeuf bourguignon, though you could say it's got a little of both. But I'm encouraged that this fervent cultural relativist grants the intrinsic attraction of certain flavors, grants that some cuisines might be better than others. In an endnote Mintz hems and haws about how his generalization applies to "sophisticated persons in the West," so I'll hedge too—I only feel comfortable universalizing into the industrialized world, although Steven Feld's account of developments in Papua New Guinea's Bosavi rain forest, in which migrant workers came back from Port Moresby leading guitar bands, suggests how permeable acculturation can be. But anyone who's ever laughed at the famous *Saturday Night Live* joke about the Voyager space probe—the one where NASA equips the probe with the Declaration of Independence and the Gettysburg Address and musical samples from Gregorian chants to Beethoven to Chuck Berry, and the first message from the outer galaxies is, "Send more Chuck Berry"—has to let me wonder whether rock and roll had intrinsic attractions too.

Some fresh way of configuring melody to rhythm, first of all. But in addition, perhaps, expressive usages that made rock and roll's values—which, as the music invaded Europe early on, were understood in quite literal if romantically distorted terms: rebel youth, universal prosperity, untrammeled sexuality—signify on a sensory as well as a conceptual level: getting loud in public, flaunting your accent, expressing your animal nature. It's even possible that in its size and regional diversity, America was uniquely equipped to transform into music a principle now self-evident, that before you try to speak globally you should act locally.

If anyone thinks I'm speculating too wildly here, I apologize—asked to go out on a limb, to debate pro the exceptionalism of American music in 2002, I figured I'd better float a notion or two to keep me aloft. Most of us pilgrims to this rock and roll monument accept the commonsense idea that American music is exceptional, at least in its blues-based forms, and that this helped it go global. Even sworn enemies of the culture industry rarely claim rock and roll was a raw imposition of American capital, and many would dissent from the Brit commonplace that rock has been Anglo-American since the Beatles. But nobody thinks this exceptionalism continues uncompromised today. Acting locally, young musicians worldwide have grabbed, stolen, distorted, misprised, and pirated whatever they wanted from it and figured out how to get their booty across, to small audiences they knew firsthand and bigger ones they could only infer or imagine. That's how Elvis and Chuck did it, and nobody who takes rock and roll to heart could want it any other way.

For twenty-five years I've been an avid fan of Afropop, regarding which I long ago adopted the rule of thumb that Africans who imitated American or European forms were doomed to competence, if that, while those who seized them stood a chance of going over the top. But I've also fallen for non-American artists whose music displays far fewer similarities to rock and roll than Franco's or Youssou N'Dour's. Bahian Tom Ze and Catalan Manu Chao and New York nuevo-Yiddish Klezmatics—all located but not meaningfully described by those adjectives—at least work in rhythmic song forms. But Mongolian Huun-Huur-Tu and Kaluli Ulahi and New York Argentinian Astor Piazzolla are something else—sophisticated formalists whose commitment to the vernacular no one needs Chuck Berry to hear, even if that was how I got there. This appetite for so-called world music sets me apart from most mainstream rock critics. Narrow-mindedness camouflaged as specialization is one reason journalists aver themselves weary of pop—or, more often, bitch that it's played out. Critically, my experience tells me this is a lie. However much it does or doesn't mean culturally, the music is there. Spending fourteen hours a day listening to it is my definition of nice work if you can get it, and it wouldn't be such a great job if there weren't always more avenues opening up, more small geniuses and cultural byways revealing themselves. In that context, however, I continue to make an exception of America, notably in two very different forms: hip-hop and indie rock.

Hip-hop's worldwide influence is inarguable—it has clearly replaced reggae as an international language of protest and has injected its usages into pop music of every provenance and description. What is arguable is first, whether hip-hop is by that very token

American any longer, and second, whether the rise in an increasingly multiracial Europe of the beat-based genre I'll call techno doesn't render hip-hop ancillary if not old hat. To me the first question seems silly. Of course MC Solaar makes sense in France, and yes, I've heard compelling hip-hop from France, South Africa, even Greenland, with more to follow. But except in the border realm of trip-hop, the beats of all the world hip-hop I've heard are elementary, relatively smooth and predictable even when, as in South African kwaito, they're highly effective. I'm not just comparing RZA and Timbaland and Organized Noize; recalling Stanley Crouch and Carl Jung, I'm talking white guys who can walk that walk, from underground mixmaster El-P to pop superstar Eminem. A paradigm shift could happen tomorrow somewhere—maybe it already has. But hip-hop will likely resemble jazz, which African Americans continue to dominate musically while the rest of the world chips in.

Techno's claims are not silly. Internationally, electronic dance music is as major a development as hip-hop or for that matter teen-pop, now blamed on the American culture industry even though it's based on a European model and was test-marketed there. Techno can be simplistic, if that's bad, all volume and beat. But it's a hotbed of predominantly instrumental innovation and abstraction with an audience ready to follow its every move. Cipher-created, DJ-manipulated, site-specific, multi-versioned, it challenges established patterns of music consumption, and its failure to break out of its subculture here is widely regarded in Europe as proof that Americans are square. If I confess that I've generally found it more interesting to think about than listen to, that's not a critical judgment—not quite. But whether you trace popular music to the industrialized 1850s or the banquet rooms of ancient Egypt, it's always been about songs. Techno is not about songs. I don't think it's going away, or that patterns of music consumption are permanent. But it's a long shot flirting with an absurdity to pretend that at just this moment in history—the millennium, right?—human beings will suddenly get tired of songs. If rhythm is destined to dominate the formal future of music, a plausible surmise, then the rhythm music that understands song form is hip-hop—a verbally explosive American music from the nation that's always had a leg up on pop song.

I wouldn't think of making the same kind of claim for indie rock. The guitar band lacks song's aura of eternity; you'd think it had already outlived its two score and zero. But since it hasn't yet, we can't assume it's obsolete. Pop pundits did a lot of that in 1990, when supposedly—Bonnie Raitt was exempted from these calculations because she has no penis—not a single rock album topped the *Billboard* chart, and a year later here comes Nirvana. I don't see any Nirvanas lurking around, and I don't expect to. But just in case, I'll note that techno tends to tempt whiz kids away from the guitar option in England. And I'll also observe that the best exceptions, from the pop Pulp to the postpunk Clinic to the roots-it-says Gomez, do what English bands have done since the '60s, only more self-regardingly and less educationally—conceptualize, keep their aesthetic distance. They're in it but not of it, by choice; they're formalists. In America, where indie is widely viewed as a synonym for irony, the myth of authenticity nevertheless holds sway, so that some kind of unmediated openness of expression is achieved not just by alt-country and postroots bands but by angular wise guys Pavement and gender-bending hobbyists Imperial Teen. Moreover, the indie circuit, with its infrastructure of hometown loyalists and rumors in a van, epitomizes act-locally-think-globally. Even the best of them remain semi-popular, emanating from and appealing to the bohemia that rock first drew on and now catalyzes. But they keep coming, and the bohemia that cares about them picks up freshmen every year. College rock is the name some still give what I think of as Amerindie.

With forty-eight hours of new music recorded every day, the biggest drawback of these last generalizations is that, empirical though they may be, my chance of inducing others to share the experience that grounds them is zero. The destiny of American hip-hop is manifest no matter how much it's misunderstood overseas; the destiny of Amerindie guitar is marginal no matter how many bands slog profitably through Europe. And statuswise, it's less than marginal. Since the dawn of cultural studies, college rock has never gotten much respect from college teachers bound up in their own authenticity myths. And for all America's impulse and natural power, the cachet of U.S. bands has been dipping in Europe since *Sgt. Pepper* or ELP or David Bowie or the Sex Pistols or Culture Club or Culture Beat or Afrobeat or ska or zouk or acid house or the Gipsy Kings or Radiohead or the Bulgarian State Radio and Television Female Vocal Choir. Our moment is over, and none too soon. We're guilty of cultural imperialism as well as the other kind. I have a rule of thumb about that, too. Any third world artist wants to attack U.S. imperialism, I listen. When our silent partners in capitalist depredation render such critiques, however, I assume I'm in a turf war. Boeuf bourguignon—yum. MC Solaar—for domestic consumption only.

But this isn't reasoned analysis, just words. Having argued from the historical basics, I've slipped back to where critics live—the realm of taste, sensibility, rhetoric. And because these imponderables are always in part a function of style, I've made jokes and made fun while continuing to adduce ideas and risk Latinate polysyllables. I've generalized irresponsibly, essayed the occasional epigram, aimed for redolence as well as precision, gone slanging, and indulged in other bits of playful demagoguery. I've avoided the jargon and dead verbs and distracting repetitions of so much scholarly discourse because they suggest carelessness in a world where there isn't enough caring, a disregard for the materials of the craft at hand—in other words, words. If the structuralism wars ended up convincing me of anything, it wasn't to distrust language but rather, I'm afraid, what I pretty much knew already—that language is very nearly all human beings have, that there's no right way to control it, that it's best deployed with love, respect, and cunning. Rock criticism, some of us still call that writerly, public-intellectual approach to pop in this country, another small American exception—in the rest of the world it scarcely exists. The hope is that in matters of taste, style matters. The hope is that if I can't prove what I'm saying is true, which I can't, I can at least induce some fraction of you to think, Hey, he's not such a tight-ass. Maybe I was too hard on Pavement. Or, alternatively, He's not a total philistine. I should try and hear Pavement sometime. And you should.

chapter 3

How Come Jazz Isn't Dead?

GARY GIDDINS

The question is phrased facetiously, but not entirely. At times even dedicated boosters like me begin to wonder if jazz isn't edging into the museum's marble tomb. In a 1968 recording, "Jazz Death?" the then little-known Lester Bowie posed effetely as *Jism* magazine's Dave Flexingbergstein to ask, "Isn't jazz, as we know it, dead yet?" After an unaccompanied trumpet solo, he answered, in his own mocking voice, "Well, that all depends on what you know." Bowie was responding to debates that were rife during the summer and winter of love. Miles Davis had said that calling him a jazz musician was no different than calling him "nigger"; jazz journals were filled with barbarians-at-the-gates prognoses. One authority confidently proclaimed that so long as Louis Armstrong lived, jazz lived, settling the matter in his mind until July 6, 1971, by which time—or shortly after—the arrival of dozens of gifted musicians like Bowie made it irrelevant.

Today, "Jazz Death?" is more frequently accessed for backup than music—a smirking rejoinder to those who believe that jazz is moribund, and an inadvertent example of the defensiveness that is a certain sign of bad times. We do well to remember that jazz coroners have been hanging crepe since the 1930s. In those years, reactionaries horrified by big-band swing and its damning popularity argued that authentic jazz was the exclusive province of small, unschooled, polyphonic ensembles with relatively fixed instrumentation and repertory. They encouraged primitivism of a kind that was southern and Negro, reversing the initial assumption (stated in Osgood's *So This Is Jazz*, 1926) that black bands, however accomplished, could not compete with white concertizing orchestras. Serious jazz lovers rejected mannerly dance bands and symphonic elaborations as advocated by king-of-jazz Paul Whiteman (making "a lady out of jazz" was an approving catchphrase) in favor of highly rhythmic, down and dirty, blues-drenched improvisations by the likes of Jelly Roll Morton, King Oliver, Bessie Smith, Bix Beiderbecke, and especially the valiant Armstrong; they belonged to an exclusive club of advanced thinkers—but not for long. Some grew to detest Armstrong's ensuing success. They were too politic to say "we resent the interest of the masses" or "we hate to see our beloved primitives grow rich." So they waved the flag of authenticity. Armstrong, they alleged, sounded the first death rattle when, in 1929, he adapted white pop from Tin Pan Alley.[1]

For half a century, each generation mourned anew the passing of jazz because each idealized the particular jazz of its youth. Countless fans loved jazz precisely *because* of the chronic, tricky, expeditious jolts in its development, but the emotional investment of the majority audience—which pays the bills—quickly metamorphosed from adoration to nostalgia. Mid-Depression America gave its heart and feet to swinging big bands, and later rejected the modern postwar school in which mostly urban listeners found their own mirror images. Buffs in the booming '50s accepted jazz as cool (West Coast), funky (East Coast), and mainstream (enduring swing heroes, including vocalists like Ella Fitzgerald and Frank Sinatra), while shunning the burgeoning avant-garde, which a dwindling '60s fan base would embrace as a reflection of political and social unrest.

The avant-garde and its small, loyal coterie proved virtually impregnable, ultimately emerging as a permanent alternative to the changing but constant (and consonant) center. In over four decades, it, too, evolved diverse factions—free jazz, new music, harmolodic, freebop, and cross-cultural fusions of every kind, which taken together suggest a kind of parajazz or jazz in exile (downtown, in Europe, out of the way). The avant-garde intersects with the center no less than Dixieland, swing, bop, cool, hard bop, third-stream, soul, and the rest intersect with each other. But every idiom has its own adherents, and when we refer to a "jazz audience," we are really conjuring up a nation of tribes that speak different dialects and rarely marry out of faith. The combined tribes ought to add up to a sizable commercial force. Yet not long after Ken Burns's *Jazz* roused a patriotic fervor for "America's classical music," record industry accountants say that the jazz business is in free fall. Jazz discs account for 3 percent of total sales, including jazz-lite (a slanderous term). What's going on?

Every enduring art has to face the issue of outlasting the world of its genesis—has to confront the day-to-day plight of sustaining and growing an audience despite a mass media consumed with mass appeal. How can we evaluate the importance of an art with a following so cultlike that it barely creases national consciousness? At what point does a vital form of expression become a museum to celebrate vital forms of expression? Born as outlying cults, musical traditions that achieve popular success invariably end as establishment cults, generating international infrastructures of subsidy and scholasticism to replace a once-clamorous public.

Jazz, at the dawn of its second century, affirms a template for the way music is born, embraced, perfected, and stretched to the limits of popular acceptance before being taken up by the professors and other establishmentarians who reviled it when it was brimming with a dangerous creativity. Duke Ellington was denied a Pulitzer Prize in 1965 because the jury commended him for his overall achievement rather than a specific work; in 1999, when he lay twenty-five years in the grave, he was awarded the prize–for his overall achievement. The jazz template, though not new (while the Three Tenors bellow the music of Lord Webber, consider that no American record label has a symphony orchestra under contract), may have a singular prognostic relevance for rock. It has four stations.

The first station might be called "native." Every musical idiom begins in and reflects the life of a specific community where music is made for pleasure and to strengthen social bonds: New Orleans fraternal societies, Appalachian fiddlers, Bronx high school doo-woppers, and so forth. The fable that recounts how jazz came up the river from New Orleans to Chicago and then leaped to New York and the world is crude, but it will do to set the stage. Jazz was brewed in a cauldron of music, including marching bands, spirituals, rag-time, blues, African drum choirs, Spanish and French dances, slave chants, minstrelsy, opera, and anything else that could be heard in New Orleans at the turn of the twentieth century. It developed a distinct and local character, applicable to every kind of social occasion from picnics to funerals. Stalled at station one, traditional or Dixie-land jazz might have remained one of the world's great folk musics, achieving a formulaic apex in King Oliver's Creole Jazz Band, which came to Chicago in 1921. One reason it didn't stall is that a year later, Oliver elected to bolster the ensemble with a second trumpet, and wired his protégé Armstrong to join him.

Those who experienced the exhilaration of Oliver's band during its residency at Chicago's Lincoln Gardens wanted it to go on forever. But the ailing Oliver knew how fickle sophisticated audiences are. Biting the bullet of progress, he soon exchanged his incomparable ensemble for a larger, mediocre, New York–style orchestra. As the "native" period faded into history, critics sentimentalized it while attempting to hold the fort. Authenticity reared its baleful head. "Printed scores are not a part of jazz," historian Rudi Blesh declared. Armstrong, he said, had abandoned jazz; "West End Blues" "narrowly misses banality," with its "dark romanticism foreign to jazz." Ellington's "tea dansant music" had no jazz content whatsoever.[2]

Blesh was neither the first nor the last critic to proclaim his love of an art by telling its artists what to do. On a radio program with Blesh, Alan Lomax introduced New Orleans clarinetist George Lewis as an example of jazz in its Arcadian purity. Lewis, an affecting musician with a fat-boned sound but limited technique, had gained attention playing with Bunk Johnson, the ancient trumpet player recently outfitted with new teeth and paraded (falsely) as a mentor to Armstrong and beacon of true jazz. Lomax told his audience that in Lewis it would hear jazz as it was before commercialism mucked it up. He repeated the claim after Lewis's solo, unaware—unlike all of his teenage listeners (including future critic Martin Williams)—that Lewis, eager to show New York he was no dinosaur, had played the latest hot licks from Woody Herman's "Woodchopper's Ball."

By 1940 it was easy to mock "moldy figs" like Blesh and Lomax (though they had a sizable following, including novelist James Jones, who wrote a short story, "The King," about the thrill of finding Bunk),[3] because jazz had long since reached its second and most important station, which might be called "sovereign." Here, music ceases to be the private reserve of any one place or people. No longer a communal craft with relatively few technical demands and a myopic outlook, it metamorphoses into a universal art with what Gunther Schuller calls the "potential to compete with the highest order of previously known expression."[4] For Schuller, Armstrong's introductory cadenza on "West End Blues" was the alarum; some would choose other and earlier Armstrong performances. But virtually no one contests Armstrong's genius as the triggering agent. A transitional moment is caught on Oliver's 1923 "Chimes Blues." Armstrong was assigned the trio episode, a brief, written melody, played twice. It offered him no improvisational freedom, yet his brilliant tone, confident phrasing, and robust swing all but capsized the ensemble. Within a year, he would cause New York's best players and arrangers to rethink everything they knew about jazz; a year after that, in Chicago, he would initiate sessions by the Hot Five (a band that existed only to record), restructuring jazz as an art in which individual vision meant everything.

I don't mean to imply that Oliver, Morton, and others who brought the New Orleans style to full flower failed to achieve a profound level of expression. But Oliver inspired musicians to play Oliver's music; Armstrong inspired musicians to discover their own. Armstrong was the one great tributary to spring directly from Oliver. Tributaries that sprang from Armstrong ranged from the Swing Era ("orchestrated Louis," it was called) to modern jazz (Miles Davis: "You know, you can't play anything on the horn that Louis hasn't played—I mean even modern") and beyond.[5] Armstrong's singing unleashed America's vernacular voice; his rhythmic and melodic liberties reversed the balance of power from song (and song publisher) to performer. Everything he did bolstered individuality as indicated in the jazz axiom, "It ain't what you do, it's the way that you do it."

The genie was out of the bottle, and no one—certainly not its liberator—could put it back. Armstrong did not initially like the extravagant intricacy of Dizzy Gillespie's playing, but as Gillespie observed, "No him, no me."[6] The music would now go wherever individual genius took it, and the status quo would never be static for long. When jazz became capacious enough to include Dixieland, boogie-woogie, swing, and modern jazz (or bop), the word *jazz* grew too large for the comfort of most listeners. Jazz had accrued a history, a chain of events, but in reality each link would attract its own followers and only a handful of critics and listeners would care to track them all. For more than half a century, music lovers had been arguing Brahms or Wagner, Tchaikovsky or Debussy, Stravinsky or Schoenberg. Now jazz enthusiasts could join in the fun. The jazz wars of the 1940s and after produced some of the most intemperate spats in all cultural criticism.

The second station is the hardest to leave, and bitterness was inevitable. For little more than a decade, 1935 to 1946, jazz had been America's pop music—to a point. *Swing* was the byword, not jazz. True, the great bands of Ellington, Basie, Goodman, Hines, Shaw, Lunceford, Herman, Dorsey, Webb, Calloway, Krupa, and many more, played jazz; they enjoyed success with dancers and recorded many of the most profitable and artistically accomplished and innovative platters of the era. But all of them, to one degree or another, at times tamped down the jazz for arrangements that allowed them to keep larger audiences. A typical Benny Goodman session would produce two jazz instrumentals and two pop vocals. "Flamingo" bought Ellington time to compose *Black, Brown and Beige*. To many Americans, none of those names meant as much as Glenn Miller, Hal Kemp, Guy Lombardo, Larry Clinton, Kay Kaiser, and the other leaders of novelty or sweet bands that flourished as swing but had little or nothing to do with jazz. For that matter, the average Basie fan had no more interest in searching for old sides by Oliver and Bix than in contemplating the flatted fifth–bebop's preferred blue note.

And yet: only in 1939 could Coleman Hawkins have scored a hit with "Body and Soul," a peerless two-chorus saxophone improvisation with scant reference to anything resembling familiar melody. Only in the "sovereign" period could jazz have so utterly taken hold of the world's imagination. It penetrated the Soviet Union and China, where listening to jazz was an offense, and was adopted by occupied nations as a statement of defiance–in response, the Nazis recorded imitation jazz records to lure listeners to its own broadcast channels. The immediate postwar explosion of modern jazz, from the release of Charlie Parker's "Ko Ko" in the first weeks of 1946 to the economic failure, in 1948, of the Basie, Herman, and Gillespie bands, also belongs to the second station. The jazz wars–trad versus swing, swing versus bop–had created a public consciousness of jazz that contributed to the rise of bop clubs and concert series. The nation never took bop to heart, but it knew something was up, if only because of the frequent radio and movie gibes. *Life* magazine explained bebop (the moniker alone made it seem trite, like hip-hop) as a clownish society of ritual handshakes, dark glasses, berets, and goatees–the humorous pretensions of Negro artists (Parker was not mentioned). Armstrong recorded "The Boppenpoof Song," and Bing Crosby and Patti Andrews followed with "Bebop Spoken Here." In *Appointment with Danger*, Alan Ladd asks, "Bop? Isn't that when everyone plays a different tune at the same time?" Maybe he was thinking of Dixieland, but the comment (in a 1951 flick) demonstrates the widening gap between jazz and the public's understanding of it.

Jazz was now sweeping inexorably toward the third station,

which might be called "recessionary." This occurs when a style of music is forced from center stage. The floating orchestras that had recently crisscrossed the nation fell victim to postwar economics and changing tastes. Swing was now associated with the hardships of Depression and war. In Denmark, jazz, which had become a popular obsession during the occupation, suddenly fell out of favor after the liberation—it reminded people of evil times. In the United States, the turnabout was not as abrupt, but returning servicemen did not expect to resume the old party, and young people wanted something to call their own. Rhythm and blues and later rock and roll gave it to them, after a transitional period in the early '50s, when the pop charts were dominated by novelties that implied an optimism and faux innocence bordering on idiocy. In that environment, the undercurrent of rebellion and excess that had always been part of jazz slid into the shade, where it flourished with fewer constraints. Young musicians who wanted to play jazz didn't look to swing veterans for inspiration, but to the rebels who were remaking jazz as emotionally introverted concert music. (The distinction between concert and nightclub lessened as wartime cabaret taxes forbade dancing in most small clubs). Ballroom habitués weren't necessarily the types to seek music in the relatively genteel setting of a concert hall.

Of course the issue of gentility disappeared as new rites of passage, like the long-running Jazz at the Philharmonic tours, introduced a level of rowdiness rivaling the Savoy during Battles of the Bands; now battling tenor saxophonists generated the screams. Yet the gap widened between jazz and an increasingly uncomprehending public that was taught to associate modern jazz with characters like TV beatnik Maynard G. Krebs, who incarnated a white, lowbrow version of *Life*'s report on bop. In movies of the early '50s, modern jazz meant jukebox platters by ineptly raucous big bands playing stock riffs overlaid with dissonance. They drive Marilyn Monroe to murder in *Niagara,* Sam Jaffe to lechery in *The Asphalt Jungle,* and Marlon Brando to sentimental malingering in *The Wild Ones.* Meanwhile, swing was now as sentimentalized as Bunk Johnson; in *The Glenn Miller Story,* Miller's swing charts are engulfed in strings to diminish the rhythm. Between stodgy swingsters and pathological boppers, one thing was sure: jazz was off the beaten path. By the time Chuck Berry sang, "I have no kick against modern jazz unless they try to play it too darn fast," everybody sort of knew what he meant, though he didn't mean anything at all.

Yet it's a mistake to think that the distancing of jazz from the commercial center resulted in a great decline in popularity. "Recessionary" means a retreat from marketplace power but not bankruptcy. As jazz began to sacrifice commercial self-reliance for the perks and miseries of classicism, it busied itself with mining the past—reissues complete with rejected takes, biographies, treatises, discographies—as well as forging an extremely exciting and diverse present, one that has never ceased growing in stature. The fan base may have been reduced and localized, but it was stable. New stars with cutting-edge personalities appeared: Miles Davis, Thelonious Monk, Gerry Mulligan, Dave Brubeck, Charles Mingus, Art Blakey, Clifford Brown, Jimmy Smith, Ahmad Jamal, and as many others as there had once been great orchestras for dancing. The jazz business prospered with a renewed luster: Smart music for smart people. The masses don't get it? That's a *good* thing—1928 all over again: We're hip and you're not.

For the next fifteen years, as youth music blanketed the culture and rock and roll's sovereignty in the marketplace brooked few incursions, jazz qua jazz—as opposed to jazz qua swing or jazz qua bop—achieved a success that, in some respects, trumped anything in its past. The factions seemed to fade and the flag of authenticity was raised only to banish the shamelessly commercial, the hangers-on. True, a lot of the great pre-bop soloists fell on dark times, but everyone at least paid lip service to their greatness. The main thing is that jazz had come to embody the sleek, affluent, postwar adult world. It was the original New Frontier, not just smart and hip but also socially adventurous, patriotic, and incredibly sexy. Everybody said so, from Lenny Bruce to Jack Kerouac to Norman Mailer to Steve Allen to Leonard Bernstein to James Baldwin to Hugh Hefner to Peter Gunn. Received wisdom says different. Ken Burns's *Jazz*, for example, is predicated on the glorious cresting in the 1930s, when swing bands resuscitated the recording industry and fueled a national craze. No one can doubt that, for the country at large, jazz peaked in those years, as (mostly white) jazz stars became famous enough to warrant Hollywood cameos and mainstream magazine covers. Yet in terms of financial rewards and cultural respect, jazz made immense strides between 1951 and 1964.

This was the era when Hollywood produced most of the jazz-themed movies and virtually all jazz-themed TV programs. These were the great years not of live radio broadcasts, which had all but disappeared, but of canned radio stations devoted to jazz on disc. Consequently, it was also the peak period for independent labels that focused on modern jazz as well as classic jazz. They prolifer-ated: Blue Note, Prestige, Verve, Emarcy, Fantasy, Cadet, Riverside, Bethlehem, Atlantic, and Impulse, for starters. Jazz hits, of which there were many, did not figure in most sales charts because they were LPs. Yet they often sold more units than the hits of the 1930s. Sales between 1931 and 1938, when many assumed that the record business was on its last legs (radio offered music free to a cash-rav-aged country), were negligible by the standards of the 1950s. In 1936, a disc that had sold 40,000 units wound up in the top 20, 25,000 in the top 100; 100,000 was almost unheard of. In the 1920s, sales had often topped a million, as they began to do again in the '50s. The reasons for the upsurge were not entirely musical.

After impressively rebounding from the Depression in the late '30s, the record industry had been on hold during the war—a victim of the rationing of vinyl, the drafting and disbanding of orches-tras, union strikes, and the focus on transcription recordings for the armed forces. Then came the revolution of tape and microgroove, which proved especially suitable for jazz and classical music. In a contest of patents, RCA and Columbia divided the business: the donut-hole 45-rpm disc replaced the 78-rpm disc as the vehicle for pop singles, while the 12-inch 33-rpm LP replaced the multiple-78s album and offered an expanded slate for more ambitious projects. Almost instantly, jazz labels encouraged artists to record longer works. Ellington was the first to compose extended pieces for the new medium—tone poems that, unlike suites, couldn't easily be di-vided into three-minute movements. Sonny Rollins extended his solos into tours de force of thematic improvisation. Sinatra, designing his fabled comeback, continued to concentrate on three-minute arrangements, but now presented them in theme-based sequences, like moody novels. Satisfied with dominion over the singles market, rock and roll was content to use the LP for anthologizing hits, until the Beatles introduced *Sgt. Pepper.*

Jazz's concept albums and live recordings sold reasonably well: Fitzgerald's songbooks, Miles's concerti, Oscar Peterson's trios, Brubeck on campus, Cannonball Adderley in nightclubs, Jimmy Smith at the chicken shack (which inaugurated a new genre of Hammond B3 organ combos), and others scored better numbers than most hit singles of the '30s. Benny Goodman's 1938 Carnegie Hall concert, first released in the early 1950s, outsold the 78s that had made him a megastar fifteen years earlier. Many jazz LPs were so successful that tracks were released as singles, and several ranked high on the pop charts—Brubeck's "Take Five" (three months, 1959), Dinah Washington's "What a Difference a Day Makes" (five months, 1959), Etta Jones's "Don't Go to Strangers" (seven weeks, 1960), Stan Getz and Charlie Byrd's "Desifinado" (four months, 1962), Vince Guaraldi's "Cast Your Fate to the Winds" (eighteen weeks, 1962–63), Louis Armstrong's "Hello, Dolly!" (number one, 1964), Ramsey Lewis's "The 'In' Crowd" (four months, 1965). Yet most of the action was in the LP market, where jazz radio boosted unlikely recordings to a prominence that superseded the presumed marginality of its audience: John Coltrane's "My Favorite Things" is a famous example, as are the consecutive hits (1963 to 1965) Blue Note enjoyed with Herbie Hancock's "Watermelon Man" (covered by Mongo Santamaria), Horace Silver's "Song for My Father" (covered by James Brown), and Lee Morgan's "The Sidewinder" (adapted for a Gillette ad). There were others, as well as frankly meretricious bonanzas like Wes Montgomery's *A Day in the Life.*

Jazz continued to infiltrate pop throughout the '60s. By the '70s, imitators of Coltrane and Montgomery were everywhere, and jazz was commonplace in movie scores and on TV talk shows. Sadly, those uses generally amounted to little more than background music. The kinds of jazz that pressed hardest for serious attention were the avant-garde, which required a lot of concentration, patience, and blind trust (Cecil Taylor might be a genius, but a four-hour concert is a serious investment, and Taylor himself took a Joycean stand, expecting preparation from his audience), and fusion, which required the same, plus a willingness to accept loud electrical instruments (Miles Davis might be a genius, but the repetitions and lack of melody—from him, of all people—were as provoking as the funny clothes and tape loops). Suddenly, the traditional history of jazz, from Dixieland to avant-garde, could be encapsulated in one odd word, "acoustic," and in the years 1968 to 1972, acoustic jazz bottomed out. Many key figures left for Europe, the studios, teaching, pit bands, and fusion. Jazz had sunk into such a slough of despond that no one bothered to argue authenticity—except as regarded producer-generated fusion, where established players were inveigled into overdubbing solos over rote funk arrangements; and there wasn't much debate there either, since everyone seemed to agree it was a thoroughly disreputable business. This was the moment when Bowie recorded "Jazz Death?" for one of the Chicago labels that were documenting a new approach to acoustic jazz—a broader, wittier, looser avant-garde. Jazz was now pulling into the fourth and final station.

The situation in which jazz is presently found might be called "classical," not to denote an obeisance to orthodoxies and traditions (though, yes, there's plenty of that), but because even the most adventurous young musicians are weighed down by the massive accomplishments of the past. In the space of a lifetime, jazz history has progressed from a carton of King Oliver 78s stored in the attic to a grand labyrinth of idioms and artists that one can hope to master only with years of commitment. For the first time, a large percentage of the renewable jazz audience finds history more compelling than the present, and young musicians, who once aimed above all else for an original voice, are now content to parrot the masters. Pundits ask the reasonable question: If a young fan enters the huge jazz section at Tower, should he buy Wynton Marsalis's rehash of Monk or an actual Monk classic? The answer is implicit in the question, which would not have been posed in any other period. (Monk or Tatum? Both, of course.) The parity between old and new no longer exists.

History keeps jazz alive in the Cultural Treasure sense—like opera—while making it almost impossible for new artists to get a hearing.

Perhaps the "recessionary" station's last hurrah was the "loft era" that peaked between 1975 and 1985. The previous decade, as noted, was rife with compromise and despair, bleak efforts to adapt psychedelic attitudes and electric instruments (remember the Varitone sax?), when even John Lewis and Bill Evans recorded on Fender Rhodes. As jazz once again raised its head as an uncompromising art in the banner year of 1975, it faced up to the reality of occupying a small and isolated section of cultural real estate. Yet the sheer number of new players and reemerging old ones engendered a liveliness that had been absent for years. A wave of major musicians who had been riding out the storm away from the limelight regenerated their careers, among them James Moody, Hank Jones, Tommy Flanagan, Dexter Gordon, John Carter, Don Pullen, Art Pepper, Cecil Taylor, Johnny Griffin, Red Rodney, Phil Woods, Frank Morgan, Jimmy Rowles, Jackie McLean, and Benny Carter. The young and not-so-young (but little known) musicians from the West and Midwest who turned up in New York as members of collectives, cooperatives, or rehearsal bands included Lester Bowie, Muhal Richard Abrams, Henry Threadgill, Sirone, Roscoe Mitchell, Leroy Jenkins, Fred Hopkins, Steve McCall, Julius Hemphill, Oliver Lake, Jerome Cooper, Leo Smith, Anthony Braxton, Hamiet Bluiett, David Murray, Arthur Blythe, James Newton, Marty Ehrlich, James Blood Ulmer, Shannon Jackson, and many more. They eschewed the mainstream (or vice versa) and transformed New York's jazz scene, organizing concerts, producing records, and gentrifying low-rent lofts into performance venues.

Most of them carved out successful professional niches in the world arena. But the world closed in on them, and their audience became true believers. Still, they were strong individualists, and the one thing that did not close in on them was jazz history. No one posited a marketplace competition between David Murray and Dexter Gordon. The younger players drew on the past; they didn't mimic or recycle it. Which is precisely what has happened in the "classical" phase. In 1981, Wynton Marsalis came to town. Working with

Art Blakey, he personified the promise of a neoclassicism he hoped would restore a virtuoso élan that predated the avant-garde but still had a lot of life to it. As his renown spread, however, Marsalis reawakened the old Rudi Blesh debate about jazz authenticity: if you didn't swing his way, you didn't swing; if you didn't play the changes, you weren't playing jazz. The ensuing jazz war was probably inevitable. In a sense, the "classical" station is defined by the question: Who will inherit the music—the classicists or the renegades? What Marsalis was slow to learn is that the audience doesn't care. By 2002, he was without a label and asking for incredible sums when his records sold no better than those he claimed were killing jazz. Marsalis is very likely the most famous living jazzman—everyone knows him. He writes books and appears on TV and in magazine ads. He is a genial, generous, and increasingly mellow spokesman for jazz, and his educational programs and big band tours merit and receive much praise. Yet his orchestra could not function without the sponsorship of Jazz at Lincoln Center (the most successful fund-raiser in jazz history), his music exercises decreasing influence, and his record sales are modest. He is the quintessential superstar for an art overwhelmed by its past.

For most jazz artists, fame will always be circumscribed. Establishment—as opposed to marketplace—recognition is in short supply. Jazz has virtually no standing with Brahmin networks like the American Academy of the Arts or the Pulitzer. The Kennedy Center Honors, which have acknowledged Chuck Berry, Johnny Cash, Bob Dylan, Paul Simon, and Paul McCartney, have been far less generous to jazz innovators of the past half-century: do not expect them to ring up Sonny Rollins, George Russell, Ornette Coleman, Max Roach, Horace Silver, Cecil Taylor, Charlie Haden, McCoy Tyner, Clark Terry, or the rest any time soon—Brubeck or Peterson maybe, Marsalis surely, in time. (A representative of the Kennedy Center Honors once asked me to recommend a jazz musician. I said that the most pressing candidate was Benny Carter, who was close to ninety at the time. She laughed and said, "That's so funny. I just spoke to Quincy Jones and he said the same thing." "So what more do you need to know?" "Oh," she explained, "this is for television.

We can't have Benny Carter. He isn't famous enough." A subsequent petition mounted in Hollywood got Carter the honor.) The idea of jazz as a stately, classical art—less stuffy than European classicism, more dignified than rock—remains an attractive one, and cities around the world are eager to launch jazz festivals, each with its own definition of jazz. Dixieland thrives in New Jersey, swing in Florida, soft-funk at Newport. In 2002, the New York JVC Jazz Festival offered its lowest quotient of bona fide jazz ever; its impresario insists there are no longer jazz stars to pack the big halls. In truth, there are a few—Sonny Rollins never fails to draw one large flank, Chick Corea another, Diane Krall a third. The one musician who unites the diverse tribes, if only in contumely, is Kenny G—the Lord Webber of jazz. Several years ago, a joke was widely repeated: You are given a gun with two bullets and placed in a room with Idi Amin, Saddam Hussein, and Kenny G. Only two bullets. What to do? Shoot Kenny G twice.

Jazz as a business is in deep trouble, despite steady sales of archival classics and various commercial uses of those same beloved records, often rendered anonymous in TV ads. How could it be otherwise? Jazz musicians have virtually no access to the machinery of capitalism, and multinationals have no patience with leisure pursuits that supply insignificant profits. Furthermore, the appalling copyright extension, sanctified by the Supreme Court in 2003, prevents smaller jazz labels from fleshing out their catalogs with competitive editions of classics that, in many cases, the majors refuse to reissue anyway. I am not convinced that the issue of commercial marginality cannot be effectively addressed and alleviated. But it will take a dot-com billionaire jazz lover. Such an individual could work wonders by creating a national jazz radio network or cable station; or by organizing an agency to plan and produce jazz tours, reviving the campus circuit and the kind of excitement that attended Jazz at the Philharmonic; or by erecting a national jazz temple equal to those that exist for country music and rock and roll. Barring that, a new Miles or Monk or Rollins could come along and attract as much excitement as the originals. Anything *could* happen. In lieu of pipe dreams, however, jazz will survive as a permanent alternative music, like the nineteenth-century symphonic repertory, sustaining its audience through word of mouth and a constant replenishing of the talent pool.

One of several remarkable musicians to appear in the last few years is pianist Jason Moran, who records for Blue Note and works regularly in New York. New York has no commercial jazz radio station; nor is there a jazz outlet on the hundreds of cable stations. Yet he is committed, inspired, prolific, and by no means alone. A critics' darling almost from the first, he achieved something rare in contemporary jazzcrit: a consensus regarding his 2002 solo album, *Modernistic*. Much of the excitement stemmed from the way he approached the wider world—that is, the jazz past (stride pianist James P. Johnson), the pop past ("Body and Soul"), the jazz present (avant-garde guru Muhal Richard Abrams), the pop present ("Planet Rock"), a probable future (originals that combine improvisation and swing with hip-hop beats and prepared tapes), and even a circumnavigation that adapts Schumann lieder as a harmonic grid for ad-lib variations. With minimal self-consciousness, Moran asserts himself as a gifted jazz artist and as a musician of his generation. He may have little if any chance of cracking the multinational monopolization of the mass audience, but he embodies a way of negotiating the margins without succumbing to traditionalist nostalgia—something rock musicians will have to master when the mantle of classicism falls over them.

Ailments granted, jazz could never be sick unto death. There is no indication that the music or the desire to master it will vanish, any more than cinema or literature will vanish. A stream of new blood enters the jazz body annually. The best young musicians invariably learn to make a living at it. The constancy of jazz's past (in 2001, Columbia Records revealed that Miles Davis's 1959 *Kind of Blue* sold, on average, 5,000 units a month) guarantees an unending succession of players who want to master the idiom, and who get plenty of encouragement in school and from the media's occasional obeisance to America's Classical Music (a phrase that doesn't seem so flattering now that the evidence is QED and jazz players are less in need of respect than work). They aim to make their own contributions and extend jazz history. If they differ from their forebears in having learned jazz from records and in classes rather than on the street or as apprentices in big bands, they embody the same spark of obstinate originality and defiant pleasure. The notion that jazz is dead or could die in the foreseeable future is predicated on one of two ideas: it is a narrow musical style with fixed parameters, or it is a passing fashion that has had its day. A century of development puts paid to both.

Indeed, the jazz press seems more upset by the obstacles than do the musicians, whose optimism ensures jazz's endurance as something more than a museum treasure. For them, authenticity isn't an issue of style but of competence and imagination, as summed up by an observation once made by John Steinbeck. "Great reward can be used to cover the loss of honesty [among other artists] but not with jazz players," he said, adding: "Let a filthy kid, unknown, unheard of and unbacked sit in—and if he can do it—he is recognized and accepted instantly. Do you know of any other field where this is true?"[7] Put another way, it all depends on what you know.

chapter 4

Sister Rosetta Tharpe and the Prehistory of "Women in Rock"

GAYLE WALD

More than any other twentieth-century black vernacular music, gospel is the forgotten root of rock 'n' roll. If blues and boogie-woogie are rock 'n' roll's acknowledged progenitors, then gospel is its midwife: the figure that assisted at the birth but isn't remembered as having been central to the creation process. Yet rock 'n' roll sounds and sensibilities are thoroughly enmeshed with the sounds and sensibilities of the "good news" music that developed in and from African American working-class Pentecostal churches in the 1930s. "All rock's most resilient features, the beat, the drama, the group vibrations derive from gospel," writes Anthony Heilbut in *The Gospel Sound*, a celebratory chronicle of gospel music published in 1971, at the height of rock's dominance as youth music for a new generation. "The gospel sound is everywhere."[1]

Everywhere, that is, except in official musical memory. The reasons for this absence vary, although they stem largely from gospel's origins in African American Christian communities. The ritual function of gospel as religious music puts it at odds, for example, with quintessential rock 'n' roll rebel narratives of the sort embraced both in the popular imagination (where the rituals of youth are conceived in opposition to the rituals of the church) and in contemporary scholarship on popular music. The characteristic tensions of these narratives—between authenticity and the market, art and commercial incorporation—are present in gospel and yet play themselves out quite differently in a context in which religious values and interests are often pitted against those of secular mass culture. Historically, gospel artists who have "crossed over" (the term itself is indicative of these tensions, and of the ways that influence has been imagined unilaterally) have been viewed with wariness for making the sounds of African American worship—sounds produced within a sphere of racial intimacy—available as "popular" music. Technologies of mass reproduction such as radio and recorded sound, which enabled music to travel through time and space and to be both owned and collected as artifact, therefore had poignant meaning for gospel's largely poor, largely female audience.[2]

The composition of gospel's audience connects back to the notion of gospel as midwife. In part because of women's predominance in African American churches, gospel is unique among U.S. popular music idioms for offering female musicians creative opportunities to develop their talents. The Pentecostal churches where gospel flourished overwhelmingly invested men with institutional power, in particular barring women from preaching. But they afforded women a variety of leadership roles as musicians: most commonly as choir directors, church organists and pianists, and soloists. Although Thomas A. Dorsey, the blues pianist turned prolific Christian composer and entrepreneur, is thus typically elevated as the "Father of Gospel," the music's most celebrated and culturally representative artists have long been women. Even people who know little of gospel recognize the names of singers such as Marion Williams and Mahalia Jackson. This "gendering" of gospel leads jazz historian Rosetta Reitz to position African American women at the center of

U.S. popular music history. "It was," she asserts, "the women swinging the congregations from the keyboards, the soloists, the choirs, and the worshippers hallelujahing, that are the base—the underneath it all—of America's music."[3]

Reitz's inspiration for this wonderfully provocative claim was one of these underneath-it-all women: "Sister" Rosetta Tharpe (1915–1973), gospel's first national star and its preeminent crossover musician from the late 1930s through the mid-1950s. At a time when women seldom commanded commercial attention as instrumentalists, and when prevailing notions of female sexual propriety strictly limited the sphere of their acceptable behavior as performers, Tharpe distinguished herself for her dynamic guitar playing and charismatic stage presence—the stage in question alternately consisting of nightclubs, church pulpits, and local auditoriums. Rather than simply catering to commercial tastes, moreover, Tharpe made music that existed at the threshold of sacred and secular: up-tempo arrangements of songs like "Strange Things Happening Every Day," "Up above My Head," and "Didn't It Rain" (the latter recorded with her long-time singing partner "Madame" Marie Knight) that reinterpreted African American gospel idioms for popular audiences in an era of swing's commercial dominance.

Born Rosetta Nubin in Cotton Plant, Arkansas, to a traveling missionary mother who played the mandolin, Tharpe gained fame as a guitarist who could make the instrument "talk" by plucking the melody as an improvised counterpoint to the voice. Her technique drew on both southern finger-picking guitar styles and Sanctified piano techniques, especially those of blind pianist Arizona Dranes, an important early influence. In adapting these techniques for guitar, Tharpe honed a manner of playing that crossed boundaries of both genre and gender. Like Memphis Minnie, the blues musician with whom she is often favorably compared, Tharpe earned the dubious reputation of playing "like a man." In fact, men and women alike aspired to imitate Tharpe, a consummate performer who reveled in pushing amps to their limits; even before going electric in the '40s, she was partial to National metal-body resonating guitars, designed for maximum loudness without electricity.

Tharpe's command of the instrument is readily evident in the few available sources of filmed footage of her playing. In one, a guest-host stint on the short-lived *TV Gospel Time* program of the early 1960s (footage that surfaced in the French film *Amélie* in 2001), she lets loose with a controlled abandon that looks remarkably contemporary even by today's standards of rock jamming. Indeed, so porous is the musical distinction between gospel and rock, and so dominant are rock aesthetics and assumptions in shaping contemporary critical sensibilities, that it's hard to imagine a language to describe Tharpe's style that *doesn't* resort to rock idioms.

This difficulty is not simply a question of semantics. Rather, and as the phrase playing "like a man" suggests, the problem of finding a language to talk about Tharpe on something like her "own" terms goes to the heart of larger issues of cultural categorization and cultural memory. How do some musicians enter the canon of popular memory, whereas others lapse into relative obscurity? How, in particular, does this process work for women, who are less likely to be remembered as innovators, musical virtuosos, or cultural heroes?

For some time now, feminist critics have confronted these issues by challenging the idea of U.S. popular music—especially rock 'n' roll—as an exclusively male provenance. This has entailed, in part, the excavation of obscured histories of women musicians; in part, the use of these histories to rescript what we know, or think we know, about popular music itself. The riot grrrl "revolution" of the early '90s—the indie/punk upsurge that launched a thousand analyses of women in rock, and that continues to inspire feminist analysis—has been particularly influential in this regard. Work done in the wake of riot grrrl has made it no easier to talk about a pivotal protorocker such as Tharpe, however. This is especially evident in the late celebration of girls with guitars, which, though powerful in addressing the invisibility of assertive women rocker-instrumentalists of the late twentieth and early twenty-first centuries, fails to address the specific versions of gender made available, in and through gospel, to African American women of an earlier era.

Tharpe's "musicking," to use Christopher Small's useful term, is not merely invisible but largely unintelligible within rock narratives that elevate the street, the nightclub, and the recording studio as privileged sites of music making.[4] It was in the feminized public sphere of the black church, broadly conceived, that early gospel artists such as Tharpe set about rocking congregations, beginning in the 1930s. In such a context, moreover, Tharpe's early mastery of the guitar was anything but transgressive. Whereas Pentecostal churches in the early 1900s generally steered girls with musical talent to the ladylike piano, certain denominations—particularly Church of God in Christ, or COGIC, the denomination of Katie Bell Nubin and her precocious daughter—welcomed the guitar as an acceptable instrument for girls.[5] For women such as Tharpe and her mother, moreover, string instruments offered the crucial possibility of physical movement. Unlike pianists and organists, string players could accompany themselves on street corners and at tent meetings—indeed, wherever the spirit moved them—and exploit the opportunities travel afforded for expanding their musical vocabulary.

Tharpe's musical ambitions found expression through COGIC's emphasis on the public expression of faith, its elevation of evangelizing as a privilege and even a responsibility of the faithful, and its valuation of missionary activity as an acceptable pursuit for women. And while the religious aspects of gospel music dictated a certain discretion regarding its dissemination outside of the church, female gospel singers used their identification with sacred music to construct a public presence in the secular realm. In fact, it was precisely by claiming music as a calling that female gospel musicians created alternatives to traditional domesticity and motherhood—and did so in ways that preserved their ability to identify with the tenets of respectable, Christian womanhood so important (given racist and sexist stereotypes) to African American women at midcentury. For example, when, in 1947, Tharpe approached the then twenty-one-year-old Marie Knight with the idea of joining her on tour, it was the notion of divine musical "gifts"—that is, of God-given talents that demanded to be put to use in *this* world—that ultimately persuaded Knight's mother to send her daughter on the road with her blessing.[6] And while Knight was briefly married, like Tharpe (who married three times, and who never had children) she chafed against the restrictions imposed by a husband who felt threatened by her career and her financial independence.

Indeed, contrary to depictions of gospel musicians as parochial, women in gospel, like the more celebrated blueswomen before them, often led itinerant lives as self-sufficient musicians, serving the needs of geographically diverse black communities. Tharpe and Knight spent years crisscrossing the country on tours, some arranged by Decca Records, some booked by their manager; for a time, the two even shared a tour bus complete with a hired driver and built-in bed, which came in handy in southern states, where it was hard to come by hotels that welcomed African Americans. In the late '50s and the '60s, when their commercial popularity had begun to wane in the United States, they found enthusiastic and informed audiences for gospel in France, England, Sweden, and Germany. Being on the road was, in fact, as crucial to the financially tenuous livelihood of gospel recording artists as it was to secular musicians. Needing only Tharpe's guitar, some microphones, and few amps, Tharpe and Knight traveled not only lightly but frequently without the company of men.

Tharpe's career—at least as conventionally defined—is studded with a series of "firsts" and "mosts": first gospel musician to sign a recording contract (in 1938, with Decca Records, with whom she would record through the '50s); first gospel performer to play the whites-only Cotton Club and Harlem's Apollo Theater; first gospel singer to do a significant European tour; for a time the gospel solo performer with the most Top 10 records on the *Billboard* "race" (later, rhythm and blues) charts. Yet her work is only partially visible if we focus exclusively on the secular public sphere as the site of her music making. Even as she recorded for Decca, toured with Lucky Millinder's swing band, was featured in John Hammond's famous 1938 "Spirituals to Swing" concert at Carnegie Hall, played with Cab Calloway, and recorded Victory disks for overseas troops during the Second World War, Tharpe also continued to perform sanctified styles for African American church audiences who had minimal investments in such secular success.

At the same time, while church audiences often disapproved of her forays into "blues" (a word often synonymous with any music perceived as appealing primarily to the body), they took pride in her achievements as an African American woman. In the African American press, Tharpe was simultaneously depicted as controversial and exemplary, her success on the *Billboard* charts construed as an indication of the universal appeal of black music and of the possibilities for blacks' success in a segregated America.

Tharpe earned her greatest notoriety as a result of her July 3, 1951, wedding concert: an event centering on Tharpe's exchange of vows with her third husband, Russell Morrison, former manager of the male vocal harmony group the Ink Spots. In the middle of an extensive tour for Decca that kept her on the road for 115 days straight, Tharpe had little time to get married; she and her manager agreed, however, that this problem could be solved with a combination wedding and show in Washington, D.C. Janis Joplin's biographers typically credit her with being the first woman in rock to draw arena-size crowds, but Tharpe's ability to attract a mass audience to Griffith Stadium, then the city's major sports arena, and to do so as a headline act on the day before a national holiday, prompts a rethinking of the notion of the stadium rocker. Factoring in even the most conservative estimates, it's safe to say that some 20,000 "guests"—more than the typical turnout for a Washington Senators baseball game, according to *Ebony*—showed up for the wedding concert, despite a citywide transit strike that limited the run of the district's streetcars. Moreover, as the magazine duly noted, spectators "had to pay just about as much"—between 90 cents and $2.50—for the right to participate in what was billed as "the most elaborate wedding ever staged" and the "world's greatest spiritual concert!"[7]

The fact that most of these concertgoers were African American women is as significant to this story as the size of the crowd itself. The trend toward stadium rock concerts in the 1970s and '80s grew out of the spectacular success of the now-iconic rock festivals of the late 1960s. Woodstock and Monterey not only heralded the emergence of a mass audience for rock, but they also became famous as symbols of popular music's power to consolidate political and cultural community. In effect, such mass cultural events facilitated mass political movements insofar as they "sounded" a community back to itself. While it wasn't associated with a political movement, Tharpe's wedding concert nevertheless resonated politically as a mass gathering of African American women in a symbolic public setting (a baseball stadium) in the nation's capital.

It did so, moreover, in the form of an event that brilliantly and unabashedly merged secular and sacred ritual. Wearing what *Ebony* reported to be an $800 wedding gown and a $350 corsage with twenty-eight white orchids, Tharpe was given away by her mother and attended by fellow singers performing the roles of maid of honor (Knight) and bridesmaids (backup vocalists the Rosettes). The bride walked down an improvised aisle leading from the dugout to a platform at second base, and according to published accounts she regaled the crowd playing a steel guitar in her wedding gown. A massive fireworks display followed, featuring a "20-foot, animated, life-like reproduction of the famed Sister Tharpe, rhythmically strumming her guitar."[8]

Such outrageous self-promotion attests to Tharpe's wit and to her penchant for performance, both on- and offstage. It also points to the iconicity of Tharpe's guitar as an aspect of her public self-fashioning. As Knight tells it, so associated was Tharpe with her guitar in the minds of her fans that they sometimes had trouble distinguishing the two women on stage if Tharpe did not have her instrument (the other telltale sign was her neatly curled bangs). In part, this reflects Decca's strategy of marketing Tharpe as a guitarist throughout her career. Early promotional photographs from the late 1930s depict her playing in full-length silk taffeta and heels, conveying competent musicianship—in addition to modest feminine charm—as an aspect of her commercial image. Although her hairstyles and her dresses changed over the years, rarely was she pictured without a guitar; so complete was this identification that she appears with her instrument on a U.S. Postal Service commemorative stamp bearing her likeness.[9]

Notwithstanding the tremendous burden Tharpe bore as a performer deemed by many in the Holiness Church to be squandering her talents (or worse) by playing for secular audiences, her decision to record complicates predictable narratives of decline and the relinquishing of autonomy that often accompany stories of commercially popular female musicians. Decca made every effort to market Tharpe to a non-church-going audience—for example, retitling the Dorsey song "Hide Me in Thy Bosom" as "Rock Me" on her first record—and Tharpe's decision to sign with the label led to her emergence as an early popular exemplar of black female instrumental virtuosity. The preserved footage from *TV Gospel Time*, a short-lived musical variety program of the early 1960s, shows her jamming on her guitar while adhering to the ideals of saintly (in the Pentecostal sense of "saints" as the saved) femininity.

More important yet, her performance reinterprets the seeming contradictions of musical virtuosity in *women*. As she wears both her matching hat and dress *and* her electric guitar, there is little tension between her image and her display of technical skill, here including her display of pleasure *in* virtuosity. This stands in sharp contrast both to Tharpe's gospel contemporaries, such as "Mother" Willie Mae Ford Smith, who maintained her church mother appearance, down to her sensible shoes, throughout her career, and to current white female guitarists, who often perform gender ironically or subversively—recall Courtney Love in her baby-doll dresses—to both call attention to and critique the notion of their incompatibility.

How, then, do we position Rosetta Tharpe amid the current popular, critical, and scholarly enthusiasm for postpunk girls with guitars? Tharpe's legacy challenges commonplaces within feminist studies of popular music: the equation of musical and cultural value with resistance (typically imagined as a rejection of the domestic and an embracing of the "street"), and the notion that women rockers transgress gender and sexual norms when they play electric guitar.

Indeed, Tharpe's career suggests different ways of approaching notions of "women in rock." For one thing, it reveals the importance of recognizing African American and female "counterpublics" that have tended to remain invisible within rock historiography. As Sherrie Tucker argues, this means resisting the urge to include women as "contributors" to popular music cultures without significantly revising our understanding of these cultures.[10] The current celebration of (white) women rockers' appropriation of the guitar, meanwhile, needs to be tempered by an awareness of those cultural spaces that historically have sanctioned and even rewarded women's musical creativity. This is not to suggest that women like Rosetta Tharpe enjoyed unlimited authority to invent themselves as musicians, or that their visibility did not threaten social and cultural norms. Yet notions of women in rock ought to be able to include, for example, Pentecostal churches as institutions central to (African American) women's musical development.

Furthermore, even within the context of the study of the gospel roots of rock 'n' roll, we need to question the sacred-to-secular teleology that so often structures rock histories. The debate over how to position Tharpe obscures the more interesting and important issue of the constantly shifting line between sacred and secular—a relation that is crucially important to understanding the cultural production of black women. Not only was black women's adherence to their "proper place" in the sacred-secular binary enforced more rigidly than black men's, but their location within the sacred realm afforded them very specific means of access to, and authority within, the secular. Moreover, the "crossover" metaphor seriously mischaracterizes Tharpe's musical and cultural practice. Along with other gospel luminaries, she moved constantly, if not always painlessly, between spheres conceived as sacred and secular, performing gospel (a distinctly hybrid form) for heterogeneous audiences in culturally and geographically diverse locations. Similarly, the notion that some gospel musicians "sold out" in their efforts to reach secular audiences implies an irresolvable tension between the music and its commercial incorporation. Yet the figure of the gospel entrepreneur has a long and distinguished history, extending back to such renowned musicians as Dorsey and Sallie Martin, who discovered the publication of gospel sheet music as a strategy of cultural ownership.

These examples gesture toward the sort of alternative narratives made possible by the project of remembering Tharpe's life and music. The literature on rock typically acknowledges gospel's contributions to rock history through reference to black churches as places where so many musicians (whites such as Elvis Presley among them)

acquired experience and developed an ear for particular rhythms, ca-
dences, and harmonies. Yet frequently such narratives conflate musicians' cultural arrival with their geographical and creative movement
beyond the church. Among other things, Tharpe makes it possible to
critique this trajectory, to ask how ideas of musical progress might be
reenvisioned so that the logic of artistic development does not assume an evolution from sacred to secular, from race particularity to
race-neutral universality. The notion of separate sacred and secular
spheres also leads to questions regarding the social construction of
musical meaning and the use of boundaries as a means for social
control of culture. Assuming music to be a social practice, what is
the basis of the secular/sacred distinction? Does the "sacred" value
of some music originate in the manner in which it is heard? In the
place in which it is performed? In the sincerity or authenticity of the
performance? In the identity of the performer?

Finally, Tharpe's career demonstrates the need to submit the ongoing (re)discovery of "women in rock" to constant interrogation,
lest revisionist paradigms become new truisms. Because problems of
language are equally and more urgently problems of imagination,
we might begin with language—with the phrase "women *who rock*" as
a substitute for the more commonplace "women in rock." Drawing
on Nathaniel Mackey's discussion of *swing* as a verb turned noun,
"women who rock" envisions rock as a dynamic practice, not an ossi-
fied tradition.[11] It likewise represents women in terms of their cultural agency, not their static presence—their doing, not their being.

Moreover, the phrase draws attention to the limitations of the canonical project implicit in "women in rock." While it is true, as
Farah Jasmine Griffin argues in the case of Billie Holiday, that African American women seldom have been represented as creative geniuses—as makers, not merely receivers, of artistic tradition—the en-
shrining of individual women's authorship is ultimately inadequate
to addressing their absence from (or rather, their selective presence
within) popular music pantheons.[12] Only by analyzing how canons
are made in the first place can feminist scholars hope to displace, not
merely diversify, them.

Tharpe rocked musically—through her explosive guitar licks, irreverent takes on gospel idioms, and fondness for playing loud—as well as socioculturally, through her audacious, spectacular rocking of black sacred musical traditions and social norms of race, gender, and social class. Although her reputation has waned since her death in 1973, her iconoclastic musical practice looks and sounds fresh in the twenty-first century. Her example suggests that the prehistory of "women in rock" lies in large part in the stories of those underneath-it-all women shouting their faith while rocking the congregation.

chapter 5

The Birth
of the Blues

LUC SANTE

The blues, apparently, began in the mists. Sometime before history, or in some side room or annex veiled off from history, the blues occurred. The old accounts would have it that the blues were the result of a gradual evolution, from African songs remembered on the American continent—eventually by people who didn't remember Africa—that became ring shouts and work songs and jump-ups and field hollers and levee-camp hollers, which at some unnameable point were formalized into what we call the blues. There is a lot of truth in this account, of course, but it leaves out one essential point: the blues is tremendously specific. It is a particular song form made up of twelve measures of three-line verse, with a line length of five stressed syllables and an AAB rhyme scheme. Lots and lots of things have been called blues because they are emotionally congruent with the blues, or because they exist in the repertoire of blues performers, or just because the word *blues* in the title sounded snazzy to the writer. But the blues, properly speaking, is this:

> *Hitch up my pony, saddle up my black mare,*
> *Hitch up my pony, saddle up my black mare,*
> *I'm gonna find a rider, baby, in the world somewhere.*[1]

African American music evolved; the musical setting in which the blues occurred evolved; but the blues form itself could not have evolved, could only have been invented, at a particular time, in a particular place, by a particular person or persons. As Samuel Charters wrote: "It is always important to emphasize . . . that there was no sociological or historical reason for the blues verse to take the form it did. Someone sang the first blues."[2] But about the specifics of this invention we know nothing.

All we possess are the vaguest sorts of lineaments. To the best of anyone's knowledge, the first time the term *blues* was applied to a song was in 1892, when W. C. Handy transcribed a tune he heard played by "shabby guitarists" in St. Louis and called it the "East St. Louis Blues"—which is not actually a blues. It seems likely that the term *blues,* meaning sadness or yearning, already existed in the vocabulary of black music. The first near approximation of an actual blues to be copyrighted was "The Dallas Blues," the work of a young white Texan, Hart Wand, in 1912, which predated W. C. Handy's "Memphis Blues" in its titling if not its composition—Handy's piece, composed in 1911, was first called "Mister Crump" and was no more a blues than his first such effort. (Handy spent quite a long time dancing around the notion of the blues.) Now, given that the first recording of a bona fide blues did not occur until 1920, with Mamie Smith's "The Crazy Blues," it is misleading to speculate too much on the basis of written compositions. The blues in its earliest decades was disseminated orally, by people who were generally illiterate and did not have access to sheet-music publishers or any of the rest of the formal apparatus of the popular music industry of the day.

So then we have to turn to accounts derived from oral history, song collecting, and folklore research. The earliest published description of what appears to be blues dates from 1903, from an account in the *Journal of American Folk-Lore* by the Harvard archaeologist Charles Peabody, who transcribed many of the songs sung by the laborers he employed on an excavation in Coahoma County, Mississippi, in 1901. Ma Rainey remembered first hearing a blues at a tent show in Missouri in 1902. It was in 1903 that W. C. Handy heard a man in the depot in Tutwiler, Mississippi, playing slide guitar and singing a blues about goin' where the Southern cross the Dog. Incidentally, both Handy and Ma Rainey, already veteran performers on the southern African American music circuit, found reason to comment on how weird and unprecedented this music sounded to them. Then the folklorist Howard Odum published field collections of songs sung by black country people in Georgia and Mississippi between 1905 and 1908, and these include quite a few that qualify as blues. Although it took a long time for anyone to begin making serious inquiries as to the origins of the blues, the first field researchers who interviewed old-timers on the subject could not find anyone who had heard blues before 1890.

So that is all we know: the blues was invented in the 1890s, somewhere in the South. This is not a minor detail. It is true that the African American musical tradition that preceded and continued to flourish alongside the blues was tremendously rich. It is true that many songs that do not fit the blues template were called blues not just by record companies and song publishers but by blues musicians themselves, and that includes both Charley Patton and Blind Lemon Jefferson. It is true that a number of items in the songster's ditty bag come very close to the blues without quite fitting the definition—"Poor Boy Long Ways from Home," for example. But the blues itself, that instantly recognizable formula, perhaps more specific than anything that ever lent its name to a musical genre, had a definite point of origin, was *invented*, the way the X ray and the zipper and the diesel engine were invented in the same decade. Somebody, somewhere made a quantum leap. This is not the way things usually work in popular culture. There are anywhere between twelve and fifty legitimate claimants to the title of originator of rock and roll, from the 1950s back to maybe the 1920s. Rap might have been born in the mid-1970s, but you could make a pretty good case for "The

Dirty Dozens" as a member of the family, and that goes back at least to the late nineteenth century. Specific people have invented dance crazes, and instrumental styles, and methods of arrangement, but besides the blues, all the other aisle markers in the record store are products of accretion and synthesis and evolution.[3]

It doesn't seem accidental that the blues should have appeared in the 1890s, between the motion picture and the flying machine. It was the decade of inventions. The twentieth century was at hand, when surely all the world's ills would be conquered—the 1890s was a terrible decade in many respects, but it was also a time of starry-eyed idealism, filled with such foredoomed notions as Esperanto and the single tax and the mucus-free diet. It saw the beginning of modernism, when the old notions were radically simplified or radically complicated or stood on their heads or smashed to smithereens. And it gave birth to modern efficiency: the assembly line, Taylorism, modern systems of accounting and distribution. Formula was all, the key to success, the basis of ten thousand get-rich-quick schemes. How coincidental was it that the decade also witnessed the invention of a musical form that was magically simple, instantly recognizable, and endlessly reproducible?

The blues must have caught on with blinding speed. The reason we don't know who invented the blues seems obvious: he, or just possibly she, was poor and illiterate and perhaps rural and of course southern black, and any one of those adjectives would have guaranteed anonymity. But the very success of the invention must also have militated against anyone's knowing who was responsible. Even if it was a front-porch guitarist rather than an itinerant songster, it is easy to imagine that within twenty-four hours a dozen people had taken up the style, a hundred inside of a week, a thousand in the first month. By then only ten people would have remembered who had come up with it, and nine of them weren't talking. By the time any folklorist or song collector was sufficiently interested to ask the question, the trail was stone cold. We have the names of a few dozen people who played blues before World War I and were dead or inactive by the time the music came to be recorded, but that's it. For all that New Orleans in the 1920s was dense with people who claimed, with greater or lesser credibility, to have been present at the birth of some version of jazz, nobody has ever made the faintest or most implausible boast regarding the primal scene of the blues, not "My uncle made it up" or "I hear it came from down in Ruleville." Nobody ever interviewed Charley Patton, who was surely playing by 1910, or Henry Thomas, who was born in 1874 and learned his entire repertoire before 1900, and more's the pity, but if Ma Rainey didn't know, did they?

Patton was from the Mississippi Delta, and Thomas was from east Texas. Strangely, both regions have been identified as the birthplace of the blues, even simultaneously, a bit like those seven or nine Italian villages that lay claim to St. Anthony. Robert Palmer, for example, suggests that the origin of the blues lay somewhere in the vicinity of Dockery's Plantation in Bolivar County, Mississippi, but he also seems to think it originated in east Texas at the same time.[4] This is not utterly impossible, considering how, for instance, at least three different people made realistic simultaneous claims for the invention of motion pictures. Still, instances of simultaneous invention occur when a need is widespread, many people are working on a solution, and the simplest and most versatile answer comes as the inevitable result of a number of lines of research. Could anything similar be said regarding the blues? Anecdotal evidence suggests that the blues did have a rural origin, since whenever they were heard, early on, in cities like New Orleans or Memphis or St. Louis, they always seemed to have been imported there by country people. New Orleans was the central laboratory for African American music research at the time, but it does appear that the term *blues* was flung around with abandon in that city, very few of its applications pertaining to actual blues.

So the X that marks the spot must be in either Mississippi or Texas, or, somehow, both. (The Piedmont was another region of great musical fertility, but all indications are that the blues arrived there just a bit belatedly, and was absorbed into an ongoing stream.) Mississippi has always been the favorite, on account of the staggering number of innovators and stars and eccentrics who arose in a period of no more than twenty-five years or so in the crescent-shaped slice of the state's western edge that is called the Mississippi Delta. Texas is a strong contender because, although the numbers are smaller, the quality of its recorded pioneers is so striking. Among just the trio of Blind Lemon Jefferson, Blind Willie Johnson, and Texas Alexander, you can somehow sense proximity to the source. None of them sounds like a thirdhand recipient. (Of course, that might be the beginning of an argument for the music's having reached Texas later than Mississippi.)

Curiously enough, proponents of both the Mississippi and Texas theories often cite as supporting evidence their state's cultural nearness to Africa. Mississippi has the raked dirt yard and the diddley bow, the panpipes and the fife and drum bands, among other things. Texas, for its part, was historically the last state to import slaves, and so claims a lesser degree of assimilation in its African American population. This is a curious argument, because the blues is a manifestation of modernism—although of course it, like so many manifestations of modernism, strikes a bargain with the past, even the distant past. The blues sounds both more modern and more ancient than ragtime, or the black ballads of the late nineteenth century. But it is as a forecast of the future that the two states' competing claims really become interesting. Here's a rough sketch of the main stream of the Mississippi lineage: the music that Charley Patton learned from largely unknown sources and transformed, he passed along to Willie Brown, to Son House, to Robert Johnson, to Howlin' Wolf, circuitously to Muddy Waters. The latter two, along with some others, took the music to Chicago and amplified it, and it was picked up by Albert King, Magic Sam, Buddy Guy, and Junior Wells, to name just a few. These men have direct descendants in Chicago and elsewhere, but the best-known inheritors of the Chicago small-band tradition are Eric Clapton, Keith Richards, Robbie Robertson, and so on—in a word, or two: classic rock. In Texas, the baton of Blind Lemon Jefferson was eventually assumed by T-Bone Walker, Lowell Fulsom, Big Joe Turner, Pee Wee Crayton, all of whom came to play in large bands with horn sections, whose influence was felt among the house bands at Stax/Volt, Hi, and other middle South–based record labels of the 1960s, which is to say: classic soul.

One possible extrapolation of this double model might run as follows. The Mississippi tradition, involving small units and the most basic instruments (amplified, but still basic) would naturally appeal principally to white primitivists, pilgrims on the road to the promised land of authenticity. The Texas tradition came to express itself in larger ensembles, with tiers of brass instruments—sometimes even matching suits and individual music stands adorned with a crest. It saw itself as existing in a continuum with what were then the trappings of the very latest jazz, and this would signify with black progressivists. African Americans had to believe in the future—what choice did they have?—while whites yearned for an arcadian past. Mississippi was identified with a tendency that could be called minimalist, perhaps conservative, if not actually luddist, because it remained for so long outside the stream of change, while Texas was forward looking by virtue of its status as a crossroads. Such a train of thought would tend to favor Mississippi as the location of the petri dish, since Texas, at least in the 1890s, would be much more subject to winds blowing through. But a counterargument could be devised, centering on the notion that welcoming novelty makes a culture likewise more receptive to innovation. I'm not entirely persuaded by this neat dichotomy. There are too many exceptions to either rule, and overall it sounds more like a parlor game than an analysis, but it's worth considering nevertheless. It has been said, after all, that the past is continually in flux, is being reinvented every day. Considering the murkiness of the genealogy of the blues, a model that proceeds from any given present and moves backward through time seems nearly as plausible as any other.

chapter 6

Richard Speaks! Chasing a Tune from the Chitlin Circuit to the Mormon Tabernacle

RJ SMITH

Some songs are composed in a spirit of upheaval. Those who write them hope the music will shake up the street, give birth to new forms, tear down old lies. "This guitar kills fascists," read a winsome sticker sported by more than one punk rocker. As for the songs written on the guitars that kill fascists, one assumes they strike with the speed of light and are written in a state of perfect seeing.

Some songs are composed, period. But from time to time what tears up the streets is the music that nobody gave a second thought to, music that arrives not as a sum of experience or knowledge but as accidents carried by the winds, landing where they will. These songs have no date of birth, because they were never exactly conceived. They are simply not there one day, not there the next day, not there . . . not there . . . and then comes a time when they are indisputably alive, and it is said that they have always been around. Such is the case with "Open the Door, Richard."

Jack McVea assembled it from the air currents one night in Oregon. His five-piece band was touring the West Coast, playing a blend of small-group swing and early R&B. It was the early 1940s. McVea never pinpointed the date when he wrote music to go with an old comedy routine he knew by heart, possibly because he never remembered the night. It hardly seemed special to him; he was just seeking, as was his wont, to clown for the crowd. That was about as deep as it got. Jack McVea's band wore goofy hats in their stage show, sombreros and applejacks and pith helmets. They danced onstage, screaming and mugging and barrelhousing for the public. And here was a number perfect for goodtime hats and people-pleasing stagecraft. The original routine was called "Open the Door, Richard," which is what McVea decided to name his little tune. Fans seemed to dig it.

The band was back home in Los Angeles for a recording session in October 1946; they were parked in a Hollywood studio, at the rump end of an eight-tune recording session for the local Black & White label. Producer Ralph Bass later claimed recording "Open the Door, Richard" was his idea. "I was doing some blues with [McVea]. I got bored to death because everything sounded alike and suggested that he do 'Richard,' which I had seen him do live."[1]

Nobody ever said what happened the night after "Richard" was recorded; perhaps McVea's band celebrated at an after-hours club, perhaps they donned their sombreros and robbed a bank. Probably nobody even remembered that night; there was no reason to write things down. But "Richard" changed all kinds of history, and its story illustrates how immensely and unpredictably a song can matter. Loved by its fans, grudgingly accepted by those who played it over and over again, "Richard" mocks the notion that what matters most is that which has the most to say. Because, truth is, nobody agrees on what Richard says. And Richard isn't telling.

The surest source we have for the origin of "Open the Door, Richard" was not himself present at the primal moment. He was not with McVea in Oregon, not there in the earlier times when "Richard" was first performed as a comedy routine. But Dewey Markham was in congress with "Richard" and knew those who might as well be described as Richard's next of kin. He was a comic himself, who performed the routine through the better part of a century on stage and helped preserve it with a memory surpassing that of most of his grizzled chitlin-circuit peers.

They called him Pigmeat, which coincidentally was also a slang term for young stuff. Pigmeat Markham was a black comic who got his start in 1920s minstrel troupes, performing for black audiences in blackface—behind the mask of burnt cork, lips exaggerated with white makeup. He was a terrific clown, with a muscular, ridiculously theatrical voice and a gift for wringing laughs out of a fat man's frame. Markham performed with the Florida Blossoms in the early 1920s, and there met his mentor and inspiration, Bob Russell. A producer and writer with many stage shows to his name, Russell had a career in minstrelsy dating back to the Civil War, and by the time he met Markham in the Florida Blossoms around 1923, Russell was a sick old man.

Segregation prevailed, and black showmen traveled the South lightly, eating when they could, staying in homes when they couldn't find colored accommodations, dodging lynch mobs. The Florida Blossoms were touring near the end of the black minstrelsy era. Whites in blackface had already faded as popular entertainment by the Depression, but blacks in blackface lingered a decade or so longer. Markham calls Russell a "genius" in his autobiography, *Here Comes the Judge!* and there's a bittersweet passage in the book; Russell is dying while they travel by train from backwater to backwater, the elder man taking the lower berth. Russell taught Markham tricks of the trade—he'd wake Markham up in the middle of the night with a tap on the bunk and they'd talk about a new skit idea or gag. A country doctor had told Russell to eat eggs fried in gunpowder to heal a condition Markham doesn't name; the young showman wandered the early morning countryside, rustling up eggs for the man who was grooming him to succeed in the ways of blackface.

Markham writes that many folks thought he had come up with "Richard," perhaps since it was so much a part of his routine into the 1960s. Others believed a contemporary by the name of Dusty

Fletcher was the creator, but in truth, says Markham, "that song was written by my old friend Bob Russell, and he wrote it for a long-ago show called Mr. Rareback in which John Mason sang the song." Henry T. Sampson's book *Blacks in Blackface* documents that claim.[2] That's as close as we can get to the origins of "Richard."

Little is known about John Mason, beyond that he, too, performed in blackface and was known as Spider Bruce. It's hard to imagine Mason didn't have a large part in shaping the success of "Richard": Russell may have written the show, but the clowns exercised right of revision, improvising and inserting their own sensibility into the scripts. At the very least, Mason was probably the first person to perform "Open the Door, Richard," and he claimed to have done it as early as 1919.[3] He took it to Broadway in 1928 with a show called *Bamboola*. Also in *Bamboola*'s cast was a younger showman by the name of Dusty Fletcher.

Much more is known of Fletcher: there are film clips of him, a skinny, acrobatic clown who performed in top hat and tattered swallowtail coat, playing a familiar minstrel figure—the ragamuffin with pretensions. Performing the stages of the TOBA circuit, the chain of black theaters sweeping from the South to Harlem to Los Angeles, Fletcher was a star in the years after blackface minstrelsy had declined, the '20s and '30s. It was a time when black comics performed as out-and-out buffoons, or as members of a team; it would be over a decade before audiences would accept a black stand-up comic who directly addressed a paying customer as an equal. Fletcher's routines reflected (without commenting on) a reality today's viewers would find harsh. "Almost all his material is about fairly horrifying subjects: abject poverty, extreme alcoholism, spousal beating, homicide and other rib ticklers," writes one modern critic, who rather likes Fletcher.[4]

In Fletcher's "Richard" he played a drunken bon vivant at the end of a night out, staggering home only to find the door to his tenement apartment locked. He hollers up to his roommate to let him in, but Richard seems otherwise occupied; he hears heavy breathing coming from within. Along the way, cops and a cast of ghetto characters are encountered. Fletcher produces a ladder and woozily ascends, all the while firing off pleas and wisecracks—"I know he must be in there because I've got on the suit."[5] The routine traveled the TOBA circuit, and like a blues guitar lick shot out of the Mississippi Delta, like a slang term for the white man fresh out of New Orleans, Richard's weird fame was absorbed in black neighborhoods around the country as communal property.

By the early 1940s, John Mason was largely forgotten and Fletcher had retired to a farm in South Carolina. It was now Pigmeat Markham's time. The last important black comic to perform in black-face, Markham was sometimes referred to as the unofficial mayor of black Los Angeles. He was a regular presence on Central Avenue, the heart of the black city, playing the Club Alabam, emceeing at the Lincoln Theater, acting in small-time independent black produc-tions shot around the Avenue. Among those who heard Markham perform his "Richard" on Central Avenue was Jack McVea, a saxo-phone player who had once been in the house band at the Club Alabam. McVea was a true child of Los Angeles, born there in 1914, his father, Isaac, the banjo-playing founder of McVea's Howdy En-tertainers, which had a regular show on KNX's *The Optimistic Do-Nut Show* in the late 1920s. Jack played banjo as well in this group. After picking up the alto and tenor saxophones, he joined several impor-tant local dance bands in the 1930s, then hooked up with the pre-miere Los Angeles band, Lionel Hampton's crew, in which he played baritone saxophone.

McVea performed on the Hampton band's landmark 1942 "Flying Home" and was a featured player at the first Jazz at the Phil-harmonic concert; he recorded with Slim Gaillard and Charlie Parker and T-Bone Walker. All of which was a pretty solid jazz résumé, but which was also more or less the straight life compared with the weirdness that reigned when McVea and Richard crossed paths.

Dusty Fletcher and McVea collided in the early '40s, when Hampton toured with the comedian. They'd play his intro music and then Fletcher would ease into a routine, and from this McVea became steeped in the ways of the missing house key. By the time he left Hampton in 1943 McVea had memorized Fletcher's signa-ture skit. He formed his own group, one based on the swank, air-cushioned proto–rhythm and blues of Louis Jordan's Tympani Five. Their records were already making a local impact–McVea and Roy Milton among others, influenced by Jordan, were soon to give birth to Los Angeles R&B. Copying Jordan's unit, McVea's had five members–two horns and three rhythm players. "We thought that was the greatest music in the world," said McVea.[6]

Between 1943 and 1946, McVea refined the hard-edged small band sound, working regularly with drummer and vocalist Rabon Tarrant. They started performing the musical version of "Richard" that McVea dreamed up that night in Oregon. "That simple melody just came to me," he told an interviewer. "Then we added some business, like this lady across the street looking through her window at us."[7] The easygoing banter of McVea and Tarrant, the bop shadings the piano player slipped in, the busybody they described looking through her window, all of it slayed them live, and when McVea booked a recording session the fall of 1946, "Richard" was set in wax. Released late in the same year, it quickly became a jukebox favorite up and down Central Avenue. Maybe that's the best thing that ever happened to McVea. Later, after "Richard" made him a national star, McVea claimed the biggest thrill of all was overhearing a little old lady tell a streetcar conductor, "Open the door, Richard."

January 1947 came with an abundance of crisis. There was the Central Avenue gossip about the bizarre carving of Louis Jordan, in town for a long stand; he was hospitalized after his wife, Fleecie, stopped trimming her corns with a knife long enough to turn the weapon on a husband she featured for philandering. That same month, the rest of the country was tuning in to "Richard," and while Jordan recuperated in Los Angeles it was symbolically, perhaps, as if the student once again was surpassing the teacher. As soon as Black & White released "Richard," under the band name Jack McVea and His All Stars (Black & White No. 792), it began selling well–perhaps surprisingly well to McVea, who never sounded all that proud of the song. Demand outstripped supply. The February 15, 1947, issue of the *Los Angeles Sentinel* announced that Black & White was sending "one of the largest single order shipments of records ever carried by air"–

10,000 copies airlifted to New York City alone—"in a C-54, which has the largest plane doors ever constructed."

Even listening today, the song moves beneath conventional radar. "Richard" starts out so casually, a few offhand piano notes, a hint of bass, it's as if the musicians didn't even know they were recording; it has the sound of an off-the-meter rehearsal, guys casually stumbling onto the one tune they can play together. McVea has a convivial, knowing voice—he's not the tipsy Fletcher, he's a sport keeping himself in check, a hipster. After the sing-along bridge, he falls into a little banter with drummer Rabon Tarrant and then the other musicians, and a good-natured jauntiness flows. One-liners bump into each other, and the loose banter points in two directions at once—back to the dozens and playground rhymes of African American folk culture and forward to Bo Diddley's "Say man" records and even to rap. Steeped in black oral traditions, "Richard" is so casual and unforced, so unplanned and happenstance it doesn't feel like a conscious effort to *say* or *reflect* anything. It just is.

Everybody smelled a payday. Dusty Fletcher and John Mason both came out of the wings to claim authorship of the tune. "It actually happened to me," Mason told a reporter from the *Baltimore Afro-American*. "If my partner and me had two suits and his was the good one, I'd wear his and he'd stay home while I attended to business."[8] Meanwhile Fletcher said *he* came up with the routine after a night of drinking in a South Carolina railroad station. A drunk was tossed out and stood in the street, demanding the bartender let him in. Fletcher claimed he wrote a routine inspired by the scene, first trying out the tagline "Open the door, John," which got modest laughs, then "Open the door, Henry," which garnered a few more, and then Richard broke the dam.

By the time the hoofer's dust had settled and court claims resolved, revised credits on the record read: "Words by Dusty Fletcher and John Mason, music by Dusty Fletcher and Don Howell." That last name came as a surprise to McVea because, he always said, he wrote the tune himself. Never, he explained, did he meet his alleged collaborator. "Don Howell" was a front, a place-holding name that allowed others to pocket half the money that should have gone to McVea. There has been plenty of speculation as to who "Don Howell" really was–a music publisher, an executive at Decca, or maybe no single person at all. McVea was gouged far worse than if Louis Jordan's wife had offered to trim his corns.

Not only do we not know who the originator of "Richard" is, we can't even discover the identity of the fake one. Indeed, we don't even know much about Richard himself. Who is Richard? A guy you never meet in the song, somebody outside its physical space; he's the person the song is directed at. And *he* isn't listening. He's subject and object and he's powerful, most of all powerful because he refuses to show himself–Richard is heedless, uncaring, and, possibly, he's not even there.

The tune first hit in the black ghetto of Los Angeles, and it fanned out to black neighborhoods coast to coast. Many black artists quickly cut covers and answer records, and many of these climbed the "race" music charts. There were hit versions by McVea (no. 3), Count Basie (no. 1–the biggest hit he ever had), the Three Flames (no. 1), the Charioteers (no. 6). Dusty Fletcher cashed in (no. 3), and McVea's mentor Louis Jordan was moved to cover the tune (no. 6).

But if by February "Richard" was a smash in the black community, the praise was far from universal. A shouting match broke out in the letters sections of black newspapers, as Richard became an unwitting lightning rod for tensions between rural and urban, old and young, zoot suits and swallowtails. Old-timers tended to view Fletcher as the originator, celebrating him as an up-from-bootstraps survivor of the Old South. McVea was scorned as a product of Hollywood, his dap band flossy and shallow compared with the keeping-it-real Fletcher. The battle in the press over Richard was about style, and whether one responded to Fletcher's ragged but right suit and top hat or McVea's draped shape said a lot about who one was. Pillars of society viewed Richard as an embarrassment, and one critic acutely summed up his minstrelsy roots as "Uncle Tom-y."[9] They sensed in the frivolity of the McVea band everything that was holding back the race.

Perhaps as well critics dreaded the young listeners who also wore zoot suits and reflected their energy back on the band. They embraced Richard, and gave him meanings McVea had never meant any more than he meant to be a symbol of backwardness. To at least some black listeners, Richard was a barely secret call for justice's doors to spring open. In 1947 students from seven Georgia colleges marched to the state capital demanding the resignation of segregationist governor Herman Talmadge, carrying banners reading "Open the Door Herman."[10]

On the road, McVea found himself thrust into the position of agitator, and perhaps pondering the true identity of somebody he alone should know. In May, Indianapolis mayor Robert H. Tyndall nixed McVea's appearance at a Teen-Agers Frolic, declaring there would be no mixed dances in town. The chief of police refused to issue a permit; McVea, his manager, and the CIO sponsors of the dance researched local law and found a loophole allowing nonpermit dances to go on if they were classified as a private club event rather than a public dance. "Bandleader McVea expressed himself to the hundreds of teen-agers gathered by working the four-hour dance period without one breathing spell," cheered the *Chicago Defender*.[11]

On Richard's adopted Main Street, Central Avenue, a civil rights theme was reflected back on the song. "Open the Door Richard" was the headline the *Los Angeles Sentinel* ran above an editorial calling for political representation at City Hall. "We are glad to see Negroes knocking at the door and we hope that they keep on pounding until our sleeping city fathers get up and open that door," it said.[12]

Just as Richard was being reborn on Central Avenue, so too was the battle for civil rights, which was embodied by the fight against restrictive covenants and other unfair housing practices. In Los Angeles, a city in which the black population had skyrocketed since the start of World War II—doubling by the end of the decade—access to housing was the paramount struggle. Leading that battle was Loren Miller, a newspaper writer, lawyer, and the author of the editorial in the *Sentinel*. Part of the NAACP's national brain trust, Miller was involved in many important cases involving housing restrictions and argued several before the Supreme Court; he probably knew more about housing law than any other lawyer in the country. In 1947, as "Open the Door, Richard" had become a national phenomenon, Miller was helping the NAACP prepare arguments for *Shelley v. Kraemer*. When that case was won by the NAACP a year later, the Supreme Court ruled that restrictive covenants were unenforceable by the courts.

It was serendipitous that the birthplace of the musical Richard, Jack McVea's stamping grounds, featured at exactly this moment the cramped living conditions and squalor related in the song. "Richard" became a mirror in which a ghetto community saw something of itself, and gave that population a voice in the creation of popular culture.

Across the country, Richard became a fair housing messenger. A March 1947 story in New York's *Amsterdam News* reported on a sermon given by Reverend Horace A. White, pastor of Plymouth Congregational Church in Detroit. The sermon was titled "Open the Door, Richard." "This ditty which is sweeping the country on stage, air and records, was made to have deep seated meaning by Rev. White as it dealt with restrictive covenants in this community . . ." the paper reported. "Rev. White stressed the fact that . . . the doors of equal opportunity for better housing for Negroes must be opened so that he can walk boldly into any house in any neighborhood where he is capable of purchasing or renting. In this case Richard (the courts) is not asleep but is prejudiced and stubborn but sooner or later will be forced to open the door when restrictive covenants are definitely broken."[13] A year later, thanks to Loren Miller and many others, they were.

Meanwhile, other audiences tuned in; white people found out about Richard. They were hearing the same song, but hearing it in an entirely different way. By March 1947, "Open the door, Richard" had become a jovial salute on national radio shows, a line uttered by Jack Benny, Fred Allen, and Phil Harris. Jimmy Durante and Burl Ives recorded versions, as did the milk-'n-cookies harmony group the Pied Pipers. Some of these covers took Richard in directions not even Bob Russell's fever dreams could have rendered. For a moment, the public thirst for all things Richard was boundless; there were hillbilly versions cut by Hank Penny and by Dick Peterson and His Vocal Yokels; there was a calypso version—a musical craze enveloping a song craze—by Tosh "One String" Weller and His Jivesters. "The U.S., which loves screwball songs, last week hit the crackpot jackpot," wrote *Life* magazine.[14]

Whites embraced all things Richard, but they tendered their affections in a particular way, adoring Richard as pure novelty. He was accepted like any other classic catchphrase, akin to "Wanna buy a duck?" or "Vass dat you, Charlie?"—akin to any other novelty song, the likes of which had been around since "Yes, We Have No Bananas" in the '20s. McVea's insinuating flow, the song's call and response, its laid-back backbeat, all were something "Richard" had in common with Joe Liggins's "The Honeydripper," another rhythm and blues smash of the moment that was being called a novelty song in the press. The mass media either patronized the phenomenon or smirked, tolerating "Richard" as sublimely meaningless—as a tonic for nerves jangled by years of war. Unable to place a musical form that soon enough would be called rock and roll, whites took "Richard" to heart by telling themselves they were taking him to their attic, leaving him in that place where all the other fleetingly seductive and slightly embarrassing bric-a-brac was stored.

Richard became a marketing craze, perhaps the first of the postwar era. Dime stores sold Richard hats, dungarees, handkerchiefs, shirts, bracelets, and other memorabilia. He was used to market Ruppert Ale, Franklin Simon perfumes, and Best Yet hair attachments. Bugs Bunny riffed on the song in the cartoon "High Diving Hare." Opera star Lauritz Melchior broadcast his version coast to coast. Ultimately, "the life of every American named Richard became almost intolerable," lamented *Life*.[15]

The contagion then jumped the border, spreading across the globe. Molly Picon sang the song in Yiddish; there was a Spanish version, "Abra la Puerta, Ricardo," and covers in Swedish, French, and Hungarian. In Cardiff, England, fans of the local football team the Bluebirds serenaded local star Stan Richards with the chant,

"Open the score, Richards, and nod one in." In Montreal, fans of the hometown hockey team the Montreal Canadiens honored their local star, Rocket Richard, by shouting, "Open the door, Richard."

In that restless summer of 1947, Secretary of State George C. Marshall came to Harvard University with an alarming message for the nation: "I need not tell you that the world situation is very serious. That must be apparent to all intelligent people," he said in what would be one of the most famous speeches of the century. "The problem is one of such enormous complexity that the very mass of facts presented to the public by press and radio make it exceedingly difficult for the man in the street to reach a clear appraisement of the situation." No documentation exists that Marshall was speaking of the shadow Richard had cast upon the globe, but, as Richard airlifted American pop culture to far corners of the postwar world, he had become a soldier of the new American realpolitik. Richard, I think, became an early tool of what was soon to be called the Marshall Plan. McVea: "Richard, open the door, man—it's *co-hold* out here'n this air."

There was global paroxysm, then backlash, and, by late summer, exhaustion. Radio stations were banning the record by late 1947, and dozens of answer records had flopped, chilling the frenzy. Richard stayed up there in the attic, however, an object white America could pull down whenever it wanted, to puzzle over and utter, "Now what was I thinking?" Black America, though, with its greater claim on Richard, was still mulling over his inherent meanings. If in the war years he took on overtones of racial progress, only a few years later, as black unemployment skyrocketed and the mood soured among African Americans, other readings emerged.

In his 1985 autobiography *The Pony Express*, alto saxophonist Norwood "Pony" Poindexter, who played with McVea in 1950, alerts us to how the song was something far different from nonsense for those in the know.

The McVea band was famous for their hit song, "Open the Door, Richard" . . . It's interesting how a novelty tune like this could bring a smile to the face of the average white American . . .

One day a bunch of us went into the city. And were brought back to reality. In Salt Lake City almost all of the facilities open to the public were closed to the black population—without signs . . .

Next we went to the Mormon Tabernacle . . . Some of us took pictures of the two attendants that were barring our entry standing in front of the signs that stated among other things when black people were allowed inside.

After taking pictures, one of the cats told the attendants, "So this is the famous Judeo-Christian Mormon Tabernacle monument to racism hiding behind Christianity. Some of us have done you one better. In Chicago Elijah Muhammad has the great Mosque, and there are no signs with special days and times for whites to enter. You're barred for all time."[16]

To Poindexter, Richard's not going to open any doors, and the song is a piece of black culture whites don't have a clue about. It's a mystery again, not an anthem, not a sermon. *You think you understand your own signs, the messages you send,* Poindexter says, *but you don't understand—not truly.*

From minstrelsy to the hepcat underground to civil rights to Bing Crosby to the Mormon Tabernacle is an amazing journey in a few short years, but that's hardly the end of our story. It is said that a comic named Lollypop in New Orleans had a routine in the 1950s that inspired a local singer named Smiley Lewis to write "I Hear You Knockin'." *That* song was a staple on the southern R&B circuit, so much so that a Georgia-born piano pounder got tired of answering requests and wrote his own answer record—the player, Little Richard, titled it "Keep a Knockin'." Richard Nixon once quoted "Richard" to reporters, and the catchphrase was chanted outside Chicago Mayor Richard Daley's home in 1992 by homeless demonstrators demanding low-income housing. While lying low with the Band at the Big Pink house in Woodstock, New York, Bob Dylan recorded a rewrite of "Richard" that inhales the incandescent informality of the original and breathes out infinite grace. If singer/pianist Richard Manuel hadn't detested the original—having been teased with "open the door, Richard" all his life—they might not have renamed the thing "Open the Door, Homer."

McVea finished his career by returning to minstrelsy in a funny way. In 1966 Walt Disney wanted to create a band of strolling Dixieland musicians to play in his nascent Disneyland. Shortly before Disney died, he told McVea, "Your type of group is what they really had a hundred years ago, that's what I want."[17] He said McVea would have to put down his saxophone, however, and learn the more "authentic" clarinet. For the next two decades McVea was the anchor of the Royal Street Bachelors, the three-piece strolling minstrel group that dressed in red striped shirts and straw hats and performed throughout the theme park.

He says he got a few thousand out of his most famous record, all told: "It didn't do nothing out of the ordinary for me, just another song," he told an interviewer in 1986.[18] McVea was to get a nice little check from the *Lolita* remake soundtrack, which had yet to arrive the afternoon in 1998 when I spoke to him as he lay in a hospital bed. He died in 2000.

Richard—flatmate, fornicator, unseen hand behind numerous all too human foibles—remains a subject of fascination, instigator of fights and fictions. I end with a pair of quotes to show that while he may not have shown his face, nothing has ever stopped us from acting like we have seen him.

Allen Ginsberg, from an interview in 1993 with poet Steven Taylor: "Late '40s, the trips that *On the Road* described [. . .] That was the influence on my poetry, "Open the Door, Richard." I would say "Open the Door, Richard" opened the door to a new sound and music, to new consciousness."[19]

From an American Nazi Web site: "After 1945, it was plain who were the real defenders of Western Civilization: The Germans were the defenders and we, the Americans were the destroyers. European classical music vanished from AM radio, save for one station. We were then barraged by Afro-pop 'culture,' such as 'Cement Mixer, Putty-Putty' (1946) and 'Open the Door, Richard' (1947) . . . Now the singers are becoming darker: more mestizo and Black. Should we be surprised?"[20]

We should not.

chapter 7

Interrupted Symphony: A Recollection of Movie Music from Max Steiner to Marvin Gaye

GEOFFREY O'BRIEN

1

What follows, in keeping with its subject, is rhapsody, not history.

Like everybody else, I came in in the middle. The picture was already in progress. History had already happened. Nobody even told me where the music was coming from. It simply pervaded the air above the canyon as the lone horseman rode toward the vanishing point, as if gods of music commanded invisible orchestras and could intervene in the story to make it stop. An opening in the sky permitted the emergence of otherworldly music that must have been there all along. Music as underground sea: prophetic sweeps of sound so large that whole lives could cluster in their overtones.

The music was about freezing the moment and removing it from time. It instilled power into the most inconsequential actions: that someone leaned on a rail or glanced out of a window became solely through music monumental. But so often the music was unbearable in its demands. It insisted that memory was painful. It required feeling even where you might have hoped to leave feeling behind, in a stretch of windblown desert or in the wake of an aircraft carrier steaming toward a Pacific beachhead.

Who were those orchestral gods? I think automatically of one such, the great Max Steiner, because he was the first film composer I was ever told of—indeed one of the first composers of any sort—as a result of asking about the theme that played every afternoon on *Million Dollar Movie*. "That? oh, that's the Tara theme from *Gone with the Wind*": a movie I had never seen, and to this day it seems absurd to limit that melody to a single movie when year after year on Channel Nine it served as the theme for all movies. It was the very signal of dusk, a doorway carved out of sound and opening into a geography whose vegetation and mountains were although unseeable almost tangible. Those layers of instrumentation were like the dark green slopes of another more ancient home of which one had been dispossessed without ever having known it: an august progression that spilled over into the rest of the day with its import of ultimate yearning, inescapable regret, divorced from any context but the desire to become lost in the murky parallel reality of *Drums along the Mohawk* or *The Hunchback of Notre Dame*. Yet in its inarticulate solemnity the music promised something beyond the capacity of any movie to fulfill. Max Steiner's theme had something like the effect of an organ chorale on the worshippers entering to participate in ritual, the organist as invisible as the maestro of the movie symphony.

The disembodied symphony came from another world: a world as different as the Vienna that Max Steiner was born into. He was a child favored by music. The figures around his cradle must have included his parents' friends Johann Strauss and Franz Lehar, and he would have grown up hearing about their departed friend Jacques Offenbach, his father being an impresario who staged operettas and who also built the giant ferris wheel in the Prater where Joseph Cotten would confront Orson Welles in *The Third Man* some sixty years and a couple of world wars after Max's birth. He would go on in those impossibly early years (or so the legend has it) to study with

Gustav Mahler and to graduate from the Imperial Academy of Music at age thirteen. By the following year his first operetta *The Beautiful Greek Girl* had opened for a two-year run.

Movies just barely existed. In nickelodeons in the low-class entertainment districts, piano players were pounding out fragments of popular melody on out-of-tune pianos to drown out the infernal noise of the projector and lend some suggestion of coherence to random sequences of tiny movies with titles like *The Kiss in the Tunnel* and *Daring Daylight Burglary* and *Moscow Clad in Snow*. But this was a half-submerged experience on the fringes of a world in whose brightly lit center the young Max Steiner was stepping up to the podium to conduct *The Beautiful Greek Girl,* a world built out of almost intolerably rich sonorities and textures, immense chords and cataclysmic key changes, a language he inhabited like a birthright, the language of *Tristan* and *Salome* and *Das Lied von der Erde,* of *Fledermaus* and *Tales of Hoffmann* and *The Merry Widow.* He would carry that machinery of sound with him as it were in his bones, he being just one among all the other wanderers and refugees from Vienna and Berlin and Budapest and St. Petersburg, the imperial honor students and violin prodigies and child composers who would make their way across the ocean to the legendary modern cities of the new world—some drawn by splendid offers, others bearing the scars of czarist or Nazi thugs—and whose music would finally be piped into every small-town theater and big-town movie palace in America: music to describe pirate attacks and Oriental gardens and Civil War battles, to underscore the hard times of frontier settlers and homefront loneliness and the shyness of young lovers meeting at soda fountains.

Like a Greek scholar displaced by the fall of Constantinople—although he has already left Vienna before the Austro-Hungarian empire collapses in ruins in his wake—Steiner reaches Hollywood by a circuitous route from Vienna to London to Broadway, where for years he's enmeshed in the arranging and conducting of musicals and revues, the *Ziegfeld Follies, George White's Scandals,* until the talkies come in and they need him out west to supervise the movie version of *Rio Rita.* A couple of years pass: he's looking at footage of a giant ape breaking out of a wooden stockade, running wild in the big city, tearing apart the subway. He hears immense themes, a symphonic score for forty-five pieces even though the studio wants stock music off the shelf—it's the depths of the Depression after all—until the codirector Merian Cooper steps in and says, "Go ahead and score the picture, Maxie, I'll pay for the orchestra." Thus is *King Kong* allowed to come into the world, an event in Hollywood scoring something like the premiere of Monteverdi's *Orfeo* in Mantua in 1607. (There had been scores and scores throughout the silent era, but never such an intimate synchronization clinging to, or winkling out, every bend of the story.) Indeed, Steiner's brilliant colleague Erich Wolfgang Korngold, whose own scores include *The Adventures of Robin Hood* and *The Sea Hawk* and *Kings Row*, will describe his trade as writing "operas without singing": the music establishing that the movie's story was not simply something that happened to happen but something that had to happen.[1]

Movie music: everybody knew what it was. As we grew up we became aware of just how contemptible many people found it, how cheap and false and tear-jerking. Those surging strings were the ultimate joke. People showed how hardboiled they were by despising them: "Waddya want, violins? I'm outa here, baby." But by then it was too late to resist, and why would we have wished to anyway? If anything was false or fragile it was not the music but what the music underscored: the lovers running toward each other across a wide meadow, the woman climbing the hill toward the ruins of her ancestral home, the great ship hauling up anchor and setting forth on the open sea, the doomed patrol weaving its way through sand dunes under the eyes of unseen Arab sharpshooters, weightless skittering episodes without the music that measured and prolonged and certified them. This was what it sounded like to have conquered either the Northwest Territory or the heart of Claudette Colbert. This was a language adequate to speaking of cataclysm, farewell, ambush, triumphant return, ghostly seduction, sacrificial death.

When we reenacted movie scenes in the backyard, as we did in the days before video, we were obligated to include an imitation of the orchestra. That's what it took to give meaning to the turns of the story. There could be no doom without horns, no kiss without strings, no mystery without snake charmer's oboe, no secret ceremony without drums, no salvation without high choral voices segueing from minor lament to major affirmation of faith, no madness without an echo chamber to distort the circling melody, no terror without the reeds playing the ominous wailing or rumbling theme that was not merely the signal for fear but what actually was feared, the very substance of the horror movie scenes of entrance to the crypt or passage through the dark hallway or fang-haunted forest. A certain number of children, and adults too, would leave the room when that music started: "It's going to be one of those." The idea that movie music existed was just as important as any specific instance of it. A hill was something other than a hill when seen to the accompaniment of an imagined orchestra.

The music was not a background but a medium through which characters made their way. Whether it happened to be Barbara Stanwyck or Zachary Scott mattered less than the peculiar density of the sound through which they moved. It was a power that each of us wanted to appropriate. There was a longing to become the orchestra, or at least have it under your control: as if that would amount to controlling the course of destiny. Remember that almost none of this music was available on records. (The classic scores of the '30s and '40s would creep out decades later in editions that were often limited or pirated.) It was out of reach, a mixture too intense to be made available to the public. If you wanted to hear it you simply had to see the movie again, and then again.

All this was created by those invisible prodigies. Think of them as tone scientists chained to a millwheel in the vaults of the studio system, turning out scores on demand in three weeks or less with (except for the magnificent Korngold, in this as in all ways exceptional) no control over editing, working with an already completed film, forced to delegate the orchestration to other artisans, hamstrung by union regulations, measuring their days in cue sheets and click-tracks (Steiner himself having invented the click-track), and as final insult signing over the publishing rights to the studio, as they mutter to themselves, "Without us it's nothing, Gable is nothing, Garson is nothing, the story is nothing, we're the ones give the picture a soul."

They make it sound like a symphony, knowing that the audience can't tell the difference. They're the only ones who know it's just fragments, loops of sound ripped from lost orders, the old forms demolished to cut a wide path for Bette Davis as she barges her way into a cocktail party or to let Errol Flynn know that he has found land. A loose chunk of Webern's passacaglia accompanies the wolf man as far as the windowsill. The composers are cutting everything they know into little pieces and recombining them into tiny disconnected stories about shadows moving in and out of rooms. The score creates an illusion of continuity and the composers are the only ones who know what a strand of shards it is. As the '40s progress the soundtrack becomes ever more swelling, its effects ever more cunningly interwoven. The movie is wrapped in music from first frame to last, the images accented and deepened at every turn by the guild masters, by Steiner Korngold Herrmann Newman Raksin Waxman Webb Tiomkin Friedhofer and Young, orchestrating fogbound coast, spirit possession, forbidden longing, trespass into locked rooms—as if to say, "You know this is more real than anything, you yourself are possessed, you have entered the darkness"— until in, say, Bernard Herrmann's track for *The Ghost and Mrs. Muir* it seems as if it might be possible actually to cross over from being into nonbeing intact by means of those chords, those fogbound harmonic fragments, that soul music.

2

The symphony, even if it had never been a real symphony to begin with, was finally interrupted by something called jazz: even if that something bore only an occasional resemblance to jazz. Its intrusions were too truncated and constrained to be mistaken for the all-night fevers toward which the movies could only gesture symbolically. Jazz existed in a city that the movies could at best peep into, through swinging doors that concealed as much as they showed about what really went on in the zone of overheated shadows always trailing off just beyond camera range.

Jazz had always been a possibility, however rarely (and at what peculiar moments) the possibility was seized. The talkies had after all started out with *The Jazz Singer* and *King of Jazz* and Fats Waller singing "Lulu's Back in Town" in *Broadway Gondolier*. At any moment, in any modern-style movie, somebody might walk into a nightclub or turn on the radio and the noise would enter the picture, source music, real-life discord. In William Wellman's secret 1931 classic *Safe in Hell*, on the inferno of a tropical island where criminals go because there's no extradition treaty and slowly rot in the corrupt flyblown tedium of the place, we cut suddenly to Nina Mae McKinney—the mulatto vamp who seduced the hero of King Vidor's *Hallelujah*—serenading the band of exiled hard cases with her rendition of "When It's Sleepy Time Down South" and it feels like the most authentic moment ever filmed. You're in the room with her.

Music is always real, all the more so in a medium where not even the sky can be counted on to be more than a painted flat. It's all true: Hoagy Carmichael and his combo doing "Hong Kong Blues" for their own amusement in *To Have and Have Not*, in defiance of the war and the agents of Vichy closing in on them, or Lauren Bacall lip-synching (or perhaps not) the Stan Kenton hit "Her Tears Flowed Like Wine" in *The Big Sleep*, or the bar band striking up "Too Marvelous for Words" as Bacall strolls after years of waiting into Bogart's South American refuge in *Dark Passage*, another place with no extradition treaty. This was music for adults to use to make the world bearable, and it felt like a way to get around all the restrictions Hollywood had imposed on itself after 1934. They wrapped it around themselves to make a temporary home inside it. In plain sight, automatically authentic, because what could be more authentic than people playing music, under any circumstances whatever?

Music not of gods but of men: in the age of the jazz score the enveloping orchestral medium is peeled away and replaced by live tunes, atmosphere for hire. No mistaking it for the natural effusion of mountains and valleys; no heavenly choirs. Jazz is simply what is playing in the big city, a permanent noise to which the characters must adjust themselves. They move to the music, the music does not accommodate itself to them. Maybe they're energized, maybe they're swamped. The music keeps playing even in the face of death, cutting right through screams and sirens.

It's the signal of danger. You've walked into a neighborhood where you might find drug addiction, juvenile delinquency, street fights, break-ins, lonely subway platforms, neon wastelands, corrupt nightclubs, individual psychosis preparing to blossom into a gaudy display of multiple personality disorder. That neighborhood begins at the neighborhood theater where you're watching the movie. This was true even back in 1942 when Elisha Cook was the half-mad jazz drummer losing self-control in *Phantom Lady*. The neighborhood gets even harder to avoid in the age of *The Wild One* and *The Man with the Golden Arm* and *I Want to Live!* when the music of Shorty Rogers and Elmer Bernstein and Johnny Mandel comes on with a sound as merciless as the choppers of Brando's gang or the drug peddlers of Chicago's South Side or the death chamber that awaits Susan Hayward.

But you don't have to be overwhelmed, you can ride it out. Jazz is an implement, a means of mastery that people can employ like a weapon or like drug paraphernalia. If you're Peter Gunn (as played by Craig Stevens on late '50s television) you live surrounded by it, you take most of your identity from its pulse even if you'd never show it more forcefully than by murmuring "Nice combo, Jerry" to the club manager. The fact that by now this is happening on television—whether on *Peter Gunn* or *77 Sunset Strip* or *Mike Hammer* or *M Squad* or *The Naked City*—makes all the more inevitable the conversion of the music of perfumed vice dens into the newest kind of easy listening. In fact the album of Henry Mancini's music for *Peter Gunn* becomes the album of the year, and the TV or movie soundtrack becomes a freestanding artifact that can be aggressively marketed.

Yet movie music stays movie music even when standing alone. It carries a phantom story with it. The idea of movie music has the further capacity to turn any music into movie music: it's the model for a kind of deliberately manipulative listening, where the listener forces the music to serve the purposes of an extraneous narrative. The real beauty of that narrative—that ghost movie—is that it doesn't quite exist. Portions of it can be discerned in the shadows, but just as it starts to become visible it turns into music again. Any recording, it becomes apparent, can become the music for an imaginary movie; you can enhance the simplest act with it, no matter if the music seems oddly diminished by that process. You're using it for a purpose other than intended, wearing it like a borrowed suit, as if Lalo Schifrin's studio jazz could turn you into Steve McQueen. Put the needle in the groove and all your surroundings will be translated to another level by those lyrical interludes for lovers, blues for sensitive heist artists finding companionship by the San Francisco Bay or on a wet Sunday in the park, the embrace on the fire escape, the glance across the water, with flute or acoustic guitar signifying the persistence of sensitivity even among the ruins.

What exactly is appropriating what? At the request of Louis Malle and Marcel Carné and Roger Vadim, Miles Davis and Art Blakey and Stan Getz transform Parisian parties and late-night embraces into modern living at its most hermetically graceful, a matter of narrow ties, shades, thin-soled Italian shoes, exquisite sports cars, all the forms that reflect and are reflected in the horn sonorities and bass lines of the imported bebop. Jean-Paul Belmondo in *Breathless* seems simply the organism best designed to flourish in an environment defined by the angularity of Martial Solal's theme: an elusive creature able to turn corners without warning and disappear into a doorway with the speed of a jump cut, who between grief and nothing chooses nothing because "nothing" somehow goes with the music. It's a way of approaching space, an instruction kit for propelling the body through the world.

3

People have fantasies about movie music in the same way they have fantasies about sex, to effect unlikely or at least momentarily unavailable juxtapositions. What would it be like if such a sound or such a song came in at such a moment? How would the world be transformed by a different choice? The frustration of the spectator is about lack of power: if only he could control the jukebox, get a shot at picking the songs on the soundtrack. To have that power would be a kind of revolution, which is almost like what happened. The spectator didn't get to choose, but at least his choices were savvily anticipated. The revolution was announced by Bill Haley over the titles of *Blackboard Jungle,* and by Jerry Lee Lewis in person kicking off *High School Confidential.* In each case the unintended consequence was to diminish the movie itself by comparison. To live up to the implications of that music you needed an altogether different movie.

The story was overwhelmed by the noise. That in fact turned out to be the story. So often what startled in '60s movies were not events as such but moments of interruption when sound abruptly usurped the place of vision. The shock of music finally acknowledged—the sheer abrasive weirdness of the fact of the music's being there at all, not deftly interspersed by the invisible weavers of the old school but dropped in with deliberate violence—made image and story suddenly fragile. This was vulnerability indeed, to be so easily roughed up by another medium. There were many kinds of interruptions, and they came from all over: the slightly astringent carnival music of Nino Rota taking command of Fellini's images; the incursion, in Pasolini's *The Gospel According to St. Matthew* (as in some crudely hacked-together temp track) of found music as anachronistic as Nina Simone singing "Sometimes I Feel Like a Motherless Child" or the battle on the ice from Prokofiev's *Alexander Nevsky* score; Akira Kurosawa bringing the samurai down to earth by switching from the sacred gagaku court music of the old Japanese costume pictures to the anachronistic honking saxophone gestures of *Yojimbo,* Masaru Sato's music ripping the traditional world apart just as surely as Toshiro Mifune is about to rip the town apart, an exercise in ronin jazz; Henry Mancini's lounge exotica in *Hatari!* a presence as alien on the plains of Africa as the team of John Wayne, Red Buttons, and Elsa Martinelli; Ray Charles (in Quincy Jones's score) singing "In the Heat of the Night" paradoxically in broad daylight, as the camera rolls through southern cotton fields.

It was a matter not of weaving but of slicing. The cut-lines were perceptible, the process laid bare. The music track functioned not to unite image and sound but to demonstrate the difference between them. The gap was as if for the first time shown to be unbridgeable, whether it was a matter of bittersweet regret (Peter O'Toole and Romy Schneider dancing to, but not merging with, Manfred Mann's recording of "My Little Red Book" in the Burt Bacharach score for *What's New, Pussycat?*) or violent intrusion (Ennio Morricone's jangling burst of howling voices and electric guitar emerging from nowhere in *The Good, the Bad, and the Ugly,* like a flourish of sonic calligraphy in the middle of Sergio Leone's widescreen desert).

In a world of detachable elements, emotions are more like furniture than like landscape. Everything can be moved around but nothing permanently joined. First the movie starts to fall apart, then it seeks to fall apart. To place unjoinable realms side by side is at once to admit impossibility and to insist with an almost too cultivated childishness on the desire for the impossible. Such were the movies that '60s pop music dreamed of: and realized in the necessarily partial and unsatisfying form of *A Hard Day's Night* or *Having a Wild Weekend* or *Here We Go Round the Mulberry Bush* or *More,* movies about goofing around and rolling in the grass and making faces at your friends, swimming nude after the all-night party, drifting in an acid-induced soft-focus haze through the gardens of Ibiza. They were unsatisfying because of the manifest inadequacy of any image to equal the implications of the music, whether it happened to be by the Beatles or the Dave Clark Five or Traffic or Pink Floyd. Here the action was not made grand by music but curiously made somewhat pitiful, so plainly improvised as it was, not fully imagined, a dramatic equivalent of lip-synching. Somehow even the briefest, most simplistic pop song suggested more than actors were capable of miming or scriptwriters of dramatizing.

All the same it was the most satisfying gesture imaginable, a revolution of the listeners, to seize the apparatus and change the sounds it was making. The idea was to use music to open up the world. Create space by letting the sounds out like a djinn from a bottle, effect a change of air, a change of regime: an idea that came closest to embodiment in that flurry of early '70s movies once filed under Blaxploitation and now recategorized, for marketing purposes, as

Soul Cinema. It hardly mattered that the movies themselves scarcely existed as anything but vehicles for their soundtracks. Here, for once, the musicians could function as the real authors of Marvin Gaye's *Trouble Man,* Curtis Mayfield's *Superfly,* Booker T. and the MGs' *Up Tight,* James Brown's *Black Caesar,* Isaac Hayes's *Shaft,* Quincy Jones's *They Call Me Mister Tibbs!* Roy Ayers's *Coffy,* Bobby Womack and J. J. Johnson's *Across 110th Street.* Here is the final triumph of movie music, the sounds permitted to take over completely as actions become only a means of letting the music have its way, in a world where the same music is on the screen and on the street, on the radio and on the turntable and coming out of the car window and echoing from the fire escape. A private soundtrack becomes the public soundtrack, the assertion of a continuum, a republic of music.

Marvin Gaye said about *Trouble Man:* "This is probably my favorite work . . . I was listening to a great deal of Gershwin at the time, and I really wanted to do something great."[2] This was around the same time he told *Rolling Stone* that he felt capable of everything Beethoven had been capable of, only it might take him a little longer because he lacked technical training. *Trouble Man* was as close as he would get to the kind of seamless symphonic work he had in mind. It was the idea of movie soundtrack as object that gave him the long form he needed for a freedom otherwise unavailable, a freedom even from lyric and song structure. There is not a movie large enough to be accompanied by that music. It is best imagined with eyes closed, in the process becoming something like Korngold's "opera without singing": a fluid spectacle not underscored but directed by music, narrative created by music's will, sound as world-creating action. The album itself is the movie.

The schism of sound and image that was a welcome shock for a time couldn't persist indefinitely. In time there would be an inclination to weave back together what had been ripped apart, perhaps into a simulacrum, in the manner of John Williams or James Horner, of the scores of the Steiner era, thinner this time around but definitely louder; perhaps into an ambient gurgle of electronica to create by another means the sense of seamless interweaving of the visible and the audible, sound effects and musical effects merging into a single entity; perhaps with a playlist of old and current hits to get an effect like watching a movie with the radio on all the time. In each case the goal would be to heal the scar of division between picture and sound, to disguise the breach that, fleetingly, had been so flagrantly demonstrated.

The desire for movie music (a desire that would remain even if movies should vanish) is the desire for a world that a chosen music might pervade, invade, shake to its roots. In the meantime, a loved song is magnified by being made part of the soundtrack of an imaginary movie, until finally the imaginary movies are everywhere. (Martin Scorsese would imitate that gesture when *GoodFellas* offered up Frank Vincent getting kicked to death to the random accompaniment of Donovan's "Atlantis" on the jukebox, or jacked up the volume on the triumphal chords of "Layla" for a Max Steiner–like underscoring of corpses retrieved from abandoned cars and garbage trucks and meat lockers. Quentin Tarantino would turn it into something like a fashion statement by announcing that his first step in putting a script together was to take out his record collection and figure out what songs he wanted on the soundtrack, to the point of using as the title song for *Jackie Brown* the title song for *Across 110th Street*.)

The landscape pervaded by the soundtrack turns out to be the one we inhabit. Earth has been made over to accommodate the need for that orchestra that did not in the beginning seem earthly, the one behind or under the screen that spoke for time and death and thunder: the music without which the movie would have no connection to the world. If all art, in Walter Pater's phrase, constantly aspires to the condition of music, so all music would seem increasingly to aspire to the condition of movie music.

chapter 8

Burnt Sugar: Post-Soul Satire and Rock Memory

DAPHNE A. BROOKS

Tabloid scandals aside, R. Kelly's most spectacularly profane act prior to his indictment on charges of child pornography may in fact have been his first single, 1995's "You Remind Me of Something." In that urban radio hit, Kelly converts romantic nostalgia into a fantasy where women's bodies transmogrify into material objects of desire. In effect, the single perverts the warm and pensive melancholic soul characterized by rap pioneers Pete Rock and C. L. Smooth ("They Reminisce over You") and, in more recent years, by Atlanta bedroom crooner Usher ("You Remind Me of a Girl That I Once Knew"). With its booming chorus, "You remind me of my Jeep / I wanna ride it," the track tenders Kelly's affections to his own "sound / I wanna pump it / Girl, you look just like my car / I wanna wax it / Something like my bank account / I wanna spend it." Seemingly unable to distinguish consummation from consumption, the single, as

Mark Anthony Neal suggests of much of Kelly's work, calls attention to the excesses of 1990s black urban materialism.[1]

To Neal's observations, I would add that "You Remind Me of Something" captures the curious manner in which memory itself has gradually worked its way to the center of the current R&B vocabulary. The increasing attention paid to heavily hyped "neo-soul" artists such as Jill Scott and India.arie, coupled with a surge in first-wave hip-hop nostalgia projects, suggest that cultural memory is now recognized as a marketable aesthetic strategy of expression in contemporary pop.[2] But ironically, Kelly's song also illustrates a critical act of forgetting: for instance, how bling-bling consumption has failed to mobilize and empower urban communities.

For that matter, neo-soul's high-profile commodification of nostalgia threatens to eclipse the ways in which African American subcultural musical movements, such as the influential Black Rock Coalition, have long placed strategies of remembering at the center of political and cultural agendas. And it is this continuing effort to specifically reinterrogate collective historical memory, and the place of rock and roll in the cultural imaginary, that remains a critical undertaking for a small yet significant number of post–Civil Rights black musicians.

With so much mainstream attention paid to neo-soul artists of late, I wish to shift the emphasis of analysis to focus on the place of black subcultural popular musicians equally invested in forging ways to collectively remember and to critique cultural memory through resistant aesthetic strategies. These artists expose the cultural amnesia embedded in rock's master narratives. Moreover, they redeploy literary tools of expression, such as satire, parody, and irony, as instruments of interventionist power in both the world of rock and more broadly in relation to post–Civil Rights American culture. Manifesting the ambiguities of this transitional era through lyrical as well as musical double-vocality, black rock satirists articulate the ironies of post–Civil Rights identity formation; their subcultural acts use parodic performance to articulate historical memory in a period dually characterized by "legislated racial equality" and the lingering residue of sociopolitical and material inequities born out of institutionalized racism.[3]

Rock in a Hard Place

An icon of cultural ambiguities, comedian Chris Rock endlessly manifests America's complex racial and class hybridity dance, particularly as he remains an entertainer invested in exploring the traumas and contradictions of growing up in an age of integrated schooling efforts. His beloved and now defunct HBO variety show mocked conventional black pop and political ideologies while also taking constant aim at dominant American power structures, generating a broad-based crossover following in the process. While Rock is anything but a "black subcultural music figure," I would suggest that his diverse political sensibilities and the musical range showcased on his program worked in tandem to articulate a "black alternative sensibility" to that of the African American mainstream.[4]

Rock's musical tastes, which of late have extended to the indie blues-rock act the White Stripes and rap-funk outfit N.E.R.D., consistently demonstrate his free-roving interest in cultural polymorphousness. His HBO series featured musical artists ranging from former *Saturday Night Live* colleague Adam Sandler to Anglo funk diva Nikka Costa and gangsta stalwarts Jay-Z and Lil' Kim. Likewise, popular music has proven central to Rock's own comedy recordings. His second album, *Roll with the New,* skewered the reckless commodification of hip-hop culture with the track "Champagne." For the follow-up, *Bigger and Blacker,* Rock shifted his genres, collaborating with rapper Biz Markie to parody the Rolling Stones' AOR mainstay "Brown Sugar."

Recorded in 1971 and included on *Sticky Fingers,* "Brown Sugar" epitomizes the band's well-documented fascination with African American culture, turning the already tenuous line between cultural appreciation and appropriation into sexual allegory. Flaunting the pornographic confluence of money, sex, and power in the Atlantic slave trade, Jagger and Richards' lyrics chart the odyssey of a "gold coast slave ship bound for cotton fields" and a "scarred old slaver knows he's doing all right / Hear him whip the women just around midnight." The track culminates with revelatory pleasure: "Brown sugar, how come you taste so good? . . . Brown sugar, just like a black girl should."[5]

It would be a safe bet to say that neither the vast majority of the Stones' nor Chris Rock's fans have an extensive engagement with the particularities of the history that "Brown Sugar" bawdily and fecklessly distorts, traffics in, and celebrates. Even pop critic Touré declared on MTV's fall 2000 *Top 100 Pop Songs of All Time Countdown* that "Brown Sugar" was "one of the great love songs written to black women"! Is it just me or is that the sound of Tina Turner gearing up to ask what love has to do with a track that blatantly weds the violent with the erotic? How is it that "Brown Sugar" persists in the cultural imaginary as one of the most recognizable tracks in the Stones' increasingly Jurassic corpus? In a pop-cultural universe where the transgressive dealings of slim shady rappers are regularly policed, this "classic" rock song curiously remains beyond reproach and re-interrogation. Indeed, it's worth considering whether the number's promotion of the colonization of black women's bodies paradoxically operates as a way for the Stones to inscribe themselves into American genealogies of racial and sexual exploitation. From this standpoint, "Brown Sugar" remains, then, one of the band's grandest performances in their career-long quest to authenticate themselves as "American" icons.

With every VH1 boomer-nostalgia countdown, with each beer commercial soundtrack, each time "Brown Sugar" rides the sonic currents of a stadium sound system during a professional sporting event, the song's historical complexities are further obscured. And thus its revered and uncontested position in the rock and roll cultural canon generates a whole host of questions as to how post–Civil Rights cultural workers should intervene in both the violence of the track and the violence of historical memory itself.

For Chris Rock, the solution in 1998 was to record "Snowflake," an extended parody of "Brown Sugar" that inverts the system of racial fetishization in ribald and self-consciously offensive terms.

Set against the original "Brown Sugar" composition, Biz Markie's Cookie Monster-meets-Louis-Armstrong vocals proclaim an undying affection for all that is Anglo: "Halle and Tyra just put me to sleep / Give me Sharon Stone, Pamela Lee, and Meryl Streep / Go tell Oprah that I know what I like / Give me any woman, just as long as she's white." Penned by Rock and Markie, the track dances in and across multiple taboos, hyperbolically replicating the dominant cultural paranoia about black male sexual desire directed toward white women and equally rejecting black female sexuality.[6]

In the mosh pit of black rock parody, "Snowflake" delivers a disruptive slam to a rock and roll ethos that renders discourses on slavery and racial and sexual exploitation invisible even as the culture is itself predicated on this history of appropriation and erasure. Rock and Markie's lewd cover forces its listeners to question the original's canonical status. Following the lead of "disturbatory" black satire from the 1930s fiction of iconoclastic writer George Schuyler to the best of Richard Pryor's stand-up material, "Snowflake" underscores which sorts of historical injustices and discriminations are deemed unacceptable and which are, conversely, at the center of an American cultural grammar. Its racial inversions defamiliarize the original track in such a way as to force listeners to hear the song differently, to pick up the long-buried and backmasked yet still troubling frequencies at its core.

What does it mean for Chris Rock to use such a strategy of narrative expression in relation to rock and roll culture? It was my godbrother (himself an enormous Chris Rock fan) who once argued that "black people don't like irony." This point, however, necessitates historical contextualization, since we might consider the extent to which signifying, in part, a black vernacular form of satire and parody, continues to resonate in African American culture. Alanis Morrisette be damned, irony remains a way of making words convey the exact opposite of their literal meaning. Irony allows for exposing an incongruity in a particular situation, while the characters in that situation remain unaware of this incongruity. By extension, satire is a genre driven by irony. Rather than merely mimicking or imitating famous figures or re-creating well-known situations, satire works to expose the weaknesses or problematics of public figures and social and cultural situations. And black folks have been doing this sort of thing since the boat touched the soil in 1619. As Henry Louis Gates, Jr., and other cultural critics have pointed out, African Americans have been crafting and stylizing satirical forms of "signifying" for more than two centuries now. Indeed, Gates has argued famously that the African diaspora's rhetorical practice of "signifying," with its "black double-voicedness" and its engagement with "formal revision and intertextual relation," depends on repetition "with a signal difference."[7]

Within this critical context, Rock and Markie's "Snowflake" operates as a satirical method of exposure that lays bare the incongruous ways in which the sexual exploitation of black women has been naturalized in the American imaginary. The signifying strategies fueling Rock's work, or novelist Alice Randall's insightfully acerbic retooling of *Gone with the Wind*, provide these "postsoul" artists with the means to disrupt and disorient historical narrative and "collective" historical memory.[8] It is a move that demonstrates the political and interventionist power of satire as a uniquely expressive strategy for artists of the post–Civil Rights era.

Importantly, Rock's decision to shift his own signifying visions to the realm of rock and roll announces a critical moment in black popular culture that demands greater critical attention on the part of music and literary critics alike. In this regard, my aim here is to look more closely at the rich and fertile correlation between late-twentieth-century black satire and black alternative musical strategies—particularly black rock—especially as each relates to matters of form, authenticity, memory, history, and cultural inheritance rites. Why black satire and black rock *now*, within the explosion of post-soul culture? To ask the question means searching for answers in the discordance between the material inequities embedded in American institutions and the putative juridical transformations manifested in the Civil Rights Act of 1964 and the Voting Rights Act of 1965.[9] Post-soul satire clearly manifests this uneasiness and queasiness with the state of the Union, the discordance and disjointedness of black postmodernity in all its quotidian ironies and inversions.

If a general definition of satire is that it encompasses "irony, derision or caustic wit," that it's often used to "attack or expose folly, vice, stupidity," then satire is the expressive mode for a generation of African American popular music artists aware of both the progress of a sweeping political movement and its seething underbelly. And this is why I'm arguing for a method of examining contemporary strategies of black cultural expression that link the literary and the musical in uniquely expansive ways. If the Harlem literary renaissance had its "blues ideologies," if the Black Arts movement of the '60s and '70s had its experimental Coltrane-inspired "ascensions," then this present era provides fertile soil for black underground musicians whose work revels in the double vocality that characterizes the dissonant turn-of-the-century landscape.[10]

Slow Buses and Satirical Movements

Contemporary black rock, like black satire, registers and manifests discordance in its very form and has flourished as a countercultural movement since 1985, when Living Colour cofounder Vernon Reid, journalist Greg Tate, and artist-manager Konda Mason formed the Black Rock Coalition (BRC) in New York City. Anthropologist Maureen Mahon has argued that in publicly aligning with rock culture, BRC members navigate a "conceptual and aesthetic terrain . . . betwixt and between both mainstream black and white worlds as well as between discourses of black nationalism and black integration." This is work intended to "critique both the dominant discourse of black authenticity and the persistence of racism in the United States."[11] In this context, black rock is an inherently ironic, vertiginously parodic art form.

We might consider reading black rock as a kind of late-twentieth-century version of the cakewalk, a dance born out of gatherings of the enslaved and designed to reference the culture of the master class (who were, in their own right, imitating and transmuting black cultural forms). Nineteenth-century cakewalking evolved into a signifying performance of innovation as well as a critique of white culture's interest in black culture.[12] And so, fundamentally at issue in relation to cakewalking as well as black rock is the question, who is the imitator and who is the imitated? To quote another black diva, who's zooming who? For millennial African American artists looking to transcend the great imaginary divide between authenticity and inauthenticity, black rock provides a way to assert the tensions of American cultural hybridity, mobility, and struggle that W. E. B. Du Bois expressed some one hundred years ago.[13]

Likewise, black rock's volatile authenticity politics clear a space for artists who work outside of traditional forms of black cultural expression to fluidly question popular culture's perpetuation of racial and class stereotypes. In other words, if there's something already ironic about a black artist playing power chords on a guitar in contemporary American culture, then one is automatically in a position to contest and mock the constrictions of racial identity formations. In this regard, black rock lends itself to rearticulating African American signifying strategies in a putatively integrated cultural landscape.

One of the more influential southern California ska, funk, and punk bands of the 1980s, Fishbone works rigorously with the politics of double-consciousness, operating out of the nexus between black rock and black satirical and parodic forms. Trey Ellis calls them "the New Black aesthetic personified," a band "brought together by court-ordered busing out to a mostly white San Fernando Valley junior high school."[14] Rock and roll affords Fishbone a mouthpiece to enact the contradictions of black cultural identity formations in radical flux. This is perhaps why they have so notoriously relied on satirical and taboo imagery both in their live performances and in their earliest recordings. Ellis describes attending a Fishbone show, where a set could consist of the group tossing dead fish at the crowd or projecting "a porno film of an oceanically fat black woman having sex with two white men during the song 'Cholly' ('I love ya Cholly with your big fat body . . .')."[15] Like Chris Rock's anti-homage to the Stones a decade later, Fishbone's use of interracial porn returns audiences to the primal scene of racial miscegenation as a disorienting backdrop to their festivals of pop chaos. But as with Rock's work,

Fishbone's pyrotechnics ultimately mount a spectacle of irony that threatens to burn the house that rock built to the ground, with dire consequences for the female figures buried at the center of their signifying wonderland.

This kind of problematic irreverence resurfaces on the band's landmark third record *Truth and Soul* and the cut "Slow Bus Movin (Howard Beach Party)." Revisiting an incident in 1986 in which several black youths were violently assaulted for having entered a segregated, all-white New York City neighborhood, Fishbone use a syncopated send-up of a spaghetti western score to evoke race relations in Wild West frontier disarray.[16] The lyrics openly recycle Civil Rights and Black Power tropes: "born in the 1940s, my parents couldn't vote / X and King were on a march for power true." But "the bus is goin mighty slow." The bus imagery here cuts both ways, since it simultaneously operates as a recognizable symbol of radical, youth-based Civil Rights activism and the challenges faced by a generation of young heirs to the movement who were often forced to integrate into unwelcome spaces (think, of course, of Boston's notorious busing conflict and controversy in the 1970s).

These ambiguities come to bear on the song's climax and the sharp, acerbic turn that it takes in its final stanza: "Well the overlords thought it would be a good idea to mix the black with the white but if you're a fly / in the buttermilk they'll chase you all through the night / So go ahead and burn your cross and rape our women in the night / cause the day will come when your cream coated daughter is gonna be my wife." The 1980s reaction to integration and the resulting rise of segregative tactics in policing public urban spaces provides a critical backdrop for Fishbone's incendiary response to conservative social anxiety—exaggerating the stereotypical dominant cultural fear that integration will lead to miscegenation. In a curiously familiar move, however, women (both black and white here) resurface as exchangeable objects, the trump cards used in the battle for social and cultural power in the song.[17] In this regard, one is forced to ask whether black rock parody itself is a "slow bus movin" in the divisive world of popular music culture.

Changing the Jokes, Switching the Notes

Mired in its own gendered repetitions (without a difference), the millennial black rock scene might do well to look to Mos Def's insurgent double vocality as a salve. For it is that wily Brooklyn MC's antimisogynist lyrics and musical signifying practices that let us see how tensions around imitation and reappropriation play out within rock—and in hip-hop culture as well. With his elegant and ambitious 1999 solo recording *Black on Both Sides,* Mos Def heightened his position as one of the more passionately imaginative rappers of his time. A key figure in the current movement to bridge hip-hop activism with countercultural poetry, Mos Def's work has evolved out of a concerted effort to wed the literary, the musical, and the political. In addition to coproducing and hosting HBO's *Def Poetry* series, he recently appeared in Spike Lee's film *Bamboozled* and is currently developing a new side project, Black Jack Johnson, an African American hard rock band featuring, among others, Will Calhoun of Living Colour and Bernie Worrell of Parliament-Funkadelic. The track "Rock N Roll" off *Black on Both Sides* anticipates this project and offers an extension of the BRC's goals to rescript rock and roll history.

Opening with a nod to Marvin Gaye ("make me wanna holler") and set against a cool, midtempo funk groove reminiscent of Sly Stone's "Family Affair," "Rock N Roll" aggressively disassembles the pop canon. "I said, Elvis Presley ain't got no soul / Chuck Berry is rock and roll / You may dig on the Rolling Stones / But they ain't come up with that style on they own / . . . You may dig on the Rolling Stones / But they could never ever rock like Nina Simone."[18] The track layers a reworking of the labor chant sung by the Wicked Witch's slaves in *The Wizard of Oz* and a spoken-word narrative that places the speaker in a culturally hybrid, matrilineal line of descendants ranging from a grandmother "raised on a reservation" to a great-grandmother who "was raised on a plantation." These were women, we are told by the speaker, who "sang songs for inspiration, who sang songs for relaxation . . . [and] sang songs to take their minds off of that fucked up situation." Immediately, Mos Def resituates the genealogy of musical expression in the Americas, placing women of color at the center of a cultural matrix that would–through cultivation and historical innovation–produce Negro spirituals, tribal folklore, gospel, the blues, jazz, rock and roll, and hip-hop. Making a bold bid to narrate an alternative politics of American popular music inheritance rites, he positions himself as the rightful heir to a matriarchal history of resistant performance. Like his literary contemporary Paul Beatty, Mos Def realigns black musical masculinity with mother (wit) here.[19]

Post-soul griot that he is, Mos Def's "Rock N Roll" town crier spoils the party at the Graceland mausoleum. Like Living Colour before him in their "Elvis Is Dead" track and Public Enemy famously in "Fight the Power," Mos Def works to unseat the hegemony of Elvis iconography. Regicide, however, merely presents the occasion to address the evanescence of "blackness" in rock memory altogether. The bitter observation, "That's just the way it goes, steal my clothes and try to say they yours . . . Try to take everything that you made," returns the cut to the problem of cultural appropriation to expose the very deep historical legacy of making black labor disappear in the public imaginary. As Greg Tate reminds us, in the funhouse of American race relations, African American culture "remain[s] the most co-optable and erasable of cultures."[20] For his part, Mos Def's revisionist anthem aims to pull back the veil shrouding black rock artistry, reminding his listeners of its foundational origins, that it has "been here forever, they just don't let you know."

However, Def's "Rock" jam ultimately builds on the aforementioned 1980s recuperative projects, shifting its attention inward, away from white cultural appropriation and toward the regeneration of black musical innovation pioneered by his ancestors. With the signifying exhortation to "Get your punk ass up," he closes with both a hip-hop vernacular challenge and an engagement with the radical subcultural subversions of punk rock culture. On the one hand, his bar-room growl inciting his listeners from Harlem to "Illadelphia" to "move!" operates as a confrontational challenge steeped in urban, hip-hop, masculinist bravado. Perhaps the "punk" is merely a weak opponent in a verbal confrontation. Yet, on the other hand, we should pay attention to how Mos Def's allusion to "punk" here, coupled with the track's literal shift into the hard-core guitar- and drum-driven velocity of punk performance, might also serve as a resistant political statement that redirects the message of the track to a second set of listeners.

If "Rock N Roll" begins by chastising dominant American culture for its exploitation of black cultural labor, it ends by shifting to address hip-hop audiences estranged from the political economy of black popular music's original roots. The track's punk crescendo suggests that perhaps the genre of punk rock might serve, ironically, as a tool to revitalize black musical culture. The very DIY (do-it-yourself) ethic so central to punk rock's etiology is redirected toward the hip-hop diaspora (with Brooklyn as its capital) and thus back into a hip-hop culture dominated by bad boys and cash-money outlaws. The song has come full circle, attempting to revise and subvert both dominant culture's perception of black rock and roll innovation and the stagnant state of black hip-hop communities in need of a bit of incendiary punk vision. Historical memory and its blind spots, black rock satire and its gender shuffle, cultural appropriation and its endless cycle of imitation are, in Mos Def's hands, scrapped and reassembled to make a new post-soul soundtrack for the millennium.

Coda: Cinnamon Nutmeg Superfreaks

To return to the problem of misogyny in the satirical poetics of the post-soul era, I want to close by addressing a question posed by feminist critic Amy Ongiri, who asked of me when I presented an earlier version of this paper: "How is this any different from *Soul on Ice?*" Meaning the misogynist 1960s black arts rhetoric that was far too often predicated on conquering and exchanging women's bodies.[21] Ongiri's point is a critical one. Black rock satire may blow open the door to multiple silences and erasures, but it simultaneously recycles its own R. Kellyish acts of forgetting the ways that gender hierarchies have crippled past countercultural movements.

For this reason alone, we would do well to push an exploration of the gender problematics in the work of a number of leading black satirists, ranging from novelist Darius James to the Ego Trip collective, artists who have otherwise produced a unique form of post–Civil Rights satire that takes aim at the legacies of Jim Crow segregation and social and material inequities in post–World War II American culture. As I have demonstrated, many of these artists use female figures (and particularly black female figures) as the violent punch lines of their comic manifestos. With women's bodies so often operating as loaded codes of signification in this "alternative" literature and popular music, we might speculate whether the next wave of post–Civil Rights cultural production will emphasize a fuller realization of a postliberated, new black feminist aesthetic that exposes the gendered politics of signifying expressiveness.

I might extend Ongiri's question to ask, Who *are* the black female satirists, and why aren't we talking about them today? Although not "traditional" satirists, we might look to Randall and *The Wind Done Gone;* to Danzy Senna and her remarkable reworking of the passing plot in *Caucasia,* with its deft attention paid to mobility, excursions, migrating subjects; or to Andrea Lee's often misunderstood *Sarah Phillips* as an irony-laden reworking of black female identity politics. Or we might turn to the avant-garde playwright Suzan-Lori Parks and her beautifully disjointed revisions of black women's history in the play *Venus* (about Sarah Bartmann, the Venus Hottentot) and more recently in *Fucking A,* a reworking of *The Scarlet Letter.* Having cast Mos Def on more than one occasion in her material, Parks has provocatively opened the door to transforming hip-hop masculinity within a black feminist signifying medium. Parks's disturbing and startling work forces us to think in new ways about race, gender, satire, and popular music. Her screenplay of *Girl 6* is, in many ways, a satire of the commodification of black female sexuality, set in conversation with Prince's Byzantine musical narratives of race, gender, and sexuality. And perhaps reading Parks as a black feminist punk rock playwright could move us out of the constrictive binds in which we tend to read black female cultural expression.

Of utmost concern to me, however, remains where to locate signifying black female musicians. Who are the black female music artists who, like Courtney Love at her peak (or her nadir, depending on who you ask), "fake it so real they're beyond fake," as Love put it on her band Hole's classic 1994 recording *Live through This?* MeShell NdegeOcello, Grace Jones, LaBelle, Macy Gray, Joi, Res, Skin of the English hard-rock band Skunk Anansie, dare I even say Cassandra Wilson—all of these women are irreverently playing with the boundaries of racial and gender authenticity in ways that the new cultural nationalists—Lauryn Hill (an unreconstructed) Erykah Badu, Jill Scott, and India.Arie—have yet to fully imagine. (Although Scott's boldly experimental performance with Moby and the Blue Man Group at the 2001 Grammys offers us hope!)

On the horizon, then, are musicians crafting an even fuller realization of a postliberated, new black feminist aesthetic that rocks as hard as Living Colour and signifies as wickedly as Fishbone. The question remains whether America is ready for this "burnt sugar."[22] Until then, I await the popular embrace of sisters who parody and one-up the slickly too-funky-for-her-own-good Nikka Costa. Sisters wielding the "jokes" of Andrea Lee's heroine Sarah Phillips who, when typecast as the maid character in a school play, belatedly and yet gradually discovers the power of mocking not herself but a world too myopic to embrace black girls who get the last laugh.

II.

Authorship

chapter 9

Bits of Me Scattered Everywhere: Ray Davies and the Kinks

ROBERT POLITO

If my friends could see me now . . .
        –The Kinks, "Sitting in My Hotel"[1]

For Ray Davies there is always a story behind the story. Starting in 1995, Davies initiated a succession of solo tours, first under the title *20th Century Man,* and then as *Storyteller,* that continue to this day. Mixing readings from his "unauthorized autobiography," *X-Ray,* and more than three decades of Kinks hits and obscurities alongside surprise new compositions, he shifted the program nightly—as he sometimes did his musical backup, customarily guitarist Peter Mathison but occasionally next-generation enthusiasts along the lines of Peter Buck or Yo La Tengo. Stripped of the elaborate musical revues he mounted with the Kinks in the early seventies and the labored arena-rock postures of the eighties, *Storyteller* appeared to release a Davies that even his most enduring fans had never before observed: intimate, comfortable inside the tangles and snarls of his history, commanding, intense.

During concerts and interviews Davies often stops to disclose a secret narrative that might not be evident from the lyric, arrangement, and his delivery. "Get Back in Line" was "inspired by" the film *On the Waterfront*.[2] "Big Black Smoke" is "a bit about" the girl who "ran our first fan club . . . She died of junk."[3] The sad woman of "Don't Forget to Dance" is the Davies sister of "Come Dancing," but "ten years later."[4]

A conspicuous if daunting instance of a concealed, entangling story is the plaintive 1971 Kinks recording *Muswell Hillbillies*. Davies's most tender album of social activism, *Muswell Hillbillies* focuses the consequences of the forced evacuation after World War II of working-class families from inner-city London to the suburban New Towns, and includes some of his most personal writing. His parents had grown up in Barnsbury, Islington, and Edmonton, and then moved north to Highgate and Muswell Hill. Rosie Rooke was a schoolgirl chum of his mother's, and there was a living Uncle Son; "Acute Schizophrenia Paranoia Blues" draws on his father's life, just as "Have a Cuppa Tea" and "Here Come the People in Grey" invoke the experiences of his grandmother. Along with relatives and family friends, the album glances at urban renewal, alcoholism, madness, suburbia, community, and the charms and devastations of nostalgia.

For all that, Davies told a 1972 audience at Boston's Orpheum Theater, *Muswell Hillbillies* is "really about" an Irish cowboy singer performing American western songs in a London pub, and its title derives from the American sitcom *The Beverly Hillbillies*. The Archway Tavern in north London, he later expanded to Jon Savage, featured "the worst country and western band in the world. They were Irish, trying to play country music. I wanted us to mimic that. Obviously it was more rock 'n' roll because we were doing it, but my vocals were slurred."[5]

Shot inside the Archway Tavern, the cheerless photograph on the cover of *Muswell Hillbillies* intimates that the Kinks are that "worst" pub country band, and that the Davies who wrote and performed this novelistic album of London recollections and American blues is no different from the displaced dreamers among his parents' cronies who retreat into a sham past—the woman walking to work who thinks she's in the musical *Oklahoma!* or the aging lad who pines for "those Black Hills / That I ain't never seen."[6]

A rejected track appended to the CD reissue tilts the insight toward fantasy, isolation, and self-loathing. Billed as a demo recorded at the end of a session, "Kentucky Moon" sounds like Davies in the guise of the last minstrel boy, improvising lyrics over his own piano and brother Dave's slide guitar. After listing some of the places *he's* never seen, from "anywhere south of the Delaware," to Kalamazoo and Timbuktu—the implication is they're just rhymes for him—the singer tries to explain his life. "Living is fantasy, traveling mentally," he starts. "Making up tunes in hotel rooms / 'Bout places I've never been to." Even though he claims he "can visualize what I've never seen," all he can summon is totemic fragments: Route 66, Chicago, St. Louis. But as he croons alone in his rented suite, this really doesn't vex the singer. "It's all imagery / From songs, films and TV . . . So I sit and dream, Kentucky moon."[7]

Ray Davies, as Dave Hickey once celebrated him, is "a tricky son of a bitch."[8] *Storyteller* too discloses its own confidential backdrop. The decisive, reinvigorated artist seen onstage across Europe, America, and Japan these past seven years? "It's like learning a new character in a play," Davies proposed.[9] And the one man of Davies's traveling one-man history of himself won't necessarily be Ray. "I thought, 'God, it would be lovely if I could get somebody else to do this, so I wouldn't have to work my guts out every night' . . . My new script, seriously, I'm trying to make it something that somebody could step into."[10]

The self-consuming reels and reversals of *Storyteller* are only the latest circuit in Davies's fascination with what Thomas Pynchon, writing in *The Crying of Lot 49*, styled the "extended capacity for convolution":

> "But our beauty lies," explained Metzger, "in this extended capacity for convolution. A lawyer in a courtroom, in front of a jury, becomes an actor, right? Raymond Burr is an actor, impersonating a lawyer, who in front of a jury becomes an actor. Me,

I'm a former actor who became a lawyer. They've done the pilot film of a TV series, in fact, based loosely on my career, starring my friend Manny Di Presso, a one-time lawyer who quit his firm to become an actor. Who in this pilot plays me, an actor become a lawyer, reverting periodically to being an actor. The film is in an air-conditioned vault in one of the Hollywood studios, light can't fatigue it, it can be repeated endlessly."[11]

"'You're in trouble,' Oedipa told him . . ." As she also might have cautioned Davies when he enthused over a 1975 Kinks show: "*Soap Opera* was wonderful. I was a man imagining I was an accountant imagining that he was me."[12]

X-Ray (1994) contributed the blueprint for *Storyteller,* if so fixed and normative a notion as a blueprint can accommodate an autobiography that recoils from ordinary notions of reliability, consistency, and stability. Davies's reminiscence joins a compact list of experimental nonfiction that includes such incidental oddities as Defoe's *Journal of a Plague Year,* Stendhal's *The Life of Henry Brulard,* Ondaatje's *Coming through Slaughter,* Sinclair's *Lights Out for the Territory,* and Sebald's *The Emigrants,* books that perform along the seam of fact and invention. We think of Ray Davies as a musician, singer, and songwriter, yet he turns out to be a prose stylist of Nabokovian guile and ambition.

As a title, *X-Ray* might promise revelations of irradiated frankness, the searing penetration of the skin of a public life, but here an X-ray is just another photograph. Early on, Davies speaks of the absence of any obvious physical deformity following a painful soccer injury at school: "I wanted physical evidence," he says. "A sign. Something for the world to see. An X-ray. But even an X-ray showed only the bones, the physical inside. The soul was not visible."[13] Later, the author of the disdainful "People Take Pictures of Each Other" restates his contempt for photography. "The camera may not lie, but it is not entirely honest," Davies submits. "It shows only a small slice, a narrow perspective. One split second of a lifetime of such small moments. It makes events which should be ambiguous turn into absolutes, and it disallows personal interpretation. Why reduce life to a series of images that shows a bias toward the objective when a person has spent his entire lifetime creating subjective, ambiguous images?"[14]

Instead of the reductive "series of images" of portrait photography—and of the memoir, whether celebrity or literary—*X-Ray* offers autobiography as the incessant evasion of a nefarious quest. During the teens of the twenty-first century, with Davies in his late sixties, a nameless nineteen-year-old archives clerk is sent to interview Ray Davies—or "Raymond Douglas Davies" and "R.D.," as he is retooled for the book. The clerk, an orphan prone to violent nightmares about his otherwise forgotten childhood, was raised and educated by the "Corporation," a totalitarian Society of the Spectacle organization that seeks to control all public and private life. Operating beyond the demarcations of conventional politics, the Corporation is fascism as global media saturation. The Corporation allows the clerk three months to investigate and craft a report on Davies, ostensibly, as he is told, "to complete a history of the pop-music explosion of the mid-1960s,"[15] but ultimately, he learns, to ruin him: "R.D., as you like to refer to him, must be exposed as a petty inconsequential dreamer. He and his kind are totally out of step with the realism of our times. We have failed to suppress the music. There are still people who listen to it and not only aspire to write and live in his outdated manner, but actually try to emulate him. We must destroy their dreams."[16]

The framing first-person narrative of *X-Ray* is thus the archive clerk's—and not R.D.'s, whose mainly first- but sometimes third-person chronicle is arrayed inside it. The autobiography is "unauthorized" in that the Corporation rather than Davies sanctioned it, but also because the book possesses no authority and, perhaps, no author. Beyond competing claims and paranoias of the rival I's, any suspicion of a single controlling intelligence implodes in a profusion of texts and styles. Raymond Douglas confesses to a "habit of mixing truth and fantasy,"[17] and the clerk notes his skills as a "liar," concluding that "his vagueness was his one consistency."[18] R.D. can recall moments when "it was like there were three people inside me," each of them apparently a gifted songwriter (and credited with specific Kinks tunes); but he revises the count a few pages later.[19] "I was two people at once: a Romantic with strong ideals . . . and at the same time a cruel observer with no mercy."[20] He shares, and occasionally reads aloud from, dubiously expansive old diaries, and presents titillating personal history to the clerk on prerecorded tapes. The disintegration of his marriage is recounted in journals he implies were kept by his ex-wife, Rasa, but subsequently emerge as a likely joint production: "two people were writing their own versions of what was happening."[21]

Raymond Douglas's doubleness emanates in an escalation of more subtle gestures. The verbal texture of *X-Ray* tends to dispose pairs of opposites—"I was both the centre of attention and the sideshow." He recasts his life through fanciful parodies. He juggles clashing dictions, skidding from the eloquence of a "rock poet" into "the language of the gutter."[22] Varying his appearance, R.D. can also wildly transform his voice. His identity in *X-Ray* might, in fact, be most accurately rendered as a medley of voices.

Nothing of R.D., of course, reaches a reader of *X-Ray* except through the archives clerk, and the Corporation biographer appears more impeachable than his subject. He signals his identification with Raymond Douglas even before they meet, pretends he is a composer to gain entrance to R.D.'s Konk Studio, and instantly judges the Kinks' songs "a link to my own past."[23] The clerk believes R.D. manipulates his thoughts, and starts to hallucinate the singer's dreams and memories. At one moment he insists that they are able to swap voices, at another moment that "I was experiencing his past in my body."[24]

This merging of shadow and icon allows the clerk eventually to disentangle from the Corporation, and also permits a flattering, inspirational elevation of Raymond Douglas as "the last of the independents."[25] Simultaneously, the archives clerk suspects that R.D. is corrupting him, may indeed be doping his tea, and redacts his musical history amid pathetic condescension. A blunt anatomy of Raymond Douglas's disagreeable, even sordid strains thus enters *X-Ray* through the agency of the clerk's criticisms, conjectures, fears, and naïveté. Few celebrity memoirs—think *Casanova,* or *Kinski on*

Kinski–appear less intent on accentuating the positive. R.D. arises from the archive clerk's report as needy, petty, vain, vengeful, bitter, a cherisher of resentments and a calculator of scores. Throughout the clerk maintains a Magooish balance of self-confidence and misconstruction, cheerfully simplifying Raymond Douglas's motives, and professing breakthrough epiphanies just before his slippery quarry lures him down another blind alley.

Amid the dead ends and impasses, *X-Ray* dispenses a surprising measure of Davies family and Kinks history, yet always obliquely. As his ticket into Konk, the archives clerk must pass a quiz of band trivia; a fantastic tableau, reflected in an apartment mirror, yields vital information about Dave Davies. Dazzling portraits abound, particularly of the early Kinks' aristocratic management, or of his sister Rene, who died on his thirteenth birthday, after giving him his first guitar; and there are arresting nuances. Raymond Douglas presents his twenty-year-old self as a precocious semiotician, steeped in the subversions of popular culture, and as a naïf who will sign anything. He is convincing as a husband, a father, and an adulterer. Yet through all the concerts and litigation, chart positions and affairs, fights and breakdowns, what is disclosed? The comic narrative counterpoint permits R.D. to ventilate his obsessions and complaints, and the clerk to tag him a crank. Raymond Douglas can display his contradictions–and the clerk might point them out. The archives clerk will register his own progress toward individuality, and R.D. will recede into the third person. The chase replaces the revelation, as the lurid tidbit sustains the mystery. Even the infamous banning of the Kinks from America after their 1965 tour stays an enigma. Another obvious sense of the *X* in *X-Ray* is "unknown."

As a search for the secrets and significance of an elusive, isolated, destructive legend, *X-Ray* executes a neat spoof of *Citizen Kane*, with the puzzling Julie Finkle in the Rosebud role. As the clerk listens to Raymond Douglas's serpentine legal saga, the Kink suddenly pauses for what might be described as a Barbara Walters moment, and tearfully requests a hug: "Will you hold me for a second? I feel afraid . . . Remember, I am not a queer and I do not want your body." His vulnerability established, however confused and creepy it may be, Raymond Douglas leans in for the Rosebud whisper: "Then R.D. closed his eyes and kissed me gently on the lips. He whispered a name under his breath as he drew away from me—Julie Finkle."[26]

Sometimes a muse, other times a succubus, and perhaps only R.D.'s improvised appropriation of the clerk's Corporation colleague of the same first name, Julie Finkle remains evanescent to the end. Raymond Douglas instantly recovers, "becom[ing] a completely different person," or a rapid succession of people: a Marxist social critic, a drunken crooner, a preacher with a Groucho Marx accent.

The film critic Manny Farber once described his prose style as "a struggle to remain faithful to the transitory, multi-suggestive complication of a movie image."[27] For "a movie image" substitute something like "my insane life as a rock star during the 1960s" and you approach the wit and urgency of Ray Davies's stylish convolutions in *X-Ray*. "It was like being held captive inside his head," the archives clerk notes of his quest for Raymond Douglas.[28] Davies represents that rock life as equivalent to trauma, even schizophrenia. Through multiple focus, fragmentation, parody, dissonance, mimicry, non sequiturs, jokes, amnesia, mood swings, déjà vu, and lies, he restores the confusion and freshness of—for instance—the recording of "You Really Got Me," when his present, future, and past all rolled together:

> Then all I had to do was the vocal . . . I suddenly remembered all those family singsongs around the piano, with my dad getting drunk and my sisters dancing with their boyfriends. I pictured Rene watching them. Then time jumbled together and I was performing on stage in front of an audience. Those thumping chords started playing down my headphones and in the first row of my imaginary audience I saw a girl. Every emotion I had was focused on that one image, and nobody could deny me this moment. I had invented myself and someone to sing for.[29]

Davies establishes slippery parallels among that audience, the archives clerk, characters in his songs, R.D., and a reader of *X-Ray*. His structure teases, rearranges, suspends, and aims to destroy time: "There is no time here. No future nor past."[30] And in the boldest violation of memoir etiquette, Raymond Douglas dies before the end of his book. The narrative of his life stops in 1973, on the eve of *Preservation*, the recordings R.D. seems to view as his musical capstone. His own interior story winds down instead to turmoil, paralysis, and failure: a marriage in ruins, drug overdoses, a public announcement he is quitting the Kinks. Raymond Douglas, moreover, concludes his history as a self-styled sellout, signing an apology to the American Musicians Union.

After the funeral, the archives clerk absconds with the manuscript we are reading, perhaps to the same Flanders attic where R.D. once took Julie Finkle in his dream. "Born again and placed in another life," he appears to have merged completely with Raymond Douglas, who is now *his* "shadowman." The clerk etherealizes into something like songwriting itself–"I was invisible and able to see people, observe and document their lives"–but absent the supports that R.D. avowed made his songs possible: family, roots, and place.[31] A third sense of the *X* in *X-Ray* is "formerly." Fixed forever at age nineteen–the same age as Ray when he joined the Kinks–the archives clerk is the ultimate ghost, the once–and maybe future–Raymond Douglas.

Questions of identity agitated and amused Ray Davies as early as September 1964, in the form of a stock "Chart-toppers" Q&A in *New Musical Express*. Each of the four original Kinks was requested to name his favorite foods, singers, drink, clothes, bands, and pets. Next to the entry for best friend, Davies responded, "Me." His most thrilling experience? "Meeting my best friend for the first time!"[32] The early Kinks singles were notoriously ambiguous, especially regarding ordinary pop gender roles, starting with their first Davies original, "I Took My Baby Home." ("She had some pile-drivin' kisses / They really knocked me out / They knocked me oh-oh-over / She had a hug like a vice").[33] The title and lyric to the follow-up, "You Do Something to Me," are almost derisively vague, a suspicion that the peppy, Merseybeat attack only heightens. Even the magnificent metallic hits of 1964 and 1965 flash their multiple declarations. In *X-Ray* Davies indicates that only incidentally does "You Really Got Me" involve a girl who ties the singer up in knots, tracing the four-line source of the song to his parents' front room and a wounded, radical anger at a complex of frustrations ("*Yeah,* you really got me going"). On the advice of a tour manager, he substituted "girl" for "yeah" during the recording session. The weary, ominous "Tired of Waiting" evokes a late date, but apparently started as a notebook poem "about being tired of waiting for success to happen."[34] Here, too, you can hear the origins in the music.

The distorted power chords of "You Really Got Me" ushered in four decades of strutting white male aggression, but everywhere on the early Kinks records Davies sounds vulnerable, hurt, and conflicted. Singles like the obsessive "All Day and All of the Night," the almost-convinced "Ev'rybody's Gonna Be Happy," the straining "Set Me Free," the androgynous "See My Friends," and the insistent "I'm Not Like Everybody Else" might be designated hymns to ambivalence, except that high-toned phrase doesn't catch the constituent confusion, the panic. These first records are hardly aloof shrugs at the complexity of things. Davies comes across as a singer struggling to convey what he thinks, and since what he thinks keeps changing with every song, sometimes every line, he sings each of these songs differently.

He advanced his moodiness as an aesthetic gambit, steadily more adept at shading his anxiety into irony and his contradictions into characters, whom he then viewed ironically—more or less. The satirical trilogy Davies embarked on next—"A Well-Respected Man," "Dedicated Follower of Fashion," and "Sunny Afternoon"—is as distinctive for the cunning, revelatory social details as for the escalating sense of his own complicity in these mocked (or are they?) middle- and upper-class figures. The camp nods in "A Well-Respected Man" and "Dedicated Follower of Fashion" wink and smirk simultaneously. The pleasure manifest in Davies's crooning vocals— to insinuate a posh accent, or deflect a choice line—also slants the tunes away from simple raillery. As he has R.D. reflect in *X-Ray,* "the only way I could interpret how I felt was through a dusty, fallen aristocrat who had come from old money, as opposed to the wealth I had made for myself."[35] Some of his ambitious subsequent songs—

"Dead End Street," "Autumn Almanac," and "Big Black Smoke"—mix heartbreaking observations of everyday English life and disorienting musical pastiche: maniacal Broadway choruses, Salvation Army trombones, and squirrelly vocals. Most "ironic" rock from the 1960s into the next century is schematically Brechtian. As Tom Waits once put it, "I like beautiful melodies telling you terrible things."[36] But Davies so eluded ready-made oppositions that his exact stance toward his material often is nearly impossible to calculate. The only unhyphenated songwriting center among the British Invasion troika of the Beatles, Stones, and Kinks, he played Lennon to his own McCartney, Richards to his own Jagger, squaring violence and yearning, bitterness and empathy, American blues and British music hall. One strain of his writing would culminate in "Lola," the story of a young man new to the city who meets someone who may or may not be a woman—though after some anxious speculation, he doesn't care: "Well I'm not the world's most masculine man / But I know what I am and I'm glad I'm a man / And so is Lola."[37] Another strain would lead to the multicharacter theatricals of the early 1970s—*Preservation, Soap Opera,* and *Schoolboys*—that saw Davies performing three or more roles on stage simultaneously, singing live against his own videotaped backdrops.

I cited those same lyrics from "Lola" for a paper on de Saussure and Chomsky I wrote in a linguistics class my junior year in college. My point, as I recall, was something along the lines that while a transformational grammar would generate two syntactic descriptions for the phrase "And so is Lola," namely that "Lola is glad" and that "Lola is a man," it—said transformational grammar—could communicate nothing about the indispensable allusion to *The Blue Angel,* thus also to Marlene Dietrich, and that only Ferdinand de Saussure . . .

Whatever. This is now my point, as I can recall those days here. Throughout *X-Ray,* Davies underscores his working-class beginnings, but for me and my friends Ray was always the heart and index of whatever sophistication we aspired to inside or outside school. The first time I can remember listening to the Kinks except on the radio was at a party in the eccentric basement of my friend John Shea's

Jamaica Plain home. There was a fake fireplace on one wall, the shingled facade of a house on another, and hundreds of old wooden bobbins everywhere. This would most likely be the spring of our sophomore year in high school, perhaps May 1967. Girls were present in that basement, but I can't tell you how they got there. We were smart but, then as much later, short on experience. Boston College High School, our Jesuit preparatory academy, was male exclusively. The high school arranged an assortment of local "sister schools"— Fontbonne Academy in Milton, Saint Gregory's High School in Dorchester—and there were even Friday-night dances in the BC High gym, one notably starring the Animals on the way down, many showcasing Barry and the Remains or Moulty and the Barbarians, but on those occasions the girls were bused in, and this party was a bit like that. Fitful attempts to dance with a stranger, much segregated whispering, the relief of music talk.

Slipping *The Kinks Greatest Hits* into a hi-fi unit that in the perilous Shea basement scheme of indoor/outdoor sat between a carved mantelpiece and a country kitchen door that opened onto a cement wall, John got me really to hear for the first time "A Well-Respected Man." The draw, of course, was the infamous pun in the line "And he likes his fags the best," but I recall hearing—or saying—what a great thing it was also to put "his own sweat smells the best" into a song, that "pater" we knew from class was Latin for father, that "regatta" and "get at her" were pretty funny as well, and soon we were caught up in the exhilaration of the whole album.[38] For a half-hour or so, it was for us as if Oscar Wilde had materialized from the hi-fi spindle, and perhaps for a decade after that night, through high school, college, and into graduate school, Davies embodied intelligence, wit, rebellion, and style. My friends and I would find ourselves pronouncing at parties, "Everyone is bisexual" or, alternately, "Bisexuality is boring." Our evidence for either claim was the same. None of us, so far as I know, had slept with anybody.

Eventually I came to believe that the contemporary literature I most enjoyed in college, from Beckett to James Merrill, Elizabeth Bishop to Nabokov, Barthelme to Robert Lowell, I first experienced through the Kinks. In "20th Century Man," Davies might shout,

"You keep all your smart modern writers / Give me William Shake-speare," but the joke only showed again that he was one of those writers.[39] Although this is rarely discussed in rock journalism or culture studies, popular music for many working-class children of the '50s and '60s performed the initiation in sensibility traditionally assumed by high culture. I've always felt that I arrived a decade or so late for high culture—at least a *living* high culture of astonishing new artists and works. But a sentimental education through popular music hardly seemed a significant deprivation. Requested to "describe the multiple forms of irony in the *Satyricon*" for a graduate-school Latin exam, I discovered that all my real thinking on the topic derived from the Kinks, with appropriate quotations hastily substituted from Petronius.

Back then, though, the mercurial misery of the Kinks' music was intrinsic to the fascination. *The Village Green Preservation Society* of 1968 is customarily viewed as the moment Davies fell out of sync with his generation and the 1960s, and during passages in *X-Ray*, Raymond Douglas appears to endorse the notion. But Ray years earlier pulled the plug on the official sixties, if his life ever was really wired that way. "It's unbelievable that Harold Wilson was part of the 'swinging' sixties," R.D. jokes elsewhere in *X-Ray*, "but I think the sixties were a con: the establishment still ruled the country."[40] His incentive as a writer was never liberation and love, but isolation, depression, powerlessness, disappointment, double binds, and secrets. The second side of *The Kink Kontroversy* (1965) shapes a pocket opera of despair—"The World Keeps Going Round," "I'm on an Island," "Where Have All the Good Times Gone," "It's Too Late," "What's in Store for Me," and "You Can't Win."

Davies in his melancholy resisted the abject, oily confessions of sixties singer-songwriters from Paul Simon to James Taylor. From the outset, he seemed less the fallen "rock poet" of the archive clerk's disillusioned appraisal than an incipient novelist, or dramatist, intent on situating the personal inside a social world. For all his inwardness, he evinced no visible gift for introspection. The individual radiated outward, personality into persona. On *Face to Face* (1966), *Something Else* (1967), and the singles around them, Davies contrived to stage his ambivalence still more indirectly, and comprehensively, across the multiple vantages of an album, and increasingly within the shifting angles of a single song. He casts himself as a mother in "Rosy Won't You Please Come Home," mourning the escape of her daughter to the "upper classes," a neat reversal of the woozy classlessness of "Sunny Afternoon." Sybilla and Priscilla in "Two Sisters" might be Ray and Dave, but they also incarnated the songwriter's double life as Kink and new husband during the early days of the band. Did the kazoos at the end of "Two Sisters," the cartoon tempos on "Situation Vacant," the ba-ba–duck call chorus on "Most Exclusive Residence for Sale," the batty singalongs on "Harry Rag" and "Tin Soldier Man"—did any of this vaudeville recant the kitchen-sink sentiments in the lyrics? Davies's playfulness only seemed to deepen the songs. The intermingling of candor and theatricality on "Days," "Wonderboy," "Waterloo Sunset," and "Autumn Almanac," their tenuous balance and taut poise no less than their tugs and losses, is unparaphrasable. Here was wit, as T. S. Eliot defined it in his essay on Andrew Marvell–"a recognition, implicit in the expression of every experience, of other kinds of experience which are possible."[41]

Davies never appeared to make a claim for the superior authenticity of any musical style, or set of styles. Bob Dylan and Ray Davies retreated from dominant 1960s cultural trends at roughly the same moment–Dylan, in early 1967, for a rediscovery of American music that evolved from *The Basement Tapes* into *John Wesley Harding* and *Nashville Skyline;* Davies, in late 1967, for a rediscovery of Englishness and music hall that evolved from *Something Else* into *Village Green Preservation Society, Arthur,* and *Muswell Hillbillies.* Each was a search for continuity amid revolution, and for roots in a past only tangentially his own. For Dylan this marked another brilliant instance of artifice in the service of a greater authenticity. Davies chose instead to track the tensions between authenticity and artifice, to frame authenticity as a form of artifice, and to embrace rather than sublimate and disguise the most artificial-sounding elements in his music.

Partisans of *Village Green* often celebrate the record as an exercise in nostalgic fantasy, a concept a 1969 Reprise "God Save the Kinks" campaign propagated with a promo box containing a Union Jack and souvenir grass from the Village Green. Davies's last words on the album, however, are "Don't show me no more, please"—rebuffing, if momentarily, in the aspect of family photographs, the nostalgia that's been luring and vexing him for fifteen songs.[42] As he later told Dan DeLuca of the *Philadelphia Inquirer:* "A lot of my songs are evocative of a time gone by, but I never thought the past was any good."[43] For Davies, reminiscence and the mockery of it are delicately bound together. His vision remains double through the final couplet of *Village Green Preservation Society.* Just before he exits on the dismissive "Don't show me no more, please," Davies sings, "Oh how I love things as they used to be."[44] The record manages to suggest that living in the past might be the only tolerable way of living in the present, and also that it's impossible to live there.

Our personal stake in this is fairly obvious. Davies was a mask behind which my friends and I could sort through our various confusions—sexual, certainly, but also class, since most of us were the first in our families to attend college. I regret to say we inflicted the Kinks on anyone who wandered into our circle, honored faculty along with students, and usually their rarest and quirkiest songs—the 1969 "Plastic Man"/"King Kong" single, among others. Since most found the Kinks annoying, Davies was a test and also a weapon. The Kinks drove people away. In this sense the sexual and intellectual were pretty much inseparable.

Arthur, Lola versus Powerman and the Moneygoround, and, particularly, *Muswell Hillbillies* shuffled constants and variables of the authenticity/artifice equation until Davies arrived at *Everybody's in Showbiz.* Inside our koterie of kultists, *Showbiz* probably marked the ultimate Kinks moment. We fixated on Davies's pitching of the everyday toward simulation, camouflage, and the grotesque. The fantastic diary of a band on tour across America, *Showbiz* focused the apparently interchangeable lives of ordinary citizens who wish they were stars and sad stars who cast longing glances back at ordinary life. In the most original songs, all experience divides into the mechanical and the painful. To those walking down Hollywood Boulevard, Davies sang, "But please don't tread on dearest Marilyn . . . she should have been made of iron or steel / But she was only made of flesh and blood."[45]

Davies's songwriting no longer merely reclaimed the mundane with style, it carried the chill of something darker. Imitating by turns a rocker, a bluesman, a music hall singer, a social critic, a satirist, and a dandy, he acted out a kind of comic repulsion toward all available styles. During the season my friends lived inside it, *Everybody's in Showbiz* shaped a worldview as bleak and thrilling as any I knew. We saw it through the twin lenses of Andy Warhol and Samuel Beckett, then my favorite artist and writer. The shattered glamour of *Showbiz* etched a chintzy aestheticism that recalled Warhol's *Death and Disaster* canvases of car wrecks, race riots, and electric chairs. Davies appeared to stroll a tightrope of elegance and despair that reminded me of Beckett's trilogy of novels, *Molloy, Malone Dies,* and *The Unnamable:* those beautiful sentences of utter hopelessness. In the next issue of our college literary magazine, we added Davies's name to a list of notable suicides.

I wish I could remember more about the one time I met him. I know the date was October 27, 1969, because it was my eighteenth birthday. The Kinks were in residence for a week at the Boston Tea Party, during their first American tour in four years. My friend Tom Coen approached Ray Davies after one of the shows and arranged an interview for the campus paper. Tom, John Shea, and I descended on the Holiday Inn behind the Boston Public Library in Copley Square the following night. Ray was alone in his room, finishing a salad. He wore, as I recall, gray wool pants and a mod shirt.

Soon after we arrived, he lit a cigar and proceeded to knock the ashes into the salad bowl. From room service he ordered a pot of tea for himself, and—for some reason—round after round of rum and Cokes for us. Ray tolerated the tape recorder, and our increasingly opaque questions. None of us had ever been drunk before, but I don't think anyone got sick.

All I recall from the interview is that Davies was the first person I ever met who paused to think before he answered a question. Tom Coen transcribed the tape, and we submitted the typescript to the arts editor of the paper.

Our interview ran the next week—radically condensed, illustrated by a series of fey photographs of Ray, and under the headline, "Iron Man Davies." The arts editor's introduction identified him as Dave Davies.

To this day I'm humiliated to think he ever saw it.

Everything in *X-Ray* appears to be leading to *Preservation, Soap Opera*, and *Schoolboys in Disgrace*, but R.D.'s hasty demise permits only hints and foreshadowing of that mirage—or perhaps displaced—conclusion. Early on, during one of his efforts to ingratiate himself with Raymond Douglas, the archives clerk tells us:

> I had heard his *Schoolboys in Disgrace* album from the mid-1970s. In it the headmaster, symbol of the establishment, sends his disgraced schoolboy down the road to ruin after he has been humiliated in front of the school, punished for a crime he didn't commit . . . [T]he disgraced boy returns as the evil dictator Mr. Flash. After a military coup the rebel armies, financed by the superpowers, invade, and Mr. Flash is overthrown by his old schoolboy enemy, Mr. Black. Again the establishment returns to haunt him.[46]

Later, R.D. sketches the social anger behind the Flash/Black cartoon:

> The sixties were like a carrot held up to youth to distract us so that we would not rebel against the ruling classes and all the backhanders and corruption that were actually present in politics. The countryside was being eroded and trees pulled up in order to build motorways, factories were being closed, coal mines were being ear-marked for the chop . . . The sick thing was, that I was heralded as a standard bearer for that deceitful

time. I was writing songs and the country was gradually being sold out.[47]

Finally, if Flash is an echo of his wounded childhood, he also crawled from the wreckage of R.D.'s divorce. Here Raymond Douglas discusses—in the third person—*Preservation* and the end of his marriage:

> Mr. Flash became R.D.'s super villain. But that was in *Preservation* land. In the real world, Rasa's side were shaping themselves up into believing that Raymond Douglas was some sort of irrational sex-crazed tyrant. If R.D. was going to be accused of participating in drug-induced orgies in LA and Muswell Hill, why not be this person and invent a character called Mr. Flash? Perfect casting . . . The fictitious Mr. Flash would then take over R.D.'s stage persona.[48]

Within the arc of *X-Ray*, the missing narrative of *Preservation*, *Soap Opera*, and *Schoolboys* smacks of a phantom limb. Neville Marten and Jeff Hudson speculate, in *The Kinks: Four Respected Men*, that "by the end of the '60s . . . chart-wise and sales-wise, the Kinks are a commercial spent force . . . And so, in his autobiography, he'd rather kill himself off in the text than be seen to lose the race."[49] This sounds improbable. Indifferent sales don't stop R.D. from chronicling *Village Green*, *Arthur*, and *Muswell Hillbillies*—or from revealing, "I rate the *Muswell Hillbillies* album up there with *Preservation*."[50] The Kinks, moreover, rebounded as a commercial outfit during the early 1980s.

My inkling is that R.D. sidesteps his musical revues chiefly because their significance in *X-Ray* would be redundant. *Preservation*, *Soap Opera*, and *Schoolboys in Disgrace* all orchestrate variations on the elaborate disappearing act he will perform some twenty years later in his autobiography. As in *X-Ray*, the flair and vitality of Davies's theatricals are conspicuously self-atomizing. Anyone who viewed the midseventies Kinks shows came away with a whiff of psychodrama. Their dramatic principle appeared to be how many different Ray Davieses could take the stage at the same time. On back-projection screens, under masks, and in voice-overs, he was everywhere, and nowhere: young Flash and old Flash; Headmaster and Schoolboy; Starmaker and Accountant; Tramp, Flash, and Mr. Black; assorted announcers, choruses, emcees.

Accenting the wit in his concept, Davies rendered the RCA *Soap Opera* album a clever bore. But his 1975 American performances recast the Norman/Starmaker struggle as a wall-to-wall nervous breakdown. This Norman didn't aspire only to rock stardom—he's convinced he is Ray Davies of the Kinks. Home from a day at the accounting office, the Starmaker rants to Norman's wife, Andrea, after she challenges him to "stop pretending you're something you're not": "I'm *not* an accountant. I'm a rock 'n' roll singer. I'm a *star*. I'm one of the world's top songwriters. Look! That's my group over there, *the Kinks* . . . Look! There's the audience, they've been watching us all night . . . You silly cow, you must be blind . . . I can prove who I am . . . Somebody bring me a guitar . . . I can prove who I am. I've got hit songs to prove it . . . This is a song I wrote in 1965." Amid applause, the Starmaker proceeds into a rote, wedding-band sing-along medley of "Well-Respected Man," "Dedicated Follower of Fashion," and "Sunny Afternoon," dragging the actual audience into his fight with Andrea. "See, they know who I am."[51]

The *Preservation* shows of the previous fall also culminated in a mare's nest of unresolvable questions, particularly regarding Davies's tangled, irreconcilable sympathies, and similarly found him everyone and no one. The Mr. Flash/Mr. Black conflict follows the comic-strip plot Raymond Douglas outlined above in *X-Ray*, except that in the original RCA recordings, *Preservation Act I* (1973) and *Preservation Act II* (1974), the intrigue is witnessed by a Tramp, who returns to Preservation after years of wandering to discover his village at civil war.

Flash might arise from the "irrational sex-crazed tyrant" of Rasa Davies's divorce petition, yet he actually operates like a more appealing fusion of Max Miller and Lucky Luciano, amid traces of Watergate-era Richard Nixon. The manipulative Black and his fanatical New Centurion "People's Army" marshal an early installment of the Corporation, although Black himself can imply Ray Davies as the other Kinks viewed him–pianist John Gosling's "detached," superior leader, or the cold, ruthless exploiter of brother Dave's 1996 autobiography, *Kink*.

The characters of Flash and Black were implicit in *Muswell Hillbillies* and *Village Green Preservation Society*, much as the Tramp distilled the anonymous observer figures of late-sixties Kinks songs. Against the vast civic vistas of Flash and Black, the Tramp's return to Preservation to obtain the forgiveness of Genevieve, the girl he seduced and left behind, is insistently personal. As R.D. recounts in *X-Ray*, "This song, 'Sweet Lady Genevieve,' was my last desperate attempt to apologize to my wife for all of the wrong I had done."[52]

Musically, *Preservation* progresses as a battle of the bands. Nearly all the songs indulge pastiche and parody. Crafting ballads for the Tramp, Davies represented Flash and Black as compositional opposites–for Flash, a noisy motley of music hall and old rock 'n' roll; for Black, a prim ensemble of Gregorian chant, medieval flutes, and, fascinatingly, chilly, reptilian vocals evocative of David Bowie and Bryan Ferry (in 1974 the sound of rock's tomorrow). He registered the complementary, mirror-twin complexion of the Flash/Black confrontation through deft echoes–the resurgence of Flash's anthem "Demolition" in Black's "Salvation Road." As Flash is routed by Black and committed to the Mad Scientist for a mind overhaul, Davies cloaks some gorgeous tunes in abrasive, angular arrangements. For melodically, too, he always fled any fixed sense of himself. To focus only on the Kinks' first decade: a new listener confronted with, say, three sets of albums–*The Kinks* (1964) and *Kinda Kinks* (1965); *Something Else* (1967) and *Village Green Preservation Society* (1968); *Preservation Acts I and II*–likely would surmise they are the work of three different composers.

Throughout the public action of *Preservation*, Davies presses two alternate futures, and refuses to choose between them. Corruption, or conformity? Flash is crooked and violent, but human; Black is pure, reformist, and inhuman. Each ultimately can only destroy the village of Preservation. In the more private *Preservation* story, the Tramp doesn't reconnect with Genevieve. Thrust aside, helpless and irrelevant, he probably will have his kinks ironed out in Black's laboratory, stripped of his history and feelings just like Flash.

For the American *Preservation* tour of November and December 1974, Davies expanded the Kinks into a road troupe of perhaps a dozen costumed actors, singers, and horn players. Judicious shuffling of the earlier order of songs and announcements shaped a stripped-down, near-mythic clash of Evil and Evil. Of course this was Evil filtered through the cheek of 1930s and 1940s British comedy. Smoother and tighter than on record, *Preservation* live proved funnier as well. Davies played Black as a German divinity student, obscure strains of perversity rumpling his snug serenity, but his Flash was an old song-and-dance man. A lurid Hogarth sketch in a trilby, bow tie, and multicolored bathrobe that recalled comedian Max Miller's famous flower-patterned suit, Flash strode among his wideboys as a genial, ingratiating monster, muttering a joke and a sad story as he slipped in the shiv. Many of the gags were musical. Dave Davies sang "Here Comes Flash" in a solemn caterwaul as the Kinks thrashed behind him like a hair metal band. The spectacle of the obviously trained voices Davies hired to trill his cracked choruses ("He was a second-hand car spiv up from the slums") enhanced the hilarity. But this *Preservation* also sounded emotionally nuanced, where the RCA recordings were flat and rote.

Perhaps because of the grand scale of the production, *Preservation* live looked even more a multiple-personality sideshow—an off-off-Broadway musical adaptation of *Sybil*—than *Soap Opera*. Through films, photographs, shadow play, and tapes, Davies routinely enacted two, and occasionally all three major parts at once. Aloft on a back-projection screen as one character, he would castigate himself below, onstage, as another character, and then trade insults back across media. But Flash and Black sometimes seemed the least of his identity explosions, for Davies also assumed roles of the broadcasters, journalists, and commentators. From the wings he might introduce Black, just before he walked out dressed as him. He served as the evening's emcee. "Ray Davies, being the fabulous actor he is, has kindly condescended to play both parts, Mr. Black and Flash," he told the audience in New York. Davies gestured toward the Kinks. "Ladies and gentlemen, it's not easy for these ordinary people to act with such a great star as Ray Davies."[53]

After viewing an early TV version of *Soap Opera*, Pete Townshend remarked, "It's just shocking to realize that it happened and it did nothing. I remember seeing it and thinking, this is either going to be ignored, or it's going to be huge. It was totally and completely out of time. It was like seeing the last episode of *The Prisoner* but being lived out by somebody. Ray was both the puppet master and the puppet, precariously living out the audience's experiences, crying and laughing in public. It was unbelievable."[54]

Soap Opera, Preservation, and the Flash/Black prequel, *Schoolboys in Disgrace,* almost didn't transpire at all. Right before he embarked on these repertory albums—in a mere twenty-four-month span, November 1973 through November 1975—Davies announced at a White City Stadium concert that he was quitting the Kinks. That same day he overdosed on pills. The years 1973 to 1975, he subsequently said, were a point "in my life, in my career, when I should not have been allowed to put records out."[55]

X-Ray of course spoofs the "as-told-to" star autobiography, still the customary genre for personal recollection among rock musicians, as well as most other celebrities. The rock memoir that so far rivals Davies's is Chuck Berry's *The Autobiography,* a claustrophobic carnival ride of obsessively metrical and punning disclosures that calls up Elvis Costello's *Get Happy!!!* more than "Johnny B. Goode." Yet we must not slight those rare masterpieces of inadvertent wizardry among the as-told-to confessionals. The celebrity tale that in artistry and transgression probably most matches Davies's is Michael Edwards's 1988 *Priscilla, Elvis, and Me: In the Shadow of the King.* Inadvertence, ordinarily the predilection of surrealists or cranks, also spikes the most plangent ghostwritten books. Remove the words "Michael Edwards" from the title page and substitute, say, "Don DeLillo," and *Priscilla, Elvis, and Me* would be an audacious, slyly sad novel of accidental revelation.

Edwards announces himself as "the most successful male model in the United States and Europe." Perhaps, although a casual poll of friends suggests he was no more visible back when *Priscilla, Elvis, and Me* appeared. His story purports to chronicle his seven-year *affaire de coeur* with Priscilla Presley, yet Edwards keeps stumbling over his history, characteristically divulging more than he might intend. On their first meeting, Edwards recalls, he passed out on Priscilla's suede couch. On their next date, an outing with Lisa Marie's friends to Magic Mountain, he vomits the beer he drank behind the Spin of Death. "I watched Priscilla and the girls climb onto the ride and, for the first time since childhood, I felt joy."[56] He finally falls for Priscilla after he hears her random-dial telephone numbers, pretending to each listener she's a hooker. "Something about it touched a place in my heart, and I felt the first stirrings of love for her that evening."[57]

Edwards's destructive ardor soon roosts elsewhere, inside the ghost of Elvis Presley and the body of the King's look-alike daughter. Successively aggrandized and shamed by "my position as Elvis's successor," he steadily derails. In his creepiest substitution, Edwards reaches a startling equation: Priscilla was to Elvis as Lisa Marie is to him. Picking Lisa up at her Catholic school, he lingers over her wool skirt, white blouse, and loafers. The young Priscilla also wore "a uniform just like Lisa's . . . I could certainly understand Elvis's feelings . . . it definitely turned him on."[58] He scarcely can conceal his erection as he and Lisa play together in the pool, and after a quarrel with Priscilla, Edwards drunkenly lurches into Lisa's room. "I wanted someone to talk to, but Lisa was asleep. I lifted a corner of the sheets and gazed at her. She was lying on her back, and her honey-colored hair was spread out over the pillow. She was my beloved, and I couldn't even tell her . . . Everything about her was exactly what I wanted in a woman."[59] Lisa Marie is thirteen.

Priscilla, Elvis, and Me traces the arc of a rent-boy *Lolita:* Edwards as Humbert Humbert, Priscilla as Charlotte Haze, Lisa Marie as Lolita, and Elvis as the spoiling Quilty. Like *X-Ray,* the autobiography reclaims the shopworn star vehicle as a literary experiment. But too strange and chilling to be spun into camp, Michael Edwards is the sort of spiritual mutant from the fringes of showbiz culture that the archives clerk and even R.D. seem always about to turn into, and that Davies shadowed in his next book, *Waterloo Sunset* (1997).

Waterloo Sunset lifts a cue from a 1993 Davies *Phobia* lyric—"Bits of me scattered everywhere"—and, if anything, thickens the self-fragmentation. In a succession of crosscut short stories, every selection is titled after and circles a Davies song. *Waterloo Sunset* evokes another Nabokov novel—the late, mad *Look at the Harlequins!* in which all sensation of a realistic world vaporizes into the allusive network of the author's prior fictions. Some stories whisper the circumstances of a song's creation; others trace a song's impact on an imagined listener. *Waterloo Sunset,* terrifyingly, is a sealed car eternally circulating Kinkdom.

Tangents abound, as in all Davies concepts. But a rough, invidious scheme surfaces. A dealmaker named Richard Tennant aims to revive the career of a fading and temperamental '60s rocker—Les Mulligan, another volatile Ray Davies stand-in. Les is widely understood in the industry to have suffered some sort of meltdown in the mideighties, after he left his original group to go solo. But behind the rumors of his ruined, spectral life in New York and London, an "evil spirit" whom Mulligan alternately views as stimulating and thwarting his songs may (or may not) be responsible for a spate of brutal rapes and murders around Surrey. All the stories in *Waterloo Sunset* loop back to a seedy busker singing for change in the London Underground, a role Davies acted in his 1985 film *Return to Waterloo.*

Familiar Davies phantoms pulse through the prose—class dislocations, vanishing local cultures, the lures and indecencies of showbiz. Accountants betray their background and embrace the ruling classes, while their wives and children come to hate them; old market-inflated houses foment ghosts; loners spill their troubles to a mute woman in Regents Park; lovers fight and draw blood. The Hollywood bottom-feeders around L.A.'s Rat Trap Club, on Sunset, prove as clueless and degraded as Michael Edwards.

The shufflings of personality, particularly as the mysteries of voice, impersonation, identity, and madness converge on songwriting, is the recurrent provocation of the *Waterloo Sunset* stories, diaries, and screenplays. Everyone seems to be a character from Les Mulligan's songs, as a few—a con artist turned painter called Fox, and even Richard Tennant—come to realize. Tennant says that Les is now only a "shell," and "the real creative part of him was down in the Underground, busking anonymously."[60] Tennant fears that Les might have "gone inside his work so deeply, he'd surrendered his own character to his songs, and they live through him instead of the other way around."[61]

The prickliest story, "Return to Waterloo," lifts an epigraph from Genesis: "God created man in his own image." But the question of who is the image and who is the originator remains. The "Surrey Rapist" mocks the Underground busker—"my creator"—for his oversights and condescension, for his "gall to believe he could penetrate my inner thoughts,"[62] before he more brutally flings his fancy, romantic art words back at him. His creator "inspired" him to follow a woman in a Burberry coat; if the "character he imagines me to be is merely a metaphor for his own . . . I won't submit"; and he, not the busker, retains God-like mastery over people's fates.[63] "Return to Waterloo" concludes with "the camera . . . reversed . . . I'm walking towards my creator, down that Underground corridor, him strumming a guitar like a subway panhandler . . . We stare at each other . . . The gust thunders through the subway once more. It takes both of us to hell. I suck my inventor in through my eyes, absorb him into me and carry me with him on my journey."[64]

Waterloo Sunset chases the riddles of writing songs and making art, sometimes wondrous and celebratory, and other moments, as here, literally hell.

Death in *Waterloo Sunset* is envisioned as a completed song. "That's when you know he's finished," the dying painter Fox is told. "Your song is done and you can go home."[65] Davies managed an approximation of his posthumous fancy of a Davies-less *Storyteller* in 1998, when the Boston Rock Opera staged *Preservation* entirely *sans* Kinks. A vivid cast of twenty-three singers, actors, and dancers, plus a canny eight-piece band, raised a smart, rococo edifice from his ancient blueprint. Directors Eleanor Ramsay and Jane Bulger restyled the design from music hall to opera. Free of the Ray Davies identity circus, *Preservation* at last emerged as what he always maintained it was: a black comedy about the masses and the media.

In *X-Ray* Raymond Douglas plays his favorite video for the archives clerk—the 1973 Don Siegel noir, *Charley Varrick*, a curious film he also dismisses as a "nice fantasy" without really going into it.[66] Walter Matthau is Varrick, a middle-aged crop duster who, after he couldn't compete against the big combines, starts robbing banks with a small crew, his wife and a few friends. During the bloody holdup of the Tres Cruces Western Fidelity Bank, he accidentally steals some Vegas syndicate money that is being laundered through the bank. Varrick ultimately triumphs over both the law and the mob—but amid stunning personal wreckage: his associates double-crossed; his wife dead.

Seeing the film again is a bit of a wonder. R.D.'s signature phrase in *X-Ray*—"last of the independents"—actually is painted on the side of Varrick's truck and stitched onto his overalls; it's the slogan of his crop dusting company. Elusive muse "Julie Finkle"—or at least her family name—may also derive from *Charley Varrick*. The anti-Semitic Western Fidelity Bank president taunts Tres Cruces district attorney Garfinkle, repeatedly addressing him as "Mr. Finkle."

In the end, Charley Varrick flies off after (shades of *X-Ray*) faking his own death, his crop dusting plane also emblazoned "Last of the Independents." "I like that," Molly, a mob enforcer, earlier remarked of Varrick's motto. "Has the ring of finality."[67]

chapter 10

Authenticity, Gender, and Personal Voice: She Sounds So Sad, Do You Think She Really Is?

SARAH DOUGHER

I have been teaching literature, writing, and Latin for almost ten years, and have been performing as a singer, guitarist, and organ player, both alone and with rock bands, for about eight. As teacher and performer, I am always aware of how these seemingly contradictory roles actually have a lot in common. There is, first of all, the situation of standing up in front of people like you've got something to say. Then there is working a long time to figure out what you are going to say, practicing, researching, and writing. And then there is the third thing, which is a little harder to pin down—it has to do with how you use your voice once you are on the stage or in the classroom: representing who you are to an audience, as well as telling them something they might be interested in hearing. What I have found is that this is a position of power. In the process of learning how to use it, I have also learned a lot about the way that contemporary culture views this voice. As a lady academic and a lady rocker, I am working in two very gender conscious and sexist fields. I'm confronted with the dilemma that women always face. Should I use my voice like I think sexism is OK (choosing the demure "feminine" or the assertive "masculine"), or should I do something different, something that challenges this? And how do you do that?

I went to graduate school in Austin, Texas, where I learned how to teach Latin and read Greek tragedies in Greek. I was allowed for the first time in many years the opportunity to sit and think, and to this activity I added a pawn shop guitar. Classically trained on violin and piano, and a veteran of a few college singing experiments, I started to reteach myself guitar and began to write music. It was in this environment that I first began to play music in front of people, and first began to teach. In both contexts I often felt like a big faker, and that someone was going to find me out and strip away the modest public voice I was beginning to gain. Slowly this feeling began to disappear as I became more adept at holding my audience of baseball-cap clad students or slumped over drag queens. I couldn't help but feel a bit ineffectual. But I was a beginner, this was my audience. The only way I could communicate effectively was to do so with as much truth and, well, authenticity, as possible.

From my background as a Latin teacher, I can barely contain myself when it comes to explaining the Latin roots of words, so I hope the reader allows me some forbearance. When I use the word *authentic*, I think about it in its oldest meaning, from the Latin (and Greek) *authenticus*, "from the author." So if you say you want to communicate "authentically" it has a meaning close to wanting to "author" something. The other things we associate with authenticity, like "truth" or "reality," are a little more nostalgic and depend on some notion of what "truth" and "reality" might be. But I do not care to venture into such deep waters here. I only want to say that in the early stages of developing my voice as a teacher and performer, I realized right away that audiences want to hear *you* speaking. They want a version of *you* that conforms to their expectations. If you are a woman, they have a certain set of expectations. If you don't conform, or if you challenge your audience, you have a mighty row to hoe.

I liked school when I was young. I liked it so much that I ended up going to a small liberal arts college. There I was encouraged to engage in dissent and discussion, cutting my feminist teeth and (mysteriously) developing an unrelenting attraction to the Greek and Latin classics. It was a safe environment in which to meet the world of adulthood, and decidedly sequestered. When I finished there, I decided to go to grad school. That was a lot different. I encountered competition I had not known before, and a distinct hierarchy of power fueled by sexism that slowly began to drive me away from academics. In the static world of classics grad school, surrounded by the exclusive cadres of male first-years and the younger of the male professors, my days were fraught with small, inconsolable offenses: Why does the senior professor think he can cut in front of me for the copier? Why wasn't I invited? Why wasn't I given the time? The nomination? The opportunity? And why was it always a man who got it instead? I realized there were only a few roles available to me: the bitchy feminist shrew; the acquiescent, understanding, supportive "teacher." If I was going to "make it," I would have to learn different ways of speaking and acting—ways that would significantly mute my rage and blind me to sexism.

The other thing about the academic world is that there are very specific ways of writing. Except for recent experiments with form and the personal essay, the voice of the academic is absent in academic writing. You will not read about why scholars became interested in their topic, what their unique life experience might bring to their interpretation. The model we have inherited from the nineteenth-century university tradition is of scientifically based, rational deduction. My own field of Greek and Latin literary studies was particularly susceptible to this, in part because the knowledge base was so specialized and rarefied. Anyone educated after second-wave feminism, and with even a modicum of knowledge about feminist theory, understands the problematic nature of this system. The disembodied text, or the voice without a speaker, has long been challenged on the grounds that it mutes the less powerful voices of the dispossessed: women, people of color, the poor, sexual minorities. The work of revolutionary educator Paulo Freire *(Pedagogy of the Oppressed)* and the notion of the "open classroom" have made inroads: the idea that a teacher could speak from personal experience and at the same time encourage her students to do the same, all within an academic context.

So there I was, about to embark on an academic career that was (A) socially and politically opposite of who I was and (B) had rules about writing that I thought were really messed up. At the same time, I started playing music. I would not say that rock set me free exactly, but it did give me a chance to really think about what exactly was wrong with the academic model. What I realized was that rock had its own rules. Often it was both (A) socially and politically opposite of who I was and (B) had rules about writing that I thought were really messed up. Maybe it was not academics, after all, but the whole world that was messed up!

As a musician, the rage and aggression I felt had a place, but the place was a ready-made—and I didn't quite fit. Fortunately, when I began playing music, it was in an environment that valued women to an exceptional degree. The reverberations of riot grrrl had begun to affect the lives of my peers, both male and female. I was sometimes belittled in guitar stores, or treated in a condescending manner by the soundman, but on the whole I was fortunate to escape most of these situations. When I looked at music in the mainstream, I was always disturbed by how repetitive the images and sounds coming from women were. It appeared that you could be angry or lovelorn, but that was about it (since 1990 there has been some improvement on these two basic models, but not much). Since I knew I didn't want to actually be in the mainstream, I was OK.

In the context of my own music making, the standards for "success" were very different from the mainstream. No one I knew wanted to get signed or become famous. At best we hoped to earn enough to live on (a tall order, I realize), and maybe go on tour. I was very far removed from the most developed and impermeable bastions of sexism in music, those institutions that hold the purse strings and the avenues to "success." My expectations and hopes for success had more to do with developing and participating in community, and trying to fuse politics with music in a new way.

My studies weren't all bad either, so long as I recognized that it was passion for the material that drove me rather than any "professional" advancement. I study the classics because of both the basic strangeness and the weird familiarity that ancient lyrics hold for me. Strange because their meaning must cross a divide through unspoken languages, languages that hold interpretive mystery and power as generously as they hold precision. Familiar because they are about emotional worlds that resonate with me: love, distance, longing, home, beauty of detail, and vastness of beauty. The question of authenticity is also one of the most riveting in the study of ancient lyrics, both in the study of sources (who wrote what) and the study of historical afterlife (each century gives you a different answer to the question, "Who was Homer?"). These issues, particularly the latter, have held my interest since I started school.

One of my enduring fascinations has been with the poetry of Sappho, and with the way that Sappho has been regarded as an author since about the fifth century B.C.E. This is partially because the enigma of her lost lines and works is so mysterious and engaging; what fragments we have fill a very slim volume and are apparently (according to ancient sources) a fraction of her work. But it is also because her unique position as a singular feminine voice from the preclassical Greek world has created a mythology around her persona that is inseparable from the mythology of the Woman Author. Her history is instructive because it shows how the assumptions about female voice and sexuality change the ways that cultures read and understand her lyrics. Suffice it to say that Sappho has, in her long life of interpretation, been reduced by various interpreters to, among other things, a whore, a corrupter of children, a school marm, a song and dance teacher, a lover of women and of men, a poet, a teacher, a suicide. In this manner of interpretation, it is only her personality that can possibly determine her lyrics.

I'm dwelling on Sappho, where the examples of Joni Mitchell or Suzanne Vega might be more contemporary, because my understanding of the way that the female voice is consistently personalized resides in this first and fundamental predecessor. Moreover, for me, as both an academic and a musician, there is not a big difference between interpretation of the personal voice and its use. I can argue in an academic context that when Sappho says "Sweat breaks on me and I turn paler than green grass" she may be inhabiting a character. We can't be sure, since we know so few details of the culture from which this poetry comes. But to make the supposition would imply the poet's ability to speak from outside her own experience, a more complex creative act, and give her credit as a manipulator of language, not simply as a woman who wanted to get her feelings down on papyrus.

Meanwhile, as a writer and performer I confront similar expectations about the role of the female "author" in pop music. In these modes I try not to think about how interpretation of my music might occur. But as a singer-songwriter—I'll just peg myself in this marketing niche for a second—I know that representation of personal experience, and authenticity, are very highly valued in this kind of music. And this is a kind of music in which the female voice is the undisputed king. This shuts down your options as a performer and also gives you a chance to manipulate them. If I say "my heart is broken," am I talking about me, about my heart in my real life being broken? Consider, in contrast to Sappho, Chan Marshall, aka Cat Power, whose personal breakdowns on stage are so real life we are positively riveted. Is she acting crazy or is she really crazy? She sounds so sad, do you think she really is?

We see the "I" used everywhere in pop music, and used to many different ends. Overall, however, when a man uses the personal voice, he speaks of himself and of a common "I," a generalized experience (and in this way, like the absent voice of authority in the academic context). When a woman uses the personal voice, she speaks about herself and only herself. It may resonate in a general sense, but it is regarded as emanating from the woman herself, as her personal, unique experience.

Historians of gender and rock 'n' roll Simon Reynolds and Joy Press trace this process as it relates to stereotypes of masculinity embodied in the "rebel" and the "mystic" (manifest in psychedelia). These categories were already well established once women began to pick up guitars in the 1960s. One reaction to already existing categories of masculinity was (and is) for women to mimic them. Another is to use a confessional voice, which is a particularly female voice, in part because the vulnerability it affords the singer mimics the vulnerability of women in a sexist world.

Reynolds and Press point to many exceptions to this tendency, and to the success of such voices as Liz Phair, Lydia Lunch, and PJ Harvey in redefining the vulnerability in the "I." Their "I" simultaneously complies with gendered expectations and defies them. Nonetheless, the pattern still holds. How many times did I read the musing of critics who supposed that finally PJ Harvey was happy and maybe even in love after the release of *Stories from the City, Stories from the Sea?* There were also critics who supposed her best music had been made in her darkest days. A critic's recognition of the history of persona in songwriting and performance can ultimately dispel this style of reductive critique, particularly when it comes to female performers.

Ultimately, the authentic voice in pop music comes less from what the speakers know than how effectively they can relate emotional states. These emotional states may or may not be communicated in a personal voice, but historically women's voices have used this "I" to convey the authority of experience. This has had the unfortunate effect of creating an identity between the speaker and the song's "I" that is not necessarily there. When the performer understands this idea, she can use the position of speaking from her personal experience to speak to experiences outside of herself, and discuss political or cultural ideas that may be potentially transformative to her audience.

I wrote a song once called "The Walls Ablaze" that is about looking at the smoldering ruins of something. My original impetus for the song was reading about the way the walls of Troy burned after the Trojan War for days and days, day and night. It is also about the view of the Trojan women, standing on top of the walls, waiting for them to fall and having to make the choice to die or become slaves to the

Greeks. They watch as the hero Achilles drags the dead body of his enemy Hector around the walls to disfigure and disgrace his corpse. This is not really normal fodder for a pop song, but it raised so many issues I thought were important, and that I thought I could write about in a way that other people might be able to understand. That's why in the song it starts with a verse that is a view from far away: "The walls ablaze / they burn for days / from miles away / through smoke and haze."

This way the song is about walls, any walls in any war, or any still-burning relic of conflict. The chorus brings the attention to the listener and singer by making a demand: "Show me a sign / of things that you can change / or keep the same," which is of course an impossible demand—it is a demand to show that you have control over any fate, including your own. As the singer, I am asking for this from the listener, but I am also trying to show a "sign" by stating that really you can't control your fate, that the walls will burn until they are all burned out. The next verse goes: "Look down below / you've got no place to go / except around / is wrath all you have found?" This verse is about making the choice to encounter conflict with rage, and being so blinded by rage you see only one way out of a given situation. By asking a question in this context, the chorus comes back with an answer, again: "Show me a sign / of things that you can change / or keep the same." And this time it appears that you can make a choice, to fight or not fight, to jump or not jump, to indulge wrath or turn away from it. It is important for me to have my own voice in this song (Show *me* a sign), because I wanted to communicate the personal nature of these ethical questions—the me can be me, Sarah Dougher, or any person who cares to repeat the lyric in their own voice, in their own head.

I am concerned as a musician with the process of translating emotional language into meaning, and emotionally based narratives into music. Continual reinvention of the public self through changes in style, voice, and even genre allow women artists a degree of mobility otherwise unavailable. This is one reason, for example, that Liz Phair's music about sex is so successful: she could sing like it is her, but is it? It also empowers women beyond the sexist assumption (initiated in the book of Genesis) that women are by nature manipulative.

I think the key to understanding the relationship between the uses of the personal voice in academics and in songs is to compare their approaches to authority. The podium and the stage are very powerful places: there is an often problematic hierarchy of authority that is automatically assumed between the teacher/performer and the students/audience. You are up there because you ostensibly have something to say. As a teacher, you've got the capital of your education to bank on; as a singer, well, you're there to entertain and you've got the capital of your voice, your body, your talent—not institutional power. So in either situation, you have variables to work with and to manipulate. In my own experience of performing, I much prefer an open, level position of communication with the audience, where I can talk with them, ask them questions, engage them about things that we both think are important. Sometimes this works—when the audience feels comfortable enough—and sometimes it doesn't (particularly in bars and other venues where the audience is interested in a conventional show, some entertainment with their pitcher). In addition, in the time before and after a show it is important for me to be where I can be in touch with the audience—maybe behind the merch table, for example—where I can have access and be accessible.

Simplistic criticism of a conference like EMP's focuses on the divide people see between the experience of rocking—very visceral and nonverbal—and the perceived antiseptic relationship that academics have with music of any kind—cerebral, unemotional. Even this lame criticism has to do with the idea that academics command a different kind of authority than rockers, which is true, but it also suggests that rockers and academics don't share any concepts of authority—and this, in my view, simply isn't the case. I teach and make music in a sexist world, a world that reads male experience as general (like the absent voice in academics) and the female voice as specific, singing only about herself.

By continuing to create lyrics outside the veil of my own experience, I am trying to manipulate the personal voice to speak from outside myself, into the personalities and situations, real or imagined, that interest me and that I wish to communicate. I inherently use my experience to inform those lyrics, although obliquely. Perhaps the most important connection is emotion. By expressing an authentic personal voice in an academic context, my teaching can model personal experience as a basis for judgments and opinions. No one would deny that this is where these come from anyway, but in academics, it is not cool to say it.

In both situations, I am asking my audiences to pay attention to what I have to say. I am also encouraging them, in my own way, to use their own voices to both speak their truths and to empathize and feel compassion for others, to create imaginative worlds where they synthesize the outside world into versions of art that speak to them and, if they are lucky, speak to others as well. These comments come into a world that is slowly changing, toppling the strongholds of sexism and centralized control of discourse. There are new places for the "I" to explain and describe emotion, and hence there are new spaces for potential transformation. What remains is the constant challenge for any person who wishes to disrupt sexism and to create cultural forms and political discourses amid the ruins of old structures.

chapter 11

All the Memories Money Can Buy: Marketing Authenticity and Manufacturing Authorship

DAVID SANJEK

"Everything mediated is spurious until proven genuine," Charles Keil memorably said.[1] Well, I don't know of any commercial music that lacks dirty hands. Rather than a cut-and-dried category, authenticity comes across to these ears as a constructed category that bedevils the distinction between the commodified and the noncommercial, the immediate and the mediated, the raw and the cooked. Seldom are we in a position to isolate these domains from one another. The circumstances under which we assess recorded music for its quantity of authenticity parallel the proposition put to movie directors by the character actor Walter Brennan: Did they want him to play a particular part with or without his dentures? Same man, with or without the incisors. Same music, with or without the apparatus that we associate with the mass media.

We can come to some understanding of the forces against which musicians must contend and regardless of which they occasionally remain true to their values only by examining individual instances of cultural production. To that end, I want to explore three narratives that illustrate how complicated the conferring of authenticity can be when a variety of interests with competing values and assumptions blend to produce a commercial recording. These moments are the 1927 Bristol Sessions, wherein the parameters of country music are assumed to have been codified; the release in 1947 by Capitol Records of "folk songs" by Merle Travis; and the 2000 and 2001 releases of the raw sessions from which Miles Davis's albums *In a Silent Way* (1969) and *Bitches Brew* (1970) were made. We will find that many hands played a role in these recordings and, therefore, no single individual or agency determined the meaning and consequence of the results.

Generating Genres and Codifying Copyrights

Whether merchandising catchphrase or cultural category, some of our most familiar musical genres owe their origins to the barriers set in front of individuals who wanted to help a novel form of performance reach the widest possible public. Take country, for example. In 1923, Polk Brockman, an Atlanta-based phonograph salesman, saw some newsreel footage of a fiddlers convention during a visit to New York and recalled that such contests were wildly popular in his hometown. Brockman contacted an executive at Okeh Records, Ralph Peer, and induced him to record one of the leading players in the South, Fiddlin' John Carson. Peer found the results not only aesthetically unacceptable but also without commercial potential. (It was "pluperfect awful," he told an interviewer years later.)[2] Peer denied the material any advertising, labeling, or even a presence in the company's catalog. In fact, he pressed only 500 copies for Brockman personally, and he was surprised to discover that in a matter of several weeks, they had sold out.

A label for the newly established genre, "hillbilly," would be proposed in 1925 to Peer by one Al Hopkins, whose musicians came from North Carolina and Kentucky yet, perhaps ironically, were based in Washington, D.C. (To compound the irony, these so-called hicks were the first in the genre to perform in New York City [1927]; the first to play before a president [Calvin Coolidge]; and the first to appear in a movie [a fifteen-minute Warner Brothers short].) *Variety* fumed that "the 'hillbilly' is a North Carolina or Tennessee or adjacent mountaineer type of illiterate white whose creed and allegiance are to the Bible, the Chautauqua, and the phonograph . . . The great majority, probably, 95 percent, can neither read nor write English. [They are] illiterate and ignorant, with the intelligence of morons."[3]

The inordinate inaccuracy of *Variety*'s vilification of country music was proven by the speed with which a number of entrants into the field sussed out how one might make a killing. A good example is Bradley Kincaid. Born in Garrard County, Kentucky, and educated at the progressive Berea College, he began his career singing "mountain music" on his "hound dog guitar" over the airwaves of Chicago's WLS in 1925. He drew an immediate response from this very urban audience and subsequently became a regular on the station's *National Barn Dance*, whose listeners sent him 100,000 letters in the course of a single year. He began to record an incredibly diverse repertoire for the Gennett label and disdained the "hillbilly" designation. Kincaid believed that the vernacular repertoire he had inhaled growing up, and whose vitality was reinforced by the cultural values taught to him at Berea, amounted to a body of material no less meaningful or valuable than any other on the American scene. His popularity and the extent of his influence have led Archie Green to state, "Our very conception today, that much American folksong is by definition undefiled, a precious elixir for national well-being, stems in part from Bradley Kincaid's achievement."[4] Kincaid also possessed considerable perspicacity about the marketplace and released songbooks of his repertoire. The first sold 100,000 copies, and he eventually racked up sales of 400,000 copies, including later editions. So much for the morons of the mountains.

Kincaid's achievement was not lost on others in the business, including the aforementioned Ralph Peer. Peer's revelation, however, was that the long-term benefit in this material was not to be had from the performers themselves or even their recordings. Fashions come and go; copyrights remain. He made a bold move in response to these conditions. In 1927, he left Okeh and signed with the RCA Victor company with the unusual proviso that he receive no salary but retain the copyrights of the material he produced. The material that he would go on to record for Victor was either "original," or so his artists told him, or of sufficient vintage and so reorganized as to be in the public domain. What this allowed Peer to do was, as Richard A. Peterson concludes, "transform tradition into a renewable resource."[5]

One of the most important events in that process was the series of recording sessions held in the summer of 1927 in Bristol, Tennessee, a small town whose main street formed the border between Virginia and Tennessee. Peer let it be known that one of his artists, Ernest Stoneman, had made $3,600 in royalties from sides cut the previous year. Little did Peer realize how effective the bait he had set would be: during the course of his stay in Bristol, he would cut seventy-four pieces by nineteen different groups, among them two performers who would go on to transform the face of country music— Jimmie Rodgers and the Carter Family.

Peer's contract with artists contained three components: a fee for the actual recording; a split of the mechanical royalty for each record sold; and, most important, the copyright to the material that he consistently retained in his own hands. At the start, Peer intended to offer $25 per song, but Victor induced him to raise it to $50. His standard cut of the mechanical royalty was in his favor, 75 percent of the 2-cent scale of the day, with only .05 cent going to the artist(s). Whether the players knew or not that they were getting the short end of the stick remains a matter of conjecture, but only one of them, A. P. Carter, made a point of ensuring that he retained the copyright to his material.

If the urge to condemn Peer for gross manipulation is strong, it must be said that he offered these people a better financial arrangement than most of his peers in the record business. At the same time, what Peer shared with his fellow A&R men was a view that artists could be used and then discarded when whatever novelty the individual or group possessed was preserved on disc. More than one commentator has compared this process to strip mining. Frank Walker, who worked for Columbia Records during this period, put the matter in exceedingly curt language. "Their repertoire would consist of eight or ten things that they did well and that was all they knew. So, when you picked out the three or four that were best in a man's so-called repertoire you were through with that man as an artist. That was all. He was finished. It was a culling operation, taking the best that they had."[6] While Peer grew to like and to have long professional relationships with a number of the artists he worked with on the Bristol Sessions—Rodgers and the Carters, in particular— he shared Walker's snide and dismissive tone. Peer spoke on future occasions of his having invented "the hillbilly and the nigger stuff," and he called attention to the necessity of keeping those spheres of performance as segregated as the lives of their makers; he deliberately separated Rodgers from his chosen group of accompanists because "the records would have been no good if Jimmie had sung with this group for he was singing nigger blues and they were doing old-time fiddle music. Oil and water . . . they just don't mix."[7] Even if much of what Peer would preserve for posterity was unmistakably hybrid, he conceived of the material, and its creators, in a rigidly compartmentalized fashion.

   What then of that material? Peer had, without knowing it at the time, the unique break of discovering Rodgers and the Carters, but what repertoire did he decide to commit to disc? Is it, as the newspaper story stated, evidence of "prewar melodies and old mountaineer songs"? That has been the impression one gets from the mythology that has been passed down since 1927 about this event. The Bristol Sessions have been characterized as the "big bang of country music," the crucial ancestor to the recent and meteoric public success of the soundtrack to the Coen brothers' 2001 film *O Brother Where Art Thou?* That picture, the soundtrack, the series of public concerts of the included material, and the film made of the shows, *Down from the Mountain* (2002), have collectively been characterized in the press and elsewhere as an overdue revival of authentic vernacular music.

The Bristol Sessions are viewed as a repository of material untouched by the commercial mainstream and resonant with the values of bygone eras. Simply put, is this so?

The answer, of course, is not simple, for the individuals who sat before Peer's microphones were not cultural absolutists. Who wrote the songs they sang, what race they themselves might have been, what religion they practiced, and what region of the country they came from seems to have had little influence on performers. Bill Malone reports a telling anecdote in this regard. When a groundbreaking body of folk research materials, the Jonathan Edwards Memorial Foundation collection, was transferred from UCLA to the University of North Carolina, Chapel Hill, a conference was convened. In the course of the affair, a ballad singer, Doug Wallin, presented a group of songs he had learned growing up in "that citadel of old-time music, Madison County, North Carolina, where Cecil Sharp had found his richest body of traditional ballads." Wallin then announced he would perform a song he had learned from his mother, which turned out to be "After the Ball"—the 1893 ballad by Charles K. Harris that was a mainstay of the Tin Pan Alley repertoire. As Malone slyly adds, "The incident nevertheless tells us much about the musical catholicity and tolerance of the folk."[8]

Looking at the contents of the Bristol Sessions, we can confirm the inescapable hybridity of that authentic genre we know as country music. A number of the songs were from the kind of sources Cecil Sharp and other professional song collectors would have thought of as legitimate. A. P. Carter was well acquainted with the dictates of copyright, but he also was something of an amateur folklorist and traveled the countryside collecting material for the group to perform, sometimes accompanied by an African American guitarist, Leslie Riddles, who acted as an amanuensis. Jimmie Rodgers provided Peer with more complicated issues of attribution. As a live performer as well as one on radio, Rodgers was well versed in contemporary repertoire, but that conflicted with Peer's agenda. A song like "The Longest Train I Ever Saw" fit the parameters, for it was a version of the folk standard "In the Pines." Two other pieces were less than traditional but somehow escaped Peer's detection. "The Soldier's

Sweetheart" was a piece from World War I, though sung to the tune of the more traditional "Where the River Shannon Flows." More to the point, the song that sold Peer on Rodgers's groundbreaking use of the yodel, "Sleep, Baby, Sleep," was a vaudeville piece from the 1860s and had received earlier treatments by other recording artists.

Less well known players similarly erased the purportedly fine line between traditional and professional repertoire. The Shelor Family's rendition of "Billy Grimes, the Rover" was actually a transatlantic act of appropriation, for the song came from the English music hall and was first sung in America before 1850. The melody to Alfred Karnes's gospel piece "I Am Bound for the Promised Land" was wedded to the structure of the blues piece "Don't Let Your Deal Go Down." Two other of Karnes's selections are from the commercial sphere: Dion De Marbelle's 1887 "When They Ring Those Golden Bells" and Fanny Crosby's 1899 hymn "To the Work." Charles and Paul Johnson's "A Passing Policeman" is actually a version of an 1884 Tin Pan Alley piece, "The Little Lost Child." It was cowritten by Joe Storr and Edward Marks, the latter of whom became one of the most successful New York publishers of the day. Finally, even Ernest Stoneman brought pieces outside the purported tradition to the affair. "Tell Mother I Will Meet Her" was from a 1903 songbook released by the Georgia-based John B. Vaughan, and "Are You Washed in the Blood" is a gospel standard by Elisha Hoffman dating back to 1878.

The authentic, then, became on the Bristol Sessions an elastic affair. Peer's genuine sensitivity to the quality of the players was coupled with a less astute sense of where the material came from. He might well have bristled when someone played him a piece he recognized as a pop song, but, clearly, the ability to distinguish the professionally written from the traditionally acquired was a hit-or-miss affair. When we think of these recordings as the ground zero of country music, we must remember that the detonating device employed was made from less than pure ingredients. Furthermore, the benefit of the sessions was far from an equal matter. The musicians, some of whom never returned to the studio after this one occasion, had their talents displayed to the public and reaped a degree of larger recognition—some, obviously, more so than others, the Carters and Rodgers being the stars of the hour. At the same time, the benefits to Peer and his publishing company, Peer Southern, continue to the present day.

Wanna Be a Folk Singer?

The considerable number of individuals who have allied their cultural capital with the body of American vernacular expression designated as folk music presume their investment is predicated on a stable currency. The vernacular repertoire they espouse disdains the use of euphemisms, grounding itself in emotions and ideas that mirror eternal verities, experiences that no individual can simply dismiss out of hand or translate into facile abstractions. Anyone, regardless of class or educational background, is capable of understanding this body of material, for it positions itself as being neither superior to nor beyond the comprehension of the average person. The seeming simplicity of its language and musical technique enables the songs to be readily absorbed and transmitted to others. Folk music has the unique property of being superficially quite uncomplicated, yet rooted in subject matter and sentiments that are anything but simple.

To complicate such familiar narratives, let us turn to the recordings made by the eminent songwriter and guitarist Merle Travis, under the title *Folk Songs of the Hills,* for Capitol Records in 1947. I want to point to three songs featured on this LP: "Dark as a Dungeon," Sixteen Tons," and "Nine Pound Hammer." Each has its roots in Travis's experience growing up in the mining country of Muhlenburg County, Kentucky, as well as in how his considerable professional expertise fused with his ingrained knowledge of musical and cultural traditions. As we shall see, these songs experienced considerable commercial success when recorded by others, most notably "Sixteen Tons" through its performance in 1955 by Tennessee Ernie Ford. They also, to varying degrees, became curiously absorbed into the vernacular repertoire as anonymous expressions of the travails of the folk. Travis's experience indicates that the demarcation between folk and pop can be tenuous indeed. What is one to make of truth-telling when a person self-consciously adopts the posture of a folk singer so successfully that the material he or she creates becomes absorbed by the vernacular community as well as the hit parade, each precinct operating under a completely different set of principles?

The origins of Merle Travis's folk repertoire date back to 1947, when Cliffie Stone, bassist and session leader, was commanded by the Capitol brass to locate a performer who could emulate Decca's successful recordings of folk music by Burl Ives. Stone contacted Merle Travis as the most likely candidate on the Capitol roster. Travis, at thirty, had been a professional musician since he left school in the eighth grade. He had established his reputation on radio when signed as a member of the Drifting Pioneers to Cincinnati's WLW in 1937. Soon thereafter the station inaugurated the *Boone County Jamboree*, a regional equivalent of the *Grand Ole Opry*. Travis's ensemble became featured stars on the broadcast along with other eminent country performers, including the Delmore Brothers, banjo player Grandpa Jones, guitarist Joe Maphis, and the duo Curly Fox and Texas Ruby. Travis, Jones, and the Delmores performed gospel material together under the name Brown's Ferry Four. When Syd Nathan established the eminent King Record label in 1943, primarily as a vehicle for country music, Travis appeared on the first piece of music released by the company.

In March 1944, financially strapped and depressed over his rejection by the U.S. Marines as unfit, Travis migrated to Los Angeles, where he quickly became a major participant in that city's country fraternity. He released his first solo material for Capitol Records in the summer of the following year. Travis established a reputation as a jack-of-all-trades: sideman and leader, instrumentalist and singer, but, most of all, songwriter. His first self-penned hit, "Cincinnati Lou," charted in March of 1946, and that same year he wrote one of the best-selling country songs of the period, Tex Williams's "Smoke! Smoke! Smoke! (That Cigarette)." This witty tribute to the joys of nicotine resembled a number of Travis's other charting songs, such as "Sweet Temptation," "Divorce Me C.O.D.," and "So Tight, So

Firm, So Fully Packed," in its skillful play with language and sense of fun. Travis was no naif but a trained professional with the aptitude to churn out what the public wanted to hear. His appeal crossed over into other media, for he appeared on both local and national radio; in "soundies," those short nonnarrative pictures that preceded music videos; as a performer in cowboy B movies; and, when the technology emerged, as a featured artist on the television series *Town Hall Party*, hosted by Tex Ritter. Travis's Capitol recordings featured an unusual ensemble of instruments, mixing his facile and influential guitar picking with acoustic bass, accordion, trumpet, and steel guitar. They stood out not just for their witty words but also for their uncustomary combination of sounds.

So, when Travis received the phone call from Cliffie Stone on August 7, 1946, that began with the query, "Wanna be a folk singer?" his immediate response was negative. He told Stone that Ives and others had recorded all the genuinely vernacular repertoire he knew, to which the bassist challenged him, "Write some." Travis countered that the very notion was an oxymoron: you couldn't write folk songs. Stone retorted, then write something that sounds like the real cigar—and make sure you've got eight of them for the record. Ever the professional, Travis let Stone know he would have the material ready for the next day. True to his word, on August 8, accompanied solely by the bassist and playing acoustic and not electric guitar, Travis laid down "Dark as a Dungeon," "Sixteen Tons," "Nine Pound Hammer," and "Over by Number Nine." He arrived for the session on his motorcycle and, in fact, had written "Dark as a Dungeon" on the way, when he stopped under a streetlight in Redondo Beach. *Folk Songs of the Hills* was not a commercial success, though it did stack up some sales in the urban market, including New York City, where the market for work like that of Burl Ives was strong. Curiously, the record company, or Travis himself, failed to copyright the songs, and he and the Capitol staff went back to their business of trying to produce hits.

The presentation of the material on the LP bears mentioning, for it includes a spoken introduction to each song, detailing its origin and setting in the personal experience of the performer. Travis also affects a more down-home accent and delivery for these elements than he did in other contexts. In the introduction to "Dark as a Dungeon," he says he'd recently been talking to an old friend of his family, a coal miner just like Travis's father: "When I asked him why he never left and tried some other kind of work, he says, 'Nawsir, you won't do that. If ever you get this old coal dust in your blood, you're just gonna be a plain old coal miner as long as you live.' He went on to say, 'It's a habit [chuckle] sorta like chewin' tobaccer.'" These passages not only established a persona for Travis but also constructed a rural past for the material, so that a song scribbled beneath a streetlight could be imagined to have been passed along from generation to generation in the singer's ancestral Kentucky. "It's a-many a man I have known in my day / Who lived just to labor his whole life away," the lyrics declare. "Like a fiend with his dope and a drunkard his wine / A man will have lust for the lure of the mines."[9]

Two things should be noted. At this point in his life, Travis had not returned to his home for some time, and, therefore, the dramatic confrontation depicted in the introduction should be taken as altogether a dramatic device. Second, and more crucially, the references to obliteration through drugs or alcohol possess an autobiographical dimension. Though he puts the information in the voice of the old man, Travis was a long-term abuser of both alcohol and pills and possibly a manic depressive as well. He shunned the spotlight and seemed to recoil from the trappings of celebrity. Embarrassed by fame or even simple compliments, he denigrated his considerable skills with a vengeance. Implicit in the song, then, is the haunting lesson that one comes to a sorry end whether through poverty or fame.

Almost immediately, "Dark as a Dungeon" began an exodus from commercial recording to take a position in the anonymous folk lexicon. The paragon of folk sensibility, Alan Lomax, included it in his last collaboration with his father, John, the 1947 anthology *Folk Song U.S.A.* Ben Botkin transcribed both the introduction and lyrics into *A Treasury of Southern Folklore* (1949) and identified the material properly as Travis's work. Cisco Houston, the confederate of Woody Guthrie, performed the song on his 1951 Folkways LP *This*

Land Is My Land, without any credit given, and three years later yet another rendition of the piece, by Bob De Cormier and Pete Seeger, appeared on the *Hootenanny Tonight* release, again without attribution. In 1953 *Sing Out!* magazine, the principal organ of the folk community, included an unattributed transcription of "Dark as a Dungeon." Members of the folk world have long railed against the commercial music industry for absconding with vernacular material, yet here is a reversal of the very same process.

Similarly, "Sixteen Tons" was transcribed without attribution by *Sing Out!* in 1952. The magazine stated in the headnote that "the traditional miner's song speaks a sharp language—with a real worker's imagery in its poetry." The editors went another unwelcome step further when, two years later, they printed "revisions" to the lyrics, again not ascribed to Travis. It was not until 1956, after the success of Tennessee Ernie Ford's million-plus-selling cover of the song, that *Sing Out!* even mentioned Travis's name. Pete Seeger suggested that since the politically inclined songwriter Earl Robinson, author of "Ballad for Americans," resided, like Travis, in the Los Angeles area, the two must know each other, and Travis had been influenced by, in Seeger's words, "Earl's manner of explaining a folk song to make it come alive to the audience."[10] In another example of the complexities of how folklore becomes pop lore, a commercial phenomenon, the editor of the *United Mine Workers Journal* wrote the first article on the vernacular origins of Travis's work after hearing Tennessee Ernie Ford perform the piece on television, the medium in which it broke before Ford committed the selection to disc.

The third selection, "Nine Pound Hammer," illustrates not so much the unwitting conflation by others of the commercial and the vernacular, but the manner in which the two realms are fused in the hands of a skillful and knowledgeable creator. One cannot check off with certainty the many possible pieces of the folk canon alluded to in "Nine Pound Hammer." Travis himself may not have been aware of them all, but he did report to Archie Green that he had heard the song first from the aforementioned Texas Ruby. To what degree was he conscious that the song has its origins in the John Henry myth and the songs constructed about it, with his reference to the nine-pound hammer that will eventually kill him? Did he hear the earliest commercial recording of the song, by country pioneers Al Hopkins and the Buckle Busters, released in 1927, or the subsequent versions by Frank Blevins and his Tar Heel Rattlers, and by G. B. Grayson and Henry Whitter, that appeared the following year? How about the celebrated Ernest "Pop" Stoneman cut done in 1934, or that by Bill Monroe and his brother Charlie in 1936? All remains conjecture. Add to this series of conundrums the fact that the work songs of African American railroad gangs played their part in the creation of the material, as Charles Bowman of the Buckle Busters told Archie Green.

The line of influence that connects these individuals and episodes rises above and then drops below our cultural radar, yet the fact that one player after another took a turn at the material proves that each possessed a sensitive ear for the vernacular influences that lay all about, in the air and on disc. If nothing else, the cultural practices that resulted in Merle Travis's tackling of "Nine Pound Hammer" validate Archie Green's assertion that "there is a given time when any traditional fragment must be captured in sound or print if it is to serve in extending large society's awareness of folk culture."[11] Whichever unwitting publicist might have been in the employ of Capitol Records at the time, he or she did not know how wisely they wrote when they stated that Travis's *Folk Songs of the Hills* LP contained "authentic folk music . . . handed down for generations."[12] Merle Travis's folk songs prove that authenticity is a slippery phenomenon, and, in the case of "Sixteen Tons" in particular, a mighty lucrative phenomenon at that.

It Will All Come Out in the Mix

Recorded music, the domain from which I've drawn my three examples, amounts to a sphere parallel to but separate from live performance. Ever since the introduction of plastic tape in 1947, the studio has become a place where the technicians play as much of a role in the final product as the people whose work they reproduce. They collectively engage in the creation of what Evan Eisenberg has

dubbed "phonography." "The word 'record,'" he writes, "is misleading. Only live recordings record an event; studio recordings, which
are the great majority, record nothing. Pieced together from bits of
actual events, they construct an ideal event. They are like the composite photograph of a minotaur."[13] But what occurs when reverse
engineering takes place and we are presented with the original master
tapes from which the product was mined, as has recently been the
case with Miles Davis's *In a Silent Way* and *Bitches Brew?* Compli-
cating matters further, some of the Davis selections take on a third it-
eration in the form of remixes Bill Laswell released in 1998 under the
title *Panthalassa*. Here is a phenomenon that would give joy to Walter Benjamin. Wherein lies the genuine "aura" of Davis's efforts at
this juncture in his career?

In the late 1960s, Davis began to explore the comingling of jazz
with the techniques of popular music, and particularly the rhythmic
patterns of rhythm and blues. He had always been a conscious editor of his own work, believing that the fewer notes the better, especially if one chose wisely what notes to use. He rarely told the other
musicians with whom he worked how to achieve this manner of se-
vere concision on their own part, instead allowing them to go out on
a limb until they ceased to be afraid that they would fall. More than
one of his colleagues have remarked about recording with Davis that
they were not sure if they had achieved what he was looking for, or
even, in some cases, if they had played with any skill whatsoever. Davis wanted them to disdain routine and reach for an undetermined
but always accessible form of communication that resisted cliché or
custom.

One of the most telling comments Davis made at this stage of his
career arose during the production of *In a Silent Way*. The title track
was a Joe Zawinul tune that Davis disassembled and played in a
form that Zawinul, a keyboard player, felt undermined if not ignored altogether what he was attempting to achieve. In response to
Zawinul's distress, Davis remarked,

Whenever Joe or somebody would bring in something they
wrote, I'd have to cut it all up because these guys get so hung up

on what they write. They think it's complete the way they write it. Like the way he wanted that "In a Silent Way" was completely different. I don't know what he was looking for when he wrote that tune, but it wasn't going to be on my record . . . You write to establish a mood. That's all you need. Then you can go on for hours. If you complete something, you play it, and it's finished. Once you resolve it, there's nothing more to do. But when it's open, you can suspend it.[14]

In Davis's defense of his radical surgery upon Zawinul's piece, an attitude of uncertainty and flux in the process of recording is not something to avoid but a goal to pursue. That acceptance of chance and indeterminacy was mirrored in how he laid down tracks in this and subsequent sessions. He let his musicians go until they appeared to have virtually reached the end of their rope and then drew the exercise to a conclusion. What resulted was the raw material for a product, not the product itself. In the case of "In a Silent Way," nearly an hour of tape was filled, then turned over to Davis's producer Teo Macero. Macero was a bricoleur of the recording board, for he treated the raw material of Davis's playing as fluidly as the trumpeter did the score. In the first round, he reduced the piece to roughly forty-nine minutes and then played it for Davis, who excised it further to twenty-seven. To fill a marketable LP, Macero then repeated some elements and built the work up to its final thirty-eight minutes.

What is astonishing about this process is not so much the degree of concision in the final product but the fact that Davis left Macero virtually on his own to make the necessary choices. To accomplish those ends, Macero used a sophisticated tool kit that relied on echo, reverb, and a self-devised slap (tape) delay. He could spend as much as four or five weeks on a single piece, rarely strategizing verbally with Davis. Macero remarks, "There's very little dialogue . . . between Miles and myself. If we say twenty words in the course of a three-hour session, that's a lot. But there's no mystery."[15] Davis appeared to treat Macero as one more participant in the process, another player in the mix, with no more or less voice in the matter than either himself or the other musicians on the track. Davis's seeming absence from the final product then, in the end, parallels his wish not to take a determining role during the recording process. Remember his statement: when you complete something, it's finished. Where, for Davis, did the focus of authenticity lie: at the moment of improvisation, when confronted with the final mix, both, or neither? Did the attribute have any meaning or significance to Davis at all? If nothing else, the fact that he rarely listened to his own work once it was released reveals that he had little interest in investing himself in a formal artifact. That was a matter for the Columbia brass to attend to.

So, how would Davis respond to the present product, which, with some alteration, includes the raw material from which Macero cooked the two releases? In a sense, I don't think he would care one whit, for it amounts to just another take on an indeterminate project. While the two sets are not bootlegs but corporately supported material, they do, in effect, offer the listener access to a kind of parallel career to Miles's formal recordings. In this context, the recent observations by Robert Polito on the voluminous bootleg concert recordings of Bob Dylan—another Sony employee—bear examining. Polito wonders whether that material might "ultimately prove, as now appears likely, his most vital, revelatory, and enduring work."[16] Likewise, might the tapes of Davis's studio activity come to take on a more important role in the estimation of his career, particularly during this complex passage, than the recordings that were issued commercially at the time?

In truth, it does seem more than likely that these releases possess the greatest appeal for the obsessive rather than the average listener. They allow us to enter the Mothership Davis piloted during this phase of his career, to tinker with the engine and observe in greater detail how, in Greg Tate's marvelous phrase, the trumpeter and his "furthermuckers" achieved their effects.[17] The engineers who reversed Macero's machinations believe that one can now more clearly hear the interplay that occurred in the studio. Sony staff engineer Mark Wilder states, "Those guys played some killing stuff that got a little lost in the technology of the mix and the postproduction.

So yes, we tried to create a feeling of people playing together. The musicality of what occurred during these sessions was paramount for us, and we wanted to remove some of the original mix technology to bring this out."[18] But should we congratulate Wilder and his confederates and, by doing so, demean Macero for obscuring what Davis *really* wanted to play, as if whipping the master tapes into shape brought them, and us, in sync with the late musician's intentions? Or is that just sheer presumption?

In an article from the magazine *Hermenaut*'s issue devoted to "Fake Authenticity," Chris Fujiwara examines the consequences of the restoration work done on Orson Welles's 1957 *Touch of Evil* and Iggy Pop and the Stooges' 1973 *Raw Power*. The tampering fails in the end, he believes, to result in material that either clarifies the artists' intentions or makes their decisions more accessible to the viewer or listener. He writes, "Those who wield the technologies of 'restoration' create the forms in which past works will be preserved and known by future generations—they can't avoid betraying these works even as they save them."[19] The flaws in both works—in Welles's case due to studio interference and in the Stooges' the tampering with the final mix by David Bowie—are incontestably integrated with their virtues, and to presume that one can separate the two makes us believe ourselves more alert and artful than the creators whom we admire. So, we lose the rawness of the Stooges if we gain the ability to hear all the instruments. We are able to see Welles's opening tracking shot without the impediment of titles but lose the percussive urgency of Henry Mancini's theme. Which are we then to call the authentic artifact? In the case of Davis, do we divest him of his sense of structure and the coherence achieved by Macero's editing by diverting our attention to the material from which he and his producer made their choices? No matter what, we will benefit the coffers of Sony by mulling over our decision, while the music Davis created will remain, whether raw or cooked, a body of work whose value and meaning we will not soon easily unravel.

Debates over authenticity really come down to distinctions about repertoire. It's almost as if each of us were programming a jukebox and endeavoring to prove our personal list superior to another's. Reducing the question of how to estimate the importance and worth of one record over another in this manner is nothing short of a collector's reflex, a conviction that catalog outweighs content. Whenever the mainstream taste of the wider public descends into a pattern that the cognoscenti consider debased, the obsession with repertoire emerges in full force. Dismissing the Top Ten out of hand and replacing it with cultish preferences bears an unappetizing similarity to the educated classes barricading themselves against the barbarians at the gates. Gina Arnold's metaphor comes to mind in this context: "That, after all, is my generation's symbol of a roving mind: great record collections in cardboard boxes, kept the way monks hoarded literature from marauding pagan masses."[20] Taste is transitory, and the belief that when someone shares my preferences, the chance increases of better things emerging on the horizon does not parallel my sense of social transformation. In the end, I'm more interested in what music people like and the role it plays in their lives than whether or not I get off on the same material. Their authenticity could easily be my ersatz.

chapter 12

Authorship Meets Downpression: Translating the Wailers into Rock

JASON TOYNBEE

It now seems that the rise of the author as a central figure in European culture can be traced back at least as far as the Middle Ages. According to Burt Kimmelman, by the twelfth century the troubadours had adopted an intense first-person voice with which to assert their "individual poetic authority" in song.[1] A hundred years later authors like Chaucer, in the emerging genre of narrative poetry, were bestowing their own attributes on their characters. This function, the representation of the persona of the creator in a work, then became embedded in a range of literary genres. It took on a significant new twist in Romantic poetry however. Now the author's sympathy and understanding of the human condition were key. As Thomas McCarthy puts it, "The successful lyric establishes a bond with the reader by stimulating the imagination such that the reader is moved to reproduce for himself the poet's emotional state."[2]

Strangely, perhaps, these developments reach some kind of destination in rock music. Whereas the author was effaced or subverted in literary modernism (Barthes's "Death of the Author" is both a historical description and a manifesto),[3] rock embraced the sympathetic and expressive author with enthusiasm, even with rapture. The new writer-performers of rock became the vanguard of a middle-class counterculture opposed not just to the mores of their parents but also to the prevailing aesthetics of modernism and the now withered canon of "official" culture. Another way of putting this is to say that authorship redeemed rock 'n' roll energy for a new, bourgeois constituency: it enabled a transformation of the people's music into art. However we look at it, though, the process occurred very quickly. Between the first rustlings of the author at work (Dylan or Lennon and McCartney, around 1963) and the full-blown shout of the rock-auteur (Pete Townshend and Jim Morrison, in 1966) there were only three years. By the end of the decade the new institution had been firmly established at the heart of the music industry, along with a new commodity form, the album, and a new marketing strategy built around long-term stardom.[4] One result of this was that when Bob Marley began negotiating a recording contract for the Wailers with Island Records in 1971 he could clinch the deal only by persuading label owner Chris Blackwell that the Wailers were capable of a metamorphosis—that they could become a rock band, something completely outside their long experience as recording artists in Jamaica.[5]

This essay explores some of the issues raised by the launching of the Wailers on the international rock market. It examines what happens when music makers from the postcolonial periphery encounter the institution of rock, newly installed in the metropolitan core. And following on from this it asks the question, posed originally by Gayatri Chakravorty Spivak, "Can the subaltern speak?"[6] In other words, did the Wailers' translation into rock repress Jamaican musical creativity, a form of "speaking" almost diametrically opposed to the sort of expressive authorship practiced in the metropolis?

The Jamaican music scene of the 1960s was characterized by a flat, interactive mode of production with a well-defined yet flexible division of labor between singers, songwriters, backing musicians,

and producers. In terms of market, records were made in the first instance for use by the "sound systems" that competed for audiences
in the dance halls.[7] As we will see, the high degree of interactivity
promoted continuous stylistic development and, in some periods,
radical shifts in musical form. This could hardly be more different
from rock in the 1970s, the domain into which Marley and the
Wailers were propelled. In rock, the key principle was that groups
or individual artists should make original albums at infrequent in-
tervals.[8] Above all it was important that the work be in some sense
unique, that is unlike the work of others. Although there was a division of labor, it tended to be suppressed in rock discourse. According to the conventional wisdom, rock musicians had to be autonomous author-performers, able to produce completely new works
with nothing but their own creative powers.

It is clear that Marley had already learned something about the
rock mode of production before he signed the Island deal. Nonetheless, making the transition was never going to be a straightfor-
ward matter. Black, Rastafarian, politically militant, and from the
postcolonial margins, the Wailers were not merely outside rock, they
were Other to it. How, then, to find a way to translate the group?
This was a key question for Island, and also for the music press, during 1972 and 1973. The influence of the press was particularly significant in the British music scene. As journalists struggled to frame
the Wailers in a way that rock fans could make sense of, they re-
sorted, perhaps inevitably, given the ideological premises of rock, to
a number of primitivizing and racist strategies. And yet the very
project of translation also invested Marley with authority and a degree of control over his creative practice. Enough control, in fact, to
enable him to dispense with the remaining two members of the original Wailing Wailers, Peter Tosh and Bunny Livingstone, in 1974.

The complex exchange at stake here was unequal and was always
limited, personally, to Marley. Other reggae artists were never seriously considered by the industry for the sort of treatment he received. Nonetheless, the moment of the Wailers' transition in the
early 1970s offers important insights, into the ideology of rock authorship and also about conditions for the possible entry of hybrid,

postcolonial forms into a global culture in which the Author still rules.

Of course, deconstructing rock to show up its cult of authentic genius as an oppressive myth has long been a preoccupation of popular music studies.[9] It is a research tradition that has proved extremely useful in helping us understand popular music as a social and economic formation–partly by pointing to how much of the rock aesthetic (and the industry based on it) is premised on the figure of the auteur. However, the critique of authentic genius has rarely addressed the question of what lies behind its allure. In particular, we haven't found out much about how authorship connects with and impinges on the practice of making music. This is one reason why the case of the Wailers is so illuminating. Their translation from Jamaican vocal group to a new kind of reggae-rock hybrid foregrounds the tension between authorship doctrine and the utterly social process of music making itself.

And that in turn begs one more question. Is it possible to characterize in a general way the nature of creativity in pop? I would suggest it is, and that such creativity can best be conceived as social authorship, a difficult term perhaps, if only because of the way "author" so strongly connotes individualism and self-sufficiency.[10] Yet it seems to me that agency is absolutely central to music making, and if we want to emphasize agency then "author" does this better than any alternatives that have been offered. For instance, the "scriptor" of literary modernism described by Roland Barthes is a shadowy figure, "cut off from any voice" and unable to act with present intent–effectively a ghost writer.[11] As for other possibilities ("cultural producer" from sociology is one candidate), these are generally too broad and don't draw attention to the specifics of symbolic creativity. Hence the coinage: my hope is that the qualifier "social" mitigates, but does not obliterate, "authorship."

There are two aspects to this. First, creating new music always involves the interaction of people in a variety of roles.[12] A short list would include entrepreneurs, technicians, session musicians, writers, singers, producers, and, of course, audiences. Clearly, the particular way in which functions are divided and interaction is organized varies historically and by place. But in all cases, and whatever the supervening ideology, we can say that making music is a continuous process of social exchange: of editing out, feeding back, arguing, sharing ideas, acclaiming some trends, and rejecting others. The second way in which music making is social is that musical materials—from the sound of particular instruments to song structures and themes—come from a historically deposited common stock. Thus no music is original. Invariably musicians are remixers who inherit, inflect, and recombine musical voices and structures. This applies to everyone in the extended field of pop, from Paul Whiteman to Busta Rhymes. It means that, against the grain of much critical discourse, musical innovation is incremental. The so-called greats may add to a style through the brute force of success. But they are never as radically original as so much journalism and fan talk suggests.

If we start to think about these issues more concretely, in relation to Jamaican music making as it took off at the end of the 1950s, there are a number of features that mark the scene out. In the first place, the stock of resources that musicians could draw on was extremely diverse. A thriving folk music called mento subsisted in town and country, and the religious cults of Pocomania and Rastafarianism kept alive certain African musical traditions. Burra drumming style, in particular, provided an important fund of rhythm patterns and textures.[13] At the same time, there was very little recording and, apart from mainstream gigs for tourists in the north-coast resorts, not much live performance to paying audiences either. In other words the commercial music scene was relatively undeveloped. As a result, Jamaican popular music making was inaugurated through copying and adapting music that came from outside.

Sound systems playing U.S. rhythm and blues records at dance halls and on open-air "lawns" had been the chief form of musical entertainment since the late 1940s. These records were a cheap repertoire source for dance music. Sometimes they could also be heard on radio sets tuned in to the more powerful R&B stations in the southern states. However, by the end of the '50s the supply of the shuffle-rhythm records popular with Jamaican dancers was drying up. In effect, the advent of Sam Cooke and the gospel sound spelled the demise of R&B boogie. So sound system operators like Duke Reid and Sir Coxone turned to local musicians to record the older style.[14] What now seems extraordinary is that almost immediately the sound began to change as more and more emphasis was placed on the offbeats in the 4/4 rhythm. In fact, it took just from 1961 to 1963 for ska to emerge as a fully formed and intensely idiomatic style, marked not only by this innovative meter but also by a series of new features.

We can hear the leap forward when we examine a pair of records made just two years apart. The instrumental "Blackberry Brandy," credited to tenor saxophonist Roland Alphonso,[15] is an orthodox swinging blues, comparable, for example, to sides made by the Tiny Grimes Orchestra more than a decade earlier in the United States. Performed at a loping 132 beats per minute, it features a theme consisting of a repeated two-bar pattern in which stabs from trumpet and trombone alternate with a short riff from the tenor sax. This pattern cycles over the twelve-bar, I-IV-V chord progression in the classical manner of the blues. As for rhythm, a walking-four bass line, well up in the mix, predominates. It is reinforced by piano in the left hand. The drums are indistinct, although a snare can be heard playing irregular figures around the beat in the generic "jazz" style of bebop and after. Guitar chords then pick out the offbeats. Crucially, though, these are still understated. The onomatopoeic "ska" guitar sound (which will come to denote the emerging idiom over the next two years) is barely more pronounced than in any number of American shuffle-rhythm R&B numbers from the previous ten years or so. In other words the new style is latent at this point.

On the other hand with the Wailers' first hit, "Simmer Down" from 1963,[16] we are immediately struck by the full force of ska power. Now each offbeat is given equal weight, and voiced loudly by guitar and brass. Although bass and piano are still pacing out a quarter-note pulse, this pattern is deep in the background, a vestige. As a result the meter ratchets forward by an eighth note, so that the offbeats assume a lurching dominance. The new rhythmic organization is completed by heavy snare hits on beats two and four. They suggest an alternative sense of time as well as a counterstress on the backbeat. The overall effect is one of urgency. At 127 bpm, the tempo lags behind that of "Blackberry Brandy," yet the perceived speed is much faster, an impression reinforced by the vocal performance. As the Wailers urge, "Simmer down," Marley's rasping tenor, on the very edge of falsetto, offers a hysterical counterpoint. Never before has a plea for moderation—the song is addressed to fractious rude-boys—sounded so desperate.

For the most part, the same group of musicians played on the two recordings. Roland Alphonso's side men had become by 1963, when they supported the Wailers, the leading session group in Jamaica. They would shortly record under their own name as the Skatalites. But the point I want to make here is that the extraordinary stylistic development between the two recordings was not at all the work of imagination of a few great men, that is, of authors as they have been understood in the European tradition—troubadours, Romantic poets, rock gods. Rather it depended on a particularly flat form of social authorship that, once institutionalized, came to underpin later developments in reggae too: the change to rock steady in 1966, the emergence of roots style in 1970 and 1971, dub and lovers rock later in the 1970s. In effect, tiny incremental changes were made over a series of single record releases, with this process of cumulative development being reinforced through intense selection of certain, style-leading records by intermediaries and the market. Rapid change was then followed by a period of consolidation and "lateral" articulation as the style, its key elements now relatively stable, became more varied.

We can explain innovation of this sort in terms of a specifically Jamaican mode of popular music production and, in particular, three main features:[17]

1. It is entrepreneur coordinated, initially by the sound system operators and DJs, and then by the record producers, who are often sound system operators as well. These cultural intermediaries call the shots, not only in business terms but also in relation to sound and choice of artists and repertoire.
2. There is intense audience feedback. The aesthetic intervention

of the entrepreneurs is based on their closeness to audiences, and their ability to judge which music works and which does not. The model here is the sound system itself where audience and DJ or operator are copresent. In this situation entrepreneurs are able to select or reject trends very quickly. Significantly, retailing of records comes relatively late, and always remains a secondary market. Recordings continue to be made primarily for "live" performance through the sound systems. Competition also contributes to intense innovation and high turnover of records as sound system operators race to find the newest sounds.

3. A strong division of labor exists between musicians, singers, engineers, and producers. Singers, unless among the handful of consistent hit makers, work for next to nothing. They often write for next to nothing too, as copyright implementation is virtually nonexistent. The small number of regularly used musicians, on the other hand, have a fairly steady session income. The Skatalites established the model here for the hot session band that is then hired by producers as a working unit. For two decades or more a small, and periodically changing, pool of Jamaican musicians constitutes a sort of collaborative research and development unit. It depends on an unusual mix of collectivity and competition.

These were the key factors that constituted the reggae mode of production. The corollary of this form of organization was that no auteur system emerged in Jamaica. The top DJs tended to have both a public profile and a degree of longevity. Yet despite their importance, they were clearly not writers. A small number of singing songwriters—like John Holt, Desmond Dekker, and Jimmy Cliff—managed to be successful for several years. But few, apart from Marley, were able to build long-term careers independently of the island's music entrepreneurs. As for producers, the most celebrated worked for ten years or more, yet none could be compared with the major rock producers in terms of the acclaim they received. Only in retrospect were Lee Perry and King Tubby consecrated as great artists through reissues, compilations, and journalistic discourse. Bob Marley and the Wailers had therefore to negotiate their transition to the international market from a completely different kind of musical culture and infrastructure in Jamaica. There was nothing of that romantic cult of the author or celebration of virtuosity that came to characterize the Anglo-American rock mode of production in the same period.

By 1970 the Wailers were managed by Americans, Danny Sims and Johnny Nash. Now in their classic vocal trio lineup, they were making records with the producer Lee Perry and had already cut versions of many of the tunes that would be presented again on the Island albums. But they rarely played live. There was little demand for this, and often group members were not in the same place at the same time, which made regular performances impossible. What's more, despite the new management and production, they were still failing to sell records outside the tiny Jamaican market. Thus, when Marley and Blackwell met in December 1971, their real breakthrough consisted in an act of imagination. The Wailers would be rebuilt as a reggae band that could record albums, play live, and adopt what amounted to a rock band ethos of self-sufficient authorship.[18] The group was quickly successful in this project—on the first two Island albums, but perhaps most spectacularly on the tours done to promote the albums in the U.K. and the U.S.

In terms of personnel, two Wailers, Bob Marley and Peter Tosh, became singer-guitarists while the third, Bunny Livingstone, sang and played percussion. Carlton and Family Man Barrett, Lee Perry's former house rhythm section, were then added on drums and bass, respectively, but now as "full" members of the band. Finally, all the musicians adopted an inflected but still recognizably rock image. Key here were Bob Marley's trademark denim shirt and jeans, which became the arch signifier of the new hybrid project. Marley took the initiative as spokesperson for the band, but initially at least, he was *primus inter pares* rather than leader.

If the packaging of the Wailers represented a significant shift toward the rock norm, what is interesting is the extent to which critics in the United Kingdom (including the enthusiasts) found it difficult to cope with the new phenomenon. There was in effect a kind of discursive gap or lag between the re-creation of the Wailers and ways of understanding them in the critical apparatus of rock. Unlike in the United States, where FM radio stations championed new rock music, in the U.K. the specialist press was the major means of promotion and mediation. Bands simply could not break into the market without press coverage. This mattered, of course, because it was the United Kingdom that was used as the launch pad for the Wailers' international success.

How were the Wailers approached by the British rock press? I would identify three broad tendencies. The first might be described, after Hal Foster, as the "primitive gaze."[19] Up until the Wailers' arrival, reggae in the U.K. had been mainly popular among Caribbean immigrants. The music was also taken up by the white working-class, skinhead subculture, and after 1968 a few singles actually crossed over into the Top 20.[20] In this context middle-class rock journalists clearly found it difficult to approach the Wailers without treating them as a lower form of life. Here, for example, is Steve Lake in *Melody Maker*, reporting on a concert in November 1973. "Goddam it, the Wailers aren't even musicians in the technical sense at all." This extraordinary judgment appears in what is actually a very favorable—even a rave—review. But the primitivist approach is summed up best by a concise paragraph in the middle of the piece. "Basically they do everything wrong and it works beautifully," Lake declaims.[21]

Martin Hayman, in *Sounds*, has a similar take. Under the headline "Wailers' Simple Message," Hayman writes, "Bob Marley looks as though he could be a heavy [with] the gleaming eye of a potential fanatic and . . . two short furrows which look suspiciously like scars." As for the performances, we are told that "the Wailers communicate very directly with the people, directing the essentially simple message through from the feet to the body to the brain."[22] This is a central trope of primitivism in Foster's terms: identification of the body as receptor of a basic, syn-aesthetic charge that can be produced only by the primitive.

The second tendency in early coverage of the Wailers is what might be described as the "(Black) Politics" reading. This begins to assimilate the projected Otherness of the musicians by setting them up as representatives of a countercultural movement. In a review of the album *Burnin'* we learn that "Marley is an angry young man with a mission" and "a real threat to society"—precisely recognizable, metropolitan social types. Yet there is also uncertainty about the extent to which such an interpretative framework can be applied to music makers who, located far outside the subjectivity of rock, remain irredeemably black and Other. Thus, "'Duppy Conqueror' is certainly a beautiful song, [but] the words relate so specifically to Rastifarian ideals that [it] is almost incomprehensible to us white folks."[23]

The last approach I want to identify sits more squarely on rock's home turf. It consists in elevating the band to the status of virtuoso artists above the primitive milieu of reggae. David Milton adopts this tactic when reviewing a concert on the first, *Catch a Fire* tour. He writes, "The Wailers use the ethnic merely as a foundation, just as Stevie Wonder and Curtis Mayfield utilize their soul roots as the core from which springs the seeds of a fertile imagination." Singling out Marley within the group as the great auteur then completes this process. As Milton puts it, "Under the leadership and inspiration of Bob Marley, the Wailers have broadened the scope of West Indian music—they have added subtlety, inventiveness and technical virtuosity to the inherent rhythm of their music."[24]

This account parallels that by Sebastian Clarke in the *New Musical Express*. Of older Wailers' material he writes, "Although some of the songs are well written, the musical accompaniment and recording quality are noticeably poor." Apparently the problem is due to a lack of funding and studio availability in Jamaica, and the impossibility, therefore, of spending "the length of time required for a record of quality." Such difficulties can be contrasted with the state of affairs on the Island recordings, where "the quality is vastly improved, as is the musical accompaniment—arrangements, variety of instruments, vocal backings etc."[25] Clarke makes a starkly ethnocentric judgment here. What he is pointing to is the fact that earlier Wailers' recordings don't sound like rock, whereas *Catch a Fire,* with its searing lead guitar and funky clavinet, most definitely does.

These awkward, early attempts by British critics to assimilate Marley and the Wailers into the rock gestalt are important because they lay the ground for the more polished (though just as contradictory) "Natural Mystic" discourse of the later 1970s. Indeed, the dominant approach to Marley that has endured posthumously is a heady new age romanticism in which the cult of the author converges with the primitive gaze we first encounter in the pages of the British music press in 1973.

I have been arguing throughout this essay that musical creativity, the making of new sounds, should be understood as a social process rather than the original work of authors. Rock, with its deeply embedded mythology of the musician-poet, would deny this, however. The denial is ideological, because it enshrines a type of creative action that isn't even practiced by rock musicians, while at the same time denigrating ways of music making that are outside the rock purview. The thrust of my argument has been that ideology of this sort is a Bad Thing. In the case of the Wailers' translation into rock, it works to assimilate subaltern creativity, but on the terms of the hegemonic culture; sometimes casting aspects of their creativity as Other, sometimes projecting a metropolitan notion of authorship onto the Wailers' practice.

The relations of power at stake here are substantial. Nevertheless there may be a case for a more complex, more ambivalent way of approaching them. First, to develop the point just made, auteurism in rock is contradictory. Because the form emerges from people's music—rock 'n' roll, country, R&B—there is always an internal Other with which the rock-poet must identify and, simultaneously, define himself against. As a result, splitting is the condition of rock authorship. Or as Foster puts it (he is speaking of Gauguin and Picasso), "Since 'the primitive' both attracts and repels these artists, since they both desire and identify with it—such oppositions are pressured to the point where they begin to falter, where the white heterosexual masculinity founded on them begins to crack."[26] The advent of Marley and the Wailers threatens to crack open rock's primitive gaze too. More affirmatively, it contributes to the critique of authorism encountered in punk and postpunk, a critique based on an investigation into musical Otherness within the rock psyche.

Second, the Wailers do speak. As Spivak emphasized several years after writing her original essay, the key issue is whether there is "a transaction between the speaker and the listener."[27] The Wailers are able to engage in such a transaction partly by assuming the role of author (the speaker who will be listened to) with real facility. On the Island albums, but arguably going right back to "Simmer Down," we hear the voice of rational anger directed against the "downpression" of the suffering peoples of Jamaica. This voice resonates so effectively with the expressionist shout of rock precisely because both rail against power. Could this be otherwise? The conjuncture of the 1960s and early '70s, with its struggles for liberation at both core and periphery, demanded affiliation and common cause between these positions, even as it produced mistrust, hypocrisy, and Othering of the sort I have described. That is to say, authorship was a common strategy of cultural resistance.

Finally, the Wailers' translation into rock presages the emergence of a postcolonial speaking position. Homi Bhabha suggests that colonialism depends on "rules of recognition" that fix the identity of the colonized. Paradoxically, though, the imperative to mark as Other (to represent colonial subjects as "exorbitant objects of discrimination") whether in art or in political discourse constantly undermines this goal.[28] It is surely such a failure of control that is at stake in the confused response to the Wailers of the music press. The drive to make the band intelligible, to fix its Otherness, actually generates divergent interpretations and opens up a range of positions between which the musicians can move, positions that do not easily fit rock's expressive ideology—Rastafarianism, collectivism, a harking back to Africa, and a listening forward through technology to a utopian musical future. In Bhabha's terms, what we encounter here are "contingent and hybrid articulations of the sacred-in-the-secular . . ., the archaic within the contemporaneous."[29] Such combinations are utterly typical of hybrid, postcolonial forms of culture.

In one way, then, the Wailers' translation into rock challenges

Western cultural hegemony. For at the very moment they achieve celebrity as auteurs—in other words, inheritors of a European tradition stretching from the troubadours through the Romantics to the rock poets—these social authors effectively dissolve the institution of the self-sufficient creator. But does that do much to upset the terms and conditions of geocultural power? Not really; the fact is that more than thirty years on, the Wailers remain the only rock superstars from the postcolonial world.

chapter 13

Creativity
and Band
Dynamics

DEENA WEINSTEIN

They all say it.

"It's like a family," reports Lars Frederiksen about his band, Rancid. "Of course you've got your little argument, your little tiffs. Just because you fight doesn't mean that you're not family anymore."[1] Kid Rock's drummer, Stefanie Eulinberg, tells us that the members of the Detroit rocker's band "work together like a family."[2] "Culture Club is important to me. It's like a family," Boy George attests in a 1983 interview.[3] "Pretty Things are like a family, really. People come, people go, but there's a wonderful camaraderie amongst the guys. Well, not always—everyone has fights and stuff," Wally Waller reflects, explaining how difficult it was for him to decide to leave the band.[4]

No matter what era or style of rock. They all say it.

Mick Jagger declares, in response to learning of Brian Jones's death, "Something has gone. We were like a pack, like a family, we Stones." A sentence later, he adds, "I wasn't ever really close to him."[5] Alice Cooper drummer Neal Smith looks back on his band thus: "We were like a family—you love each other but there's always tension."[6] "We are basically like any family—we fight like a family, we love each other like a family—but like most families, we also work things out in the end," Keith Knudsen, drummer and vocalist with the Doobie Brothers, chimes in.[7]

"Like a family"—it's the mother of all rock clichés. Who knows if the only time the phrase is uttered is when some rock scribe is within hearing range? And if truth be told, not all musicians describe their relationships with their bandmates with that cliché. But in my research, admittedly neither thorough nor extensive, the only bands I found that didn't use the phrase "like a family" are Creedence Clearwater Revival, the Kinks, AC/DC, Dire Straits, Black Crowes, and Oasis. And, yes, there is a family resemblance among these bands, despite their different musical styles: they all feature siblings.

Regardless of the real-life exceptions, the ubiquity of the family metaphor does beg the question of its meaning. Some musicians use "like a family" to stand for the warm fuzzy feelings they have for those in their band, while for others it seems to reference that very first family, the one from which Abel was summarily purged, without the possibility of some reunion decades later. What does "like a family" mean when it includes positive or negative attitudes? Reading interviews, you'd think that bands were held together with nothing more than emotions. The metaphor seems to have a rhetorical flavor that erases the sense of a rock band as a small corporation with objectively evaluated workers.

"Groups are a very complicated thing," says Mike Campbell of Tom Petty's Heartbreakers, in one of the few more nuanced invocations of the family affair cliché. "'It's like a family, it's like a business relationship, it's a very emotional thing. You care about each other, and you tug just like brothers; you're jealous, and then you love each other. It's a very complicated monster."[8]

Rock bands are like jackalopes, amazing freaks of nature. With their full racks of antlers, you'd think that the top-heavy jackrabbits would fall over and die rather than hop about the western prairies. Rock bands, of course, are not mythical monstrosities. They are all-too-familiar features of the mediascape and can't help but be sighted. Yet a sociologist has no trouble seeing that rock bands are as unstable as jackalopes, ungainly groups gluing together characteristics that are usually kept strictly segregated.

The basic strain that predisposes rock groups to crash and burn comes from the difference between a close-knit circle and a specialized impersonal organization. In the close-knit circle, members are valued simply because they belong to the group. In an organization, members are valued only for their contribution to the achievement of the group's goal.

Rock bands have characteristics from both sides. They are work groups with a specialized division of labor and goals to accomplish (although you'd never guess that from the mountains of words about them in magazines, newspapers, books, and online). Their interviews rarely if ever mention this aspect. Journalists and musicians fail to discuss the details, or even to mention what goes on in the extensive hours of rehearsal. But bands are also small groups that impose an intense intimacy on their members, through the long and odd hours spent in rehearsal and recording studios and the weeks and months spent together on tours. This leads band members toward becoming friends, if they hadn't started off as such, with all of the attendant personal strains brought on by prolonged nearness.

Work and intimacy have been combined throughout history, particularly in premodern societies but also in modern small family businesses. However, that blend has traditionally been stabilized by preordained roles (like the gendered division of labor and authority based on age) that help to reconcile the inherent tensions. In contrast, in rock bands there are no such cultural forms to balance practicality and emotion; each band must resolve the tension in its own way or break apart.

The tension between the values of community and efficiency is also intensified by the role that bands play in the contemporary business economy. The entertainment giants minimize the risks of creativity and innovation for themselves by relegating those functions to the bands, which must engage in a Darwinian struggle for survival. The need for rock groups to be creative introduces acute strains into their structure that are related to the balance of influence and power. Bands are also enveloped in the romantic myth of the authentic creative artist; a requirement dictated by a corporate economy is perceived as the demand of a cultural ideal.

Pearl Jam is a case in point. "We were hanging out a lot, Eddie and me, talking politics, life, surfing, music," notes guitarist Mike McCready. "I remember telling him we need to be very cognizant of the powers that be, because it's critical to our survival. We needed to go out and play music, and enjoy it, within this capitalist structure. To still support those causes, but to work through the established channels."[9]

The (Romantic) Creative Ideal

It's ironic that the requirement that rock bands create their own music originated in the protest era of the 1960s. Creativity was tied to a desire to oppose the fabrications of the entertainment machine with the alternative of an authentic culture expressing genuine passions and commitments. What would immediately be co-opted by the entertainment machine for its own advantage was, at first, understood as a liberation.

Before the mid-1960s, it was only the performance that mattered. Although the audience cared about the songs, it wasn't concerned, and didn't really know, if the songs had been written by the performer (as Chuck Berry and Buddy Holly had done) or by songwriting specialists in the Tin Pan Alley tradition. The Beatles and especially Bob Dylan provided the model for genuine creativity. Initially bands like the Rolling Stones and the Who were urged by their savvy managers (Beatles manager Brian Epstein wrote the book for them) to write their own songs, given the financial benefits that accrued from songwriting royalties. As the 1960s became the cultural '60s, the value of creative sincerity (what Johnny Rotten sarcastically proclaimed a decade later—"We mean it, man") became central.[10] It provided another and, for the audience, a major reason for bands to write their own material.

But the '60s ethos also valued the group, which privileged collective performers—the band—over solo artists. Most band names reflected an egalitarian collective, rather than individuals. Think of the Animals, the Beatles, the Byrds, and even the Monkees, in contrast to the older '50s model like Buddy Holly and the Crickets. One of the few exceptions was Crosby, Stills, Nash and Young. Stage moves and especially the posed photographs emphasized this "all for one, one for all" collectivity.

At first the discourse of genuine creativity was not centered on the unique voice of the unique person, but on "authentic" cultural traditions like African American blues and working-class folk music. That was soon to change, however, as middle-class rock musicians broke free from the "prestige from below" that had nurtured their fledgling rebellion and took their music into their own hands.

Authenticity was quickly married to a romantic ideology that harkened back to the nineteenth-century *poèts maudits* like Baudelaire. These déclassé avant-garde romantics of the middle and late nineteenth century, forerunners of 1950s-era movie roles played by James Dean and Marlon Brando and other sensitive-guy juvenile delinquents, carried on the myth that had first arisen in the 1820s of the creative individual, uncompromising in passion and bearing unique gifts. It is here that the major ideological tension present in the creative process of rock bands entered the mix; the band, which remained the creative focus, or at least was thought of as such, took on a myth adapted to a radically individual practice.

This romantic understanding and value of creativity came into rock, in part, due to the influence of British art schools. As Frith and Horne document, many of the major figures of '60s rock—Keith Richards (Rolling Stones), Pete Townshend (The Who), Eric Clapton (Cream), Syd Barrett (Pink Floyd), Ray Davies (Kinks), and Jimmy Page (Led Zeppelin)—had gone to art colleges, the destination of choice for smart and unruly British boys.[11]

Despite heavy doses of irony, let alone postmodern influences, romantic ideology still permeates thought and discussions about rock. How many interviews have you read that included some quote about "staying true" to one's art? It places a host of destabilizing burdens on bands, beyond the transfer of an individual ideal to a collective one. The romantic aesthetic privileges novelty, in contrast to what Umberto Eco calls classical aesthetics—good versions of an ideal form. "The pleasurable repetition of an already known pattern was considered, by modern theories of art, typical of Crafts—not of Art—and of industry."[12] Bands face the demand that a new album must show growth by going further than previous efforts. Critics praise a new release when it does so and denounce it as the "same old same old" if it is too similar to earlier recordings.

The romantic legacy also sees the values of authenticity and creativity as opposed to or even fully inimical to commerce.[13] Selling out (note ironic references in album titles—*The Who Sell Out*—and band names—Judas Priest) became a sin just when bands were destined to be absorbed by the entertainment machine (Pink Floyd's "Welcome to the Machine"), causing innumerable battles among band members and, at times, within musicians themselves (for example, Kurt Cobain). It is telling that so many of the bastions of rock authenticity (Dylan, the Beatles, Bruce Springsteen) have been artists supported by strong and knowledgeable managers (Albert Grossman, Brian Epstein, and Jon Landau, respectively).

Still another problem created by romantic ideas about art is that the music is generally seen by the audience to be a creative product of all of the members of the band, regardless of whether each member had a hand in creating, or even approving of, the songs. Thus each individual in the group is seen in the same light as the others, regardless of actual authorship. Finally, the creative process itself is seen not as a craft or a learned skill but as the response of suffering or mad artists. And if suffering or madness doesn't come naturally, the ever helpful nineteenth-century poets provide rock with a way into those states: drugs and alcohol. Privileging substance-induced irrationality may, either actually or because of belief, enhance one's creativity for some period of time. But living and working with a person in such a condition hardly improves a group's stability.

That creative individuals are allowed and even expected to be less than stable encourages their worst sort of social behavior. If bands survive under the domination of a "difficult" creative musician, they often have a revolving-door lineup. My favorite case in point: Ritchie Blackmore's Rainbow was a five-man band whose slots were filled by sixteen people over its seven-year life.

Spheres of Creativity

The structural and ideological strains endemic to rock bands are played out in a number of spheres in which creativity is demanded, all of which can become flash points for conflict and disaffection. Songwriting is the main focus in discussions of rock creativity, for a variety of reasons. Foremost is the fact that it is the only instance of creativity that is singled out for special payment.[14] (Probably the best literature on rock band creativity is contained within the law suits dealing with plagiarism.) The areas beyond songwriting in which rock bands are called on to be creative–sonically, verbally, and visually–are extensive. They include everything from concert set lists, stage moves, clothing, and hairstyles to facial expressions in the posed and not fully posed photos that accompany the "stories" they give to the press.

Bands, of course, are brands. Establishing a band's identity, its name, visual image, and signature sound, is the foundational creative activity. This crucial set of activities remains in the shadows, unacknowledged. Each of these spheres of creativity involves not merely "coming up with something" but is preceded by a more or less voiced "We need." Recognizing a lack, proposing a solution, and reacting to that solution can be–but rarely are–the province of only one person in the band. Saying, "We need an up-tempo song that can raise the energy level at the show" requires different skills than writing such a song; a suggestion that "we all ought to turn our backs to the audience when we play this song" takes no real skill to execute but can cause disagreement.

The number of creative decisions that bands confront is endless. In light of the individualistic ideology of the rock band, each is a possible bone of contention. This vulnerability to conflict is only partly alleviated by the tendency of bands to develop an authority structure and a division of labor. Such stabilizing structures are threatened not only by romantic individualism but also by the myth of a closely bonded community of equals.

Reacting to suggested solutions is so fundamental to a band's functioning that roles tend to emerge. The critic evaluates the quality of a work in a variety of ways. For example, if it's a new song, the critic may ask: "Is it a good song?" "Is it a song that fits with others on the new album or on the set list?" "Does the song violate the band's image or clash with its signature sound?" "Is it a song that sounds fresh?" In contrast, the emotional appreciator—the audience-within-the-band—provides immediate feedback: "That sounds great" or "It's good but it needs something near the end." Of course, some emotional reactors are extremely stingy with praise, more given to hisses and boos.

Creativity and Band Stabilization/Destabilization

"I have spent eight months transforming this band and our new songs into an unstoppable juggernaut, and sadly Twiggy wasn't able to make himself a part of it," said Marilyn Manson in a statement explaining the departure of his band's bassist. Twiggy Ramirez, who cowrote Manson's biggest hits, like "The Beautiful People" and "The Dope Show," had been in the band for eight years. The split, *Rolling Stone* reported, "was a result of creative differences."[15]

Rock bands start from scratch. Most groups with which we involve ourselves—at work, at home, in recreation, religion, politics, and other pursuits—have a model for roles and authority that precedes any specific set of people. This structure serves as a blueprint that newly formed groups can more or less follow. Bands have no such models, except for genre requirements; which members sing, write the music, focus on the finances, mediate disputes, and so on is left up to each group to devise. The media's inattention to the working life of bands and, worse, their promulgation of the nearly impossible all-are-creative egalitarian model, leaves each set of young musicians to reinvent the wheel themselves, and this hasn't changed over the years. Then when they bring in outsiders to help with some of these functions, there are no expectations about which band members will be the liaisons. Indeed, there is not even an expectation about the originating point—a band can be a set of friends coming together to play music or a group of musicians previously unknown to one another who start a band and then develop emotional relationships.

Once a band has a commercial goal, various leadership roles become prominent. Writing songs is a major form of domination: "Play my song," "Play these notes in this precise tempo," "Sing these words with this emotional tone." The egalitarian myth of bands is almost always violated. Not all of the other members even serve as critics, and the reactions of some are seen as more significant than the reactions of others, causing power imbalances that call for adjustments in attitudes and expectations. And as mentioned above, in bands where one person writes almost everything, there is usually one faithful member who serves as the critical and/or emotional reactor. The creator and reactor then form a strong controlling dyad.[16]

Some, perhaps the majority, of famous bands have two major songwriters, and it is their relationship that makes or breaks the group. The list is long. Among them are John Lennon and Paul McCartney (Beatles), Keith Richards and Mick Jagger (Rolling Stones), Joe Strummer and Mick Jones (Clash), Chris Difford and Glenn Tilbrook (Squeeze), Morrissey and Johnny Marr (Smiths), and Bob Mould and Grant Hart (Hüsker Dü). It may be a complementary relationship (for example, lyricist and music writer) in which each has crucial abilities that the other lacks, or one may be better at expressing the band's romantic side while the other is most proficient at writing the energetic or musically sophisticated songs. Together they create a body of work that attracts a far larger audience than either could alone.

Another type of songwriting pair doesn't specialize in any way but works synergistically, each providing energy and ideas to the other. In yet a third pattern, each member of the pair is, either originally or over time, capable of writing full songs alone, and does so.

The relationship between the two may serve as a friendly and appreciative rivalry that spurs them on. Or it can be, or can become, nastily competitive and fraught with bitter jealousy—of the other's ability, of the other band members' or the fans' greater appreciation of his songs, or of the fact that the other's songs earn him more money, since more of them find their way onto the albums. When such a pair forms the central relationship of the band, the whole band is destabilized when that relationship becomes conflicted. "We shan't work together again" is the line ending the long-term relationship between spot-on rock-band spoof *Spinal Tap*'s creatives, Nigel Tufnel and David St. Hubbins.

The relationship between the creators and the noncreators in a band rarely remains constant. The dynamic equilibrium in a band results from a variety of pushes and pulls relating to the issue of creativity. Shared backgrounds, history (especially struggles to "make it" that involve the whole band), and tastes in music promote close bonding. Then, too, musicians may want to stay in a band for reasons having nothing to do with the other members: the bond may be with the band itself, because of an appreciation for the music that the band creates; the goodies the band brings, like money, "chicks," and fame; or the sense that they have no other options in life.

Counterbalancing the stabilizing factors is a host of stressing conditions, many of them involved with issues of creativity. Musicians may change their aesthetic preferences and, thus, their appreciation for the creative elements of the band's repertoire—its sonics, its lyrical themes, and its visual presentation. Rarely do tastes change in the same direction or at the same time for all members of a band. Some members are more plugged in to a changing zeitgeist, are more sensitive to the shift in audience taste, undergo an emotional maturation, or achieve greater musical proficiency or sophistication. Thus, bands whose members were once on the same wavelength (or at least appeared to be so) develop aesthetic conflicts, aka "creative differences."

Judas Priest's leather-clad multioctave singer Rob Halford wanted to focus on newer trends in metal, to head toward a more aggro than power music and toward reality-based lyrics rather than the band's "fantasy, fictional matter." Given the band's reluctance to make these changes, he tried to channel his interests into a side project. The situation became untenable, and he left his decades-old job fronting Priest.[17] (The Hollywood version of this, *Rock Star*, badly distorted the facts of the story.)

Creative abilities within a band also change. Those who once weren't able to write songs may learn to do so, for instance. Moreover, it's common for those who were once the creators in the band to lose their ability at some point or at least to experience its decline. The deterioration of the Beach Boys' ingenious genius, Brian Wilson, is an especially poignant example. In addition, given the romantic ideology that encourages the use of drugs and alcohol to find one's muse, as well as the psychological evidence that "creatives" are statistically more likely to be mentally ill than "noncreatives," a band's creative members are often more fragile, volatile, and difficult than the others. If not incapacitated altogether, they are a constant source of instability and crisis: the rest of the band needs the creative one, yet the latter's vagaries can destroy the group. This problem is mitigated somewhat when a band crystallizes, achieving a signature sound and becoming associated with certain themes. Then the same level of creativity is no longer required; other band members, or "ringers" from the outside, can create new songs on the basis of the established code.

When destabilizing factors increase, members of the band may resort to compromises to allow them to exist in a less favorable situation. In the past decade, especially, many alienated or unfulfilled musicians have taken up side projects in which to express their new or different tastes and release the creativity that is suppressed in the band. It's not clear whether the growing number of such side projects is a testimony to the stability of rock bands (if not their friendships or pride in their sound, then their financial rewards) or to the gradual demise of the rock group itself as a way of making music. In either case, it is usually creative differences that lead a member to undertake some extramural activity, either to try something new (like a style of music that is outside the band's signature sound) or to do something similar but with a new partner (which allows them to assume a new creative role or power position). Blink-182's singer-guitarist Tom DeLonge started an old-school punk band, Box Car Racer. As the Drive-in's front man, Cedric Bixler, and guitarist, Omar Rodriguez, put together a dub-music group, Defacto. Phil Anselmo, Pantera's front man, formed Down in 1996 with members of Corrosion of Conformity, Crowbar, and EyeHateGod. The group's releases sold well and the band has done several tours in support of them. Anselmo has, or has had, several other side projects, including Superjoint Ritual, Viking Crown, Southern Isolation, and Necrophagia. Faith No More's Mike Patton, almost as promiscuous as Anselmo, is in the cult-fave avant-metal band Mr. Bungle, and in Fantomas with Buzz Osbourne from the Melvins. "It's like having an affair without breaking up the marriage," Stevie Nicks said in 1981, when she made a chart-topping solo album while still in Fleetwood Mac.[18]

Then there are the side projects that start off as supplementary affairs but are found to be so rewarding that the straying partner seeks a divorce and sometimes winds up destroying or badly diminishing the original band. The Allman Brothers Band guitarist Warren Haynes and bassist Allen Woody got a yen for an "improvisational power trio" at a time when the ABB "was in a stagnant state. There wasn't a lot of writing or rehearsing. We were basically going through the motions, playing the same songs all the time. Gov't Mule was all of a sudden the opposite of that," Haynes reflected.[19] Gov't Mule did so well that the pair eventually quit their main band to devote themselves full-time to it.

At times, the remaining members of a band jealously demand the divorce. The departure of Rob Halford from Priest, noted above, is a case in point. Jason Newsted, long-time bassist for both the '80s and '90s versions of Metallica, admitted that the "band's tight control of his side projects finally caused him to leave." "'I keep chasing music all the time and they kept saying, 'Don't do that! You can't do that!'" Newsted said.[20]

Creative Differences

The rock band is a jackalope, a close-knit circle with characteristics of an impersonal organization that is dependent upon and destined to an environing corporate society. It has no cultural traditions and models to stabilize it, and it is burdened by the transfer of the myth of romantic individualism to a dynamic group. Over the years, as the specialized role of the producer has come to the fore and been publicly recognized, and band management has been rationalized, some of the uncertainties of band organization have been partially dispelled. Still, it's a wonder that rock bands survive at all. Most don't; those that do learn to mitigate the inherent tensions. Success helps, providing extramusical incentives for cooperation. (Although sometimes, of course, success can break a band, as when the creative center thinks it's all due to him and his ego swells to intolerable proportions.) More important, bands that survive either develop an authority structure that violates romantic mythology, creating a gulf between the way the band presents itself to the outside world and how it actually operates, or members reach an accord on a division of labor that all can live with, acknowledging the value of one another's contributions.

When the imbalances of creative power are not mitigated, bands crash. According to the romantic myth, the only legitimate justification for a band to break up is "creative differences."[21] That phrase is used as an excuse for any breakup—and there can be many reasons that have nothing to do with the actual creative function. Yet the appeal to creative differences is at least one case in which mythology is often not so far off the mark—creativity is the rock band's most sensitive function, and creative differences and accords often genuinely determine whether or not a band will survive.

chapter 14

"O Secret Stars Stay Secret": Rock and Roll in Contemporary Poetry

STEPHEN BURT

When Dan Treacy of the Television Personalities crooned (or tried to croon: his grainy voice wouldn't quite let him), "If I could write poetry, I would . . . and tell the world that I love you," he wasn't just displaying the wistful ineffectuality that won him the hearts of indie fanboys worldwide.[1] The TVPs' 1981 single played on our assumptions about the differences—no, the *contrasts*—that separate poetry from rock and roll. Rock is easy, poetry hard to create; rock is spontaneous and simple, poetry intricate, enduring, reflective. Rock is ephemeral, while poetry endures. And rock songs (for all those reasons) belong to the young, as poetry maybe did once but sure doesn't now—or so we assume.

Treacy wasn't just speaking (or singing) for himself. Despite a few outliers and performing celebrities—and despite the *very* different relations linking jazz, blues, and African American poetry—both rockers and poets kept just those contrasts in play from "Rock around the Clock" all the way to the end of the 1980s. While a few rockers sought "poetic" grandeur (a story I won't tell here), baby boomers who published books of poems used rock to invoke youth, rawness, energy, spontaneity, sex—all the supposedly adolescent qualities they couldn't claim for poetry itself. They wrote about rock when they wanted to think about the youth they felt they had lost. Then things changed: over the past ten years young poets have used postpunk and indie-rock culture in new ways. Those poets (I'll claim) now write poems just as immediate—and no more obscure—than the songs they imitate, namecheck, or praise.

Rock's ties to youth are as old as the music itself. No wonder, then, that rock-inflected poems so often depict either actual young people or characteristically adolescent states of mind—imperiled innocence, hunger for independence, sexual excitement. Philip Larkin famously wrote that "Sexual intercourse began / In 1963, / Between the end of the *Chatterley* ban / And the Beatles' first LP."[2] Paul Muldoon's *Sleeve Notes* follows the poet's life through records, from his youth in Northern Ireland to his current New Jersey home. In one sonnet named for the Rolling Stones' *Beggars Banquet*, the adult poet compares the unworldly child he once was with the adventurously sexy music that that child heard. Though the young Muldoon still takes piano lessons from "Miss Lattimore,"

> *In next to no time I would be lost*
> *to the milk bars*
>
> *and luncheonettes*
> *of smoky Belfast,*
>
> *where a troubadour*
> *such as the frontman of Them*
>
> *had long since traded in the lute*
> *for bass and blues harmonica.*[3]

In this sonnet about changing musical tastes, each stage of life boasts its appropriate music, setting, and "diction": Miss Lattimore's parlor piano lessons for childhood; milk bars and early Van Morrison ("the frontman of Them") for adolescence. The two stages reprise their quarrel (mapped onto the sonnet's reversed octave and sestet) within the adult who remembers it all.

Exceptional in his crafty, evasive forms, Muldoon (born in 1951) resembles other baby boom poets in his attitude toward rock and roll. Jim Elledge's anthology *Sweet Nothings* (1994), devoted to "Rock and Roll in American Poetry," focuses on this demographic, for whom, Elledge writes, "the elements of rock and roll incorporated into their poetry . . . almost always represent . . . a time of innocence—or an era of innocence turned sour."[4] Nancy Schoenberger's "Epithalamion" equates its favorite songs with her favored youth: when "Van Morrison sang *brown-eyed girl*," Schoenberger recalls, "those songs were always me in my green time."[5] Ronald Wallace's near-sonnet "Sound System" casts similar memories in a present tense: he imagines "necking / to 'Little Darlin'" and other fifties hits "as my father from his wheelchair in his study / calls out to keep it down, and Buddy Holly, / The Big Bopper, and Ritchie Valens leave the ground."[6] To Wallace, rock means youth, innocence, sex, rebellion, hope, and immediacy. Poetry, *by contrast,* frames those qualities and compares them with a disappointing present; poetry, unlike rock, makes us notice loss—the father's lost legs, or the loss of Holly, Valens, and the Bopper in their plane crash.

Reviewing *Sweet Nothings,* Thomas Swiss complained that "most [of the poems] embed their rock-related references in stories about adolescence."[7] Poems about rock—until quite recently—have turned on such reflections: the reasons lie not only in the history of rock but also in the history of poetry. Since at least the turn of the nineteenth century, poems and poets have wanted—or said they wanted—to champion an authentic individual against a larger, impersonal world. And the adolescent, by twentieth-century definition, does exactly that—fights for himself, or herself, against society. José Ortega y Gasset wrote in 1932 that "poetry is adolescence fermented and thus preserved."[8] Wallace Stevens in 1943 described "The Figure of the Youth as Virile Poet." If these equations strike you as implausible, or as way too abstract, rock and roll may be one reason: rock music brings with it a far stronger claim to represent adolescence, and to convey immediate, authentic feeling, than any claims U.S. or U.K. poets can now make. In asking readers to compare poems about rock songs with the songs that these poems describe, poems about rock can admit their own failure to find, or to keep, the inner independence or autonomy that we often hope poems can give—and that we associate with youth.

One of the first poems about rock and roll—perhaps *the* first—outlines just that conundrum. The poem is Thom Gunn's "Elvis Presley," published in 1957:

> *Two minutes long it pitches through some bar:*
> *Unreeling from a corner box, the sigh*
> *Of this one, in his gangling finery*
> *And crawling sideburns, wielding a guitar.*
>
> *The limitations where he found success*
> *Are ground on which he, panting, stretches out*
> *In turn, promiscuously, by every note.*
> *Our idiosyncrasy and our likeness.*
>
> *We keep ourselves in touch with a mere dime.*
> *Distorting hackneyed words in hackneyed songs*
> *He turns revolt into a style, prolongs*
> *The impulse to a habit of the time.*
>
> *Whether he poses or is real, no cat*
> *Bothers to say: the pose held is a stance*
> *Which, generation of the very chance*
> *It wars on, may be posture for combat.*[9]

Each stanza reevaluates, and elevates, the Elvis of the stanza before: each seems designed to answer high-culture objections. Yes, Elvis seems limited, but therein lies his strength. Yes, the words are hackneyed, but his delivery gives them style; yes, it's an act, but it's also genuine. When we have worked out all the stanzas' oppositions we have come from a reflexive rejection of Elvis all the way to seeing in him the icon of a new culture: self-consciously adolescent, and proud of it. Yet Gunn's admiring poem about Elvis never sounds like the singer it lauds: in fact, it never tries. Instead Gunn shows off precisely the virtues (self-control, logic, reflection) Elvis's singles seem to lack. (Gunn's poem would later furnish the title for George Melly's *Revolt into Style*.)

Poems like Gunn's sound "sentimental" (or "reflective," *sentimentalisch*) in the German writer Friedrich Schiller's famous sense of that word. Modern poets, Schiller wrote in 1795, "will either *be* nature or they will *look for* lost nature": the first are naïve and need only "feel" to create, the second *sentimentalisch* and self-conscious.[10] Poets who put rock music into their poems can thus cast rock as "naïve," natural, authentic, youthful, and their own poetry as "sentimental," reflective, artificial, grown-up. James Seay's poem on Chuck Berry and "Johnny B. Goode" relies on the changes it brings to Berry's lyrics:

> *What a wonderful dumb story of America: country boy*
> *who never learned to read or write too well, but could play*
> *a guitar just like ringing a bell and his mother*
> *told him he would be a man, the leader*
> *of a big old band, maybe someday his name in lights.*[11]

Seay's lines end up deliberately less euphonious, and much less regular, than the line breaks we would hear in the lyrics themselves. The poem comes off as secondary, belated, dependent: Seay's poem, unlike Berry's song, *sounds* older and less hopeful than the "country boy" it describes.

Such contrasts can also guide a story. David Wojahn's *Mystery Train* is a history of rock in thirty-five poems, most of them off-rhymed and highly colloquial sonnets. Wojahn begins by admiring the young James Brown, but his later sonnets mostly upend or gut the clichés of a rock history told by and for baby boomers: Wojahn finds poems in Jerry Lee Lewis's cradle-robbing marriage, in the Altamont killing, and in faith healing at Elvis's grave. Lucie Brock-Broido's prose poem "You Can't Always Get What You Want" also relies on baby boom landmarks, and it, too, likens rock songs to a lost faith:

There are no sorcerers left, only mechanics to fix things as they break down.

You get what you need. I am invited, with religious frequency in parking lots, to be Saved, to convene, to partake in redemptive ritual, to come back to the small circle of prayers. I go on, alone, ever aware of the great algebraic equations which keep this world aloft.[12]

Brock-Broido—like Mick Jagger—may get what she needs, but she does so by distancing herself from these parking-lot audiences, which recall both the circles of Philip Larkin's famous poem "Faith Healing" and the crowds at any arena rock show: she feels too old, and knows too much, to join in.

So American baby boom poets see rock as lost youth: what about the Brits? Though it kept its associations with rebels and youth, after about 1966 rock and roll took on a different valence for British verse. For one thing, by that point British people (even older ones) could see British rock as a prestigious cultural export (thus the Beatles' knighthoods). For another, British poets in the 1970s and 1980s had fewer ties to the academy, and more public presence (book sales, TV appearances) than their U.S. counterparts. British poets (if they so desired) could thus imitate, or claim to imitate, rock stars as American poets could not. The "Liverpool poets" of the midsixties helped to establish the British performance-poetry scene. Jeremy Reed claimed in "Rock and Poetry" that his own "Poetry needs street-cred, an energy / vital to youth"; two years later he published a book called *Pop Stars,* with admiring profiles of Mick Jagger ("still energized, youthful . . . rebel"), Madonna, Lou Reed, and David Bowie.[13] The so-called New Generation poets of 1994 found themselves saddled with the publicist's slogan, "Poetry is the new rock and roll"; one cartoonist depicted them as the Monkees.[14]

And yet—though they may use rock stars' names more freely—when they write poems directly about rock and roll, the British and Irish poets of recent years largely repeat familiar links between rock and youthful promise, poetry and adult retrospect—albeit with a corrosive ironic overlay. The Irish poet David Wheatley's "Fourteen" pivots on a musical original that's already self-conscious and comic: "My alarm increasing, as year wore on, at Morrisey's *bouffant—* / Was

I This Charming Man, Still Ill, sure, even, What Difference It Made?"[15] Wheatley expects us to know that the Smiths' own answer to "What Difference Does It Make?" is "It makes none." Similar jokes on sad record-collecting boys pervade the English writer Paul Farley's prizewinning 1998 debut, *The Boy from the Chemist Is Here to See You*. Wheatley's and Farley's dark jokes about gloomy youth reflect changes in teen life as grown-ups see it: outside of literature we're less likely than ever to consider young people as naïve, or to see a bright line between adolescence and adulthood. At the same time, these poems present a sort of dead end: can rock and roll—as poetry portrays it—represent anything *except* a youthful, innocent energy, now dissipated or gone bad?

That question now has a new answer: the answer is yes. A cluster of young American poets are flaunting different ways of using rock and roll. The power these poets find in rock remains linked to youth and strong feeling, but the rock they depict has become not a culturewide touchstone, nor a property of youth in general, but a subcultural quasi-secret. Most of these poets identify strongly with the self-conscious subcultures of indie or underground rock that emerged in the eighties—subcultures in which their own poems try hard to take part.

This is not the place to define indie rock, and there's no need for me to do it myself. Beat Happening boasted that their scene would remain "Our Secret"; Drew Daniel (ex-Crain, now in Matmos) went so far as to call "the commercial hopelessness of most underground music . . . not only its surface badge of 'authenticity' but a genuine regulator of artistic motivation."[16] Authenticity in indie rock isn't, or wasn't, about *innocence* (though "the kids" got invoked as much as ever), nor did it connote an *unspoiled* sexuality. Indie rock instead sought honesty and energy in its freedom from capital imperatives, in its comparative obscurity, and in its limited means. If fifties and sixties rock recalled romanticism (with its spontaneous, sexy, sometimes-doomed young heroes), indie rock (with its resistance to popularity and its unsexy secret societies) looked more like a JV version of literary modernism.

Poems that compare themselves with this sort of rock music can take a different attitude toward it than baby boomer poems about Top Ten hits. If rock energy comes from obscurity rather than universality, from quasi-conspiratorial collaboration rather than from innocent inarticulacy, that energy might be something a carefully made poem could emulate, rather than just commemorate. New poets' different generational attitude toward a rock music that has itself evolved means that in recent American poets' first books, rock may represent youth or irresponsibility, but only in qualified and relative ways: older poets' contrasts between a naive musical *then* and a grown-up, reflective verbal *now* no longer seem to fit the facts.

Let's look at examples. Joshua Clover published rock criticism himself (sometimes under the name Jane Dark) before and after his first book of verse appeared. The first poem in *Madonna Anno Domini* (1997) makes fun of baby boom rock fandom, which Clover equates with the pre- or apolitical naïveté of someone's "Mom":

> *Imagine mom: pre-postModern new teen,*
> *innocent for Elvis, ditto "Korean*
> *conflict," John Paul George Ringo Viet Nam.*
> *Mom's one state west of the glassworks, she's*
> *in a tree / K*I*S*S*I*N*G . . .*[17]

That's the rock culture Clover promises *not* to use: allusions to bands and songs in his other poems instead ally them with his own jittery knowingness. "Zealous" imagines a "continental breakfast" somewhere in a "new New World": there

> *A cloud floats by looking exactly like a*
> *Word, a boat looking for all the world like a*
> *Xebec, perhaps this is the Mediterranean? You won't tell me,*
> *You're a ghost, la la la la la la la . . .*[18]

Just as Clover wants clever readers to recognize the poem's alphabetical acrostic pattern, he wants them to recognize his concluding line as the chorus from John Cale's "Paris 1919." Clover calls a prose poem "Stories about Mecca Normal"; the poem describes not the Canadian duo who recorded *Dovetail*, but "'Mecca Normal, the capital & market town'" of a nameless Arabian nation, "a burnished city just past our southern sight."[19] Cale's song, like Jean Smith and David Lester's rock band, exists not in an innocence Clover remembers but as part of the knowledge he wants to evoke.

Other young poets deploy obscure band names too. Jen Hofer brings together the Sixths and the Cows; in Mark Bibbins's *Sky Lounge* (2003), "Godspeed You Black Emperor skewed a flower shop's ambience." Lee Ann Brown's oblique "Transisters" poems ("Belly," "Breeders," "Polly") imitate the rough guitars favored by the tough women rockers the poems name.[20] And yet one need not rely on knowing allusion in order to make new claims about rock, poems, and youth: all one must do is take fairly recent rock on knowing, intimate terms. Saskia Hamilton thanks the band Rites of Spring "for letting me borrow the title of a song from their first record."[21] The song, "For Want Of," describes a yearning almost too intense to fit any words: "I woke up this morning," singer Guy Picciotto exclaims, "with the present in splinters on the ground / And then I found . . ."[22] Hamilton (who shares D.C. roots with Rites) makes "For Want Of" not a touchstone for a lost adolescence but a formal model. The poem (like the song) deploys repeated short phrases, and then abrupt silences, to describe raw mourning and searing loss:

> *I have to wake up again and again.*
>
> *I have to take him and show him the gate.*
>
> *Something unconscious yesterday lifted*
> *the edges with a shovel and slipped in.*
> *It wasn't alive, it was no living thing.*[23]

Hamilton's poem has everything to do with loss, but nothing to do with lost youth: instead, she treats "For Want Of" as a work of art greater than (or equal to) her own, a work whose technique she wants to translate from rock (one medium) into verse (another). She also hopes we'll recognize the song—and knows that only some of us can.

D. A. Powell's 1998 debut, *Tea*, uses songs and scenes from gay disco clubs almost exactly as other poets of Powell's generation use indie rock: "heaven is a discotheque [*why don't you take me*]" one poem begins, quoting Sylvester.[24] Other disco songs and scenes pervade the book: each one reflects a promise of queer freedom threatened or flattened by HIV. "He must have been a deejay this one," Powell reflects at a "'lost companion' sale"; in these "crates of vinyl" full of twelve-inch singles "the past is actively recaptured" along with the esoterica of Powell's own gay youth: "not a whiff of poppers and halston z-14 / no brief encounter with a surviving negative. just a soundtrack undergoing reconstruction."[25] Not coincidentally, Powell emerged from the same schools and journals as Clover and Hamilton (both Powell and Clover are Iowa Workshop grads): he learned to use disco just as they learned how to use rock. And though his record collection may not look like theirs, Powell—very much like Clover, like Hamilton—wants readers to recognize songs as emblems of the imperiled subculture whose "queer argot" informs his own verse.[26]

Of several first books from the past few years to pursue these new uses of rock and pop songs, the best just might be Ange Mlinko's *Matinées* (1999), which imagines the adventures and misgivings of educated young people in Boston and Providence. Mlinko declares that her own poetics and her favorite rock songs occupy common ground. "I turn off their songs to hear my song hearing nothing I wait," she writes in "Immediate Orgy and Audit," directing us to the "sound of action in nothingness."[27] Her poem "'No one shone there'" recalls trips through New England; each stanza ends on the name of the same Boston band:

> the blind men & in wheelchairs down by the winged memorial
> wash hands in the bathroom, sit cemetery cadillac
> baby Old Glory over gravesite, lawn toy of snuffling hamlet
> town center to town center
>   O Secret Stars stay secret[28]

The poet shares with the quiet duo she names a "secret" world of peregrinations and distances to which the flag, the Cadillac, and the older men cannot belong.

Mlinko's prose poem "Editorial for Compound Eye #2" hints that playing her kind of rock feels just like making the poems she writes: "I was told once, 'When you're in that hypnagogic state where your drumsticks become one with your drums and you're afraid you can't unstick them, then it's time to put the book down and go to bed.'"[29] Listening, here, becomes an extension of reading, as playing the drums becomes an extension of writing. And Mlinko can think of rock in this fluidly personal way because she can think about youth in that way too: as a realm of conspiratorial, virtuous circles, where "the whole group is in lyrical motion."[30] Mlinko has discussed her use of rock music:

> The imbrication of *Matinées* with Boston, indie rock, etc., is al-most too overwhelming for me to summarize. I will probably never *not* respond emotionally to the music that came between Nirvana and Elliott Smith (after whom many of the quieter po-ems in *Matinées* were written). But most importantly, I was at the same time involved in an alternative poetry scene in Boston and Providence that seemed a direct parallel to indie rock: DIY; the Kill-Rock-Stars Impercipience of Burning Deck; photocopied zines; a communal identity outside the "mainstream." Did we, like indie rocksters, luxuriate in peer-group security? Indeed we did. Were the stakes high? Yes they were.[31]

American poetry has certainly lost (to quote Christopher Beach) the "high cultural status it enjoyed in the 50s and 60s, when poets like . . . Eliot and . . . Lowell were . . . cultural heroes."[32] In response, recent poets (as Beach's book shows) set up, and celebrate, small-scale networks of their own, often with left-wing or anticorporate ideologies. These structures resemble those that support indie rock—as the poets (and not just Mlinko) have noticed. American writers have self-published small-scale poetry journals since the 1950s, but only in the past ten years have poets begun to call such journals zines. (The Minneapolis poetry zine *Swerve* even included a 45-rpm seven-inch record along with issues number four and five.) With these rock and roll analogies and celebrations of obscurity come, predictably, quarrels about young poets' "selling out," parodies of those quarrels, and parodies of the parodies, in verse and prose (say, Gabriel Gudding's: "I have felt for some time that I am writing inside a butt").[33] The poets who learned from indie rock's introspection must now try hard to avoid its clannish demerits. Some of them ought to know those demerits perfectly well, having been (or being) rockers themselves: the Silver Jews' David Berman won widespread praise for his book of poems, *Actual Air*, while Franklin Bruno of the witty indie rock band Nothing Painted Blue regularly appears in advanced West Coast litmags.

Like the Secret Stars—and unlike the Stones—young poets know what "fit audience though few" they might find, and they acknowledge it in their new work. Poets inspired by indie rock now find in it not just models for individual poems, but models for their (largely obscure) careers. These poets know that they won't become celebs, or even earn much of a living at their work (except obliquely, through teaching): the obscurity of their new verse both mirrors, and alludes to, the acknowledged obscurity, and the sense of community, indie kids tried to create. (And yes, Powell's disco fits this model too—the contexts he gives his divas and DJs are not the mainstream dance floors of *Saturday Night Fever* but the later, less visible space of gay male subculture circa the mid-1980s.) Literary poetry nowadays (spoken-word performance is something else altogether) will never take on the innocence, the uncomplicated gusto of "I Want to Hold Your Hand"—nor can poetry grab for itself the incendiary immediacy of "Blitzkrieg Bop." Some parts of rock and roll just have to stay beyond the reach of written art forms—just as some kinds of experience really do recede after the teenage years. And so long as poets who cared about rock music took those parts of rock as their examples, the poets got stuck with retrospect, with nostalgia, with poems about the rock and roll youth they had lost. Rock and roll can, however, spread other effects—and other emotional affects—over that persistent 4/4 beat; it can represent other, more knowing youth subcultures. And poetry can take those other effects as its own: poems can whisper or ring with the gritty insularity, the wiry ironies, the conspiratorial secrets, the economy of means, and the contrarian obscurity devoted listeners find in the subcultural scenes of the eighties and nineties—scenes that reimagine both rock and youth, in ways the newest poets have made their own.

chapter 15

Compressing Pop: How Your Favorite Song Got Squished

DOUGLAS WOLK

The history of CD technology, if you ask most people, is a history of perfectibility, just like the history of sound recording technology in general. Every generation of equipment is supposed to make recorded music clearer, stronger, louder, more vivid, closer to the actual sound musicians intend to be heard. CDs have certainly gotten louder—pull out any hit pop albums from ten years ago and from last week, play them side-by-side, and the difference in volume is instantly evident.

But if you ask many CD mastering engineers, that's a big problem. They'll tell you that, in fact, their own work isn't what it could be because they have to give their customers what they want, and what customers want is loudness at the expense of subtlety and listenability. The culprit is compression, a tool so useful in gaining a competitive edge that the music business learned to make it impossibly powerful. But their cure-all turned into an addiction: the music is now so economically dependent on compression that its overuse has helped to turn CDs and pop radio into a harsh, throbbing mess.

I'll be throwing the word *compression* around a lot for the next few pages, so I'll explain it before I go on, and I'll try to take it easy on the tech-speak. Everyone's seen pictures of sound represented as a waveform; if you look at one, you can see that the wave's amplitude is constantly changing. What that represents to a listener is the sound's *level* from instant to instant. If you raise the level of something, it gets louder; if you lower the level, it gets quieter. When you record a voice or an instrument, it's not going to maintain the same level, even for a fraction of a second. There are fluctuations in level going on all the time, and some of them can be intense and distracting. In most cases, you're going to want your recording to sound more consistent than its source actually is—or at least to make sure that your recording's major inconsistencies in level or in sound are intentional.

A compressor is essentially a tool to make levels more consistent by limiting their range. To use compression, you first decide where you want it to start working. You pick a threshold level—say, 12 decibels (dB)—and set the compressor to affect everything above that level (and ignore everything below it). Then you set the ratio for the compressor—three to one, say. So when the compressor processes the recording, for every sound that's louder than the threshold, it will take the *amount* by which its level is higher than the threshold and reduce it according to the ratio. If a compressor is set as we've described it here, and a particular peak of a recording is 18 dB, the compressor will change that peak so it becomes 14 dB: 18 dB minus 12 dB, times 1/3, plus 12 dB.

So compressors make things quieter, right? Technically, yes, but in practice it's the other way around. The reason you use compression is so that you can then raise the *overall* level of the recording so that the loudest parts are as loud as they were before. What you effectively do is make the quiet parts louder—bringing the stage up, so to speak, instead of bringing the ceiling down.

That's a really, really useful trick to be able to pull off. Compression is like salt: a little of it makes everything sound better. Compressed voices sound more authoritative; compressed instruments sound more precise and energetic. Done properly, it gives sound more oomph. Analog recording media actually have a certain amount of compression built into the format. Recording engineers *love* compression—very often they'll apply a little bit to most or all of the instruments in a mix, and then a little more to the whole thing. But compression also affects the sound—changing the waveform of a sound, no matter how slightly, alters its timbre, and there's no getting around that. If you apply compression to certain kinds of sounds on the low end of the spectrum, especially bass guitar and some drums, you can actually hear it making a whooshing sound as it kicks in. That's a bad thing unless it's part of your artistic intention, which it very occasionally is—U2's "Beautiful Day" is a rare example of a song that deliberately uses that whoosh as an effect.

There's another, more extreme kind of compression, called limiting. Limiting prevents a sound from going over a certain dynamic level more than a tiny bit, or at all. You set your compression ratio at 10 to 1, or 20 to 1, or 50 to 1, and you'll severely squish down any part of your signal that goes over the threshold level. If your threshold is 12 dB, and your ratio is 50 to 1, then to get an output of 12 dB, you put in 12 dB; to get an output of 14 dB, you have to put in 112 dB.

There are two areas of the music business that use a lot of compression. The first is pop radio. Radio wants everything to be as in-your-face as possible, because a lot of its listeners are in cars. Pop radio stations use as much signal strength as they're allowed to by law, so that the signal comes in loud and clear, and doesn't fade in and out all the time as you drive. That also means they don't want the quietest sounds you hear to be all that much quieter than the loudest ones. Two pop radio stations can be transmitting at exactly the same power from exactly the same place, but the one that's compressing its signal more will sound like it's stronger and louder.

The biggest rock stations in urban markets, like K-ROCK in New York, have a very, very limited dynamic range—the exact size of the range tends to be proprietary (and their engineers aren't willing to talk about it), but it can be as small as 1 dB. The decibel scale is logarithmic, so a difference of 10 dB means doubling or halving a signal's level; that means that the quietest sound you'll hear on K-ROCK is practically as loud as the loudest sound. Generally, a pop radio station will run its signal through a compressor—at, say, 3 to 1—to smooth off the biggest peaks, and then a limiter—20 to 1 or so—and finally an infinity-to-1 limiter, so it can push its signal strength exactly as high as it can go. (There's a multistage compressor-limiter called an Optimod that's widely used in radio.) And stations don't adjust the settings on a song-by-song basis; they just set up the limiters and let them work.

(Note that these practices are specific to pop radio. In general, classical radio stations would much rather have a lot of dynamic variation than a lot of level, because their listeners are a lot more likely to be audiophiles—they're specifically listening for the dynamics of the performance, from pianissimo to fortissimo. That's why when you frequency-surf on FM radio, classical stations almost always sound a lot quieter.)

There's also a lot of compression that comes into pop music in the recording, mixing, and mastering process, long before radio adds its own, and it tends to be more nuanced and adjusted for the needs of a particular recording. Part of what recording and mastering engineers have to keep in mind, of course, is how their work is going to sound on the radio. Vic Anesini, one of the head mastering engineers at Sony Music, told me that "you don't want the station's compression to have to work on your music—you give it to them as a compressed brick, and the station's compressors don't change the sound." The parts of the audio spectrum that generate the highest levels and the most peaks tend to be the low end and the high end; the midrange is not nearly as peak-prone. Radio stations have been compressing their signal for decades, but the technology got more efficient in the '90s; a lot of songs from the past five or six years that have been prepared with radio play in mind are centered almost monomaniacally on midrange. (The more heavy the bass is to begin with, the less loud the whole production will sound on its own on the radio, and bass gets sliced away by limiters anyway.) The Goo Goo Dolls' "Iris" is basically a doctrinaire "brick": squarely in the midrange, vocals way up front so that broadcast limiters don't squash them into the mix.

Even so, if you take a heavily compressed recording and run it through a radio station's superintense compressor-limiters, you'll very often get a sound that's squished to a pulp. The notes are the same, but it sounds small. Songs that rely on dynamic variation can have so little dynamic range that the quiet parts effectively sound louder than the loud parts. (Next time you're in a car and "More Than a Feeling" or "Smells Like Teen Spirit" comes on the radio, listen with this in mind—it's pretty shocking.) Sometimes, when you hear badly recorded early hip-hop on the radio, the rapper's voice will almost disappear for a moment every time the kick drum hits; that's the same effect at work.

Of course, radio stations aren't the only contingent that wants their music to be loud. Artists and labels often demand that their CDs have to be louder than everyone else's. That's not the recording engineer's problem; it's the responsibility of the mastering engineer, whose job is to prepare the finished recording to be duplicated. Mastering engineers report that artists (or label executives) take home their test CDs, put them in a five-disc changer, note that they aren't as loud as the new Madonna or Jay-Z album, and bring them back in to be "corrected."

This isn't exactly a new phenomenon. It goes back to the days when vinyl records had to "pop out" of the jukebox, so they were mastered as loudly as possible. But that was a phenomenon of singles much more than of albums, which were mastered with an eye to their flow rather than their moment-to-moment impact. The dramatic increase in CDs' loudness isn't just a sign of technology getting better—it's actually affecting the way contemporary pop music sounds. Scott Hull of Classic Sound, a veteran who's mastered recordings by the likes of Alanis Morrisette, Limp Bizkit, Ani DiFranco, and Bruce Springsteen, told me that the quality of CD mastering has gone *dramatically* downhill over the past half-decade, and virtually every other mastering engineer I spoke to agreed with him.

The way it happened is a good example of how mechanical "perfectibility" can go wrong. When CDs were introduced, they had to be mastered from a special digital tape, called a U-Matic, or 1630. The music industry's advertising spin for compact discs (and the expensive equipment that played them) was that they would eliminate the flaws of vinyl reproduction—their slogan, in the early days, was "perfect sound forever"—and the kind of distortion that was sometimes heard on vinyl was supposed to be absolutely out of the question. One of CDs' advantages over vinyl, in fact, was that digital recordings could be mastered quietly enough to give something closer to the full dynamic range of the original performance. The machines that read the U-Matic tapes had a maximum level; if the recording went above that level at all, a light went on, it was considered an error, and the plant would reject the master. A tape sent to a manufacturing plant had to come with a written annotation of every pop and click. (The original CD edition of Frankie Goes to Hollywood's fastidiously recorded *Welcome to the Pleasuredome*, released in 1984, included that annotation on its back cover!)

At that time it was also considered a serious technical flaw when CD mastering engineers used digital limiting, which meant that the consumer wasn't getting the "perfect sound." They could nudge sounds into place with a little compression, but if they actually put a limiter on, it was called "clipping." (It's obvious what "clipping" means if you hear what happens when you apply a limiter to a solo instrument. It comes out sounding harsh and somehow defective.) But mastering engineers could get more work if they were willing to use limiting to make recordings louder, so the taboo gradually fell away. And some engineers invented workarounds to evade the U-Matic machine's light of doom. According to Greg Calbi, one of the most experienced mastering engineers in pop, around 1989 or 1990 his studio, Sterling Sound, invented a device that would eliminate the "overs"—the moments where the levels were too high—by disguising them. They'd tweak the data on the tape so that it'd still have the peaks but the machines at the pressing plants wouldn't detect them.

Pressing plants essentially threw up their hands at this. There was nothing they could do. A few years later, the technology of CD manufacturing changed and stopped requiring 1630s. Now pressing plants could manufacture CDs from whatever media you gave them, and pops, clicks, and distortions were the customer's responsibility, not the plant's. So slightly higher levels became possible. Around 1995 or 1996, a company called Wavez came out with a piece of equipment called the L1, and later the L2. The L1 is what's called a "brick-wall limiter." It's also known as the Ultra-Maximizer, which should give you a good idea of what it does. You set your threshold level on the Ultra-Maximizer, and *nothing* gets above it. It has zero attack time, it has an infinite compression ratio, you can push your levels as high as you can bear, just skirting the edge of digital distortion. (If you've ever heard serious digital distortion, it's incredibly unpleasant. It doesn't have that kind of sexy raw sound that analog distortion can have. There are a couple of artists who can use it in an intentional way, but they are very few and far between: most of them are noise or extreme metal artists, like Rehberg & Bauer or Napalm Death.)

Once the Ultra-Maximizer was available, record companies' gentle pressure to make new records sound hot turned into an all-out loudness war—and sent the community of mastering engineers into a permanent state of disgruntlement. I've talked to about a dozen fairly well known engineers, and every single one of them hates being asked to make a CD as loud as it can get. Mastering engineers can do all sorts of things to the sound of a recording; they generally like to make it sound complicated and vibrant, and to play up its dynamics and overall flow. But that's not what bands and labels want very often anymore. When I went to visit Greg Calbi in his studio, he told me that the day before, a guy from a well-known young rock band had come in with some new material to be mastered. Calbi asked him if he had any particular things he wanted to play up in the mastering process, and the young musician said, "I don't know anything about mastering—I just want it to be *really loud*." As he told me the story, Calbi gave me a sort of "well, what can you do?" look. Similarly, Scott Hull says he's had a few clients who have told him they came to him because they initially took their album somewhere else to be mastered, and when they got it back and listened to it in the subway it didn't drown out the subway noise.

Presumably, they've got some CDs that do. As Hull puts it, "It kind of washes your hands of the quality issue at that point." Why are these engineers so unhappy? Because making CDs very loud means that you can't do much else with them. When a recording is ultramaximized, its dynamic range is severely limited and it loses what's called "headroom"—the amount by which a recording can get louder than it is, the sound-engineering equivalent of available space. Without headroom, the entire recording starts turning into one dense, undifferentiated clump of sound. (For some diagrams of what this does to a recording, see engineer Rip Rowan's essay "Over the Limit" at *www.prorec.com,* a lengthy and very funny rant against the way Rush's 2002 album *Vapor Trails* was mastered.)

There are some recordings that are fatally damaged by brick-wall limiting—they can be loud or they can be professional sounding, but not both. Vic Anesini at Sony says that he's tried to make loud versions of recent Bob Dylan songs to plug to radio, and it just doesn't work—Dylan's voice starts crackling badly, just because of its natural timbre. It's likely that there are artists who can't get played on the radio now because their voices no longer sound right when they're made loud enough to get programmers' attention.

Compression and limiting can't determine the sound of pop music all by themselves, but like any kind of pervasive technology, they privilege some kinds of expression above others, and alter the way anything that passes through them is perceived. Just to see what would happen, I asked engineer Jesse Cannon to choose a very familiar rock song, and to master it three different ways. He picked Led Zeppelin's "Houses of the Holy"—a curious choice, since it doesn't seem at first blush like it has much dynamic variation. It does, though; listening to the commercially available CD version (mastered to sound as much as possible like the original mid-'70s LP), there's a lot of give and take between the individual instruments, and all the parts have clearly discernible phrasing and fluidity. It's mastered at a fairly low level compared with current standards, but it has plenty of definition when it's turned up. That's our control version for this experiment; it's not value neutral, and it's not an exact representation of what Led Zeppelin sounded like in their practice space or even on their master tape, but it's a pretty close approximation of how that kind of rock record was meant to sound twenty-seven years ago, or even fifteen years ago.

Imagine, now, that young Jimmy Page walks into a mastering studio today with a copy of the freshly recorded *Physical Graffiti*. The mastering engineer asks what Jimmy wants him to do with his album. Jimmy says, "Well, first of all, I want it to be *really loud*." The result is the second version of "Houses of the Holy" Cannon mastered: the same sounds, ultramaximized. The solo guitar part at the beginning of the song suddenly sounds like it's being played by a robot, with unvaried intonation, and it comes off as more metallic and synthetic, since the overemphasis on the distorted guitar's natural overtones gives its tone an unpleasant buzz. Once the full band kicks in, the bass is much lower in the mix than it is in our control version—almost feeble. It's very in-your-face; it's also very constricted, and claustrophobia inducing, heavy in a way that suggests repeated impacts rather than a steady gravitational pull.

So take that extremely loud, heavily brick-walled mastering job—on the same recording, mind you—and play it on a big rock radio station, where they run it through their compressor-limiters that squish whatever dynamic range is left to about 1 dB, and what happens is Cannon's third version of "Houses of the Holy," which barely sounds like the same song. It's really bracing—it jumps out of the speakers and grabs you—but it's not jumping at you from very far away. The headroom of the original recording is entirely gone. It's got no flexibility and no real dynamics; the full band is at exactly the same level as the solo guitar at the beginning. And it's distorted to the point that everything just goes *crunch*. If you think that sound might be familiar, you're absolutely right: that's the sound of nu-metal, right there, from Puddle of Mudd to Slipknot to System of a Down. Even if those bands wanted to reproduce the timbres of, say, Led Zeppelin, they might not be able to, just because of what happens between their amplifiers and our ears.

Note, though, that this process affects guitar-based pop recordings more than other kinds of music; it's a lot easier to make hip-hop records loud than to make rock records loud. Hip-hop generally uses either preset keyboard tones that don't have a lot of overtones (the parts of a sound that distort more easily) or samples that have been "cleansed" to have simple waveforms. And hip-hop rarely relies on dynamics, so it can usually be compressed pretty ruthlessly without changing its effect much. But when rock bands want their records to be as loud as Nelly's, they run into trouble, since their instruments are a much more messy proposition.

Within the mastering community, there's a lot of discussion of "the loudness wars." Clients just want their disc to be the one that leaps out on the CD jukebox or the music director's stereo; they won't pronounce it ready for manufacturing if it's as quiet as a typical CD of the early '90s, and that effectively means an engineer has to compress it to within an inch of its life. A few engineers have even floated the idea of trying to make a deal across the business to roll back levels a little, since at this point compact disc levels are basically maxed out. (I asked a few if they might have more leeway with new formats like DVD-Audio, and they just gave me a "let's not even go there" look.)

The first practical effect of all this is that new CDs, in general, are much more aggressive and present than they were even in the mid-'90s—but many of them, especially rock CDs, sound distinctly worse than they used to. Hypercompressed CDs are actually very hard to listen to for more than a few minutes. They tire out the ears; they don't flow well for a full album's running time. (In fact, a lot of the recent loud rock records that listeners appreciate most as albums are not as compressed or as loud as the current norm—a few engineers mentioned Tool's *Lateralus* as an example of a hit CD that had been mastered carefully and at a reasonable level.)

The second practical effect is that, if you're writing or recording a song meant for the radio, you can't include much dynamic variation—but you can also make the dominant technology work to your advantage. One thing that does work is dynamics based on on/off, sound-or-silence ideas, especially if the sounds have very simple waveforms (synthesized tones, or heavily processed samples). Timbaland, for example, is brilliant at playing to radio limiting's strengths: Tweet's "Oops (Oh My)" and Missy Elliott's "Work It" sound dynamic as anything, but their arrangements concentrate on spikes and near silences.

That's the direction taken in a lot of the most popular hip-hop and R&B recordings right now: complicated arrangements whose component parts are very simple sounds and lots of space. Another way to work with the expectation of a heavily compressed CD and brick-wall-limited radio is the flirting-with-disaster route of hard rock, aiming for something that sounds very harsh and punishing, and accepting that you're going to get a certain amount of distortion. The third and final way is to go for the "compressed brick" that Vic Anesini spoke about, which yields a recording that's heavy on the midrange, with vocals way up front, no real low end, no real high end, and no risk of being changed much by radio: the sound of the Dixie Chicks and "Your Body Is a Wonderland." And if the juxtaposition of those three techniques sounds like contemporary hit radio, well, that's not entirely a coincidence.

chapter 16

Rapping about Rapping: The Rise and Fall of a Hip-Hop Tradition

KELEFA SANNEH

This story starts in a pool hall on West Twenty-first Street, sometime around two in the morning. I was interviewing a rapper named Beanie Sigel—a roly-poly guy from Philadelphia who rhymes more or less exclusively (and wittily) about the pleasures and frustrations of selling crack. He was giving me a foreshortened version of his autobiography, running through a familiar fairy-tale narrative. "My story is like a Cinderella story," he said.

It was a routine he had undoubtedly rehearsed in dozens of interviews before this one, but he has a marvelous voice—slow and snarly, with lots of dropped consonants—so I was happy to listen. I asked him what I thought was an obvious question: When did he first know he wanted to be a rapper?

Beanie Sigel sighed and shook his head, getting ready to clear up a common misconception. He explained that he'd never really wanted to be a *rapper*—he emphasized the word to underscore his disdain. Eventually, he said, some friend of a friend got him into a studio, but still, he kept it a secret. "Where I'm from, it wasn't cool to be a rapper," he said. "If you was a rapper, you was a sucker, straight up. So I kept it under my hat. I'd say, 'Nah, man, I ain't no rapper.'"

I wasn't sure if I believed him, but the sentiment sounded familiar—and not just because he'd used the exact same line on his first album.

Time was, rappers were eager to tell you what they did for a living, and how well they did it. In fact, that seemed to be the only thing they wanted to talk about. Like generations of three-card monte men before them, they rapped about rapping, explaining how the trick worked even as they pulled it off. You can hear this on virtually any earlier hip-hop record; one of the most amusing examples is Jimmy Spicer's absurd 1980 single, "The Adventures of Super Rhymes," in which he battles Howard Cosell, Dracula, and anyone else who crosses his path. It starts with the rapper being born:

> *My mother said, son, that's the way it should be*
> *Your name is Super Rhymes—You'll be an MC*
> *so then my father put me on a meteorite*
> *sent me to earth, to rock the mic*[1]

But by the late 1990s, things had changed. On one hand, rappers were achieving extraordinary success, succeeding even where they probably should have been failing: there were movies and clothes and lucrative record imprints, and the music itself had become the most popular genre in the country. At the same time, though, rappers were facing a problem that no one could have predicted: low self-esteem.

Maybe it wasn't low self-esteem, exactly—they still thought pretty highly of themselves as people, as hustlers, as master criminals, as sexual athletes, as businessmen. But they were in no rush to tout their own credentials as rappers.

The obvious conclusion was that rapping was a lost art, buried in the mad rush of capitalism and tough-guy (and tough-girl) posturing. There were, perhaps, more great rappers than ever, only lots of them were doing pretty much the opposite of what their predecessors had done: they rapped about everything except rapping itself. In fact, they sometimes went to absurd lengths to avoid admitting that they were rappers at all. On September 11, 2001, Jay-Z released his sixth album, *The Blueprint* (Roc-A-Fella/Island Def Jam), which includes an unusual boast:

> *Look, scrapper: I've got nephews to look after.*
> *I'm not looking at you dudes, I'm looking past ya.*
> *I thought I told you characters: I'm not a rapper.*[2]

From "Your name is Super Rhymes—You'll be an MC" to "I thought I told you characters: I'm not a rapper." In twenty years, the rapper had gone from Superman to Invisible Man. How did it happen? And—more important—why does it matter?

It makes sense to start in 1984, with the release of the first Run-D.M.C. album. Run-D.M.C. helped invent (and popularize) rapping as we know it, severing the ties between hip-hop and disco. They didn't dress as if they were going to a party, and they didn't rhyme like it, either.

The earliest rappers often sounded as if they were killing time: they'd keep running their mouths until the beat stopped; the longer they kept it up, the longer people could dance. Jimmy Spicer's single, for example, lasted sixteen minutes—the form far outpaced the content. But Run-D.M.C.'s songs were shorter and more urgent, as if they had something they really wanted to say.

Of course, what they really wanted to say was that they were really good at rapping:

> *Two years ago, a friend of mine*
> *asked me to say some MC rhymes*
> *so I said this rhyme I'm about to say*

the rhyme was def, and it went this way
took a test to become an MC . . .[3]

You might say that Run-D.M.C.'s style was an illusion: their voices promised something that their words couldn't quite deliver. You can hear this tension in a lot of their best songs—the energy pulls you forward, but the words just keep going round and round:

It's tricky to rock a rhyme,
To rock a rhyme that's right on time, it's tricky . . .
It's tricky, tricky, tricky, tricky.[4]

By the late 1980s, rappers were broadening their lyrical horizons by creating better-defined characters: KRS-One was a teacher, Slick Rick was a storyteller, Too $hort was a pimp, Rakim was a mystic, and the members of Public Enemy were, well, public enemies. It was inevitable, in retrospect: hip-hop was getting topical, and its cast of characters was diversifying.

Still, these rappers all saw a link between their identity as rappers and the characters they portrayed. Sure, Chuck D. delivered black nationalist sermons, but he also wanted to remind listeners that he was a "rhyme animal." Too $hort told convincing stories of drugs and prostitution (and he knew his way around a dirty joke, too), but he also said, "I'm just an MC rapper and nothing else / I keep rhyming, and I do it by myself."[5]

Things changed with N.W.A. They were riveting storytellers, and they realized, long before many of their peers, that hip-hop storytelling was built on a paradox. How could any rapper be convincing if he kept reminding his audience that he was merely a rapper? How could he draw listeners into his narratives if he refused to stay in character? These are the famous opening lines of N.W.A's classic album, *Straight Outta Compton*:

Straight outta Compton, crazy motherfucker named Ice Cube
From a gang called Niggaz With Attitude
When I'm called off, I got a sawed-off
Pull the trigger, and bodies get hauled off.[6]

There's no mention of microphones or rhyming, and even the rap group itself is disguised as "a gang called Niggaz With Attitude." Later in the album, Dr. Dre talks about the art of rapping, but he's not impressed. On the contrary, he argues that rapping compares unfavorably with everyday life:

Some musicians cuss at home
But scared to use profanity when up on the microphone
Oh, yeah—they want reality, but you will hear none
They'd rather exaggerate a little fiction.[7]

It was an odd turn of events, to say the least: a rapper was speaking out against exaggeration. Isn't that a bit like a drummer speaking out against rhythm?

The biggest rap star of the 1990s took this gambit one step further. Where N.W.A acted as native informants, giving listeners a tour of their neighborhood, 2pac gave listeners a tour of himself. He was the hip-hop answer to Madonna, with a persona so big that the music seemed secondary. In early 1996 he released "All Eyez on Me"—notice that it's not called "All Earz on Me." He's far too deep into his own mythology to brag about anything as trivial as lyrical prowess. Instead, he says things like,

The feds is watching, niggaz plotting to get me
Will I survive, will I die?
Come on, let's picture the possibility.[8]

A few months later, he was dead, and in the years since, his confounding mishmash of art and life has made him a hip-hop icon—which is to say that, in death, 2pac just about succeeded in making people forget that he used to be a famous rapper.

A lot of the hip-hop stars of the late 1990s weren't really rappers at all. Following the example of Dr. Dre, who split off from N.W.A. to become the first superstar hip-hop producer, there was Master P, Jermaine Dupri, Sean "P. Diddy" Combs—big-money titans whose main talents lay somewhere besides rapping. You might say that life had overtaken art: you could brag that you had the best lyrics, but that wouldn't help you save face when Master P responded—truth-fully—that he had made the cover of *Fortune*. When P. Diddy tacitly acknowledged his reliance on ghostwriters, he became, I think, the first major rapper to brag about his *lack* of skill: "Don't worry if I write rhymes—I write checks."

What about those performers who *were* great rappers? Well, they had to convince their listeners that that wasn't all they were. As usual, the Notorious B.I.G. put it best, in this rhyme from his second album, released in 1997, a few weeks after he was killed:

> *I'm a criminal: way before the rap shit,*
> *bust the gat shit. Puff won't even know what happened*
> *if it's done smoothly. Silencers on the Uzis,*
> *stash in the hoopties . . .*[9]

To make his story more convincing, he has to establish that he had another life "way before the rap shit." More than that: the fear is that being a rapper has already undermined his credibility. In the middle of an engrossing story about a revenge killing, he has to interrupt himself and find a way to reconcile his career with his persona.

This conflict between career and persona spawned something like a hip-hop identity crisis. And so, in the late 1990s, rappers seemed eager to disparage their art. There was Jay-Z, of course, whose mega-lomania intermingled with an odd sort of self-loathing. "Back to Shawn Carter the hustler, Jay-Z is dead," he rhymed. There was Juvenile, saying, "I ain't no pussy-ass nigga / I'm a rapper but I'm still a gorilla."[10] In this couplet, the important word is *but*. Dead Prez took a slightly different approach, belittling the music as a way of advancing their political program. "It's bigger than hip-hop," they insisted, to make sure no one would mistake them for mere rappers.

And then there was Missy Elliott, who tackled this conundrum with a characteristic combination of self-deprecation and sly wit. On her 1997 CD *Supa Dupa Fly* (Gold Mind/Elektra), she mockingly boasts about her lyrical prowess. The words convey tongue-in-cheek bravado, but when she croons and giggles them, it sounds as if she's making fun of those old-fashioned rappers who are preoccupied with their craft:

My style of rapping
I'm su-su-such a good rapper
I give you good and plenty
My style's the bomb-diggy.[11]

The subliminal message is clear: Who cares?

The late 1990s was an odd time. Rappers themselves were doing better than ever, in every place except one: their own songs. In rap lyrics, "the rapper" was the enemy—a hokey literary device that was no longer necessary. Most of the time, rappers didn't even bother to distance themselves from the art of rapping. They just went on telling stories about their implausible lives, hoping we'd forget what they did for a living.

When many people talk or write about hip-hop, they talk about this trend as if it were a bad thing. Commentators and historians are always reminiscing about the good old days, when rappers aspired to be nothing more than great rappers. The assumption is that hip-hop has lost its mythical purity—and what could be purer than lyrics about lyrics?

But it's also clear that the decreasing popularity of rapping about rapping has helped broaden hip-hop's range of subject matter. Rappers were forced to invent alternate worlds, and so the narratives got more complex. Acts like Wu-Tang Clan, Jay-Z, Eminem—to name just three—took very different approaches, but they all created specific identities for themselves, identities that were only tangentially related to their identities as rappers.

Who wants to listen to someone huffing and puffing about lyrical skill, when you could be listening to the members of the Wu-Tang Clan reinventing themselves as Shaolin warriors? When Jay-Z insisted that "Jay-Z is dead," he tackled the paradoxes head-on; the conflict between persona and profession provided him with some of his richest material. And Eminem filled his verses with different versions of himself, including Slim Shady and Marshall Mathers. The decreasing viability of "the rapper" as a protagonist forced them to tell bigger and weirder and more complicated stories.

Perhaps more important, this lyrical evolution is closely intertwined with the musical development of hip-hop. Over the 1990s, as the rapper became a less dominant character in the hip-hop landscape, rappers became less dominant in the music, too. If P. Diddy could breezily tell listeners, "Don't worry if I write rhymes," it was because he figured they cared more about beats and choruses, in any case. And the rappers' own eagerness to downplay their skill only bolstered this trend—you might say that rappers came close to talking themselves out of a job.

If you go back and listen to old Run-D.M.C. records and concentrate on the music, not the lyrics, you'll notice that there's almost nothing there. On many of their earliest and greatest tracks, there's just a drum machine keeping a steady beat while the guys recite their verses about verses. The lyrical focus matched the sonic arrangement: it was all about rapping. Make no mistake, listeners certainly expected to hear a good beat, but a good beat was defined, in part, as a beat that didn't get in the way of the rapper.

By the 1990s, things had started to change. One of the decade's most important hip-hop stars was Dr. Dre, who was adequate on the microphone and brilliant in the music studio. It's worth noting that the figure most closely identified with so-called gangsta rap is primarily a musician, not a lyricist: Dr. Dre's hard, heavy, tuneful beats probably had a greater influence on hip-hop than any lyrics ever did. When Dr. Dre went looking for a protégé, he wanted someone whose voice would fit the beats, and he found Snoop Dogg, who excels at intonation, not wordplay. Snoop Dogg's appeal stems from his lilting delivery, and from his ability to complement the music without drowning it out. Expectations had changed—listeners wanted a rapper who didn't get in the way of the beat.

By the end of the decade, hip-hop was increasingly dominated by producers such as Timbaland and the Neptunes. If rappers remained the biggest stars, they nevertheless knew that to maintain their popularity they had to learn how to make do with fewer words.

New York City has a long tradition of hip-hop verbosity, so the renewed emphasis on beats and music favored performers from different parts of the country—it's no coincidence that the pioneer of the laid-back, sing-songy style was Snoop Dogg, from Long Beach. Missy Elliott, from Virginia Beach, took an even more extreme approach, emphasizing form while dismissing the importance of content. She built her career around her playful, casual delivery, paired with her partner Timbaland's avant-garde beats; it didn't much matter what she was talking about. Other southern rappers—Trick Daddy, from Miami; Juvenile and Mystikal, from New Orleans; OutKast, from Atlanta—succeeded by concentrating on vocal tone and texture, and by aligning themselves with adventurous beat makers. It's not overstating the case to argue that the rebellion against old-fashioned hip-hop, against rapping about rapping, helped make hip-hop listeners more receptive to acts that might once have been consigned to regional success.

By 2001, a couple of rappers had taken this approach one step further. The year's two best-selling rap albums were by Nelly, from St. Louis, and Ja Rule, from Yonkers. Both of them practice a style that might be called "sing-rapping"—neither is a great lyricist, but both found mainstream success by setting their words to music, emphasizing melody over meaning. In a sense, this is the logical conclusion of rappers' disavowals of rapping. Once rappers stop claiming to *be* rappers, why should they keep *sounding* like rappers?

So what comes next? Is sing-rapping the end of the road—the final spasm of a genre that talked itself to death? Does it mark yet another rebirth, signaling the beginning of an era in which hip-hop isn't so reliant on the old-fashioned practice of rapping? Or will sing-rapping prove a short-lived trend, destined to be yet another footnote in hip-hop's evolution?

Whatever the case, it now seems clear that the belittling of the rapper was a kind of constructive criticism—the perfect antidote to hip-hop bravado, as well as its logical conclusion. It somehow seems fair that, after years of boasting, rappers had to confront the banality of their own lives. They responded the way rappers always respond: with bullshit and belligerence and plenty of wit, confident that they'd be able to talk themselves out of this jam, too. They were right, I think: you might argue that the death of "the rapper"—the character—helped extend the life of his genre, creating another decade of viability for "the rapper"—the musician.

As I write, the country's most popular movie is *8 Mile,* and its most popular album is the *8 Mile* soundtrack—no matter what the state of hip-hop, Eminem is more popular than ever. He contributes three extraordinary songs to the soundtrack, in which he spends most of his time rapping about rapping: "Sometimes I wanna jump on stage and just kill mics / And show these people what my level of skill's like."[12] The subject matter is old-fashioned, and so is the music: the beats are hard and simple, so as not to get in the way.

But this isn't exactly a return to a traditional way of doing things. If Eminem doesn't sound like himself on the soundtrack album, it's because he's rapping in the voice of Jimmy "Rabbit" Smith, Jr., the aspiring rapper he portrays in the movie, which is set in 1995. And so a once-dominant hip-hop tradition is revived as a Hollywood tie-in—Eminem's logocentric verses are proof of his commitment to acting. And "the rapper"—a hip-hop character whose time has past—finds a home in the place where all great American archetypes go to die: the movies.

III.

Values

chapter 17

Bread and Butter Songs: Unoriginality in Pop

ANN POWERS

During the 1990s I spent countless nights standing in dark rooms with excited strangers. Overheated, rowdy, very often drunk or alternately rapturous and silent, the crowds around me demonstrated the strange parameters of passion. Though the job description "pop critic" landed me with them, I came to feel that my deepest role was as witness to these devotees pressing all around, or more precisely to the spiritual exchange they had with the musicians whose bills they paid and reputations they made. Most pop critics consider passing judgment their primary task, but for me that was the surface work, important but not profound. The real challenge came in accepting that even music I found offensive or dull really moved people, sometimes stadiums full. The next step, even harder, was figuring out why.

That's the task all of us accept, on some level—to create a framework for understanding pop music beyond our own preferences.

Academics and journalists alike have come a long way in getting inside the heads of music fans. Reams have been written on fan culture since the early 1980s, when rock and roll students like me were eager to enlist in the Cult Studs Brigade. At the same time, rock criticism has continually challenged high-culture notions of quality and meaningfulness, first in arguing for the worth of rock itself, and then keeping watch over false distinctions within the rock canon. The recent recuperation of 1980s hair metal through the noteworthy efforts of the Chucks, Eddy and Klosterman, is a case in point.

But on the way from subcultural studies to MTV's *Fanatic*, some essential questions got sidetracked. While the explosion of the pop canon has been thrilling and generally beneficial, especially to the aging one-hit wonders of VH1, the canonization process itself remains essentially the same. Studies of fan culture offer insight into the art worlds people so lovingly build around their favorite icons and genres, but in letting fans speak for themselves, scholars often sidestep the question of whether the music is intrinsically interesting. And pop criticism inevitably returns to questions of value grounded in personal taste. Though the element of memoir has broadened the range of views expressed, we critics nearly always end up back with those *American Bandstand* kids, saying, "It has a good beat and you can dance to it, I'll give it an 87."

Critics treat taste the way celebrities treat their abs—working it under the headphones makes our opinions ring true. If a critic embarks on a mission to recuperate "bad" music, she does so under the assumption that conventional notions of "good" and "bad" are faulty and need to be replaced or at least expanded. Chuck Eddy's *Stairway to Hell: The 500 Best Heavy Metal Albums in the Universe*, the book that arguably made the whole critical/popular reclamation of trashy post-1960s rock possible, is after all an expanded Top Ten list.

One reason it's so difficult to break the habits of value judgment in pop is that ordinary music lovers express their own experiences in those terms. Simon Frith has done more to unravel music's ties to identity than nearly anyone, and in his opus *Performing Rites: On the Value of Popular Music*, he asserts that deciding what's exceptional is always the heart of the matter: "First, it is clear that we need concepts of good and bad music even if we know full well that we won't be able to agree on how the labels should be applied." In Frith's view, such judgments are emotional and moral as well as aesthetic. The distinctions made by critics and average people alike reflect the listener's standards of originality, appropriateness, authenticity, and intelligence; arguing for those standards constitutes fanship and, for many people, identity itself. What we advocate is always, to our ears, extraordinary: "We all hear music we like as something special, as something that defies the mundane, takes us 'out of ourselves,' puts us somewhere else."[1]

But the process of forming identity is not a constant chain of exceptional moments. Nor is life as a music lover. What if the tendency to talk in terms of "good" and "bad" identifies not the ultimate truth about music or identity but a gap in the language music lovers have developed? After my time in those countless rooms of fans, I know that "good" and "bad" don't always matter in the heat of a musical connection, at least not in the way those terms are usually understood. When a woman swoons, enthralled, as Enrique Iglesias sings a ballad, she is not merely thinking, *Wow, this so outranks Ricky Martin's last one!* She's receiving some kind of sustenance or inspiration, despite the fact that by any critical assessment—even, perhaps, her own in a "rational" moment—the music is utterly banal. If that woman does later declare "Bailamos" great, that statement and its qualifiers allow her to enter into a social discourse that pop creates. But such judgments aren't adequate in capturing the full experience of loving music, which is as much about breaking down distinctions as determining them.

Actually, "Bailamos," or whatever represents your personal nadir in packaged pop, can't really be mediocre—with nearly 30,000 recordings produced each year, any one that makes it to the public's ear must possess some charismatic quality, puzzling as it may be. As critics and music lovers, we need a framework for understanding that nondescript essence. There needs to be room for the unexceptional in our thinking about music. If, to paraphrase Frith, music gives us a way of making sense of the world, then it must include utter familiarity and even tedium as well as revelation. We all know that music is the ideal vehicle for communicating exceptional emotions; perhaps its mediocre moments give the listener room to make sense of all that intensity. At any rate, ordinariness must be part of pop. Yet we who write about music have no way of expressing its subtleties.

Take one aspect of ordinary music: the problem of unoriginality. Or is it really a problem? Reviewers still commonly dismiss works as derivative, but culture producers have turned unoriginality to their advantage. The new paradigms established by dance music and hip-hop give the lie to the notions of romantic heroism that propped up classic rock. Sampling and remixing grant proud authorship to those most skilled at cutting and pasting, and digging in the crates has replaced bedroom riff memorization in the education of future superstars. Fresh girls Alicia Keys and Pink squeeze surprise from warhorses by James Brown and Diana Ross, as Britney Spears plays grown-up by donning Elvis's white suit and Joan Jett's black leather roar. This beautiful borrowing reaffirms that all music has come from other music, making neotraditionalism cool again and causing Bob Dylan, that old real McCoy, to grow a con man's mustache and call his latest album *Love and Theft*. Prometheus, stealer of fire, has replaced Orpheus, the transgressor, as pop's favorite god.

Chuck Eddy was on to this in the mid-1990s, when he called unoriginality the essence of rock and roll, writing, "I'd go so far to argue that more bands should rip off my favorite records."[2] Musicians themselves seem happy to fulfill his mandate. Covers albums abound, making influences obvious, and pop reconstructions such as the Verve's Stones-quoting "Bittersweet Symphony" and Mariah Carey's Mariah-quoting "Heartbreaker" laugh (or, after the lawsuit, cry) in the face of copyright. The Name That Tune game is an essential part of music expertise now, as the references that have always littered pop reviews become positively kaleidoscopic.

Borrowing has always been acceptable in pop, so long as it's done cleverly. It's triteness no one can tolerate: the embrace of the "easy," the obvious, or the familiar. Accepting unoriginality as either inevitable or virtuous seems to solve the problem, but while playing flip-flop with standards has become common in this era of Duran Duran tribute bands, I think most critics, myself included, almost always fail to take the needed extra step and revamp their criteria. Critics who say they love the packaged mainstream still seek innovation there. Taking artists seriously means uncovering their distinct contributions to pop's evolving language, celebrating how they tweaked it to "make it new."

Thus firebrands have declared that Shania Twain made country new by sexing it up with hair-metal guitars, that Mary J. Blige made soul new by singing like a man from a woman's perspective, and that even Creed made blowhard rock new by sandblasting that style's grand gestures until they shone clean again. (Okay, I'm the rebel behind that last one.) And everyone enjoys the way Timbaland, Missy, and the Neptunes prove that the sound of a million-seller can be lushly weird. Yet read through an issue of *Rolling Stone* or *Blender* and you'll still encounter the frequent use of the words *formulaic, cliché,* and *imitative* in negative reviews, and *startlingly new* and, yes, *original* in the positive ones. Beyond the narrow scope of reviewing, that old rock and roll standard of defiant novelty influences which artists gain critical and scholarly attention: Eminem, for example, and not his equal in cultural significance, J. Lo.

I've begun to wonder what would happen if the qualities of pop music that even populists normally disdain were given fair due. With rock so old that it's repeating itself repeating itself, and hip-hop entering its own early middle age, it's time to reconsider the relationship between the more esteemed aspects of creativity, such as innovation, eccentricity, and rebellious self-expression, and those normally derided, such as consistency, mastery of cliché, and the gift for fulfilling an established type. When less glamorous qualities are given equal weight within the pop equation, rather than being dismissed as a sign of middling ambition or failed talent, they soon reveal themselves as key to the pop experience. They serve their own purpose, and also play the essential counterpart to that relentless subversive thrust so treasured by rock and roll fans.

Unoriginality is pop's bread and butter, its safe haven, its base. Giving it credit means rethinking pop's basic function in people's lives. Music can still carry forth the messages of modernity—it can open minds to much more than new sounds—but it also serves as an antidote to the confusion change can bring. The nostalgic aspects of pop most obviously play this role—"Don't rock the jukebox," Alan Jackson sings, sounding a cautionary note against all those social forces rocking his world. But even, and perhaps especially, within songs that deal with change and confusion, unoriginality allows for a less disruptive, more absorbable experience.

"Music is our myth of the inner life, a young, vital and meaningful myth, of recent inspiration and still in its 'vegetative' growth," wrote Susanne K. Langer in her groundbreaking 1963 treatise *Philosophy in a New Key*. Langer used classical music to demonstrate how art can reproduce not just particular feelings but an entire morphology of feeling; that is, art reveals the shape and chemical content of anger, joy, jealousy, contentment. Emotion, even at its strongest, is not merely unsettling. It always has a side that's familiar, that calmer edge that allows the rest to flow forth and not destroy us. According to Langer, art, and particularly music, offers a reflective encounter with all sides of an emotion, its gasping breath in and its calming breath out. Music, she wrote, is "not transparent but iridescent. Its values crowd each other; its symbols are inexhaustible."[3]

Langer herself would probably be bemused to see her philosophy applied to pop; she was a formalist who believed that music's nonrepresentational purity offered a perspective on emotions quite separate from simple feeling. Her analysis dismisses as mere sound the expressive gestures of performance as well as essential popular musical elements like electric noise and distorted volume, and she had no use for lyrics. Yet bring Langer's music down from its pedestal, add in the "nonmusical" elements she found suspicious, and as a last step combine music with words, and her insight into music's ability to guide us through emotion's form and structure becomes extremely useful for understanding pop.

Contemporaries of Langer, including Raymond Williams and John Blacking, similarly saw music's potential to help listeners grasp the subtleties of emotion. It's hard to keep a handle on how this process works, however, when considering popular music, because the mountain of rhetoric about rock and roll's chaotic soul makes its more measured elements seem like negatives. What memorable songs offer, including banal ones, is a way not just to feel but to better grasp the structure of feeling, by re-creating the sense of becoming enraged, turning on, or falling in love. This re-creation is formal and visceral at the same time. The thrill of that ritual draws in the listener. But it's music's more grounding side that keeps us coming back—otherwise its violence would be too scary, too intense. And because those emotions can be overwhelming, sometimes they're most palatable when framed within something familiar. That's why dull songs mean so much.

It was a very ordinary song that got me thinking about all this. "Hanging by a Moment," by Lifehouse, is a dime-a-dozen midtempo ballad; there's always one of these hovering around the bottom of the Top Ten. Starting with a dropped bass line that you've heard somewhere before, the song is almost a round, it's so repetitive. The lyrics are standard loves-me-loves-me-not, delivered by the twentyish heartthrob Jason Wade in a quaver that gets louder but never bolder. The song surges forward like it's on training wheels, another anonymous power ballad from a not-so-secretly Christian band that suckled at the breast of Pearl Jam.

Two weeks after September 11, I stood in a New York crowd and watched kids cry and grin and sing along wholeheartedly to "Hanging by a Moment." I've been taught that it's the right kind of banal. It doesn't demand catharsis; it's gentle while being strong. The generic jangle-rock instrumentation creates a clear path for Wade's vocals, which order the song without pushing it. Describing the agony of unfulfilled young love, he rightfully sounds tremulous; the music's steady, reassuring drive makes the emotions the lyrics invoke bearable. The song contains the extremes of joy, resentment, and uncertainty first love stimulates, and the containment seems all the more profound when one learns that Wade wrote the song not for a girlfriend but for that ultimate hard-to-read lover, God.

"Hanging by a Moment" works a variation on the power ballad, the ultimate bread and butter form. But meaningful unoriginality factors into all forms of pop. Even iPod-toting snobs get hooked on stupid hits; the critical listener can determine when their seeming

staleness or corniness actually increases their power, providing necessary ballast against the forceful ambiguities at their core.

Different genres need their trite sides for different reasons. Hip-
hop "hardness," which can translate into flat rhymes and packaged
beats, offsets the tensions of a music exploring the tricky territory
of black masculinity and the battleground of sex. Country music's
sentimental melodies and Amerikitsch instrumentation equalize its
often maudlin explorations of a crumbling domestic sphere. And
teenpop needs its candy clichés more than any other genre, since
adolescence is all confusion, the time when music offers for many
the first map to adult emotions.

All of these genres have their own champions, who understand
the nuances of their formulas and can identify when they're being
put to best use. Some artists, however, still seem critically irredeemable, even under the shifted standards I'm suggesting. Sometimes a
song's popular ascendancy is not simply confusing to critics, but
horrifying. Despair sets in when one realizes that ordinary people crown their most treasured moments with renditions of "Wind
beneath My Wings." One particularly confounding example of mediocrity triumphing at a time of great consequence occurred when
Enya's "Only Time" became the unofficial anthem of the post-9/11
age.

Proud middlebrow that I am, I've enjoyed the work of this Irish
priestess. She's great for yoga class or any other formal moment of
deep relaxation. New age music, Enya's genre, is devoted to exploring music's functional qualities, its effects on the nervous system as
well as the soul, and within that definition she is an auteur. Even so,
she is the auteur of anonymity, creating sonic spaces of light and air
in which her voice plays the role of mist. To say Enya's songs all
sound the same would be to underestimate her devotion to consistency. It sometimes seems that she intends her music all to fade into
one massive minimalist project, an undifferentiated Orinoco flow.
Her journeys into monotony offer their pleasures, but they can't really be linked to established ideas of musical greatness.

Why, then, did people seek the soporific balm of Enya when the
Twin Towers fell? Because their souls were stabilized by the lunar

calm of "Only Time," the song that graced nearly every World Trade Center tribute Web site not bearing the national anthem, the song that makes many remember that burning even now. I lived through New York's darkest hour, and I would have thought I'd want fury, sorrow, something bigger than a drift of synthesizers and some platitudes. Yet the ascendancy of "Only Time" made sense to me, because at that moment real life's horrible contradictions demanded seamlessness—music as silence. I'm not embarrassed that America nourished itself on Enya's white diet after its largest modern disaster. I'm glad it existed for people to swallow, to fall into, a safe simulation of the void we all feared. Enya's profound unoriginality was a pathway to relief and a proper response to a time when silence was unbearable yet seemed the only appropriate response. "Only Time" will likely be forgotten to history—it's hard to imagine it's becoming an aural *Guernica*. Arguing for its greatness is not the point. Respecting its attractions is enough.

As the pop canon expands like the universe itself, heading toward infinity or implosion, even Enya and her equivalents will likely find thoughtful defenders. Yet we who stand up for the complexities of pop can all use to keep reminding ourselves of the importance of empathy, especially when considering music that seems instantly dismissible. I'll end these comments with an embarrassing example of my own.

I had serious doubts when the White Stripes began their rise to hipster world domination. In fact, reviewing them in one of those rooms crowded with rapt acolytes, I allowed disdain for both artists and audience to overtake me. These kids! I scoffed to myself. They're so green—not only do they not know the blues, they don't know white-boy blues, a style as old as Jim Crow and as perpetually risky to revive. The thrift-store collegians enticed by Jack White's Plant-ish yowls were so much like me twenty years earlier, though I had discovered this music mostly through the records of "originals" like Robert Johnson and Zep itself. They were like my little siblings who loved Jon Spencer in 1992, too. My hype allergy activated, I panned Jack and Meg.

They didn't go away. In fact, their popularity and credibility grew, and as irritating as I found it, I had to keep listening. It still all seemed redundant—the faux primitivism, the gender-switching covers, the red and black color scheme—hadn't the 1980s played all this out? Sure, the clatter offered pleasure and emotional release. But I remained disappointed—I expected mainstream music to thrive on unoriginality, but not the semi-underground.

Finally, just the other day, the White Stripes' latest release came blaring from the other room and something clicked. It's not like the music's innovation suddenly hit me. But the way the Whites were using the blueprints they'd inherited started to make sense. Their tightly wound, high-concept whack at the blues-rock legacy appeals to an audience for whom rock history was first a possession of their parents, then a used thing that couldn't stand up to the shininess of hip-hop. It's not that the White Stripes' fans have never heard the blues before; it's that they have heard it way too much, in beer commercials and Hard Rock hotel lobbies, and they love Jack White's bloody, irreverent, egotistical simulation because it acknowledges just how worn out this magic is. The relevant struggle in the White Stripes' music, the one that requires the element of unoriginality, is its love-doubt relationship with the history it assaults.

You can see how this approach to criticism might turn into a bit of a parlor game, a way of reducing songs to formulas of chaos and order. My thoughts here don't go far enough in exploring how unoriginality specifically operates, either musicologically or rhetorically; I'm just trying to encourage an attitude, a place to jump off. My White Stripes problem was a humbling reminder that even those of us who consider ourselves champions of the people can still unthinkingly limit the range of fans we really bother to try and understand. The fact that somebody out there loves a song doesn't mean I can't despise and eventually dismiss it. But it does mean I have to really think about what that song becomes when it's played in a crowded room.

chapter 18

Good Pop, Bad Pop: Massiveness, Materiality, and the Top 40

JOSHUA CLOVER

Everything's Different Now

Art forms tend to inherit ways of thinking and judging from older, similar forms, and it takes a certain amount of time to develop criteria proper to the new form. We haven't finished doing that yet for pop music. We still assume virtues that are by now anachronistic. The two I want to look at here are those of lasting value and difference; by the end I hope it'll be clear that these two assumed virtues are inextricable if not identical. It should take only a single gesture to shove them in the attic.

These are *assumptions* under consideration, not necessarily claims. Many music critics, especially those who follow the bouncing ball of cultural theory, would know enough not to announce their faith in such values: it would sound positively premodern (or "PreMo"). These are more like beliefs so naturalized we don't experience them as beliefs, even as they set the horizons of our analyses. The politically minded reader will recognize that as a definition of ideology.

What's meant by "lasting value" should be self-apparent. By "difference," a more culturally loaded term, I mean something rather simple: distinction, or that which makes one thing distinguishable from another. This will be divided, shortly, by ideas of meaningful and disingenuous difference.

The other bit of preliminary business is to define what I am calling pop music. Critics and fans will often forward some band as "pop" despite even limited cultural exposure, generally because of the way they sound (that is, the term is used as shorthand for "music that sounds like it *could* be popular," or maybe just shorthand for "somewhat Beatlesesque")—but herein I refer to songs that are actually popular; that is, music with the character of mass culture. So I really mean the Top 40, or something like it. Importantly, "pop music" is a metagenre: it's based on something anterior to musicological form and has included within itself, just to name a few genres, metal, fusion, punk, country, hip-hop, and tubthumping.

It's a recent enough metagenre that it's reasonable to worry the issue of what's particular to pop, what makes it itself and not something else. A strong parallel is film's inheritance of theater's critical concerns. The first generations of movie criticism were invested almost entirely in screenplay, mise-en-scène, and acting. There was a considerable span before the things that make movies movies—camera moves, montage, special effects, and so on—came to the fore. Tellingly, the most famous document concerning art in modern times—Walter Benjamin's "The Work of Art in the Age of Mechanical Reproduction"—concerns itself largely with film and the sea changes, both material and cultural, that underlie a panoply of modern forms, pop music not the least of them.

In tracing the shift from "the unique" to "a plurality of copies," and its concomitant "shattering of tradition," the landmark essay generates a remarkably common reading: that the essential change is from the organic-real to the synthetic-fake. This is perhaps simply because the distinction between organic-real and synthetic-fake remains deeply ingrained beyond the margins of Benjamin, and the

tendency to prefer the former (both aesthetically and ethically) is te-
naciously ubiquitous among the actual consumers of culture. Just
ask Alicia Keys and Milli Vanilli.

I'm going to return to the issue of whether the shift from organic-
real to synthetic-fake is entirely what's at stake in the "shattering of
tradition" that coincides neatly with the invention of mass culture.
But first I want to inquire after mass culture itself, and when exactly
its character came to pervade music.

'62: A Model Kit

1962. In the '50s, local character persisted; even after the rise of Elvis,
it was perfectly possible for the most popular song in St. Louis to be
relatively unfamiliar half a continent away. The music of your town
was still different from the music elsewhere. But fairly shortly thereafter, the *Billboard* charts could substantially reflect the soundtrack
of Anytown, U.S.A. Nonetheless, this date is a sort of comic answer,
especially since I don't mean organic-real 1962 but synthetic-fake 1962,
specifically a synthetic-fake 1962 small-town California summer night,
with autumn closing in. You could figure out the year easily even if
no calendar were in sight, because the night is filled with songs, and
the songs of latest vintage are the Beach Boys and Del Shannon.

There's a moment in this night when our heroes do this familiar
heroic thing: they travel vast distances, ford rivers and scale mountains, to visit a great sage and learn the meaning of life. Except in
the synthetic-fake Modesto of *American Graffiti*, the Dalai Lama is
Wolfman Jack, and he happens to be spinning the hits of the day
from a radio station on the outskirts of town ("XERB"—get it?).

The entire invention of mass culture, the mystery and anxiety of
it, unfolds in this moment. The Wolfman *is* mass culture: a bodiless
voice, everywhere in general and no place in particular, producing
the same hits and slang that unite all youths within fifty miles of any
relay tower anywhere. He is diffusion itself. The idea that he might
be an actual guy, who lives just down the road, is fantastical. It's
an impossible imagining, and its very impossibility stages the ur-
moment for which nostalgia always longs.

The film invokes many nostalgias: for an era, for the music of that era, for social and sexual innocence, and for adolescence as such, to name just the classics. It summons also more specific nostalgias—e.g., for an Edenic moment before the banalizations and homogenizations of mass culture turned every radio station into a Clear Channel, every Mel's Drive-in to a McDonald's.

Yet this moment with Wolfman Jack requires ghostlier demarcations. Its nostalgia is all the sharper in longing for a moment that can never be recovered, insofar as it never existed: the moment when we had all the good stuff of mass culture, without its afflicting the intense particularities of the local—as if there could be "pop music," but it could *come from your town.* One can see how this loads the movie's drama, about whether Steve and Curt will leave home to go to college in someone else's town. It's not just that childhood ends at the boarding gate. Maybe at the far end of that plane ride, the disc jockey won't even know about "Surfin' Safari" or "Runaway."

But if Curt Henderson's plane takes off from difference, it touches down in diffusion—in a world where pop music has reached its perfected form. Their DJ will know exactly the same songs, will in fact *be* Wolfman Jack. All there is now is the same songs. The music now comes from nowhere and reaches everywhere. That night—when infinite diffusion and intimate difference balanced one on each shoulder and no one had decided which was the devil, which the angel—is irrevocably gone. No, wait, I have to keep reminding myself: it never existed.

I promise you that when the perfectly nostalgic narrator of Bob Seger's "Night Moves" wakes in the middle of the night, with autumn closing in, it is in no regard by chance that he starts "humming a song from 1962." But what song is he humming?

The Land of Milk and Honey

One would like to imagine it was "Surf City," though that comes a year or two later; anyway, some song of abundance, even if it's the unjust and vacuous "two girls for every guy." The shift from scarcity to abundance, I would argue, is as much a part of Benjamin's "shattering of tradition" as the move from organic-real to synthetic-fake.

If you lived in western Europe's version of Modesto in, say, the twelfth century, you didn't encounter a lot of fresh material; the songs you knew had better be built to last. If you were very lucky, Marcabru would come riding through and teach you a new ballad, or perhaps William of Aquitaine's armies would annex your territory, leaving behind a handful of new lays composed by the troubadour duke himself.

But well before the twenty-first century dawned, there were hundreds and hundreds, and then thousands, of new songs every year, available to anyone with a radio. Don't like this one? We'll make more! *Love* this one? You'll hate it next week, but did I mention we were making more? At some point there were more songs than a person could plausibly listen to; at some point, driven into a kind of sensuous vertigo of consumption by the sixth or eleventh entrancing song they'd heard that day, someone thought for the first time that it might be swell if there were some way to listen to two songs at once. Impossible, but a tell-tale fantasy—a point of no return in the invention of the particular form of mass culture known as pop music.[1]

The shift from scarcity to abundance resides, fundamentally, within the concept of consumption—and mass consumption accounts for only half of mass society. Mass production offers its own historical shift, with its own shattering of tradition: the shift from diachronic to synchronic. These terms come from Saussure's discussions of linguistic change, but they're tremendously useful for the topic at hand. For a seventeenth-century drama to reach a large audience, to communicate to the many, it had to stick around awhile, possibly across generations. It's a diachronic form, happening over a span of time. A movie can present itself to 15 million people in a weekend; it really puts the mass in mass culture. Thus it is a synchronic form par excellence, revealing itself more or less in a single moment. The investors in a $100 million movie are unlikely to be interested in waiting several generations to recoup.

Crucially, it's the conditions that change, not the forms. That is, a play remains in more or less the same position it held before the appearance of mass culture–unless it's made into a movie. Material conditions don't change art forms; they call into being similar but new forms that take advantage of the new conditions.

It's essential to see pop music–the metagenre, independent of musicology–as a new form, not as a natural progression from many sources, from murder ballads, gospel, love lyrics, and the thousand other old forms whose traces can be found. Yes, those are all present. But for all that evolution, pop music is essentially a new animal. Tradition is shattered.

For a poem to reach 2 million Americans, it would probably have to last not decades but centuries, barring being read at a presidential inauguration. This has many aesthetic implications, which can be filed under the rubric of *durability*. It must have lasting value not because lasting value is a magically inhering good but simply to finish saying what it has to say–the pill that dissolves over centuries. That's an inescapable determination for diachronic forms. If *Nsync has something they would very much like to communicate to 2 million people, it's a matter of a single week. It isn't simply that an *Nsync song is not built to last but that, as a synchronic form, it has no need to be.

This isn't to say that there aren't pop songs that will last for centuries, or poems that are charming for a minute and just as quickly forgotten. But within their contexts of both consumption and production, the objects in question have different basic demands. In general, the idea that one would use congruent aesthetic criteria for scarce and abundant, or diachronic and synchronic, art forms is absurd.

Nothing's Different Now

Maybe the tune Seger was humming was "The Man Who Shot Liberty Valance," smash novelty song of 1962. It's an answer that would appeal to Theodor Adorno, who must always appear in discussions of music and mass culture in the dual role of angel and devil. He was contrasting "popular" and "serious" music as early as his infamous essay "On Jazz," on which he was likely working at the exact moment Gladys Presley was giving birth to twins; five years later he published "On Popular Music," detailing more directly the problem of what is charmingly translated as the "song-hit."[2]

"The whole structure of popular music is standardized," Adorno declared in 1941. This is in contrast to serious music, wherein each part goes toward constituting a holistic, autonomous artwork where "every detail derives its musical sense from the concrete totality of the piece." Serious music is a delicate relation of differences; change one, and "all is lost."

"A song-hit," however, is allowed only the most minimal difference. It "must have at least one feature by which it can be distinguished from any other, and yet possess the complete conventionality and triviality of all others." This is a familiar complaint about the Top 40.[3] All the songs sound the same. They're filled with clichés, assembled from prefab parts, all about the same thing—and as if that weren't enough of an insult to our discernment, the songs are also damned, through these very failings, as incapable of speaking to us about our own lives.

Adorno understands this not simply as an example of laziness or unoriginality but as a necessity of the form. Said distinguishing feature can be of any sort, for it has no aesthetic goal; it exists only toward "product differentiation," so that the song-hit in question can be "sold automatically, without requiring any effort on the part of the customer," immediately replacing the last, perfectly disposable song-hit.

One implication of this is that all song-hits are novelty songs, that their existence is provided by their capacity to signal newness and nothing else. This is worth considering, as it's not something we, as critics or fans, think we think. Certainly we recognize the existence of novelty songs, in which the element of difference is so exaggerated as to dominate the song rather than simply distinguish it: "Convoy," or that song where Serge Gainsbourg and Jane Birkin simulate orgasm, or anything with the phrase "fo-fana." Still, our concept of the novelty song suggests that it encompasses a relatively small percentage of Top 40 hits. Not "Say My Name," not "You Light Up My

Life" or "I Want It That Way." "Rapper's Delight" appeared as a novelty song before it became visible as the foundation of a genre; the same could be said of "Smells Like Teen Spirit."

That doesn't mean that we aren't as interested in difference as Adorno, even if we flatter ourselves that we are so *over* Adorno and his European elitism. I want to propose that we still basically employ his apparatus, having merely adjusted it to account for why we like a couple Top 40 songs.

Because this is not a survey, I don't want to cite a thousand reviews. This essay counts on an act not of faith, exactly, but of recognition, so it may turn toward the last act with some measure of timeliness. When people, including critics, describe why they like a hit single, they almost invariably appeal to exceptionality—to how the song at hand is not like the general run of popular music. This is so consistent that it seems positively natural. And the celebration of the exceptional is naturally connected to ideas of transcendence, or escapism, depending on the critic's mood. Anyway, unless we are admitting we like only novelty songs—and I don't believe that for an instant—we are simply displacing Adorno's logic (whereby the songs with significant aesthetic difference are the good ones) onto popular music. But what I've been suggesting is that this isn't natural at all; that difference is inextricably linked to lasting value; and that both are proper to a previous age, and to previous forms.

In this regard Adorno remains the devil, offering a reductive elitism disguised as aesthetic insight; our modification has been to discover upstairs and downstairs even in the house of Top 40, which one might have thought would have been cleansed of class division some while back. Still, Adorno will have his turn as the angel. If one takes even the much-reviled "On Jazz" in the context of his greater thinking, particularly the critique of the "culture industry" he and Horkheimer formulated in *Dialectic of Enlightenment*, it's clear he isn't writing about music but about economy and modernity. Popular music, and other products of the culture industry, with their standardization, specious distinction, triviality, and the rest, are meaningful for him insofar as they're reflections of, and producers of problematic social relations proper to late capitalism. That was a long sentence, but it's a long book.

And what I'd like to say is, he's right. And furthermore, in for a penny, in for a paving stone. If you don't listen to Top 40 radio because it's a morass of sameness and disposability, then don't waste your time demanding better songs from the back section of *Spin*. Put this essay down. Throw bricks through the windows of Bank of America and Niketown and Starbucks. Start now.

But before you head off to do some real culturework, I want to mount a defense of sameness. Adorno is great on modernity, but he doesn't handle modernism quite as well. Here I want to borrow a contingent definition of modernism from the art historian T. J. Clark: Modernism is formalism's response to modernity. Is it possible, one might ask, that the sameness of the Top 40 is not just a tale of commodities and reification but a formal, intransigent account of modernity?

I've Been Afraid of Changing

I wouldn't be the first to make such a claim. It is present, for example, in the work of Georg Simmel, who did a great deal of thinking about the social relations of the modern age. Here he summarizes the fetishizing of the idiosyncratic, the different:

> In order that this most personal element be saved, extremities and peculiarities and individualizations must be produced and they must be over-exaggerated just to be brought into the awareness even of the individual himself. The atrophy of individual culture through the hypertrophy of objective culture lies at the root of the bitter hatred which the preachers of the most extreme individualism, in the footsteps of Nietzsche, directed against the metropolis. But it is also the explanation of why indeed they are so passionately loved in the metropolis and indeed appear to its residents as the saviors of their unsatisfied yearnings.[4]

For "metropolis," read "mass culture" (a sort of secret metropolis, a distributed conurbation), and not much changes. The story is still of a new social formation defined by scale, density, and industry—in a word, modernity—that stands accused of homogenization, of producing legions of sameness where once individual difference reigned. *Once* is the key term, for such visionary gazes always glare back to before the shattering of tradition. And, as Simmel keenly notes, the residents of this modern world find great appeal in the call backward, as if it could satisfy all the desires not met by the new order of things.

That nostalgic leap is merely one of the directions in which such fantasies lie; utopia is always elsewhere. It's always outside, that is—like Adorno's serious art that perforce exists outside the culture industry, beyond, before, or in opposition to the quotidian depredations of the market, numbed tastes, and lowest common denominators. Hence the abjection of pop music, which by definition occupies the inside. It has only false differences. Sameness, mass culture, the modern—they all run together, and within that territory one finds the Top 40, with its ludicrous love ballads, hip-hop ego trips, and angst anthems.

And so in celebrating occasional song-hits, most pop music critics, walking the path Adorno laid out, trumpet how these select triumphs depart from the banal aesthetic turf generally enclosed by the hedges of Arbitron and *Billboard*. The songs are figured as successful exits from the morass of mass culture; the supremacy of serious art, of high culture, is implicitly saluted once again. But this doesn't account for what is specific to the art form of pop music, as opposed to symphonies or the still life. Given an abundance, a surfeit of songs, and absent the need for lasting value, one might expect that pop music would appear very much as it does: a series of repeated attempts at the best, most extreme version of a known form. The modality of the song-hit is not invention but intensity. In the terms of T. J. Clark, it would "*not* be the World Turned Upside Down [but] an imagining of the world as it would be if it were more fully itself—with its basic structures unaltered." And you shall know it by its hyperbolic scenarios, outsized expressions, and superfected sonic gestures.

Clark is not speaking of pop music; he's an art historian, after all. The writing in question concerns Cockaigne, a particular Renaissance imagining of a fantasy land of sensual surfeit. But Clark's is the most intense account of the popular urge not for great art that eludes the banalities of daily existence, but for a hyped-up quotidian, one that "dreams the impossible in terms of the everyday, but also—always—in terms of the everyday world's extremity, the way it every day never ceases producing the horrible, the preposterous, the luxuriant, the eternal." The Land of Cockaigne is, in its grotesque excesses and exaggerated pleasures, the land of the Top 40 as well: "The World the Same Way Up, Only More So."

One might accuse the Top 40 itself of a kind of disingenuous utopianism: the sounds and the stories do, after all, tend to be scrubbed clean of the blemishes, particularities, and complexities that lend daily life its imperfect character. But no one believes in the Top 40, just as "no one *believed* in the Land of Cockaigne. It was a (comic) thought experiment: not a vision, not a utopia (it did not posit itself as perfection nor as perfection gone wrong), not even really a wish-fulfillment. Wish-fulfillments do not spell out their absurdity as they unfold. It was a product of the oral culture of the European peasantry; and the legend's unseriousness, its cynicism and materialism . . . all tell something central about the texture of that culture."[5]

I do believe he's on to something. Cockaigne is not the empyrean of Dante or Milton; it's a popular conception, and as such less of a pure, ecstatically noble paradise. It's a place of pleasure more than ethics; the pleasures of the world, the same but more so. But if the Top 40 is to live up to this comparison, musn't it also tell us something central about the texture of our culture, despite the commonly held faith that it is defined by its failure to do so; despite its repetitions, prefabrications, and clichés?

To answer this question, I will have to stop wondering what song the narrator is humming in "Night Moves." No song can stand in for a year, for 1962 or 2002. Just as much, no one song can sing back to us the particularities of our lives, though some astonishing songs have died trying. I love individual songs, each of which remains for me a primal unit of pleasure, including every one I've mentioned. Even "The Name Game." But I'm always staggered by what happens if one listens to the Top 40 as a unit of communication itself—if one listens to the metagenre as a metanarrative.

It's not a story of transcendence, or escape, or difference; it's a story not just same but *about* sameness, told as much through rhythms and chord progressions and melodies as through lyrics. The story unfolds slowly, over an afternoon or a weekend at home or a week in traffic, as the collection of song-hits collates itself in your consciousness: a story shaped by relations that extend themselves to some all-too-near, all-too-human horizon of risk before returning to the security of the root form, a story in which moment after moment is rifted with yearning for change, dreams about transformative love and fame and transformation itself, yet the figures do not change much, must instead repeat the familiar joys and sorrows like, well, a broken record, and within that, find the pleasures available and keep going. That's a long sentence, but it's a long story; what's astonishing to me is how well it captures our lives, though we continue not to find ourselves there.

chapter 19

The Carly Simon Principle: Sincerity and Pop Greatness

CHUCK KLOSTERMAN

I spend a lot of time thinking about greatness. Now, this does not mean that I think *I'm* great, or that I have any intentions of *becoming* great. However, I am eternally fascinated by what *qualifies* something as "great," or—perhaps more accurately—what qualities make people *agree* that something is "great." And it's interesting how detached the second notion is from the first, particularly in pop music.

The attribute of "greatness" is the epitome of a subjective qualification, but the consensus on what's generally conceded to be "great" is remarkably irrefutable. *Bright Lights, Big City* is a great novel, and just about everyone seems to agree on that (sans the most elitist of literary critics). However, virtually no one classifies Jay McInerney as a great novelist, even though 99 percent of the people who make that criticism can't write at anywhere close to his level of proficiency. But both of those opinions are agreed-upon assumptions of greatness (or the lack thereof). There are film critics who despised *Dune* and *Wild at Heart* (Roger Ebert even dislikes *Blue Velvet*), yet if asked whether David Lynch is considered to be a great director, virtually all of those same critics would reluctantly say, "Oh, of course." Rarely do people classify Deep Purple as a great band, yet most would concede that "Smoke on the Water" has a great riff; nobody thinks Dexy's Midnight Runners was driven by great artistry, but everyone thinks "Come on Eileen" is a great tune to play at a wedding dance. I constantly hear people debating *degrees* of greatness (Zeppelin versus Sabbath, Kubrick versus Scorsese, and so on), but members of the intellectual community seem to be uncharacteristically compliant about who and what can (and can't) be part of such a debate. In fact, there tends to be more agreement about the vague, subjective topic of "greatness" than there is about what caused the Civil War, what killed the dinosaurs, and whether or not the White Stripes are actually related.

Then there's the relatively postmodern notion of critical greatness being detached from personal opinion, a schism that has always existed but, starting around the middle '90s, has slowly become the norm. There was a time when rock critics would advocate Bob Dylan, Bruce Springsteen, and Talking Heads as the most important artists of their respective eras, while noting—not coincidentally—that these were also their personal favorites. If a pop writer said a performer was great, one could assume that this writer was also a fan; conversely, any band cited as a personal favorite was supposed to be taken as worthy of being adored. I rarely see this relationship anymore. More often, I see *uber*-hip cultural commentators conceding a musical artist's greatness as a preface to mentioning how they find that music unlistenable (Radiohead, Eminem, System of a Down, Tori Amos, etc.). Even more common is the journalistic device of insisting that you earnestly love something (like Pink, Andrew W. K., or Destiny's Child) *because* they're not great—almost as if their lack of objective greatness makes them *better*.

Personally, this detachment has always made perfect sense to me, perhaps because Kiss is my favorite band of all time; it's never been difficult for me to separate what I like from what I know to be true.

However, I've often noticed that one criterion for greatness has never changed, and it's something I refer to as the Carly Simon Principle. If a musical entity aspires to unconditional greatness—be it a song, a band, or an entire aesthetic—it has to be grounded in some kind of espoused reality. And I'm pretty sure pop music is the only artistic idiom where this is true.

According to almost all mainstream cultural barometers, the *Godfather* films are just about as good as the cinematic art form gets. These are gangster movies, and they paint a portrait of the gangster experience. Yet no one discredits the films because Francis Ford Coppola, or Mario Puzo, or Al Pacino hasn't actually killed anybody. (This is especially odd when one considers that Coppola was central to the 1970s Hollywood auteur movement.) Stephen King writes horror novels, but nobody expects him to murder his family with an ax. *All in the Family* is viewed by some as the finest situation comedy ever produced, despite the fact that Carroll O'Connor wasn't really a bigot.

Now, I know all of this probably seems obvious and oversimplified, but it creates a weirder paradox than we tend to realize: in film, literature, television, painting, sculpture, and just about everything else that's viewed as artistic, "greatness" is derived from how creative something is; in modern pop music, greatness is derived from how creative something *isn't*.

Granted, there are exceptions—David Bowie's Ziggy Stardust phase might be the best dissenting argument—but it is true far more often than it's false. The classic example is Carly Simon's "You're So Vain." Certainly, this is a nice song by any gauge: good voice, great chorus, excellent use of the word *gavotte*. However, how much of this song's lasting "greatness" is directly related to the unilateral realization that it's about someone we supposedly know? (Probably Warren Beatty, although possibly Mick Jagger.) I would suggest that this is the single biggest reason "You're So Vain" is regarded as one of the greatest pop songs of the 1970s, even though it doesn't change anything about the actual product. I have never met anyone who didn't like this song more upon discovering that the track was directed at another celebrity; I've also never met anyone who didn't find Eric

Clapton's "Layla" more intriguing once they learned it was about George Harrison's wife. "Layla" profoundly benefits from the Carly Simon Principle; knowing who that song is about doesn't improve how it sounds, but it alters the perception of why it's worth listening to (or talking about). In a way, this is a microcosm of the connection between what we like and what we know: "You're So Vain" and "Layla" can now be appreciated for reasons that go beyond sonics. And that's ultimately what pop greatness is—forced transcendence. We force our understanding of what a song is supposed to mean into its notes and lyrics, and—when we play it back—we hear greatness for the first time. In rock music, the audience is always more important than the artistic product; that's why rock music is important.

Having been a pretty hardcore heavy metal fan during the 1980s, the first thing I do whenever I find a music guide or rock encyclopedia is check what it says about Guns N' Roses, since this usually tells me how reflective the guide's tastes will be of my own individual zeitgeist. In Ira Robbins's *Trouser Press Guide to '90s Rock*, the analysis of GNR is generally dismissive, but one positive sentence has always struck me: "Combining an incisive pop sensibility with a fist-pumping classic rock stance, *Appetite for Destruction* was probably the first *real* rock album that a lot of metalheads had ever heard." Fifteen years later, that's become the universal take on that album, and I wouldn't necessarily disagree if some bozo made this claim at a cocktail party. But what's weird is that I wouldn't disagree even though I know it's not true. When my metalhead friends and I first heard *Appetite for Destruction*, nobody commented on how "authentic" it was; nobody felt it was any more (or less) visceral than Motley Crue's *Girls, Girls, Girls* or Ratt's *Invasion of Your Privacy*. We just liked the songs on *Appetite*—better than everything else that was available at the time. It would have been more accurate for Robbins to say this was simply the first *good* rock album any of us had ever heard, regardless of how "real" it supposedly was.

A related sentiment was expressed to me by Jason Flom of Lave Records when I interviewed him about glam metal's ultimate destruction: "When Nirvana came out, they were just better than everybody else," Flom said. "It wasn't the cultural revolution everybody claimed. It was just better music." This is a deceptively bold statement, because it suggests that all those people who spent the 1990s writing about how Kurt Cobain saved rock 'n' roll by bludgeoning it with a dose of much-needed "reality" were kidding themselves; so far as Flom was concerned, the grunge explosion might never have happened if Trixter had released a totally killer album in October of 1991.[1] Now, Flom's hypothesis may or may not be accurate. But either way, I think it raises a valid question about what it means to call a band "real." From what I can tell, "real" translates as "great." Rock writers see those two words as synonyms. Cobain wore a flannel shirt, which is what normal people in Seattle wear, so he was real (and therefore great). Run-D.M.C. wore Adidas, which is what normal ghetto kids wore, so they were real (and therefore great). However, that's only how the equation is explained; that's not how the equation works. The members of Korn wear Adidas because that's what normal white suburban kids wear, but I never hear anyone telling me how great they are. The fact of the matter is that Nirvana made a record that critics liked and that kids loved—it was intrinsically great in a very tangible sense. But to explain that greatness, people tried to deduce what was real about it (and the most obvious thing was Cobain's shirt). Kurt Cobain's not great because he was real; he was real because he was great.[2] As a freestanding designation, however, being "real" is meaningless. Take Hootie and the Blowfish: all they ever did was watch *SportsCenter*, play music they adored, and embrace their own utter lack of cool. Technically speaking, the band was more real than Nirvana. But they were never great, and nobody (except maybe the cast of *Friends*) would claim that they were. This is another one of those things that everyone just agrees on.

Here's where the Carly Simon Principle really kicks into gear. Carly's song was about a living, breathing man, but—at this point in time—that doesn't really matter. We're going to hear reality in that song, because we've already conceded that it's great. As the audience, we create our reality; we're the creative force in this sonic transaction. There was a time when Fleetwood Mac's *Rumours* was just seen as an album that sold incredibly well; over the past five years, though, it's become more acceptable to classify *Rumours* as great in and of itself (VH1 ranked it as the sixteenth-greatest album of all time). And as more and more rock historians call *Rumours* "great," the more I hear them discuss how that album is the soundtrack for the erosion of love and a metaphor for how people viewed the normalcy of divorce and self-preservation during the late 1970s. That's the New Reality of *Rumours*. And that reality is true, I suppose, although nobody seemed to care about the psychosocial meaning of Stevie Nicks until we felt the need to convince ourselves that she was so damn important. When explaining why *Rumours* sold 18 million copies, all you needed to say was, "Well, it has some really likable songs, especially on side two." That's more than enough of an explanation for popularity. However, that's no justification for greatness.

An even better example of the Carly Simon Principle might be the difference between Britney Spears and Madonna, a pair who are often compared for the sole purpose of contrast (and generally to the benefit of the latter). Musically, it's difficult to make a convincing argument that the early years of Madonna's career were significantly stronger than Britney's first three albums; it's hard to find a reasonable, objective adult who finds either catalog stunning. Yet Madonna was on the cover of *Spin*'s fifteenth-anniversary issue and the very first performer profiled in its "Heroes and Anti-heroes" section, and she has become another one of these agreed-upon icons of greatness. That may eventually happen to Spears—it's still too early to tell—but something about her will have to change. And what will need to change is the belief in her artistic sincerity, which is currently nonexistent.

Not long ago, I was asked to write an essay about Britney, loosely built on the premise that she represented an emerging sexual duality (put simply, Spears is the first artist to consciously and overtly dance and sing like a slut while aggressively—and openly—marketing her virginity). From a commercial perspective, this is brilliant; it allows Spears to sell her entire identity the way Brooke Shields sold Calvin Klein jeans. The "virgin-whore" contradiction makes her musical product desirable to multiple demographics and it keeps her persona fascinating to the media. However, that dichotomy hurts her chances of becoming "great" in the omnipresent, publicly consensual sense, which is how Madonna is embraced by just about everyone (critics, academics, Camille Paglia, even people who don't own any of her records).

Madonna apologists would say she represented ideas about sexuality and feminism that had never been seen before, and that her greatness is social and cultural and empirical. But what Madonna technically said as an artist—and the way she played with sexual stereotypes—wasn't that radically different from anything Spears has done. Madonna didn't write "Like a Virgin" or "Material Girl." Some faceless dude came up with those phrases, just as some faceless dude came up with "Hit Me Baby (One More Time)" and "Oops I Did It Again." But the difference is that we thought Madonna somehow meant her words, even though they weren't hers. Nobody believes that with Spears.

"Pop artists used to want people to buy the image they presented," said Larry Flick of *Billboard* when I asked him about Britney. "I mean, Madonna really wanted people to believe she was a big old whore. Britney wants people to think there's no relationship between her real life and show business."

In the short term, that's fine; modern teenagers are amazingly adroit at making that kind of distinction. But this will hurt Britney in the long run. And if future revisionists eventually conclude that . . . *Baby One More Time* is an underrated classic, they'll be forced to find a realism we're all missing in the present. Perhaps they'll try to convince themselves that they hear realism in the delivery of the lyrics, which is almost as good as discovering that they're autobiographical. There's no air-tight argument as to why Carole King's "It's Too Late" (cowritten by Toni Stern) is a greater song than Journey's similarly fictional "Don't Stop Believin'," but everyone seems to agree that the former is a classic and the latter is cheese. Why? Because King does a better job at replicating sincerity. It's the same thing with political bands. Were we really supposed to believe that MC5 and Rage against the Machine wanted to overthrow the government every night they went on stage? Evidently, yes. And that's obviously crazy. But if an audience truly believes the artist felt that

way once, they're willing to hear the rasp of anarchy on the eighteenth night of a thirty-three-show tour, even if that rasp is really
just a sore throat. You have to convince most people of something
only once; after that, they convince themselves. Rock realism is self-
perpetuating.

So what does this ultimately mean? Perhaps this: songwriting is a
creative process, and live performance is a creative act, but pop music
is not really a creative art form—at least not in the same sense as the
other cultural idioms we normally associate with that term. The
creativity of rock and pop comes from its audience; in the larger
scope of experience, fans of a band like Hole are much more creative
than Courtney Love. They take the raw product of her trivial songs
and—assuming they believe those songs to be depictions of reality—
construct their meaning as something important. In rock 'n' roll,
the value of something (or someone)—the greatness—is *designed* by
the people who want to consume that greatness. But they need to
start with something (or someone) they believe to be sincere. In the
minds of both underwhelmed rock writers and wide-eyed teenagers,
the art of myth making always needs to reflect life. Otherwise, it's
just a collection of popular, likeable sounds.

Which brings us to Moby.[3]

As I type this essay, I have been paging through the March 17,
2002, issue of the *New York Times Magazine,* that publication's annual music issue. Moby just happens to be on the cover, and there's a
profile of the artist inside. Much to my surprise, in analyzing the significance of Moby's use of sampling, author Gerald Marzorati directly addresses the issue I've been writing about:

> The problem such thievery presents to the mainstream popular-
> music culture is its transgression of that most cherished of youth
> (read: chief music consumer) virtues: authenticity. Pop music
> musicians since the '60s have been expected to (or at least ex-
> pected to *appear* to) write or sing wholly original songs, prefera-
> bly drawing on or, anyway, aligning with their own experiences;
> play their own instruments, unless they are singing; and live in
> some unwavering countercultural or subcultural or teen-cultural

way commensurate with the music they play. Even in hip-hop, where sampling began more than 20 years ago, there remains an impetus to "keep it real."

Marzorati brings this up because these are all things Moby does not do. "I don't have too many issues with authenticity," the bald one says. Critics of Moby would certainly agree with that sentiment, citing the fact that all eighteen tracks on his *Play* album were sold to at least one TV show, commercial, or movie. What's even more egregious to some (though I personally find this kind of fascinating) is that he says he hopes his 2002 follow-up (a record titled *18*) will be consciously marketed to soccer moms (!), whom Moby sees as an untapped market.

Now, whether or not Moby's strident unreality is admirable or tragic doesn't really matter to me. However, I do think it will be important to see if Moby can translate what Marzorati calls his "21st Century Paradigm" into the classic definition of pop greatness. Yes, he moves product (*Play* sold 9 million copies). Yes, he's sort of a genius (at least in a technical, production sense). But at the moment, most of Moby's support comes from one of two sources: sophisticated hipster contrarians and people who don't really care about the music they listen to. He's loved by people who listen to music in order to define their coolness, and he's loved by people who just want background music. But will a guy like Moby ever appeal to the kind of people who want (and maybe need) music to change their life? Will he ever be important to those vast unwashed masses of the populace who ultimately decide which songs become transcendent pieces of our sonic culture? To be honest, I sort of doubt it. In the grand scheme of understanding our reality, Carly Simon will stomp the shit out of him.

chapter 20

Groove as Niche: Earth, Wind & Fire

ROBERT WALSER

"People tell me all the time: 'We got married to this music.' And I'm like, married?! OK, then: did you listen to the lyrics? If I was a lady, I wouldn't want to go to bed with somebody that just said that these reasons were a lie, they had no pride, they'd disappear, I'm in the wrong place to be real with you; I mean the whole thing, come on."[1]

Singer Philip Bailey marvels at how perversely Earth, Wind & Fire's fans interpret the band's ballad "Reasons," and he's right; even the most cursory consideration of the song's lyrics reveals its subject to be immediate physical desire, accompanied by open doubt about the long-term viability of the relationship and even a frank prediction of shame come the morning. What these fans have understood as a romantic accompaniment to their marriage vows is perhaps the most beautiful, persuasive, and thrilling tribute to a one-night stand ever crafted.

But the literal meaning of the lyrics doesn't much matter, because listeners aren't analyzing poetry, they're identifying with the music's rich sensuousness, the passion, vulnerability, and earnestness of Bailey's voice, his sustenance of desire and straining for transcendence. It shouldn't be surprising that people would prefer to experience these things rather than the cynical sentiments sketched by the lyrics, but it does remind us that we often too easily equate meaning with language. In fact, within the conventions of a certain historical context, the lyrics describe a problem for which the music enacts a solution.[2]

This is by now a familiar argument: that music is a means of signification, and that its processes and details can therefore be a source of knowledge. Yet it continues to be a point that is worth emphasizing, given the current state of popular music studies. For despite the many valuable things that are done by journalists and scholars in cultural studies, American studies, English, sociology—and, for different reasons, ethnomusicology and music theory—they don't usually talk about music in this way. It seems to me that this is precisely where those of us who are committed to what might be called musicological modes of scholarship ought to be taking our stand.

It's not a forthright and stable stand, to be sure—more like a game of Twister. With our right foot planted firmly on the blue dot of musical signification and our left on the red spot of historical perspective, we must somehow also reach our left hand to the yellow dot of social analysis and place our right hand on the green dot of ethical criticism. And before we know it, the spinner of disciplinary progress calls out a command and we must stretch and shift.

The music of Earth, Wind & Fire often depends for its most profound meanings on the repetitive patterns of rhythm, harmony, and counterpoint we call grooves. We have inherited a lot of thinking about grooves—and the repetition that is at their core—that will not, I believe, much help us understand their power. From Adorno's denunciation of repetition as fascistic mindlessness, to Barthes's celebration of *jouissance,* to Lacan's dialectic of repetition as mastery and loss of subjectivity, the focus has been too individualistic. Even

Richard Middleton, the musicologist who has written the most and best on repetition in popular music, addresses the topic in terms of the individual subject in isolation, in terms of the profoundly atomistic traditions of philosophy. But when musical grooves are cut off from the dialogic relationships that produce them and mark even private experiences of them, thinking about repetition circles endlessly and unpleasurably.[3]

But there has also been some tremendously useful and provocative work on grooves done from a variety of subdisciplinary perspectives, for which reason it has rarely been considered as a whole body of thinking on the topic. John Chernoff's theorization of music as a means of socialization, first of all, highlights dialogue and interaction to portray repetition as a means of building a richer social environment. Christopher Small extends this idea to analyze all aspects of music as contributing to the experience of ideal social relations. Michael Bakan confirms the broad relevance of this view in his analysis of how Balinese drummers prize virtuosic interpersonality as the basis of rhythmic success.[4]

Charles Keil and Steven Feld's 1994 collaboration *Music Grooves* put the word *groove* on the scholarly playlist with their insights into how we might learn about rhythmic patternings by tracking their subtle changes against their regularities. Feld's theorization of "lift-up-over-sounding" among the Kaluli people of Papua New Guinea tracks a specific cultural groove ("in synchrony while out of phase") that articulates meaningful responses to features of the natural environment in which the Kaluli people live; their grooving is shaped by the bird songs they hear, and the way the dense forest refracts sound.

Ethnographic work with jazz performers confirms that grooves are interpersonal, interactional processes.[5] And in his analyses of popular songs, David Brackett foregrounds social competence, the idea that a groove exists only if audiences know how to recognize and respond to it. Ethnomusicologist Thomas Turino made similar points about repetition, using Edward Hall's notion of "being in sync" to gain insights into Peruvian music: "Music and dance bring the state of being in sync—of being together—to a heightened level of explicitness. With each repetition of a piece . . ., the possibility of 'being in sync' is extended and the social union is intensified, contributing to an affective intensity. In such contexts, extended repetition does not lead to boredom: it is the basis of aesthetic power."[6]

I would similarly argue that in music such as that of Earth, Wind & Fire, grooves establish rhythmic relationships that are experienced as qualities of motion and structures of feeling. They are sometimes regarded as the underpinning for lyrics or other more easily analyzed forms of signification, but they are in fact more fundamental than that. Music without words (either entirely or momentarily) is still music; words without music are not. For an enormous range of styles, grooves are the primary source of music's affective response, and thus of its cultural power. A groove seems to furnish in sound a special kind of niche for the listener to occupy: a way of being, a path for moving, a means of relating, a place of ideal existence, an environment.

As Anne Danielsen writes in her pathbreaking dissertation on James Brown and Parliament: "When in a funk groove, the experience of time is—somewhat paradoxically—not really an experience of time. There is no distance to the events: one is continuously engaged in the co-production of gestures; there is a total presence in the groove. Time dissolves. Repetition never becomes repetitive. The distanciation required for time and repetition to become time and repetition for us does not take place."[7] When we are in the experiential niche enabled by a groove, in other words, we are experiencing one version of the ideal social relationships that Christopher Small theorizes as the purpose of all musicking. This way of understanding repetitive musical patterns reminds us that the whole idea of "musical structure," which has come to seem so natural to us, is in fact a spatial analogy that can seriously misrepresent temporal experience. Music is far less a static, mechanical object than a place to be, a context for relating, a niche.

This complex way of understanding a groove is not generally a part of the relevant critical discourse, with the result that a group such as Earth, Wind & Fire has been nearly written out of popular music history, despite their artistry, originality, and popularity. David P. Szatmary's widely used rock and roll textbook has no entry for the group in its index. Paul Friedlander's narrative history mentions them only in passing, within a list. The *Rolling Stone History of Rock and Roll* includes the band's name only within a quotation from rival funk entrepreneur George Clinton. There is no mention of Earth, Wind & Fire at all in *The Oxford Companion to Popular Music*.

There are those who have taken critical notice, and written positive evaluations, however brief. Writing in *The New Rolling Stone Record Guide*, Dave Marsh credits the group with "some of the most joyous moments in modern music." *The New Rolling Stone Encyclopedia of Rock* calls them "innovative yet popular, precise yet sensual, calculated yet galvanizing."[8] Yet *Rolling Stone* magazine itself never covered the band in a way that was commensurate with their popularity or commercial importance—more than 20 million albums sold and constant, successful touring through the second half of the 1970s and beyond. By one account, in 1978 they were the most popular band in the world.[9] But if a group of musicians succeeds in touching so many people so deeply yet garners only vaguely approving reviews or is even ignored, it suggests that we have not yet developed a language for understanding what they did and why people cared about it.[10]

Worse, there were those for whom Earth, Wind & Fire stood for all that was wrong about popular music: in *Rock: The Rough Guide*, they are described as having achieved an "over-reaching funk-pop-jazz synthesis with smarmy production values and cloying lyrics," their "hokey African-roots schtick" appended to "saccharine self-sufficiency lyrics."[11] This sort of response is not really shocking, given the history of rock criticism, and to account for it is not difficult: many rock critics value cynicism more than sincerity, artificiality more than artifice, negation or irony more than affirmation, anger more than love.

Robert Christgau, obviously moved by some of the band's grooves, nonetheless is annoyed by their lyrics and polish; he gives their first best-of collection an A— but backhands them: "Ten exquisitely crafted pop tunes in which all the passion and resonance of black music tradition are blended into a concoction slicker and more sumptuous than any white counterpart since Glenn Miller."[12] And this response reminds us that analysis can never be solely concerned with its object; it also always tells us something about the analyst and the community that is being addressed. It also raises questions about race, among other things, that deserve complex answers. What exactly is this "black music tradition" that was gussied up and, perhaps, betrayed? "Black music" and "American music" are not easily distinguished from each other, as no less than Amiri Baraka pointed out in a criticism of his own book *Blues People,* and questions of who has inherited what cannot be assumed to be answered by what Paul Gilroy calls "raciology's destructive claims."[13]

Consider the complex musical identity of Earth, Wind & Fire's leader, Maurice White. He grew up in a world filled with music and dancing, his grandmother a gospel singer and his Memphis environment clamorous with the sounds of blues, jazz, and country, Mahalia Jackson and Elvis Presley. He soon encountered the music of Ray Charles, James Brown, Fats Domino, Little Richard, and doo wop groups like the Spaniels, the Platters, the Moonglows, and the Flamingos. Later on, White studied Miles Davis, Coltrane, Bach, Mozart, Sly and the Family Stone.[14] For five years, from 1962 to 1967, he was the house drummer at Chess Records, backing such musicians as Etta James, Howlin' Wolf, and Sonny Boy Williamson. He then spent three years in the funky jazz trio of Ramsey Lewis. Finally, White formed his own group—the Salty Peppers. This was eventually changed to Earth, Wind & Fire because "somehow the name 'Salty Peppers' didn't feel universal enough." White found a kalimba in a Chicago music store, was attracted by its "Africanness," and taught himself to play the "thumb piano" in funky Afro-diasporic settings.[15]

Or consider co-lead singer Philip Bailey, who joined Earth, Wind & Fire after leaving a Denver cover band that played songs by Blood, Sweat, and Tears, Three Dog Night, and Carole King. The mélange of influences that Bailey, White, and others brought together was fused into what the band regarded as a bold new attempt to combine Miles Davis's hipness, James Brown's black consciousness, and Sly Stone's pop catchiness.[16] This was sensed by some critics, who credited them with tearing down musical barriers, calling them "the Black Beatles," though others somehow concluded precisely from their eclecticism that they were not original, that they "never set out to break any artistic barriers."[17]

Earth, Wind & Fire developed a complex identity, partly through sartorial innovations: "We were the only group wearing tights, platform shoes, and no shirts; and our audiences were hip, young, black and white." And their reception was also affected by the place of their home base in the American imagination: "When we started to become big, a lot of media thought we were kinda 'woo-woo,' real Southern California. Some folks thought we were pretentious. The truth was, I [was] writing about my life. There were people who relied on us for the message: we had a responsibility to our community."[18]

The band's members conceived of their mission in very different ways. Maurice White felt that he was carrying on the legacy of great jazz musicians such as Davis, Coltrane, and Monk, and that his music was important because it was a positive response to a messed-up world: "There are a lot of things wrong on this planet—starvation, poverty, negative thoughts, racism, a lot of weirdness. So somebody has to communicate something to try and balance that, if it's possible."[19] In the band's video documentary White added: "Music has always been sacred to me." Verdine White, the bassist, emphasized both the music's ability to affect a lot of people personally—"people fell in love on our music"—and also its resonances with the Civil Rights movement, with freedom and risk. Drummer Fred White was pragmatic about the band's technical prowess, linking it both to black masculinity and to a meritocratic musical culture where race doesn't matter: "The objective was to be the best band in the world, bar none." Other musicians, such as Ralph Johnson, stressed the social and personal good done by the music: "There's something that people pick up on when they hear these songs that helps them get through the day." Philip Bailey was proud that audiences recognized their music's "sincerity and realness"; following Stevie Wonder, he valued their ability to speak for people and have them recognize it.[20]

This rich array of perceptions challenges us to reach not for singular, correct meanings but rather to include these actually existing cultural complexities in our analysis. Theorizing in static, individualistic ways about one-dimensional identities won't account for this music. Instead of assuming that we know what is meant, thought, and signified by "a black musician" (or "a white critic"), we need to pay sensitive attention to the complexities that constitute lived lives and cultural contexts.[21] Paul Gilroy argues that music such as Earth, Wind & Fire's reflects "the desire to find a new political and ethical code in which the contradictory demands for blackness on one side and postracial utopia on the other could be articulated together under the bright signs of progress, modernity, and style."[22] Yet my own response to Earth, Wind & Fire over the years has not been simply a "problem" of cross-cultural or cross-racial identification, since Maurice White and I have many of the same cultural heroes, black and white. We share certain ideas about masculinity (for better or worse). We both like horns. We both hear in this music the performance of values to which we respond positively and on behalf of which we dedicate our professional efforts, and it is to the issue of values that I want to turn next.

Much of the power of Earth, Wind & Fire's music results from its affirmative strength and celebration of community. Certainly people identify with such music at the levels of the genre, the band, the concert, the album, but at the level of the individual song, there is much work to be done in analyzing the particularities of different grooves. Unlike the funk of James Brown, which is often harmonically static or blues based, many of Earth, Wind & Fire's songs are based on a groove that is complex both rhythmically and harmonically. "September," for example, exemplifies what Anne Danielsen calls the "song vs. groove tension," the tendency for grooves to locate us within an endless, repetitive but rich present moment, as opposed to the song's tendency to pull us through a series of events: verse, chorus, bridge, and so on. The basic groove in "September" is a four-measure pattern, used with only slight changes for both the verse and the chorus. Harmonically, it cycles around the circle of fifths in reverse, seeming to be goal oriented yet moving further away from the tonic through the course of each measure.[23] We hear this cycle three times before we suddenly land on the tonic–but it appears as a dominant seventh chord, simultaneously confirming a point of arrival and pointing beyond it toward the next cycle. Thus harmonic details contribute much to a sense of purposeful motion that remains open-ended and dynamic.

The lyrics similarly sketch an affective state of having it both ways: they are nostalgic about the past while still suggesting that the present is better. Vocal syncopations against the groove and pervasive call-and-response patterns create a rich social environment, where, as John Chernoff has written in comparing European with West African social ideals, society is not conceived as constricting individual freedom but rather makes that freedom possible. The voices soar over the groove, without which they would have nothing to celebrate and transcend, no social context to give shape to their individual impulses and make them meaningful.

Strength and celebration of community are often taken to be values that are essentially good, yet of course they needn't always be. Consider what might well seem the musical antithesis of Earth, Wind & Fire, the racist, "neoclassical gothic metal" white power song "Might Is Right" by Rahowa (the band's name is an abbreviation of "Racial Holy War").[24] There are obvious contrasts with EWF's music: Rahowa celebrates force, not love, white racism rather than an inclusiveness built around Afrocentric pride and generosity. Rahowa constructs a ponderous, monolithic sound instead of one that is polyphonic, dialogic, and polyrhythmic.[25] They are rather more vulnerable to criticism at the level of musical craft; from the meritocratic point of view of a musician such as Fred White, they command less respect, no matter how effectively they fill their performative niche.

There are, however, important similarities between the two. Both strive to articulate an ideal community, as they quite differently conceive of it, offering the powerful experience of a groove, of being in sync with a crowd of like-minded people. Both evoke historical precedents (ancient Rome in one case, Egypt in the other) to add mystical depth. Both work to produce grand, dynamic music to infuse their visions with power. All of which underscores the point that moral issues cannot be decided at the level of musical form or procedure.

My colleague Mitchell Morris has recently called for musicologists to make clear their ethical investments, particularly with respect to philosopher Charles Taylor's analysis of the features of the modern self: atomistic individualism, disengaged instrumental reason, and expressivity of an internal deep self.[26] Such an analysis lays the groundwork for answering some of the fundamental questions that Christopher Small has posed: "Each question about the value of a work of art is in reality a double one. We ask not only what there is about the work of art that makes us want to treasure it but also what there is about us that we should want to do the treasuring."[27] With much popular music, we enjoy the sense that we are expressing a deep self at the same time that we feel we are resisting, contradicting, or even affirming the other features Taylor identifies, individualism and rationality.

Music doesn't in fact resist; it can't. But while musicking we can assert and confirm alternatives as well as what is dominant. Punk doesn't resist capitalism or fascism; it affirms anarchy or socialism. Earth, Wind & Fire doesn't resist atomistic individualism or racism; they affirm an Afrocentrism that is not separatist. Rahowa responds to some of the same conditions in ways that are not entirely unlike, though only a criticism that admits to no moral basis whatsoever could fail to distinguish between them. By following Morris and Small in calling for ethical criticism, I don't mean to tell punk or metal musicians that they should be making more loving music when the musical, social, and ethical materials they have inherited don't easily lend themselves to such statements. But we can recognize and value loving music where it exists, all the more powerfully if we admit our ethical positions. This is not easy to do, and neither is it easy to analyze musical meanings in ethical terms. Popular musics have often been denounced according to simplistic perceptions of violence or other qualities that are deemed socially negative.

Consider the Earth, Wind & Fire song "Fantasy," which contains punches on the last sixteenth note of each measure that are in some sense as violent as anything I've ever heard. But although everyone on stage tenses up with that frightful jerk just before the downbeat of every measure, they do not allow it to disrupt the groove: their social coordination goes on.[28] And when they pull out of that single-chord groove into the verses and choruses, we find the same kind of purposeful harmonic motion, a longer, eight-measure romp through the circle of fifths with a couple of tricky moves that land us on the dominant to set up the repeat.[29] Although the mode is minor, the lyrics celebrate liberty, equality, and fraternity no less positively than "September" seemed to, but the song presents a more obviously negative environment (through its mode and the violent punches) over which the soaring vocals, purposeful chord progression, collaborative repetition, and peculiarly loping groove enact perseverance and harmony.

Earth, Wind & Fire's music includes a wide range of grooves, each offering a different quality of motion, a different experience of bodily action and social interaction. Take "Serpentine Fire," for example, which includes within its groove an extraordinary number of levels of rhythmic motion operating at the same time. There is a slow basic beat, emphasized with huge downbeats and backbeats at the quarter-note level, but the keyboards and guitars stress the eighth-note level with their choppy patterns. Meanwhile, the vocals and the bass work primarily with sixteenth notes, while the horns chatter away with fills in thirty-second notes.

All of this constructs an extraordinarily spacious groove, where there is room for anything to happen, even while the collective control of so many simultaneous rhythmic levels constructs an experience that is oddly tight and secure, too. In concert, you can see each musician choosing one or more rhythmic levels to articulate through bodily motion, and the audience is free to do the same.[30] The band's athleticism, and its balance of free individual motion with coordinated dancing, support the music's negotiations of individual and social identity in a way that recalls gospel music's ecstatic reconciliation.

There are limits to Earth, Wind & Fire's vision, of course. Although millions of women have been powerfully moved by it, its production has been exclusively male, and homosocial. It is profoundly artificial, since it takes discipline, work, and hierarchy to create such experiences of freedom, play, and equality. And it is historically fragile. Philip Bailey sees a shift in social values over the course of the band's career: "We came up in an environment where it was a little more community-minded. It was the in thing to be spiritually searching, to be aware of one's self, one's environment, one's humanity. We came along in a time when all that was fashionable and our message was in keeping with all that stuff. I don't think it would fly so much today because it's just become a me/mine society: Get yours, forget everybody else."[31] Touring recently without Maurice White (on a tour sponsored by Viagra), the band played many private parties in the homes of very rich people, selling affirmation to those who need it least because they've already inherited it.

In his recent book *Freedom Dreams*, Robin Kelley argues that any improvement in our lives "must begin with thought, with how we imagine a New World, with how we reconstruct our social and individual relationships, with unleashing our desire and building a new future on the basis of love and creativity rather than rationality." Similarly, Craig Werner has written that Earth, Wind & Fire, like Bruce Springsteen, Stevie Wonder, Bob Marley, The Clash, and Al Green, "refused to accept the idea that the dream had always been a lie." Or as Greg Tate put it in a discussion focused on racism: "If we don't exercise our capacity to love and heal each other by digging deep into our mutual woundedness, then what we're struggling for is merely the end of white supremacy—and not the salvaging of its victims."[32]

I mean for this essay to contribute to a defense of affirmative culture that is not uncritical but that also does not play along with the hip cynicism that is the dominant tone of so much writing about popular music. Writings of that sort serve to reinforce the disengagement of which Taylor wrote, fail to account (except misanthropically) for why some people respond powerfully to certain performances and others do not, and categorically dismiss musicians who affirm in favor of those who protest. Such protests can, paradoxically, lead to disengagement and acquiescence, while affirmation can make starkly clear the deficiencies of the world we live in. As Maurice White put it: "It's so tough out there and people are looking for more. They want more, and without sounding preachy, I hope our music can give them something positive . . . some encouragement and peace."[33]

chapter 21

Unpacking Our Hard Drives: Discophilia in the Age of Digital Reproduction

JULIAN DIBBELL

When I was starting out as a pop critic, back in the twilight years of the vinyl LP, a certain dubious scientific factoid circulated more or less unquestioned in my professional circle. According to a report I don't think any of us had actually seen, researchers had established that when monkeys were exposed to round, black plastic objects, they got erections. Never mind that anyone who's been to a zoo knows monkeys get erections about pretty much anything. We cherished the report not because we believed it told the truth about monkeys but because we knew it told a kind of truth about us: that our attraction to records wasn't simply an attraction to the music they contained. It was a passion, erotic at heart, and like all such passions it approached the soul of its object through the body. We had hardons for the hardness of records; or not to be phallocentric about it, we quickened to their touch, to the sight of them, to the thought of picking them up at the record store and taking them home with us.

We still do, I believe. CDs don't have quite the voluptuousness of LPs, certainly, but they're shinier and cuter, and if it's only the collector whose lust for them approaches the pornographic, I'm confident there remains a dash of the erotic in even the most casual of record purchases. What I'm not so sure about—and the question I want to pose today—is what becomes of this kind of eros when its once-solid object begins to melt into digital air. Can the erotics of pop consumption, in other words, survive when records live unseen and untouched on our hard drives, and if so, how? Where is the love in the age of the download?

What we need to do first if we're to start answering these questions is to look closer at the nature of the love in question. Having failed to track down that monkey-boner report, I turn now to a perhaps less conclusive but probably more productive text: Walter Benjamin's brief essay "Unpacking My Library: A Talk about Book Collecting." I look to Benjamin mainly because I know of no other writer who has thought as deeply and as feelingly about the relationship between modern individuals and the artifacts that modernity piles up around them. But there's another reason: twenty years ago I had my first encounter with Benjamin, refracted in the pages of Simon Frith's *Sound Effects,* and what I read then has had an almost totemic place in my thinking about media and culture ever since.

What I encountered was Frith's reading of Benjamin's best-known essay, "The Work of Art in the Age of Mechanical Reproduction," which is a kind of reverie on the radicalizing potential of the technologies of mass reproduction. For Benjamin, both the beauty and the tyranny of the traditional work of art lay in what he called its aura: the halo of authenticity generated by its uniqueness in time and space. The technology of the copy, he argued—of the photograph, the phonograph, the cinema—had effectively shattered that aura, removing artworks from the ritualized contexts that secured their meaning and letting them into the daily lives of ordinary people, where, as Frith put it, their "ideological meaning was decided in the process of consumption."[1] Pointedly contrasting Benjamin's enthusiasm for mass media with the sour pessimism of Benjamin's friend Theodor Adorno (who essentially saw the relationship between the culture industry and the culture consumer as one long, miserable episode of *The Prisoner*), Frith located in Benjamin a politically redemptive argument for pop music as an arena of cultural struggle, from which liberatory meanings were as likely to emerge as repressive ones. And as a nineteen-year-old pop critic wanna-be and budding cultural democrat, needless to say, I thought that argument was the shit.

Not that that would be worth mentioning in the context of this discussion, except for the fact that a lot of other people seem to have thought just as highly of it back then. Since reproduced in hundreds of doctoral dissertations, journal articles, and coffeehouse conversations, the argument, in its broad outlines, is now almost invisible to us as the founding assumption of cultural studies, but in 1982 it still had the force of revelation. And if it no longer does, I'm here to suggest that familiarity is not the only reason.

For now, I'll proceed by taking note of the damnedest thing: of the basic points on which "The Work of Art in the Age of Mechanical Reproduction" rests, "Unpacking My Library" essentially disavows the lot. Where the first essay proclaims the death of the aura in the era of the copy, this one reincarnates it, insisting that each copy too has its halo of uniqueness, generated not so much by the copy itself as by the unique history of its passage through the market to the consumer. *"Habent sua fata libelli,"* Benjamin writes, explaining that the phrase, which translates as "books have their fates," is usually interpreted to refer to the fates of particular titles—of the *Divine Comedy*, of Spinoza's *Ethics,* of *The Origin of Species.* "A collector, however, interprets this Latin saying differently. For him, not only books but also copies of books have their fates. And in this sense, the most important fate of a copy is its encounter with him, with his own collection."[2]

What excited Benjamin as a book collector, then, was not the words his books contained so much as the indissoluble blend of content, craft, and wear and tear that told the story of each book's journey to its place in his library. He loved their bodies, and more than that, he loved what was uniquely, irreplaceably *authentic* about them, which was above all the fact that they had come into his possession. "The most profound enchantment for the collector," he writes, "is the locking of individual items within a magic circle in which they are fixed as the final thrill, the thrill of acquisition, passes over them."[3]

Let's leave aside the contradictions for now, though, and assume that Benjamin has a meaningful handle on the nature of the collector's passion. How does what he says help us answer the questions we set out to pursue? Simply, it suggests that our response to the physical presence of records—again, as distinct from their musical content—is nothing so elementally carnal as a simian stiffy. What's erotic about records, rather, is our possession of them—a possession secured and signified by the physical solidity of the disc yet at the same time firmly embedded in an abstract, socially constructed system of property relations.

In short, there are some very tricky libidinal mechanics going on here, and I don't claim to know precisely how the erotic energy they generate functions within the larger political economy of pop music. Is it the record market's motive fuel? Or merely a by-product? Like I said: no idea. What I do claim, though, is that the eros of possession is central to how we feel about and how we make sense of popular music as the last half-century or so has defined it. Just as the sale of records lies at the heart of music's economy, so the acquisition of records, I'll argue, lies at the heart of its meaning.

Of course I'm aware that there are extremely significant modes of pop consumption that don't require the purchase of records. There's radio, for one. And there are dance clubs. But listening to radio, let's face it, is just a dance itself—a flirtation with the unfamiliar, enjoyable and exciting in the way of all flirtations, but only insofar as it carries the risk of leading to the deeper emotional commitment of a record purchase. And as for dance subcultures, well, there's a reason they're called "sub," isn't there? Where many of modern pop's musical antecedents were essentially just accompaniment for the more culturally central act of dance, today any scene that rates dancing as more central than records automatically slots itself into the cultural margins, often as not drawing its own dose of libidinal energy from the thrill of the outsider status thus conferred on it.

If you take exception to the cultural picture I'm drawing, though, let's not quibble. Because my next claim is basically that this is all headed for the dustbin of history anyway, and soon. Yes, I know you've heard it all before: the Napster-headed hipsters sitting naked at their PCs spamming chatrooms with the news that the record is dead, the record industry doomed, and the people's republic of free music waiting in the wings.

But if that's one part of the story, there is another. The banner of revolution has been brandished so flamboyantly by the advocates of Napster and other online file-trading systems (in the wake of Napster's famous legal defeat, the wily, thriving Kazaa currently reigns as the record industry's public enemy number one, to be replaced in time, no doubt, by some new entity even more resistant to legal attack) that it's easy to assume their opponents are reactionaries. Nothing could be further from the truth, though. The record industry wants a revolution, too; just not the same one. Celine Dion fans got a glimpse of it in early 2002, when the singer's aptly titled album *A New Day Has Come* debuted as one of the first digitally locked-down CDs on the market. Designed not to function in hard drives, the CD also crashed many computers in which it was tried—an unintended side effect, surely, but not a lot more invasive than the ways the record industry *does* hope to control the mechanics of digital consumption. Records that play on one machine and no others, that play in one geographical market and no others, that require payment for every month of play, for every week, for every single listening—these are all technically achievable possibilities awaiting only the cooperation of electronic hardware manufacturers and/or the mandate of well-lobbied legislatures.

The endpoint is a vision of the pop fan not as consumer but as tenant farmer, never owning anything at all, never enjoying any uses of her music, fair or not, except those the record company explicitly grants. Techno-anarchist claims to the contrary, the technology of digital networks makes this utopia of the marketer just as feasible as Napster's utopia of the consumer. As usual, it's not technology but political and cultural struggle that will determine the winner.

And who will that be? Your guess is as good as mine. But since there's virtually no constituency for the technological status quo—or rather the status quo ante Napster—you're pretty safe betting on one revolution or another to win. Maybe decisively, and maybe soon, but more likely after long, protracted, and ultimately not quite entirely resolved cold war–like coexistence.

Any way you slice it, though, what matters for our purposes is this: neither of these revolutions makes room for the category of possession in its understanding of the pop consumer's relationship to music. And so, after a century of comfortable residence at the heart of pop meaning, the simple act of purchasing and possessing a copy of a piece of music—your very own, to have and to hold—is packing its bags.

Benjamin, too, had his good-byes to say. "I do know"–he wrote in the final pages of "Unpacking My Library"–"that time is running out for the type I am discussing here."[4] In an age of mass publics, he conceded, the book collector's intimate possessiveness seemed more and more a relic, out of sync with the spirit both of commercially driven spectacle (like the movies Benjamin admired) and of civicly responsible archivism (like the libraries and museums he depended on). Convinced that his species was headed for extinction, Benjamin allowed himself one consolation. "Only in extinction is the collector comprehended," he wrote, and if, as he further argued, collectors knew the inner life of cultural objects better than anyone else ever could or would, then perhaps it was better that the collector be comprehended than that he survive.[5] Extinct, the collector's privileged knowledge could be, as it were, donated to science—dissected and laid out in less passionate but more intellectually useful form, much as Benjamin's essay itself proposed to do.

And if that consolation was enough for Benjamin, then shouldn't it do for those of us who now will mourn, in whatever small measure, the end of record collecting as we know it? We may soon forget forever what it was like to lust after round, black plastic objects, but let's keep in mind that we have never been better equipped than we are right now to grasp the meaning of that lust. As the physical reality of records fades away, their social reality grows starker, lit up in the glare of the digital music wars. We see more clearly now what has always drawn us to the recorded object, and lo and behold, it's the same thing Benjamin recognized, in spite of himself, as the source of the enduring aura of the copy: its status as property.

This may seem rather an obvious attribute to zero in on, and yet, as the media theorist McKenzie Wark has lately observed, a full half-century of otherwise politically sophisticated cultural studies has more or less defined itself by overlooking the obvious.[6] Why, Wark asks, has the Marxist-inspired media and cultural theory of the twentieth century—from Gramsci and Adorno up through the late canonical cultural studies of Raymond Williams, Stuart Hall, and company—so studiously skirted what Marx and Engels singled out as the focus of all truly democratic critique: "the property question"? Why, even as the information economy was coming into its own, did these thinkers focus so emphatically on information's function as a shaper of consciousness, more or less ignoring its function as a piece of property?

There are answers, of course. The economic reductionism of Marxist orthodoxy, after all, was precisely what the culturalists sought to escape; their entire project rested on the notion that culture had a life of its own, not quite independent of political economy but autonomous enough to need explaining in terms strategically remote from the economic. And as long as the economics of information were still overshadowed by those of industry and agriculture, it was easy enough to believe that the forms and ideas of culture circulated through a system ultimately separate from, however intertwined with, that of the commodity.

But nowadays that's a harder trick to pull off. As Disney, the RIAA, and other lords of intellectual property press on with their enclosure of the cultural commons, as copyrights, trademarks, patents, and brands become pivotal assets in every economic sector from higher education to the soybean market, it grows increasingly difficult to remember how I—how any of us—could have thrilled as we once did to the politics of pop consumption. Yes, to repeat the mantra, it's true: consumers wrest their own meanings from mass culture every time they pull one of its products into the context of their lives. But just as cultural technology once made this insight possible—just as the age of mechanical reproduction, that is, ushered in a new understanding of the work of art—so now technology has rendered it a bit jejune. The age of digital reproduction is upon us, and its lesson seems to be that it was never enough to ask who makes the meaning of a work of art. We first have to ask who owns it, because as Benjamin, unpacking his library, also tried to tell us, it's in possession that the power to make meaning first flowers.

He did get one thing wrong, though: the collector wasn't headed for extinction quite so soon. New media begat new passions, the book hoarder was joined by the record hound, and the erotics of consumption continued to thrive. Should we, then, trust our own intuition that with the digitalization of all media the jig is finally up, that no eros can survive the dematerialization of its object?

Once upon a time I might have thought so. But a couple years ago I saw something in a college dorm room that suggested the shape of consumer passions to come. What I saw was a pirate's treasure: a thick loose-leaf album stuffed with some three dozen naked CD-Rs, each one burned with about a hundred MP3 files. The boy who showed me this trove had gathered its roughly 350 LPs worth of songs over two years of assiduous downloading. He was a warez trafficker, a member of various groups dedicated to moving pirated digital goods—software, games, movies, music—as fast as high-bandwidth Net lines allowed.

"The zero-day scene," he called it. "It's a competition. A race to see who can get the latest stuff up first. Way it works is, say some CDs are being released tomorrow. These groups have people that go out, buy these CDs, or get them however they can, rip them, and then put them up on our site."

The boy talked fast, his knee bouncing with nervous energy. I could see in his eyes, and in the hasty ballpoint scrawls with which he'd labeled the MP3s in his binder, that it wasn't the songs themselves that interested him, it wasn't even how many he had. What he collected was the speed with which they'd traveled from their corporate origins to his computer. His lust was attuned to their fluidity, not, as in Benjamin's case, to their history. The whole obsessive idea, in fact, was to compress a record's history to nothingness, to a vanishing sliver of time: zero days.

But the erotics of piracy corresponds, of course, to the corporate revolution. It's a romance of resistance, necessary perhaps as a response to the fantasy of total control, but something in the vibe of the jumpy pirate boy told me it was the kind of passion that burned you out quick. Wasn't something more sustainable a possibility? I couldn't picture it, but then I hadn't seen Napster yet. Nobody had. And once I finally did, the answer was easy enough to make out. Without the physical body of the disc to rub up against, without the economic muscle of the corporation to throw itself at, a post-Napster consumer erotics comes to rest on the body of information itself.

This may sound like metaphysics, and maybe it is. But it should be clear by now that the eros I'm talking about doesn't need a physical object as its focus. All it really needs is something to push against, some resistance, and in the absence of the physical, legal, or economic variety, there remains always the brute chaos of information to overcome. "There is in the life of a collector a dialectical tension between the poles of order and disorder," wrote Benjamin, and those who've found themselves at play in the fields of the post-Napster perplex can tell you there's pleasure to be found in that tension.[7] The pleasure of sorting, finding, pursuing memories or schemes. It can be as simple and schematic as a kind of musical trainspotting, as, for instance, setting yourself the task of downloading every Top Ten single from the last ten years' worth of *Village Voice* Pazz & Jop critic's polls. Or it can be something subtler, a pursuit of pop epiphany through the thickets of oblivion and vague recollection.

What do I mean by that? Maybe something like this:

One warm May afternoon two years ago I heard coming out of a passing car three seconds or so of an old familiar song—the words "Why waste your time, you know you're going to be mine" repeated over an ecstatic *Psycho*-esque shriek of synthetic strings—and I had to hear it again. I couldn't remember the song's title or the group's name, but instead of the gnawing unease this might have caused me in previous years, I felt a tingle of anticipation. As soon as I got home I tossed the lyrics I'd heard into Google, looking for a clue. I got zero hits. Then I pared it down to "Why waste your time" and got 1,100. I scrolled through 200 of those before finally scoring a relevant link: to an Ace of Base discussion board where, three months earlier, one Alex Schmelkin had posted the exact same question I was pursuing. There were no answers on the board, but I e-mailed Mr. Schmelkin and learned that someone had eventually sent him an additional lyrical snippet or two, including the phrase "I'm gonna get you, baby." I plugged that into Napster and—bingo!—within a few seconds I was downloading my very own copy of Bizarre Inc.'s 1992 dance floor hit "I'm Gonna Get You." I proceeded to have almost as much fun listening to the song as I had finding it.

Would Benjamin have recognized in this networked treasure hunt the same "thrill of acquisition" that drew him to book collecting? Maybe. Maybe not. But he was attuned enough to the centrality of the property question, I think, to have recognized in the mirrored figures of the knee-jiggling warez pirate and the butterfly-chasing Google surfer the yin and yang of all genuinely revolutionary politics: the negative energy of resistance and the positive reach toward utopia. For in the end what rises from the struggle over online music won't be just a new legal and commercial structure but a new structure of feeling—and if anything is going to save us from living in the corporate design for that structure, it won't be the posturing of technolibertarians or the lobbying of activist lawyers or even, as I might once have believed, the quotidian pop poiesis of consumers. It might just, however, be the passion of collectors.

chapter 22

Lost in Music: Obsessive Record Collecting

SIMON REYNOLDS

Until recently, I'd never thought of myself as a collector—I'd always reserved that word for people who cherish rare artifacts like coins, stamps, antiques. The stuff that I hoarded I conceived of more in terms of material with use value, whether that was pleasure or research.

But at some point I couldn't help noticing that after more than twenty years I'd stockpiled a pretty immense personal archive of cultural artifacts. First as a fan, and then as a rock critic, it seemed normal to live surrounded by stacks of records, some binge-bought for "research" but never played even once; books, piled up like good intentions; most recently (a worrying development, this) vintage music magazines. The collection had gotten so large that I wasn't using more than a minuscule fraction of it at any given point (especially as a substantial portion of it resides in a storage unit in central London and has essentially been inaccessible for the past eight years while I've lived exclusively in New York). And it had started to exert a sub-liminal, oppressive pressure on my mind, possibly related to reach-ing that ominous point in your earthly span when you start to grasp the fact that you don't have enough life ahead of you to listen again to all the records you own.

Most people don't amass sound like this. Your average record collection numbers in the scores or hundreds, not thousands, and there's a haphazardness to the way it's accreted: lots of semitrendy albums bought while at university, a few token classical and jazz CDs, maybe an obscure world music cassette heard at someone else's dinner party. Generally you won't glean much sense of a journey through taste, an attempt at defining a self through aesthetic choices. Typically there'll be a definite cutoff point, when the intake of new music tapers to a trickle. Or less: my parents' collection abruptly ceases circa 1965 with a Dudley Moore Trio album.

Obviously not a matter of genetics or upbringing, my compul-sive hoarding of records can also only partly be explained by my vo-cation. Getting sent more records than you can physically listen to is an occupational hazard for rock critics, sure, but long before I be-came a "professional fan," I was bringing home more music than I could process: taping albums from public libraries "just in case," buying new records that to this day remain in the shrink-wrap, com-pulsively stopping to flick through a cardboard box of secondhand LPs being hawked on a street corner.

And yet the fact is, I dwell on the lowest slopes of collector mania. I've never bought a bootleg, never spent more than twenty pounds on a single item of vinyl, I have no interest in records that are "collectible" per se (limited-edition picture discs, foreign ver-sions, etc.), and I am not fixated on a specific genre whose every third-rate manifestation I obsessively track down. My "sickness" is an omnivorous craving to explore virtually every avenue of sonic plea-sure or stimulation, be it 1970s U.K. folk-rock, modern Jamaican dancehall, musique concrete, or ethnological field recordings.

For real behavioral dysfunction, check Evan Eisenberg's clas-sic book on "phonography," *The Recording Angel*, where there's a chapter on Clarence, an obsessive collector of interwar 78-rpm records, who's frittered away his inheritance and now subsists on social security, in a freezing-cold house whose every available surface is cluttered with teetering towers of shellac.[1]

Twenty years ago in Oxford, a friend of mine had a similarly demented approach to record buying. In the first week of term, Steve would spend his entire student grant, every last penny, on albums. In collector terms, he was way ahead of his time, purchasing Arthur Lyman's faux-Polynesian easy-listening classic *Taboo!* a good fifteen years before "exotica" became fashionable, and anticipating the current vogue for field recordings with LPs like "Venezuelan Vomit." This was our nickname for a document of shamans tripping out on the hallucinogen DMT—a record whose howling and mucoid retching became a favorite party soundtrack. These gems of vanguard taste were accidentally discovered, as Steve in his indiscriminate buying frenzies would trawl in all manner of tat and piffle: brass bands, Highland jigs 'n' reels, nursery rhymes. His potlatch heedlessness also came through in his utterly nonfetishistic relationship with vinyl. His floor was covered shin-deep in an undulant morass of unsleeved albums, layered like shale. Eventually, when he had to move in a hurry, the collection was divided up, cached with different friends, ultimately forgotten.

Voraciously "oral" in his buying habits, Steve wholly lacked the other side of the chronic collector: the "anal" obsession with storing, preserving, organizing, classifying. In Ian McEwan's short story "Solid Geometry," the emotionally starved wife of a repressed antiquarian insults him, accusing him of "crawling over the past like a fly on a turd."[2] (In addition to the property-feces link, McEwan adds more heavy-handed Freudian symbolism: the collector's prize possession is a pickled penis.) Serious collector culture—the world of record fairs, pricing guides, discographies, auctions—is the kingdom of flies. When I open a magazine like *Record Collector* or *Goldmine*, I feel queasy—this is passion misdirected, a monomania that began with pure devotion but has somehow detached itself from the actual original object and become a locked groove, a treadmill of runaway desire.

Here you find the completists who accumulate every single thing that a band has put out (remixes, B-sides, mono seven-inch mixes from the sixties) plus anything in bootleg form (outtakes, demos, unofficial live albums). Nutty behavior, from my p.o.v., but still vestigially about the music: the desire to hear every variation, every version. Beyond lies the realm of pure commodity fetishism, the sados who collect every last format and packaging incarnation: colored vinyl, promos, Japanese editions, and so forth. Deeper still into the mire of anality, there's the trade in ephemera: concert programs, tour posters, badges, press kits, tickets, promotional items, spin-off merchandise. There are individuals who sell videos that compile every last TV appearance made by the band in all territories of the world.

There is something redolent of the medieval traffic in sacred relics here, although these are mass-produced copies rather than material shards of the divine being itself. Perhaps, by accumulating as many different instances of a given recording as possible, the fan seeks to compensate for the loss of "aura" through mass production? Fred and Judy Vermorel, pioneering analysts of fandom, would diagnose obsessive collecting as one form of "consumer mysticism"—the literal idolatry of pop stars.[3] Collecting is a surrogate for connecting, a fantasy of total possession through hyperconsumption.

Mind you, collectors tend not to resemble Saint Theresa that much. Keeping any gushing mystic tendencies tightly leashed, they talk a drier, droning language: for instance, collectors are always complaining about a dearth of "documentation." Enthusing about a live Vibrators album recorded in 1976 on a portable cassette player "and frankly sounding like it," a *Goldmine* writer argues that "so many of rock 'n' roll's crucial moments have been lost forever, that, even if this were absolutely unlistenable . . . its existence would still be a cause for celebration."[4] This is the reductio ad absurdum of the documentarian pretext.

"Lost moments, captured forever" is the big lure behind bootlegs, along with the notion that the definitive versions of songs occur in performance rather than in the lifeless studio environment. A few artists do endlessly and significantly rework their material onstage, like Bob Dylan and the Grateful Dead (who encouraged their audience to tape the shows, thereby creating a massive trade in tapes). But most rock bands aren't capable of, and aren't particularly interested in, improvisation; they essentially aim to replicate as closely as possible some definitive Platonic form of each song. The fans who scroll down the tiny print of whole-page ads in *Goldmine,* checking out the 117 Springsteen boots offered by a single dealer, are clearly motivated by something else. There's a sort of redundancy at work here, a syndrome of reconsumption. It reminds me of those Roman feasts where gluttons would withdraw to the vomitorium midbanquet to regurgitate the first six courses, in order to make room for more of the same.

This stalled and stagnant desire, self-trapped in closed loops, is at its root motivated by a fear of change, of time itself. It's almost like a form of cultivated autism, one symptom of which is an obsessive need for things to stay the same. There's something idiot-savant too about the way collecting involves the accumulation of data as well as artifacts: catalog numbers, changing lineups, the locations and dates of gigs, the details of recording sessions. Fan sites on the Web often list every gig ever performed by a band—say, the Fall—complete with the slightly different set list of songs played on each occasion.

In the U.K. they call such hypermeticulous and data-hoarding fans "trainspotters," after the teenage boys who spend the day at stations collecting the serial numbers of locomotives. Trainspotter means someone who's missed the point and is engaged in pointless if busy and unstinting activity. There's an argument about trainspotterhood, what you might call the Hornby Thesis: that it's basically a way for emotionally repressed males to relate without really relating. Whether it's sport or music, these external obsessions provide men with a "legitimate" outlet for passion—something they can get worked up about emotionally, even shed tears over, while steadfastly avoiding the real world of sexuality, love, relationships. In his novels *Fever Pitch* and *High Fidelity,* Nick Hornby offers a critique—a partial self-critique, in fact—of masculinity in retreat from the mess and risks and compromises of adulthood into a more orderly, organizable world of obsessive consumption.

I had avoided the book for fear it would prove too close to the bone, but *High Fidelity* the movie slipped through the barricades. Sure enough, the John Cusack character, with his alphabetized collection, agonizing over the sequencing of mix-tapes and endless Top 10 lists, did resonate uncomfortably in a sort of there-but-for-the-grace-of-God way. Still, the movie's denouement was depressing, the predictable closure of normative hetero coupledom implying that emotional maturity entails putting obsessions in their place. Actually, most of the avid collectors I know are married or involved, hardly running scared from intimacy or commitment. If their collector selves represent a form of arrested adolescence, this is a protected zone of retardation (a sort of "nerd-life sanctuary") that runs in parallel with their "real," relatively emotionally mature lives.

Elizabeth Wurtzel has argued that women would do better to develop more "impersonal" obsessions, as opposed to those related to appearance, health, relationships. In effect, she has suggested provocatively, women would be happier if they were less like Bridget Jones and more like the trainspotter protagonists of Nick Hornby's novels. It's not that women don't collect stuff—vintage clothes, dolls, knickknacks, books. The number of women involved in book collecting has risen dramatically in the past two decades, according to John Gach, an American dealer-collector of psychoanalytical texts.[5] Maybe the same thing will happen with records: witness the steadily rising number of female DJs (the DJ being the ultimate curator-turned-creator).

For now, though, it's true that record collecting remains overwhelmingly boys-own: just check the gender imbalance at your average record fair. If there's a distinctively masculine "sickness" here, it's perhaps related to the impulse to control, contain, master what actually masters, ravishes, disorganizes you: to erect bulwarks against the loss of self that is music's greatest gift. Or is it the other way round: collecting as a perverse consumerism, a literally consuming passion that eats up your life? Music is conventionally regarded as the soundtrack to one's life: the favorite song as commemoration, a Proustian rush. For collectors, the obsession increasingly becomes independent of anything going on in their life. Collector friends, I've noticed, tend to narrativize their collecting, talking about turning points, the records that "changed my life": meaning both that their ideas about music were transformed and that new vistas of obsessive consumption were opened up.

So the obsession operates as another life running in parallel to the putatively "real" one. On one side, the life of loves lost and kept, family tribulations, "civilian" friendships; on the other, the world of music. One collector acquaintance talks about "the thrill of the hunt"—a buzz that is actually more rewarding than finding the vinyl grail in question (which may never get played more than once or twice). *Goldmine*'s name evokes the idea of prospecting or looking for treasure, and another collector pal describes tracking down specific records in terms of "dowsing": being attuned for vibrations, going out on a quest for one elusive record, "and it's almost manifested itself in the store." Record collecting lends itself to serendipity: its intensified version of everyday consumerism is the epiphany-rush of spotting something of value amid a pile of dreck. This momentary thrill often exceeds actually playing the record in question. For collectors the tensed anticipation of the search becomes an end in itself. Even the physical toil—the crouching, bending, flicking, the dust and discomfort—is part of the tension-release rhythm.

Hard-to-find becomes the definition of desirability (the obvious analogy here being "hard-to-get"). When arcane records become easier to obtain through being reissued on CD, they lose something of their allure—and not just for reasons of hipster elitism. Rare records, in their very scarceness, have recovered some of the specialness lost to mass-produced, commodified artworks. This is why collector crazes for specific genres or eras have an in-built dynamic that drives them up an exponential curve of esotericism. The cults for sixties garage punk or Northern Soul began with the rediscovery of a genuinely neglected style. But as the market for rare records develops its own momentum, dealers need to keep finding new "lost classics," while collectors want to believe that buried treasure still exists. Original copies of third-rate records go for astronomical prices, while the reissue programs and retro compilations start dredging up justly forgotten dregs. This happened to the garage punk compilation series *Pebbles*, which was essential up until about volume eight, then took a nosedive into no-fi, clone-of-clone amateurishness, stuff that never should have been let out of the garage. And it happened with psychedelia, with dealers hyping such Johnny-come-lately U.K. acid-rockers as Grannie and Dark, whose early seventies albums originally came out in private pressings of a few hundred or less. Amazingly, collectors gull themselves into coughing up sums between $1,000 and $2,000 for original copies, based on little more than rumors of greatness.

Some modern genres of music—Japanese neo-psych noise, New Zealand drone-rock, the outer fringes of postrave electronic music—exploit the obscurer-than-thou collector mindset by producing small-pressing releases in unusual formats: gatefold double-seven-inches, three-inch CDs, ten-inch singles, one-sided records with designs engraved into the other side's vinyl. As with impossibly rare records from the past, these ultralimited releases with their eccentric, often handcrafted packaging pander to a sort of anticonsumerist consumerism, driven by a longing for the aura of the unique and the one-off.

True record collecting, though, is about old stuff; it must have that whiff of necrophilia. There's a downtown New York record store called Wowsville! that's like a mausoleum of rebellion. The store resembles the deluxe interior of the Cramps' collective brain: every form of long-dead bad-boy music, from rockabilly and surf to sixties garage and seventies punk is there, along with trash aesthete talismans like Russ Meyer and Elvis kitsch. It's a particularly vivid example of the way people set up shop (literally, in this case) in some sealed region of music history, and insist that after a certain point, everything turned to crap. One example is Terry Zwigoff, director of *Crumb* and *Ghostworld* (the latter features some hilarious scenes based on the musty milieu of jazz/blues/ragtime collectors, who pore over dusty 78s and squabble about "incipient cracks" in the shellac). A collector himself, Zwigoff believes that 1933 is the cutoff after which radio and record created an ever more homogenized music culture that wiped out any regional eccentricities.[6] In sixties Britain, there was an entire youth movement, "trad jazz," based on this premise. And for every forward-looking subculture, there's been another timewarp tribe—from the Deadheads to that contradiction in terms, the mod revival—nostalgic for something they never actually lived through.

I never thought it would happen to hardcore rave, the first subculture I'd ever participated in while it was still in its prime, a little less than a decade ago. Hardcore was probably the most future-focused, neophiliac music scene ever. All genres, though, inevitably reach that midlife crisis when the early days start to look better than the present, when it feels like the music took the wrong path. And sure enough, around 1997, people started talking about "old skool hardcore," waxing nostalgic for a lost golden age that had peaked only five years earlier.

"Old skool" comes from hip-hop but has disseminated throughout pop culture as a shorthand term for notions of origins and roots. In addition to the epigonic sense of the present as less distinguished than the past, old skool usually contains the idea that an ignorant and insufficiently reverent generation has emerged, one that needs to be schooled in historical arcana and foundational principles, and shepherded back onto the right path.

As a fan and critical supporter of hardcore, I've observed the curious evolution of "tomorrow's music" into an antiquarian culture and collector's market. Back in the day (1991 to 1993), hardcore records were at their lowest value ever. A few months after their release, nobody wanted them: certainly not the outside world, which despised rave as barbaric drug-noise, but not the hardcore kids either, because they were only interested in the very latest tunes. "Oh, that track's old," the sales clerks at specialist stores would say when I'd ask for a record that'd been around for more than a few months. This wasn't because they accepted the outside world's view of the music as disposable trash, but because hardcore was moving so fast it was discarding its recent past like a rocket jettisoning fuel stages as it reaches escape velocity. Track titles like "We Bring You the Future" and "Living for the Future" proclaimed that sense of acceleration and anticipation. The idea of old skool was inconceivable then because the best was still to come.

Today, through a combination of nostalgia on the part of original participants in the subculture and the subsequent hipster legitimation of hardcore (making people want to buy into the history of something disdained at the time it was actually happening), those worthless twelve-inch singles can go for anywhere between $20 and $200, sold through sale lists on the Internet, or auctioned on eBay. Old skool Web sites and mailing lists have sprung up, with fanatics uploading thousands of tunes in MP3 form.

Old skool is not just an archivist phenomenon, though. "Back to '91" and "Back to '92" raves are now so frequent you can talk of an old skool circuit. In London today, pirate radio stations that cast listeners back to '92 are second only to 2step garage stations in popularity. The scene has run into the problem that afflicts all retro-based scenes: the sheer finiteness of the past. Hardcore was a DIY explosion generating thousands of small-pressing tunes and white labels that were in stores for just a few weeks. But as with garage punk and sixties psychedelia, all the nuggets have long since been excavated. "People who've been collecting for a while are moaning at old-school events that no one is playing any 'undiscovered' anthems," says DJ Twist, a twenty-four-year-old veteran of hardcore who's a prime mover on the retro-rave scene. "This partly kicked off the thinking that for the scene to survive we need new music pumped into it. So people are writing new 'old' stuff."[7] Not only does the notion of "yesterday's futurism" seem self-contradictory and contrived (you'd have to deliberately shun the much superior music-making technology available today), but any music that's really "of its time" *is* charged with an electricity sucked down from the zeitgeist, and you can never re-create that after the event. No matter how painstaking the attention to period detail, bad faith palpably infuses any form of "new old" music, as it does with, say, Lenny Kravitz's reproduction antique sound.

Then again, nostalgia gets a bad rap. Certain periods in the life of an individual or a culture are more intense, exciting, plain "better" than others; the impulse to go back there may be counterproductive, but it's understandable. Nostalgia-driven movements can also function as ways of getting through cultural doldrums, keeping faith until the next "up" phase. The past can be used to critique what's absent in the present. As a precursor to punk, Malcolm

McLaren opened the boutique Let It Rock as a repudiation of all things hippie: its jukebox was stocked with fifties rockabilly singles, and its clientele was largely Teddy Boy revivalists. In America, record collectors helped lay the aesthetic foundations for punk, from Lenny Kaye (Patti Smith sideman and compiler of the seminal sixties garage anthology *Nuggets*) to Greg Shaw of *Who Put the Bomp* magazine, which popularized the term *punk* and published Lester Bangs's protopunk manifesto, "James Taylor Marked for Death."

The curator-turned-creator is not an especially new phenomenon. The Stones started out as obsessive collectors, and might never have gone beyond being reverent fanboys covering blues songs if Jagger and Richards's manager hadn't persuaded them to write their own tunes. At some point in the mideighties, though, a shift began that led to the phenomenon I call "record-collection rock," where a band's total sonic identity is reducible to its members' listening habits. The first examples of this syndrome were groups like the Jesus and Mary Chain and Spacemen 3, who disengaged punk from its outside-world imperatives and set themselves up as custodians of a canon of mavericks and marketplace failures: Velvets, Stooges, Love, MC5. As the CD reissue and box-set boom escalated, and retro culture made the past accessible like never before, this mode of creativity became more common.

Take Stereolab and Saint Etienne, two of the most critically acclaimed groups of the last decade. Saint Etienne are essentially nonmusicians (one of them, Bob Stanley, started out as a fanzine editor and music journalist), and their songs aren't so much torn from the soul as lovingly pieced together from sounds either inspired by or sampled from their favorite records: pop as object, rather than expression. Jon Savage nailed this sensibility in his sleeve notes to the group's 1991 debut, *Foxbase Alpha*, which describes a trek to Camden Market in search of "raw material." The pop aesthete weaving through this overcrowded bazaar of cultural jetsam becomes a figure for navigating through the chaos of urban postmodernity itself. "Go with the flow, find what has been forgotten, put it together in a new way. Today's hauls are: 'Mash Down' by Roots and 'Bamba in Dub' by the Revolutionaries, a battered single telling you how to convert

LSD into decimal currency, a couple of Northern Soul compilations on Kent, overpriced UK psych single on labels like Camp and
Page One."[8] Stereolab don't use sampling but their sound is essentially a "musaic" pulling together various strands of retro-cool: the
Krautrock of Neu!, Moog music, Françoise Hardy–style French pop
of the 1960s. Interviews around a new release are couched in terms of
what the group has been listening to recently: with 1996's *Emperor
Tomato Ketchup*, for example, the coordinates were Yoko Ono and
Don Cherry.

Music today seems to reflect inward on itself in a way it didn't
when I entered rock culture in the postpunk late seventies. Looking
at vintage music papers from that time, it's quite striking how bands
didn't really talk about the music. Instead, they spoke about politics,
or the human condition, or about "pop" in a very general way: as
an arena of possibility, a site for subversion or mischief. When inspirations were discussed, they'd most likely stem from other areas of
culture: literature, movies, art. Bands would discuss their debts to
J. G. Ballard or Burroughs, not Can or Velvet Underground. Critics,
too, tended not to break down a group's sound into its constituent
parts and identify precursors, but to operate on the assumption that
the group was "about" something. "Muso"–meaning both excessive
technical virtuosity but also someone decadently obsessed with music for music's sake–was a potent insult in the postpunk era. This
avoidance of sound-in-itself was unbalanced, but what we have today–a situation where music is almost exclusively talked about in
terms of other music, and creativity has become reduced to taste
games–seems equally off-kilter. Record-collection rock has infected
music with some of the sickness of collector culture, making it an
arena increasingly compartmentalized and separate from life.

"Irony and reference points are the dark destroyers of music,"
railed the KLF's Bill Drummond a decade ago, clearly conflicted
about his own knowingness.[9] There is a sense that too many groups
today neither draw from deep within nor are especially engaged with
the world outside music. Instead, they assemble their identity along a
flat plane, ahistorical and postgeographical: a sort of global economy of influences. Where financiers invest in futures, bands specu-

late in pasts. There's a kind of stock market in which hot influences, high-risk options, and reliable perennials jostle: buy Brit folk, sell Krautrock, take a gamble on the BBC Radiophonic Workshop or Swedish musique concrete. "Subcultural capital" is what they call this kind of thing in the academy, a concept derived from Pierre Bourdieu's theories about taste and class distinction. Although the sixties saw pop develop its own internal version of high/low (*Sgt. Pepper's* versus bubblegum, basically), it's gotten much more complicated since then. Art-rock or rock-as-literature (Dylan/Costello) was soon regarded as middlebrow by hipsters, who created their own "dark stuff" pantheon (Velvets/Stooges, all that stuff beloved by Jesus and Mary Chain). When that countercanon, too, started to seem a little predictable, all hell broke loose with a welter of squabbling taste tribes and counter-countercanons. Some plight their troth to heavy metal (deemed superior for its very lack of "socially redeeming value") or to manufactured teenpop ("the little girls understand" stance beloved of thirtysomething men who crave some authentic inauthenticity), while still others try to move so nimbly across the terrain of hip they never get trapped inside an emergent consensus.

This ability to disinvest and reinvest your subcultural capital is what the art of "cool" is all about these days. Avoiding the obvious is paramount. (Although that can also be a trump card—"I love the Beatles; you can't beat them, really"—indicating you've transcended the game altogether.) But as with collecting a specific period genre, the past in totality is not limitless: most of the striking taste postures have already been adopted, and most of what's left is just plain crud. Daft Punk pulled off a coup in 2000 with their *Discovery* album, transforming the disregarded strains of seventies soft rock and eighties lite metal (Electric Light Orchestra, 10cc, Supertramp, Buggles, Van Halen) into a sort of "camp sublime" that was genuinely ecstatic rather than just a cheap frisson. Everybody but the most earnest futurists bought into it, but this speculative transvaluation could so easily have backfired.

Most old records never enjoy the resurrection of hip canonization, or even ironic reappraisal, but are destined to remain irredeemable dreck. As a by-product of countless hours spent poring through dusty used vinyl, I've long been fascinated by the notion of the Least Collectible Records of All Time—the unlovable albums that have left the most grime on my fingertips over the years. I posed the question on I Love Music, the hyperintelligent Internet forum, defining "least collectible" as not just bad music but an excess of supply over demand: typically, the sequel to a megaplatinum blockbuster, when millions were confidently pressed up only for the album to underperform drastically (Led Zeppelin's *Presence* is a classic example). Millions of copies, often still shrink-wrapped, circulate for perpetuity. Least collectible could also encompass genuinely popular records that have dated terribly or suffered from a capricious reversal of mass taste.

The response revealed interesting transatlantic differences. America's unfaves included many that had scant impact in the U.K.: Seals & Crofts, Alan Parsons Project, Styx, Chuck Mangione, Asia, Bob Seger, Bread. And Britain has its own distinctive antipantheon of novelty tack, expired teen crazes, and light entertainment—Chas & Dave, Mud, Bros, Geoff Love, Leo Sayer, Bert Kaempfert, Winifred Atwell, Mrs Mills—along with U.K.-specific blockbusters that punters bought like sheep then offloaded like lemmings (Oasis's *Be Here Now*). Overall, Herb Alpert's *Whipped Cream and Other Delights* clinched the title of least collectible record of all time. Its cheesy, nude-concealed-in-white-goo cover is horribly familiar to all vinyl rummagers.

The record industry is predicated on the notion that most of the product it puts out is pure waste. And this throw-shit-against-the-wall-and-see-if-it-sticks strategy means that there's a lot of shit that sticks around. The Canadian academic Will Straw might be the first theorist to seriously ponder the fate of all that failed product. In the essay "Exhausted Commodities: The Material Culture of Music," he notes the emergence of a parallel economy—car boot sales, charity shops, jumble sales, flea markets, stoop sales, and yard sales—in which items of dead culture-matter "persist and circulate," their value and meaning depleting even as their physical forms refuse to biodegrade. In New York, the lowest rung of all is represented by those plucky entrepreneurs who set up shop on the street, splaying on the sidewalk a choice array of soiled LPs (baked and warping on the griddle-like pavement), scuffed paperbacks, used magazines, semifunctioning appliances, and even garments.[10]

In a striking word choice, Straw talks about the "monumentality" of the records that no one ever buys, that will never be revalorized by hipsters, even as kitsch. In his hometown, Montreal, the usual suspects—late-seventies prog-lite, hair metal, unsuccessful musicals, budget classical, Mantovani's massive oeuvre—are augmented by local Quebecois delicacies: "the fake Tijuana Brass albums produced in Montreal, the French-language Hawaiian records, the disco symphonies celebrating the 1976 Olympics." But wherever you live, what you can glean from this monumental parade is a sort of shadow history of pop culture, the massive-selling tack that never makes it into the official account.

Even this lowly stuff may have its day, though. There are collectors who specialize in "crap records" and there's a mini-genre of electronic artists who venture into the mass graves of mass-cult in search of samples nobody else will touch: Wagon Christ, who prefers to sample "shit records"; the Australian outfit the Avalanches, who combed Sydney's charity shops for a year, then built their wondrous *Since I Left You* album using 1,000-plus samples from 600 cut-price albums; Position Normal, who chops up old spoken-word records and tape-to-tape reels discarded after festering for decades in the family attic. Perhaps the most heroic of these bottom feeders are the electronic pranksters V/Vm, who take up the option offered by secondhand record dealers desperate to get rid of unsellable stuff: the "lucky bag," where the purchaser will hand over, say, five quid for a sealed box containing 50 albums or 100 CD singles. Driven equally by some weird ecological recycling impulse, a conceptual art critique of mainstream pop, and a simple delight in mischief, V/Vm creates "new" music by digitally desecrating the unlucky contents of these lucky bags—Shakin' Stevens, Russ Abbott, Xmas records.

Artists like V/Vm and the Avalanches are just the extreme edge of an increasingly general approach to sampling: the alchemy of turning stale cheese into soulful gold. There are record stores that specialize in albums highly sought after not as listening experiences but as resources for sampling. A few blocks from my apartment in the East Village, there's a store called The Sound Library, named in homage to a specific genre of sample-fodder records: the series of incidental music albums put out by labels like KPM and Boosey & Hawkes in the early seventies. Imagine the scene: a recording studio near Denmark Street, circa 1973. A failed composer frantically scribbles an arrangement on a score, like Shakespeare finishing the third act while the players are halfway through act two. The session musicians, paid by the hour, rest their violins and trumpet on their laps, grumbling and puffing on Benson & Hedges. These albums, with their helpful back-sleeve mood descriptions of each track ("light relaxed swingalong," "industrious activity," "neutral abstract underscore," "pathetic, grotesque"), were originally intended to be used in TV, radio, and cinema advertisements, but today they are prized by hip-hop and dance producers because they don't require sample clearances and nobody's going to hunt them down for a share of the publishing.

Alongside these rent-a-theme collections with their uniform artwork, at stores like The Sound Library you typically find a vast, overpriced selection from the other oft-sampled genres: film soundtracks, fusion, jazz-funk, disco, black rock bands like Mandrill, and psychedelic-soul groups from the late sixties like the Rotary Connection, who specialized in overarranged cover versions. Sampling totally transforms the aesthetic criteria. Many of these records are essentially terrible but contain flashes of brilliant playing: a single twenty-second percussion break, a swath of string-swept grandeur. Whenever I enter The Sound Library, I'm surprised by the records by rock groups from the late sixties and early seventies of the kind that never make it into rock histories.

During this boom period for the rock album, record labels signed almost anything that moved, and sometimes created "heavy" bands from scratch using session musicians, wrapping these pseudo-groups in a package that included a "deep" or trippy name (Secret Oyster, Zzebra, If); sleeve notes full of progressive guff about blending styles and blowing minds; and lavish, gimmicky gatefolds. Staring from the back covers, with their waxy sideburns and mustaches, these groups—Ekseption, Jam Factory, Gas Mask, Solar Plexus (many seemingly from Scandinavia or Eastern Europe)—totally tanked in the crowded marketplace of the day; you'll find no mention of them in even the most compendious rock encyclopedia. Yet because of the session-level caliber of the playing, their records contain slick licks ripe for sampling, and the chances are minuscule that lawyers will come looking for payback. A few of these sampler-beloved figures have been plucked from obscurity and reinvented as auteurs, like the arranger David Axelrod, whose checkered CV includes composing and orchestrating the Electric Prunes' Gregorian chant–inspired psychedelic folly *Mass in F Minor,* and who's been coaxed out of retirement to record a solo album for the trip-hop label Mo' Wax.

The latest development in sampling culture strikes me as the ultimate example of the record collector mindset transposed to music making, resulting in a kind of meta-pop. I'm talking about the craze for bootlegs, also known as mashups or "bastard pop." Not to be confused with bootleg recordings of a band in concert or bootlegs of demos and studio outtakes, but similarly grounded in misappropriation, these bootleg mashups are essentially unofficial remixes of pop hits. This has been going on in dance culture for a long time, but mashups are different because the practitioners aim to avoid using any original sonic material of their own: most of the new bootlegs operate on the principle of the chimera, the mythological monster made out of different creatures, bird's head on top of dog's body, that sort of thing. Two or more pop hits are combined, ideally with a combination of both maximum incongruity and seamless execution. For instance, some of the more interesting mashups will take an R&B vocal by Missy Elliott or TLC and put it over a harsh electronic backing track by Gary Numan or The Normal, creating a "soul on ice" contrast. Others are done by concatenation rather than superimposition: one of the most striking of the bootlegs, called "Intro Introspection," is a twelve-minute piece woven together out of hundreds of famous pop intros.

People have come up with all kinds of interpretations of this fad, mostly modeled on punk ideas—the pop consumer fights back, seizing the means of production, do-it-yourself. To me it seems more like pseudocreativity based on a blend of mild irreverence and simple pop fandom: we like these records, let's double our pleasure by welding them together. Although mashups are sometimes sold in vinyl form, for the most part they circulate free of charge as MP3s: this bootlegging is very much bound up with the post-Napster file-sharing culture. Indeed, mashups might well be the definitive aesthetic expression of file-sharing consciousness, where history and geography are transcended, the linear flow of pop time is suspended, and there's a free-for-all in which individuals can amass or access unimaginably vast collections of music, albeit in dematerialized form as pure information. The result is a kind of sonic grand bouffe, a harvest banquet predicated on reaping what others have sown: all the bounty left over from more creative eras. For all their aura of mischief and cheeky fun, these new bootlegs exude the pathos of living in a belated era.

The punk interpretation of mashups is a kind of retaliatory vomiting back up of all the pop force-fed down our throats: as I write, Kylie Minogue's omnipresent and endemic "Can't Get You Out of My Head" is a current favorite of the bootleggers. But as with the 117 Springsteen bootlegs of the other sort that I mentioned earlier, I think it's more a syndrome of regurgitation and reconsumption: as if rearranging and compressing two or more beloved pieces of music could somehow renew your pleasure, give it a faint frisson of novelty. The pleasures of mashups are entirely bound up with pop knowledge and pop knowingness: listen to "Intro Introspection" and you smile with recognition or surprise as you identify each intro. It's pop about pop, self-reflexive, meta-meta to the point of decadence, not to mention supreme lameness. Underlying all this seems to be a tendency toward entropy: indistinctness, inertia, indifference—the heat-death of terminal cool. Which circles round to the title of this essay, "Lost in Music": the sense that you can have too much of a good thing. For an individual, there's a certain point where your collection is so vast it defeats its original motivation, it's literally unusable. The same applies on a collective level: file-sharing culture is basically an infinitely vast communal record collection. As that Sister Sledge song goes: "caught in a trap / there's no turning back / we're lost in music."[11]

Now, if only I could work out where exactly I *put* those Sister Sledge records . . .

chapter 23

Topless at the Arco Arena: Looking for the Line between Abandon and Irresponsibility during the Dot-Com Explosion

TIM QUIRK

One night in April 2001, I jumped into a white stretch limousine with the CEO of Listen.com, the vice president of business development, one of our strategic account managers, and several cases of beer. We drove from San Francisco to the Arco Arena in Sacramento to see AC/DC in concert. In the middle of the show, while the band played "The Jack," cameras connected to the giant TV screens / panned the crowd of 20,000 rock fans wearing blinking devil horns emblazoned with the AC/DC logo, looking for a female willing to strip. While several ladies appeared ready to undo a button or two on their blouse, the cameras seemed able to tell they were poseurs and finally settled on a young, exuberant blonde. As the band vamped, she began to remove her shirt, timing her moves perfectly so she could flash her breasts in Diamond Vision as the music climaxed and the crowd went wild.

A couple weeks later, that VP got laid off, the CEO stepped aside, and I was battling to save the handful of editorial positions that remained in a department that had once included fifty passionate music geeks. It wasn't the first round of layoffs we'd experienced, and it wasn't going to be the last. We were in the very early stages of a hangover that now seems like the inevitable result of the late-'90s dotcom binge, and as I popped aspirin and filled out spreadsheets designed to calculate how many Full-Time Equivalents my department could afford to jettison, I kept thinking about the lady at the Arco Arena.

Even though I am a guy who writes about music for a living, hers was not the first pair of breasts I had ever seen. I will confess, however, that I had never seen a pair projected on such a giant screen, so they were quite literally the biggest. And I had never heard 20,000 screams unite in quite the same way when they finally appeared.

The experience left me with a lot of questions for their owner. I wondered what she said the next day when friends asked her how the concert was. I wondered if she thought the crowd had been applauding her breasts or her daring. I wondered if maybe she was a plant, and had actually gotten paid for her performance. That last one was just a specific way of asking a more general question, I guess—mostly I was wondering exactly what she got out of it.

There's a slight chance it was one of those transcendent moments rock and roll is supposed to be about—a joyous release of inhibitions when everything in the world and inside your head briefly hums in harmony, and the only way she had to express the ineffable power of that feeling was to yank off her shirt.

But see, Listen.com's rock editor had told me this was going to happen (that women would strip, I mean—not that I would obsess about its significance forever afterward). His exact words, when I told him I was going to an AC/DC concert, were, "Cool. You're gonna see titties." And some casual post-gig research on AC/DC Web sites revealed that not only do AC/DC concerts regularly compel attractive, tipsy women to disrobe, but that they almost always do so at that exact moment in that precise song. It's like a ritual. Which makes it harder to argue that it was a genuinely uninhibited moment—even in rock and roll, apparently, there is a proper time and place to remove one's clothes.

So I don't feel at all goofy when I insist that I felt a strange kinship with the naked woman, who for all I know went back to work in an office much like mine the following day. The little band of content providers I managed at Listen.com and was in the process of winnowing down to a more sustainable number had basically had the same experience in reverse. Many of us were in bands ourselves, and before the dot-com explosion had spent most of our time writing, playing, or watching music being made. But the tech boom had brought us out of the world of nightclubs and concert halls and into the land of cubicles, and our adventures there proved just as heady, about as brief, and equally packed with contradictions. That's what I really want to talk about, but before I do I need you to understand that, at the height of venture capital mania, we felt every bit as sexy and powerful as the topless lady.

Not that our jobs were particularly glamorous. When I first joined Listen in the summer of 1999, the company was building a directory of all the legally downloadable music on the Net. Because most labels were being notoriously cautious about releasing songs online, the vast majority of that material was being posted by unknown acts on sites such as MP3.com, Riffage, and Iuma. There were already tens of thousands of such acts, and our mission was simple: we were supposed to listen to every fucking one, rate them, assign them two to four musical styles from the more than 500 branches on Listen's incredibly detailed genre tree, assign two to four similar artists (so that, when visitors to our site typed "Rolling Stones" in the search box, we could point them to the 536 Stones-like bands in our database, by way of an apology for not having any actual Rolling Stones tunes). Finally, we were supposed to type up a brief "review."

I put quotation marks around that word because Nick Tangborn, Listen's original editor-in-chief, had made the very wise decision to avoid explicit value judgments when we wrote up our twenty-five- to thirty-five-word blurbs about a particular act. The goal was to describe what the band sounded like rather than to state whether the band sounded any good.

The reason for this decision became evident after just two or three days on the job: almost all the bands we listened to were abysmal. Actually, I sort of wished that were the case—after a week or two I came to crave finding a genuinely horrible act, because those were at least interesting, and usually worth sharing with coworkers in need of a laugh. Most of the groups were only boringly mediocre—competent musicians without a shred of imagination aping more successful bands who weren't necessarily so thrilling themselves. Reviewing for Listen in 1999 was basically like watching an average bar band do a sound check. For eight hours. Our unofficial motto was: We listen to shit so you don't have to.

But we loved it. I kid you not, every Sunday night I went to bed happy, eager to get to work the next day and slip on my headphones. Partly this was because I am one of those assholes who had muddled along just fine without a legitimate job for the first thirty-odd years of my life, so getting up from an actual desk to get a drink from an actual water cooler was still an exotic adventure for me. And partly this was because the editorial department comprised first fifteen, then twenty, and eventually fifty genuinely engaging, intriguing, hilarious individuals whom I will always consider it my great good fortune to have known. But mostly it was because every one of us, to some extent, cherished the strange combination of absurdity and good luck that had landed us full-time jobs with health insurance and stock options and free beer every Friday at five for doing exactly what we'd always done with our free time, anyway. Namely, eat, drink, sleep, and breathe music and then be insufferable wiseasses about it all.

That's why the fact that we were listening to shitty music forty hours a week was beside the point. Ninety-nine percent of it sucked, but I'd been a freelance rock critic for the better part of a decade by that point, and this particular ratio of shit to Shinola seemed little different from the one I found going through the stacks of CDs that wound up in my mailbox at home. Besides, it was much easier to forgive naked peasants than naked emperors—I would spend eternity with the worst crap I downloaded off MP3.com before I'd agree to buy back all the horrid Dreamworks CDs I've sold to Amoeba over the years. And of course, when you did stumble across a truly wonderful act, the pleasure was undiluted and you felt obligated to share your discovery with the world.

But the real joy came from the sudden sense that a lifetime spent listening to records and going to shows and making friends with people just because they were wearing the right button was now weirdly *valuable*. Career paths for people with an encyclopedic knowledge of popular music have always been limited. And the editorial department at Listen, again by the founding editor's design, consisted almost exclusively of those misfits who *hadn't* parlayed their strange obsessions into freelance or full-time gigs at the handful of alternative weeklies or monthly magazines that the Bay Area supported. Half our writers were musicians, or DJs, or ran their own label, or some combination of all three, but almost none of us was accustomed to making any money from those pursuits.

Our rock editor, Mike McGuirk—the same reprobate who gave me the heads-up about titties at AC/DC concerts—summed up the gut-punching wonder of this development best when he said, "I thought I was gonna be a cook forever."

He didn't say that to me, though. He said it to a legitimate journalist, who was writing a feature about Listen's editorial department that eventually ran under the headline, "Revenge of the Music Geeks." That writer was just one baton-twirling majorette in a seemingly endless parade of oddly bright-eyed reporters—from the *Wall Street Journal*, the *New York Times*, CNN, ABC, and even a jovial documentary crew from the Czech Republic—all of them using the newly empowered music hounds at Listen the same way I'm using the topless lady at the Arco Arena—as framing metaphors, telling examples of a moment when the normal order of things has flipped and the meek, if they haven't exactly inherited the earth, have at least been temporarily upgraded to first class.

We weren't special; we were simply a convenient symbol for the rambunctious energy that characterized the dot-com explosion. Just as giddy women were pulling off their blouses in every city AC/DC visited on their North American tour, our experience was being shared by newly employed misfits across the country. And, just as the naked ladies made the show seem that much more exciting, every newspaper article about the pierced and tattooed dot-commies at companies such as mine made the "new economy" seem that much more unstoppable.

We all know how this story ended—eventually, time-honored business realities reasserted their incontrovertibility, and the summer camp atmosphere dissipated seemingly overnight. But for a good long while that outcome seemed anything but inevitable, as otherwise reasonable commentators were yammering on about paradigm shifts and each day we met the business world head-on and watched it get a contact high from our boozy breath.

Some examples: one of the first business decisions I made after getting promoted to managing editor was that, given all the parties our company kept throwing, we could save a lot of money by purchasing our own DJ coffin and PA system instead of renting them every other week. During a helpful lecture by the financial firm that was handling our stock option packages, the lady in charge of teaching us about strike prices and vesting periods chose to illustrate our potential windfall by repeatedly proclaiming, "And that's when you'll be able to buy that brand-new SUV." The fifth time she said this, our country editor politely raised his hand and asked her if she could please start using a different example—he suggested a Fender Twin Deluxe. And at South by Southwest 2000, the gap between my old life and my new one was thrown into particularly sharp relief. Before, I'd only come to music conferences like that one as another guy in another band, pulling into town in a beat-up van and sleeping four to a room or crashing on some kind soul's couch. This time I had my own room at the Four Seasons and a sweet little case to hold my brand-new business cards.

My favorite memory, however, is of a pep talk given by one of the venture capitalists who'd invested ungodly sums of his own and other people's money in Listen.com. The entire company—about sixty of us by this point—was gathered amid the sawhorses and stacks of uninstalled pipes in the old sheet-metal factory that was halfway through its transmogrification into Listen.com's corporate headquarters. The VC told us that the number one band on MP3.com that week had over half a million downloads. Granted, they were all free downloads, but everyone recognized there was some kind of value there. The VC confessed he wasn't yet sure how we were going to monetize that, but he was sure that we would. "Because the ultimate goal," he said, "is to monetize everything."

If I were a courageous dwarf in a fantasy novel, that would have been the moment I espied a raven or some other dark omen on a nearby branch. It was the first time I felt—and I mean felt as opposed to understood in an abstract way—that people were paying my new friends and me semidecent wages and buying us lots of drinks and letting us keep odd hours and wear whatever the hell we wanted to at work because they expected something bigger and better in return.

My moment of disquiet passed, naturally, and I went right back to enjoying the party. And like any good rock and roll show, we got carried away and took things too far. The editorial department grew, partly because building the Leading Directory of Legally Downloadable Music on the Internet required an ever-growing number of hamsters on an ever-accelerating array of exercise wheels—even at 150 bands reviewed per writer per week, musicians were uploading more songs than we could ever hope to catalog—but mostly because spending money was briefly considered just as good as actually earning any. Rapid growth was a sign of good health and greater prospects, and the VCs wanted to see us expand. The number of employees tripled, and our days got progressively weirder. We launched a coventure in Tokyo called Listen Japan. I started interviewing editor-in-chief candidates for the bureaus we were planning to open in London and Latin America. The company flew in a friend of mine to pitch ideas for the Listen.com TV show a cable network had proposed.

It all sounds so stupid in retrospect, but it's too easy to gaze back from a distance and laugh at the foolish things we do when we drink too much and decide we're invincible. Listen's PR guy and I both used to boast to reporters that we had the biggest full-time editorial department of any music publication in the United States, and while we might have benefited from asking ourselves if maybe there was a *reason* no other business tried to maintain such a large contingent of staff writers, once the spotlight finds you it becomes nearly impossible to think about consequences. You're frozen in an ecstatic present, and just about anything you do while you're there seems perfect and natural and right. Of *course* we should have our own TV show. Of *course* the 100,000 casual dismissals of amateur acts that we'd written ("Militant Christian Contemporary with sweeping rock guitars and drums that make you want to go burn down an abortion clinic") should be translated into twenty different languages. We'd been chosen. Our breasts were beautiful, the world wanted to see them, and we were gonna give the world anything it asked for.

Well, eventually the world asked for its money back. The day we had our first round of layoffs, half of our writers were let go, along with the VP who'd built the department in the first place. Everybody—those who were staying and those who'd been given ninety minutes to put their personal effects in boxes—walked to the bar across the street and had what amounted to a wake for our dead illusions. We'd lost something much harder to replace than our jobs—we'd lost the belief that our moment of glory had been necessary or real.

Now, I obviously have no idea how the lady who flashed the crowd at the Arco Arena felt the next day. But I think it's possible she experienced the same mix of emotions that I've still got today—a combination of embarrassment and glee. Part of me thinks the lady was ill used, that she sacrificed something personal for the aggrandizement of the four millionaires on stage, and that the freedom she presumably felt was a lie, since her moves were preordained. But the rest of me realizes none of that changes the way it felt at the time.

AC/DC needed a likely lass to flash the crowd at that particular moment in their set, and experience had taught them there was at least one in every arena. Nonetheless, the woman who obliged them got something of her own, something ephemeral, but real just the same. For a few seconds, she was the show. Forty thousand eyes swiveled away from the stage and drank her in. In my memory, even Angus turns around to watch her breasts sway on the giant screen, although that part might not actually have happened.

Do I think this was a fair exchange? Not really. But a couple years at a dot-com teaches you that equity is overrated. It's possible to be complicit in your own exploitation, and it's easy not to mind. Tempting as it is to repress the rush and promise yourself you won't ever fall for that again, doing so might mean you lose the only tangible thing you received in the transaction.

Despite all the attention I continue to pay to those breasts, I don't think the thrill of their unveiling had any more to do with sex than my own adventures in the new economy had to do with money. Tits, cash—those are just the sparks that fly out of the magician's wand while he's pulling the shit that's *really* gonna wow you out of a pocket.

Back when the roller coaster was still heading up, up, up, our original indie rock writer decided to take a three-month leave of absence, at the end of which he informed us he wouldn't be returning to his desk after all. When we asked him why, his response was, "I guess I'm just not down with commerce."

Me, I got down with commerce. I still work at Listen, and while the rush of anticipation I used to feel on Sunday nights has been replaced by a punier but far more common relief when Friday finally rolls around, I still dig my job. I wouldn't go so far as to say I'm a legitimate businessman, but like everyone left in the editorial department I'm a lot more realistic about the odds of our eventual success, and the bursting of our bubble has forced us to come up with more useful ways to utilize our musical expertise.

I suppose the writer who opted out early would say the forces of commerce prevailed in their struggle with the musicians and writers who stayed behind, and shaped us the way they required. But I'm not convinced it's that simple, 'cause I'm not so sure it was the folks like us who were really acting crazy. After all, we were just doing what we'd always done, only now we didn't have to tend bar to support our habit.

It was the folks my old bandmates and I used to refer to as civilians who got dangerously distracted by the tits and the cash: the commentators on CNBC, the analysts at Merrill Lynch, the VCs who assumed you could monetize anything. They became hypnotized by all the pretty sparks coming out of the magician's wand.

And when the sparks sputtered out they decided the show must be over.

Maybe I'm kidding myself, but I like to think that the naked lady and I knew better, that we kept our eyes on the magician's other hand.

So . . . what'd he finally pull out of that pocket?

Well, it's nothing you can quantify. That's why the accountants all went home, muttering that the whole thing had been a trick and there wasn't any such thing as magic. It's more like an idea, a suggestion of something that isn't there, but could be. Try to imagine a handkerchief that looks like a bird that flaps its wings and flies out the window, and then pretend there wasn't any handkerchief to begin with.

Promise is too strong a word, and reeks of lawyers, so I'm going to settle on *possibility*. That's what the naked lady breathed in, that's what the crowd sniffed, that's what I tasted, that's what a lot of people in this country briefly felt. Possibility. The possibility that the naked lady would remain more interesting than the band for the rest of the evening. The chance that a gigantic record collection could substitute for an MBA. The understanding that if anyone can be a millionaire, nobody should. The feeling, always fleeting so never scary, that someone new is in charge.

The takeaway (as I've learned to call important nuggets of information) is not that the new boss is the same as the old boss, or that the old boss always returns, although both things are equally true. The thing to remember is just how important and powerful the moments in between can be.

Sometimes the audience plays the band. And sometimes the band plays with the audience. And every once in a while, nobody's really in charge.

chapter 24

More Rock, Less Talk: Live Music Turns Off the Voices in Our Heads

CARRIE BROWNSTEIN

As an artist, it is most frightening to feel that the meaning in your work is slipping away from you. I think that this is a natural by-product of placing art into the world. But it's especially true in a medium like music, one that is populist—where the audience naturally adopts it as their own. In some ways it should belong to them. Listeners are each allowed their own interpretation, without the need for any kind of theoretical or technical understanding. Their belief that they can have a unique response or a visceral relationship to the art is what removes it from an elitist, academic realm. However, for every individual vision of the art there is also an individual definition of who the artists are and what they represent. If the audience for the work is large, you wind up with a multitude of definitions, and these are likely to vary enormously. Eventually there comes to exist, separate from the artist, an entity that is externally defined, one that embodies the expectations inhabited by the outside world. This external entity, a veritable artistic doppelgänger, is difficult to ignore. It can feel like a demanding evil twin, and artists can begin to ignore or lose sight of their own motivations.

Since my own goals in music lie in forging a connection with people, with an audience, it's disheartening to feel as though my message is misinterpreted or no longer of my own design. I struggle to tune out the external expectations and definitions. At the same time, I cannot wholly ignore those to whom I am trying to relate, who are sharing the experience along with me. It is a precarious position.

Recorded music, by fixing the sound in a specific time and place, can't help but form a definitive sonic blueprint for a band. The recorded medium is much more likely to be categorized and posited within the ever growing—and ever limiting—list of genres. We can hear the same instance replayed over and over, and though the listeners bring their own experience to the songs, and may hear new textures with each pass, the sonic nature of the song is fixed.

In contrast, the context of playing live allows for fluidity and continuity between the otherwise disparate past and present, the fixed (recorded) and the ephemeral, and the artist's private and public identities. The live experience elevates the art of music by making it permeable and improvisational. To me, the dialogue in a live context exists in the sonic and visceral relationship between the artist and the song and between the artist and the audience. Essentially, the live show is nothing more than an impromptu conversation. It's a moment that lets us connect on a level free from the restraints of everyday discourse. It welcomes as opposed to shuns lexical ambiguities. Our translation of the experience is not reliant on our intellectual grasp of the moment; it operates more spontaneously, as an intuitive and physical response. In addition, the language of any given live show is unique, a spontaneous and instantaneous negotiation of sound, utterance, and gesture. It is useful only in this moment. Few other forms of communication or art achieve this evanescent beauty.

*   *   *

For myself, the moment when the live aspect became the most crucial was when the identity of my band, Sleater-Kinney, became uncertain, when there became a joint ownership between us and the audience. We had been split into two: there were two distinct definitions of the band, our own and that of the audience. Often, the dichotomy felt irreconcilable.

To us, Sleater-Kinney was a dialogue among three people. It was our source of salvation, escape, strength, and joy. Sleater-Kinney was nothing more than the sounds that traveled from our mouths, fingers, hands, and our hearts. It traveled no further than the walls of our practice space. All of the meaning was both surrounding us and inside of us; there existed little disparity between the internal and external worlds of the band. Whatever sounds came out of us at that moment, that was who we were, we owned it. Yet the moment we left the practice space, recorded the songs, and placed them into the world, our formerly insular identity, or lack of conscious identity, became public and therefore open to debate.

Though we had no intention of remaining obscure, we also had no way of preparing for the outside definitions and expectations. Suddenly, we were defined by specific songs, albums, photographs, quotes, politics, and genders. We were a "girl group," a "feminist band," we had "risen from the riot grrrl ghetto," we were *Call the Doctor,* we were *Dig Me Out.* We went from mutable to fixed identities.

But live we remained and remain nothing except the moment itself. The audience, hearing it brought together in front of them, senses the congruencies in the music. Two seemingly disparate songs suddenly come off as unified. People tend to fear growth and change in artists, but live performance has a way of proving that this evolution contains a common thread, a core that is true to the original artistic vision.

My early relationship to performing live music is best described in the song "I Wanna Be Your Joey Ramone," which we wrote in 1995. Joey Ramone was a performer who embodied both diffidence and grandiosity. To me, he was a man who was simultaneously awkward, with his spindly legs and his hair falling into his face, and also larger than life. This contradiction seemed to be an ideal metaphor for my own relationship to performing and music. Part of me wanted to own the stage while the other part of me remained uncomfortable with such power. The song was also about stepping into someone else's shoes (in this case Joey's) as a means of exploring my own fears and dreams.

When Sleater-Kinney first began, it seemed to me that the only way to get a sense of rock 'n' roll was to experience it vicariously. At least that was the message coming to us from the outside world: the archetypes, the stage moves, the representations of rebellion and debauchery were all male. The song has us exploring a role typically associated with male performers. By doing so, we get a glimpse of the absurdity, the privilege, and the decadence that wasn't inherently afforded to us.

Some people are born with the certainty that they own sound or volume; that the lexicon of rock music is theirs to borrow from, to employ, to interpret. For them, it might be nothing to move around on stage, to swagger, to sing in front of people, to pick up a guitar, to make records. I set out from a place where I never assumed that those were acceptable choices or that I could be anything but an accessory to rock 'n' roll. Coming out of a tradition that historically didn't allow women much of a voice, then finding myself helping to create a sound that filled an entire room, that reached into every person in that room, that is a power that I had to learn. I needed to try it on before I could call it mine. I had to find a means to make it my own.

The transition from a vicarious exploration of power to empowerment could happen only in live environments. There one faces not only the audience's expectations of what it means to be a performer on stage but also one's own mental catalog of the archetypal images of rock, which are often affirmations of adolescent male sexual identity. Playing live felt like battling history, icons, images. It is hard not to be reduced to the category of "women in rock." I didn't feel like I could *be* rock 'n' roll. Instead, we were women imitating and participating in rock 'n' roll, something we didn't create. To feel comfortable with the power, I couldn't feel like it was being lent to me, and certainly no one was passing it to me. I had to claim it. I had to carve a space for myself in my own imagination and in the imagination of the audience.

Because the live moment is fluid, so too is the identity: it passes back and forth from audience to performer; it presents a form and then turns that form on its head. On stage, questions of identity, gender, or categorical indexing begin to feel obsolete. They are obliterated by the visceral. The live performance allows gender to take on an ambiguous or even androgyne role; it smashes the historical assumptions about who owns rock 'n' roll. Whoever is on stage at that moment owns the music; whoever is watching and hearing it at that moment owns it as well.

Live music also frees me from the restraints of the rhetorical. Art historian Anne Middleton Wagner writes: "It is a necessary consequence for working 'as a woman.' Making art from such a position is inevitably rhetorical; it must often be strategic, must often employ assertion, denial, tactical evasion, subterfuge, deception, refusal."[1] I certainly feel that this is the case with Sleater-Kinney: talking about the experience has become part of the experience itself. In interviews, we are constantly asked the question, "What is it like to be a woman playing rock?" More than anything, I feel that this metadiscourse, talking about the talk, is part of how it feels to be a "woman playing rock." There is the music itself, and then there is the ongoing dialogue about how it feels. The two seem to be intertwined and also inescapable. This dialogue also began to appear in our own songwriting. The songs responded to and addressed the fans, the critics, and even our own work: the new songs (such as "Male Model" or "#1 Must Have") explaining the old ("I Wanna Be Your Joey Ramone," "Little Babies"), discussing what we had already done and why we had done it.

The metadiscourse and the rhetorical form a disconnect; a psychological, linguistic, and identity fissure. However, these elements are made congruent and whole in the live context. Here the rhetoric ceases; there is no explanation but the sound itself. I am not talking about the music, I am the music.

For all the freeing possibilities that live performance opens up, it also introduces another dynamic that is more problematic: the inherent hierarchy assumed between performer and audience. There are few moments when this imbalance is effectively dismantled. Recently, however, I experienced a disruption of this dynamic. It was at an outdoor show, at the moment when night fell upon the stage, when the sky was fixed for an instant, holding elements of both night and day in its hues. This was a moment that could never happen indoors, a straddling of two contrasting environments and moods. It came to me that you could see it as nature's way of illustrating how a concert is simultaneously a public and a private experience.

Whatever form it takes, live music draws on both individual and collective elements, for performer and audience alike. Outdoors, however, the dichotomy is exaggerated. During the day, everyone is made much more aware of just how public and shared the experience really is. Not only can you sense how close you are to the strangers in front of or next to you, but after a few hours you know every detail of their faces, every whisker, every blemish, every twitch. In the midst of a song, you can watch their faces change in response to the lyrics and the music; you know how they look with their eyes closed, mouthing the words. In the light of day, the private experience is exposed and the collective experience is no longer merely visceral—it is also visible.

When I play outside I am constantly aware of this visibility. I like the way the environment lends itself to demystifying the performer and removes some of the artifice. Aside from the stage itself, there exists less of the performer-fan hierarchy perpetuated by elements such as elaborate lighting. Everyone is under the same indiscriminate glare of the sun. I can look out into the crowd and see individual faces and expressions, I can see the dimensions of the space, where the crowd begins, where it ends; there is nowhere to hide for me or for them.

Naturally, there is a drawback to a heightened awareness of one another and the fact that the private has been made public. Many people come to rock 'n' roll and punk out of desperation. They like the anonymity provided by a dark room, where emotions are less transparent, where appearances can be obfuscated. Thus, there is often a feeling of reservation at a summer concert, a reluctance to allow oneself to be exposed. And this brings me back to my favorite moment, which is when the spotlight of the sun begins to fade. Often, by the time night falls, we have been participants long enough to be acutely aware of the collective nature of the event. By this time we are yearning for a moment that is our own, a moment that goes unseen. The onset of darkness is that moment, the one where the private and public experience converge. We at last have the privacy to feel and express ourselves without anyone watching. At the same time, there is a relief in knowing that we're not alone.

In general, I feel that live performance is the truest and most organic way to experience the tradition of music, for the listener and for the artist. It frees us from our own intellectual restraints—the kind of analytical discourse that we use on a daily basis that distances us from an interior emotional landscape. Appearing live is also a way for artists to ward off static or reductive definitions. The moment relies on movement, connection, continuity, spontaneity. We are reminded that music is an experience, not merely an object, and thus it becomes difficult to separate it from our own bodies. It feels crucial to form connections with one another, to be aware of how our private and public selves intertwine. Lastly, live music is about breaking free of restraints, of tradition, of roles. This is possible because the live moment is ephemeral, it leaves no singular residue. All that exists once it is over is the potential in ourselves to be transformed.

chapter 25

The
Persistence
of Hair

JOHN DARNIELLE

Lisa's Incredible night!—Saturday, May 13—Last Stop on Tour!

Hey Hey BAZMANIACS!

Went to see Sebastian this past Saturday night with Kathy (Fire-sign2) for the last night of the tour, and let me tell ya how incredible it felt to see him! the best show I have seen of his. . . . check this out. . . .

You all very obviously know the song "I remember you" (Obviously you do or ya wouldn't be on my mailing list, right?. . . .)

[. . .] Well, insted of singing "Who my darlin', I looooove youuuuuuuuuu", . . . holy shit! He looked at me, caught my eye, pointed, grinned really REALLY BIG and sang "BAZ-MANIACSSSSSS, I loooooove youuuuuuuuuuuuuuuu!"

I coulda hit the floor! [. . .] I looked at Kathy and Glit and was like "Did that really happen or am I fuckin' dreamin'?!" [. . .] Baz has pointed me out in the audience one other time, but he has never directly

*serenaded me using my screenname or real name, ya know? [. . .] It
feel great to have the consistent show of appreciation by Baz. He really
lets his die hard fans know that he appreciates them and cares.*

*Could you imagine your favorite rock star singing right to ya and
substituting your screenname or real name in your favorite song on the
last night of their tour? It was fuckin' immortally amazing! [. . .]
Rockin' on . . .*
Lisa[1]

It's Got a Good Beat, I Can Dance to It

Many critics spent the nineties coming around to the conclusion
that just because people like something, that doesn't necessarily make
it bad. Chief beneficiaries of this awakening have recently been
Madonna, whose "Like a Virgin" was universally reviled on its release but whose self-determining icon status now seems firmly set
in stone; teen heartthrob bands, who routinely get cover stories
in even the most prestigious music magazines; the worst strains of
Neptunes-produced bling-bling sell-out hip-hop, which, incidentally, do not amount to a pimple on N.W.A's collective ass; and a
generous handful of bands, mostly from the U.K., who put vaguely
trip-hop beats underneath what are essentially Crosby, Stills, Nash
and Young songs minus the thirteenth chords and then get called
"innovative."

This impulse, whatever its consequences, has been an essentially
healthy one for criticism. It comes too late, however, for the men and
women who made commercial heavy metal in the mid- to late eighties. If you were to read all criticism penned in the eighties, you
would have to dig pretty deep to find a few words written in favor of,
say, Warrant, Motley Crue, Poison, Ratt, Skid Row (the inspiration
for the fan writing captured above), Trixter, Kix, Jackyl, Giuffria,
Tesla, Twisted Sister, Great White, Dokken, Firehouse, Autograph,
Britney Fox, Dangerous Toys, L.A. Guns, Steelheart, Saigon Kick,
Nelson, E'Nuff Z'nuff, or Stryper. Most critics were fairly well appalled by these bands, and not without reason; Nelson, in particular,
seemed to many at the time like the surest sign imaginable that the

fiery and horrible end of the world was imminent. But people liked these bands; they bought their records and went to their concerts; and a number of people were confused, disappointed, and eventually marginalized by the replacement of the above-named bands on the charts by a new breed of rock bands like Pearl Jam, Alice in Chains, Soundgarden, Stone Temple Pilots, Silverchair, Radish, Bush, and, of course, Nirvana, about whom more later. More recently, another hard-rock changing of the guard has taken place, welcoming such mostly unwelcome names as Nickelback, Mudvayne, Staind, Creed, Korn, Slipknot, Sevendust, Skrape, Mushroomhead, Nothingface, System of a Down, Linkin Park, Static-X, Papa Roach, P.O.D., and the Insane Clown Posse. Most critics, myself included, are hard pressed to say nice things about these bands, and I would be lying if I were to deny that their success has caused me to sink into a deep and crippling depression from which I despair of emerging with the same joie de vivre that once was my trademark.

One can be fairly confident that history will have its way with these bands. One can be just as confident, however, that for a fair number of people the very times in which we are now living will someday seem like the good old days. To the surprise of no one save the historically naive, there is a community of listeners for whom eighties metal, commonly and I think rightly remembered as "hair metal," represents a style whose passing signaled the end of most of what was fun and exciting about music, and this community's interpretation of what exactly happened when the torch was either passed along to the next generation or wrenched involuntarily from the old guard's grasp is worth a minute or two of our time.

All Child Stars Go on to Either Rob Banks or Work at Seven-Elevens, But the Sun Never Fully Sets on a Hair Metal Band's Fame

When we begin to talk about "communities" of music listeners, we often begin with a set of presuppositions that the phrase "true believers" describes succinctly. The first thing worth noting when we look at hair metal fan communities is that this image of the dedicated megafan whose life revolves around the object of his adoration is at best a gross exaggeration and at worst a caricature. Such ultrafans are of course common in many musical communities: in black metal, for example, where to dress in a manner socially acceptable enough to qualify one for even the most menial and degrading job can be construed as selling out, or in goth subcultures, where a host of personal behaviors—styles of dress, extramusical tastes in film and literature, philosophical leanings, or sexual proclivities and activities—are often part and parcel of the fan experience. But the hair metal community, such as it is, is distant kin at best to these, and bears only cosmetic resemblance to them. Casual involvement seems to be the rule rather than the exception, and even the most established, high-ranking-in-Google hair metal fan sites on the Web are mixtures of personal pages and tribute sites that seem to arise from a different set of assumptions about paying tribute to one's musical heroes than the set that governs the traditional fan club or site.

Why is this? For starters there's the impossibility of making any new hair metal. While retro versions of now-outdated styles of music are common, and while such rehashings of once-popular genres can develop their own new communities with their own sets of stylistic codes, such reimaginings of genres tend to fetishize niche styles: seventies stoner rock, for instance, or postpunk that relies heavily on the Pop Group and the Gang of Four—in either case, and in other similar cases, styles that were highly specialized when they were current and remain so in their various revivals. Even fifties retro follows an unwritten, internal law of reverse entropy that states, roughly, that the smaller the target of historical canonization, the greater the existing audience for its revival. (This is why Skip Spence's *Oar*, which you could not give away free with a tank of gas when it was new, is now generally acknowledged to be a masterpiece.) Hair metal, however, was at its peak tremendously popular. The ubiquity of Warrant's "Cherry Pie" is an unpleasant memory for most of us, to say nothing of the once-unavoidable Guns N' Roses. Implicitly and explicitly, bands like these relied for validation on the supposed existence of a large audience that shared their musical tastes and general worldview. One can find evidence for this in some lyrics of the period (Twisted Sister's "We're Not Gonna Take It" being the easiest example to parse), but you'll find the style's most commonly understood codices in videos, which, one after another, pit the Establishment against Youth, whose strength lies largely in numbers, and in those numbers' willingness to tear down without rebuilding. The images are still with us today, even after years of therapy: Milton Berle in Ratt's "Round and Round" video, playing both parents of a rebellious teenager who, assisted by Ratt themselves as they crash through walls and duck-walk across the dinner table, trashes the family dining room in a gesture meant to indicate the displacement of the old order by a newer and more powerful generation; Twisted Sister, who played this trope more than once; Ozzy Osbourne's "Shot in the Dark," which, while Ozzy seems to have beaten the odds and survived his engagement with a genre that doomed most of its adherents, is an almost era-perfect example of the metal video's seemingly contradictory, all-present message: that true individuality rests in conformity to a mass movement variously but invariably depicted as greatly persecuted but ultimately irresistible and unstoppable. These acts and many others worked hard to codify the requirements of the genre, placing its own popularity (obvious to those within it, but denied and feared by those without) high on the list of qualities vital to the genre's being. "You can't stop rock and roll," as Twisted Sister informed the world on its second album: "it's an angry steed / on a never ending course / with grace and speed / it's an unrelenting force / his head thrown back, defiantly proud / under constant attack." When, in the commercial aftermath of the success of Nirvana's *Nevermind* and Pearl Jam's *Ten*, it became clear that no one cared enough about Twisted Sister's style of rock and roll to attack it, the genre lost much of its reason to go on.

In the absence of a reason to go on, however, the genre undergoes an automatic and radical recontextualization. It emerges from the ahistorical and chaotic present into the warm, comfortable environment of the past. It steps through a mirror, shedding much of what had previously defined it (its own conceptions of power and popularity, for example, or its ultimate irresistibility), assuming qualities abhorrent to its old self but now vital to its continued survival. To put it another way: it loses currency but takes on narrative. What liking these bands whose hour has passed represents is a preference for narrative over engagement, or at least a desire for there to be a strong narrative element to the fan experience. That element is easier to come by within the context of a now-crystallized time, which, for the fan, is naturally a context not only of time but of place and person. The music now carries with it its own narrative, which may vary according to the listener's whim but is set in comfortable and usually pleasant parameters. The music tells a story without even trying to. And this, to the people who like the stuff, makes all the difference in the world.

Bobby Dall You Make a Difference

In real terms what we are talking about is this. In 1987, your hopes of gaining much personal insight into the daily habits of Great White's Tony Montana or Poison's Bobby Dall would have been slight. Your best bet would have been to go the way of the groupie; your chances of getting fan mail answered would have been slim at best. In April of 2001, however, Tony Montana administered and posted regularly to the Yahoo! Group "Tony Montana's Rockin News," which was founded in February of that same year and had twenty-three members, including myself.[2] To put it a different way: on Poison's Web site, one finds, along with obligatory band bio and discography, a number of pictures taken in the operating room during the surgery Bobby Dall required on his back after suffering an onstage injury in 2001. The captions to these pictures are of the family album ain't-life-crazy variety: which is to say, they're reminiscent of a trillion other captions on innumerable AOL Hometown and Geocities pages across the Web. They smack not of the glitz of stardom—of the willful, sustained distance between performer and audience in which hair metal gods reveled in their glory but now either can't muster or, more probably and certainly more interestingly, no longer care to affect—but of the genuine zeal that makes artists popular in the first place, but that they often lose as soon as their paychecks are guaranteed. Sites like Poisonweb feature bulletin boards on which long-time fans post their thoughts, dreams, comments, their thanks for the good times and their best wishes for the future—postings to which, surprisingly and charmingly, the singer or guitarist in question will often post direct responses. Even more remarkably, the acknowledged presence of the idol as known lurker in these discussions doesn't seem to inhibit the discussions at all—as in so many relationships that involve icons, the icon becomes almost secondary to the act of reverence. Fans casually address their idols on these boards as though it were the most natural thing in the world; some of this can probably be attributed to the anonymity afforded to a person who's typing words onto a screen instead of setting pen to paper or speaking to a human being, but enough back-and-forth takes place that one begins to wonder whether a fan-performer relationship of distinctly radical qualities isn't taking place.

If this were indie rock, this would be no surprise—at least, it oughtn't be, were indie rock true to its premise, which is a question for another day. But this is not indie rock: it's a music whose entire culture once predicated itself on the language of bombast, the vocabulary of power and force. So there's something disarming about going to the Delphi-hosted bulletin board on Sebastian Bach's self-designed Web site—its white text on a black background will burn your retinas quicker than staring directly at the sun—and finding, on a front page that will lead eventually to a message board rich in angry rants about a cancelled show at the Stone Pony in Asbury Park and birthday wishes for the recently-turned-thirty-four Mr. Bach, something like this:

> *My dad's name is David Bierk. Most of you know that he did the cover for Skid Row's Slave to the Grind record. Here is a timeline website of just some of his art, including the painting above which is of me & my Grandpa Bill in a laundromat in 1975. This painting is part of the Art Gallery of Peterborough collection in Ontario, Canada & can be viewed in person by the public, along with other paintings there by my dad.*[3]

The text speaks eloquently for itself: practically all of the posing and posturing that defines not only hair metal figures but to a greater or lesser extent popular figures in all realms of music is absent. The give and take between hair metal figures and their fans approaches a kinship that is almost excruciatingly personal. Fans are granted a level of access unheard of anywhere save in the life of, say, grindcore bands touring Europe, who of necessity sleep on a lot of floors and eat a lot of communal meals. But there's nothing humbling in that: the grindcore band, after all, began at that level and is obligated by its vocation to remain at that level or be scorned by the community that supports it. The hair metal figure, on the other hand, has undergone a remarkable transformation: his status has changed from idol to peer. In a sense, his experience of his popularity's decline so exactly mirrors his fans' dislocation with more current music that of necessity the two halves of the performer-fan relationship are merged, blended, joined at the hip.

To put a finer point on it, consider the "Poison, You've Made a Difference in My Life" site on Geocities, a five-page creation of such shattering fragility that it must be left to speak entirely for itself. It pays tribute to the way in which the members of Poison, individually and as a group, have "made a difference" in the author's life. Each member receives a personal tribute; the collective tribute to the band as a whole reads as follows:

> open dedication to the members of the band Poison . . .
> you have made a profound difference in my life,
> and once and for all, I'm telling the world.

> TO POISON:
> Who You are Makes a Difference
> You guys have made a tremendous difference in my life. Truly a profound impact, beyond making me want to name a child after you or something like that. I can honestly say that I would not be alive were it not for you. I wanted to let it be known to the world just how profoundly you have impacted my life, and just how much I owe and love you guys.
> As a group, you have in the past decade brought to my life happiness, light, and often a will to live. In times of my deepest despair, you

touched my heart where no one else could reach and cleansed away all of the hatred and sorrow I held inside me. Like an angel, you were there whenever I needed you. I cannot tell you the number of times that I have had a razor to my wrists . . . or throat and full intentions of doing myself in. But somehow you always managed to intervene: a song on the radio of a passing car, someone humming as they walked past my window . . . there was always some incarnation of you to bring me to my senses. You've always managed to bring me back from the ledge I was balanced on, sometimes literally. When there was nothing but darkness in my life, there was you to light a path to somewhere better. You were quite literally my "Something to Believe In." In all my life, you've been the one male constant. A father figure during some times, and friend during others . . . there are so many hats that you've worn to improve the quality of my life. In addition to you're effect as a whole, you've had a profound effect individually. Each of you bringing something else to my life that made me more whole, and more alive than I could ever have hoped. Your meaning to me is difficult to word, except to say that one of your songs states almost exactly what you mean to me "Only Time Will Tell." In the many horrors that I have endured in my life, from drugs to rape . . . you guys have been my life preserver. Keeping me afloat above all of the garbage and muck around me. You are oxygen to me. I cannot imagine my world without you. I would truly be lost. There is no me without you. I would not be the person I am today were it not for your immense influence in my life.

This is how you've made a difference as a unit. Each of you has also made a profound difference as individuals, which I would also like to share.[4]

The site's guestbook, which contains twenty entries, includes an entry reading: *"i have to say that i understand how poison could touch some ones life in a dramatic way. they are so wonderful. they show love for their music where others show the want for money. they care for their fans where others could care less. i love them,"* one reading: *"Rikki is my Guardian Angel. I am battling cancer for the second time and Rikki was there for me. I know Rikki can't be there for me now, but i'm sure he's thinking of me. You have a wonderful website God Bless you! Nicole,"* and a third that reads in its entirety: *"They are the best band that I have ever seen in my fucking life."*

The Nineties Are Over So Burn Your Pearl Jam Flannels

There is another quality, at least as important as all the others and perhaps more so, that unites hair metal performers and their fans, and it isn't pretty, and I'm sorry to have to report it to you. It first came to my attention when, morbidly fascinated with Ratt's 1997 album *Steel River,* I went searching online for evidence that there was anybody anywhere calling for the return of Ratt. What I found was the now sadly defunct *ratt-n-roll.com,* whose trendsettingly Day-Glo javascript headline read: *"Welcome to Ratt-n-Roll.com!!! The '90's are over, so burn your Pearl Jam flannels!!!"*

Eighties metal bands and the people who love them are of one mind on the question of how it came to pass that the Warrants and White Lions and Poisons of the world fell from popular grace. The watchword is *grunge,* and the rage they feel toward the dressed-down rock music that came to be viewed as a movement in the wake of Nirvana's and Pearl Jam's great success is a seething, hateful beast. As part of a brief questionnaire, I put the following question out to a number of mailing lists: *"Why do you think most of the '80s bands saw their popularity fade shortly after the start of the new decade?"* and the following answers are typical of the responses I got:

> *Grunge music was becoming popular. That was kind of a new sound and style. I believe that Nirvana and Pearl Jam were the main grunge bands that made people turn away from 80s metal and focus more on grunge.*

> *It was getting to be like a broken record. More and more of these bands with long hair and screaming singers were coming out. It was an overflow. Too much of a good thing isn't always good. And some of the longhaired bands that came out were more like jokes, they couldn't really sing that well and were giving long-haired bands a bad name (not that they needed much help but a bad name in a different way). The new good*

bands were lost in the mix of jokes and wanna-bes. Then Kurt Cobain came in and changed everything.

The glitz and glammer was no longer cool. it was more cool to be depressed and misunderstood.

Most pointed, though, was the one who first responded with the single word *"Metallica"* but then amended his response thus: *"Metallica selling out and the fact that an unwashed junkie piece of shit named Kurt Nobrain destroyed everything that we stood for."* While the replacement of one style by another in popular music is an observable, regular phenomenon, and while some fairly strong reactions are common ("Disco sucks" being the most memorable I know of), no one bears a grudge with the tenacity of a hair metal fan. It is part and parcel of the need for narrative: To more fully contextualize the experiences that crystallized their taste in music, there needs to be an era-ending event about which the community can agree. Although some fans offer musical explanations for the turning of the tide (*"it was getting cheesy,"* suggests one respondent), the overwhelming majority believe in a loosely defined conspiracy theory that posits the so-called grunge movement as an all-powerful villain whose victory permanently impacted music for the worse. Without a trace of irony, hair metal fans argue that grunge was a music based on fashion, while hair metal focused first on music and then on spectacle—costumes, flash pots, light shows—a quality that these fans conceive of as somehow entirely distinct from the empty, mindless dictates of fashion to which Nirvana is thought to have been responding.

"Kurt Nobrain" and "everything that we stood for"—what, exactly, did "we" stand for in those times? Could "we" have expected to continue unabated for a thousand-year reign without the interference of the grunge bands? Of course not; musical styles are transitory and have been since men and women first banged rocks together in time. But the arrival of the grunge barbarians at the gates effectively forms a hermetic seal around the entire era, so that all future efforts of the hair metal bands are given new context within the narrative: kings in exile, or saviors rejected by the world they came to improve. Narratives like these feed on themselves, ensuring that, whatever its size, the community of hair metal enthusiasts will only become more firm in their conviction that they have seen the best and the brightest, and that they were right to elect to leave themselves behind rather than moving forward with the new bearers of a false standard.

Notes

Introduction: Who'll Write the Book of Love?

1. As of spring 2003, the Music Museum Alliance included sixty-four members.
2. Presentations from two of the earlier conferences are collected in Andrew Ross and Tricia Rose, eds., *Microphone Fiends: Youth Music and Youth Culture* (New York: Routledge, 1994), and Karen Kelly and Evelyn McDonnell, eds., *Stars Don't Stand Still in the Sky: Music and Myth* (New York: New York University Press, 1999).
3. Paul Morley, *Ask: The Chatter of Pop* (London: Faber and Faber, 1986), p. 55.
4. With understandable overstatement, Ted Ottaviano called Book of Love's poor-selling 1991 release *Candy Carol* "the most misunderstood album in the history of music." Kurt Reighley, "Who the Hell Was Book of Love?" *Resonance* 26 (Summer 2001): 60.
5. Paul Théberge, *Any Sound You Can Imagine: Making Music/Consuming Technology* (Hanover, N.H.: University Press of New England, 1997); Bernard Gendron, *Between Montmartre and the Mudd Club: Popular Music and the Avant-Garde* (Chicago: University of Chicago Press, 2002), p. 310.
6. Tony Mitchell, ed., *Global Noise: Rap and Hip-Hop Outside the U.S.A.* (Middletown, Conn.: Wesleyan University Press, 2001).
7. Motti Regev, "The 'Pop-Rockization' of Popular Music," in David Hesmondhalgh and Keith Negus, eds., *Popular Music Studies* (London: Arnold, 2002), p. 261.
8. One exception is Nick Tosches's exemplary inquiries into the buried history of blackface minstrel Emmitt Miller. See *Where Dead Voices Gather* (New York: Little, Brown, 2001).
9. Hobey Echlin, *V* magazine (Spring 2001), reprinted online at *www.bookoflovemusic.com*.
10. Lawrence Grossberg, "Reflections of a Disappointed Popular Music Scholar," in Roger Beebe, Denise Fulbrook, and Ben Saunders, eds., *Rock over the Edge: Transformations in Popular Music Culture* (Durham, N.C.: Duke University Press, 2002), pp. 25–59. In the

same collection, Robert Fink offers an iconoclastic defense of pop musicology much in keeping with the spirit of this book. See Robert Fink, "Elvis Everywhere: Musicology and Popular Music Studies at the Twilight of the Canon," ibid., pp. 60–109.

1. "And I Guess It Doesn't Matter Any More"

1. The report, *Make or Break: Supporting UK Music in the USA*, was finally published by the British Council at the end of May 2002.

2. This quote taken from the *Daily Mail*, April 25, 2002.

3. The veteran dee jay and chart commentator, Paul Gambaccini, did blame the BBC for the situation: "Radio One has made a deliberate programming decision that acts against the interests of young British artists . . . Their current policy is to fill the airwaves with an American urban sound. US rappers receive airplay that is totally disproportionate to the sales, or the merits, of their music. Meanwhile British artists are losing out" (*Daily Mail*, April 25, 2002). But this seemed to reflect the *Daily Mail*'s animus against the BBC (and Eminem) rather than any industry thinking, and Gambaccini went on to give his own reason for Britain's export problem: unlike their American counterparts, too many aspiring British musicians can't play their instruments properly.

4. The British Council, long funded by the Foreign Office to promote British culture abroad, has recently started publishing a music magazine, *New Routes: A World of Music from Britain*, and syndicating a radio show, *The Selector*, to celebrate Britain as a multicultural society. This is a deliberate break with past policy: "Thankfully, it's no longer possible to easily define what is British music," as the editorial in the 2002 *New Routes* puts it. On the other hand, as Kevin LeGendre points out in the same issue, the British music industry continues to treat black British artists rather less seriously than their African American peers.

5. See Tim Fleming, "Awfully Affecting: The Development of the Sentimental Text in the Lyric of the British and American Popular Song," Ph.D. thesis, Department of English Studies, Strathclyde University, Scotland, 1999. Fleming shows that in the early nineteenth century the sentimental song was strongly associated with the Irish and combined nostalgia for a pastoral utopia with sympathy with the suffering of the peasant poor. The Irish experience

stood for the broader disruption of industrialization. The "Irish song" was still a genre advertised by British and American music publishers at the start of the twentieth century.

6. See Simon Frith, "Playing with Real Feeling–Jazz and Suburbia," *New Formations* 4 (1988).

7. See Simon Frith and Howard Horne, *Art into Pop* (London: Methuen, 1987).

8. For example: "Our music industry is a U.K. success story–it is something we do well–and I believe that we lead the world in creativity and innovation. The history of U.K. popular music is littered with all-time greats of world pop and rock music. Our consumption of music is massive–greater than that of any other nation." From a speech by Pete Wishart, MP–and ex-member of the Scottish band Runrig–opening the first House of Commons debate to be held exclusively on the music industry, June 12, 2002.

2. U.S. and Them

1. Janice Radway, "'What's in a Name?' Presidential Address to the American Studies Association, November 20, 1998," *American Quarterly* 51, no. 1 (1999): 4–5. Wise quoted in ibid., p. 5.

2. Michael Denning, *The Cultural Front* (New York: Verso, 1996), p. 431.

3. Ernest van den Haag, "Of Happiness and Despair We Have No Measure," in Bernard Rosenberg and David Manning White, eds., *Mass Culture: The Popular Arts in America* (New York: Free Press of Glencoe, 1957), p. 520.

4. Philip Rahv, *Image and Idea* (Norfolk, Conn.: New Directions, 1957), pp. 3, 1.

5. Nichola Tawa, *A Music for the Millions* (New York: Pendragon Press, 1984), p. 18.

6. Albert Murray, *The Omni-Americans* (New York: Avon, 1970), p. 88.

7. Stanley Crouch, *The All-American Skin Game, or, The Decoy of Race* (New York: Pantheon, 1995) p. 148.

8. Murray, *Omni-Americans*, p. 38.

9. Sidney W. Mintz, *Sweetness and Power: The Place of Sugar in Modern History* (New York: Penguin, 1985), pp. 192, 190.

3. How Come Jazz Isn't Dead?

1. Rudi Blesh, *Shining Trumpets: A History of Jazz* (New York: Alfred A. Knopf, 1958 [1946]).
2. Ibid., pp. 281–287.
3. James Jones, "The King," *Playboy* 1955, reprinted in Jones, *The Ice-Cream Headache and Other Stories* (New York: Akashic, 2002).
4. Gunther Schuller, *Early Jazz: Its Roots and Musical Development* (New York: Oxford University Press, 1968), p. 89.
5. Nat Hentoff, "An Afternoon with Miles Davis," in Martin Williams, ed., *Jazz Panorama* (New York: Crowell-Collier Press, 1962), p. 165.
6. Conversation with author, 1977.
7. Quoted in Tony Bennett, *The Good Life*, with Will Friedwald (New York: Pocket Books, 1998), unnumbered page.

4. Sister Rosetta Tharpe and the Prehistory of "Women in Rock"

1. Anthony Heilbut, *The Gospel Sound: Good News and Bad Times* (1975; reprint, New York: Limelight Editions, 1985), p. x.
2. Heilbut calls gospel singers "the most underpaid in America, and the fans, surely the poorest of any mass audience." Ibid., p. xi.
3. Rosetta Reitz, "Sister Rosetta," *Hotwire* (May 1991): 16.
4. See Christopher Small, *Music of the Common Tongue: Survival and Celebration in Afro-American Music* (New York: Riverrun Press, 1987).
5. According to Jerma A. Jackson, "The Church of God in Christ was virtually alone among religious communities"—even among those congregations that rejected restraint as a normative temperament for worship—"in its enthusiasm for the guitar." See Jackson, "Testifying at the Cross: Thomas Andrew Dorsey, Sister Rosetta Tharpe and the Politics of African-American Sacred and Secular Music," Ph.D. diss., 1995, p. 138.
6. From an interview with Marie Knight conducted October 18, 2002, in New York City.
7. "20,000 Watch Wedding of Sister Rosetta Tharpe," *Ebony* 6 (October 1951): 27–30; p. 27.
8. "Sister Rosetta Tharpe to Wed Russell Morrison: Costly Gowns,

Fireworks, Concert Added Features," *Washington Afro-American,* June 30, 1951, p. 13.

9. The stamp was issued in July 1998 as part of an American Music Series block of "Gospel Singers" including Tharpe, Mahalia Jackson, Roberta Martin, and Clara Ward. Like other commemorative issues, this one came about as a result of significant lobbying to celebrate gospel musicians as an important part of America's musical heritage.

10. See Sherrie Tucker, *Swing Shift: 'All-Girl' Bands of the 1940s* (Durham, N.C.: Duke University Press, 2000).

11. Nathaniel Mackey, "Other: From Noun to Verb," in Krin Gabbard, ed., *Jazz among the Discourses* (Durham, N.C.: Duke University Press, 1995).

12. Farah Jasmine Griffin, *If You Can't Be Free, Be a Mystery: In Search of Billie Holiday* (New York: Free Press, 2001).

5. The Birth of the Blues

1. Charley Patton, "Pony Blues," 1929 Paramount single. See Charley Patton, *Screamin' and Hollerin' the Blues* (Revenant, 2001).

2. Samuel Charters, "Workin' on the Building: Roots and Influences," in Lawrence Cohn, ed., *Nothing but the Blues* (New York: Abbeville Press, 1993), p. 20. I am indebted to Charters for inspiring the speculation in this essay.

3. There is one other exception: bluegrass, pretty much the invention of Bill Monroe.

4. Robert Palmer, *Deep Blues* (New York: Viking Press, 1981), passim.

6. Richard Speaks!

1. Tony Burke and Dave Penny, "Opening the Door on Richard," *Blues and Rhythm* (March 1986): 28–35.

2. Pigmeat Markham with Bill Levinson, *Here Come the Judge!* (New York: Popular Library, 1969), n.p.; Henry T. Sampson, *Blacks in Blackface: A Sourcebook on Early Black Musical Shows* (Metuchen, N.J.: Scarecrow Press, 1980), pp. 481, 538.

3. "Two Daddies Claim 'Richard' as Their Own Goofy Brainchild," *Baltimore Afro-American,* February 15, 1947, n.p.

4. Jake Austen, review, *Roctober* (Summer 2000): 23.

5. *Music and Comedy Masters*, vol. 6 (Hollywood's Attic, 1996).
6. Jack McVea and His All Stars, *New Deal*, liner notes (Juke Box Lil, 1989).
7. Jim Dawson, "'Richard' Opened Doors," *Los Angeles Times*, October 26, 1986, p. 82.
8. "Two Daddies," *Baltimore Afro-American*.
9. Wendell Green, "Show Time," *Los Angeles Sentinel*, February 6, 1947, p. 19.
10. Ibid.
11. "'Richard' Opens Racial Door in Indianapolis," *Chicago Defender*, January 30, 1947, microfilm, n.p.
12. *Los Angeles Sentinel*, January 30, 1947, microfilm, n.p.
13. "Minister Airs 'Open the Door Richard!'" *Amsterdam News*, March 1, 1947, microfilm, n.p.
14. Dusty Fletcher file, New York Public Library for the Performing Arts.
15. Ibid.
16. Norwood Pony Poindexter, *The Pony Express: Memoirs of a Jazz Musician* (Frankfurt, Germany: J.A.S. Publikationen, 1985), p. 61.
17. Dawson, "'Richard' Opened Doors," p. 82.
18. Ibid.
19. Panel discussion, "The Beat Legacy," *www.naropa.edu*.
20. "Aryan Greetings!" *www.faem.com*.

7. Interrupted Symphony

1. Amanda Holden, ed., *The Penguin Opera Guide* (New York: Penguin Books, 1996), p. 193; see also Mark Evans, *Soundtrack: The Music of the Movies* (New York: Hopkinson and Blake, 1975), p. 27; Tony Thomas, "Korngold: Vienna to Hollywood," liner notes to Erich Wolfgang Korngold, *The Warner Bros. Years* (Rhino, 1996).
2. David Ritz, *Divided Soul: The Life of Marvin Gaye*, 2nd ed. (New York: Da Capo Press, 1991), p. 164.

8. Burnt Sugar

1. R. Kelly, "You Remind Me of Something," *R. Kelly* (Jive/Zomba, 1995). Words and music by Robert Kelly. Copyright 1995 by Zomba Songs Inc. and R. Kelly Publishing, Inc. Mark Anthony Neal has observed of Kelly's shamelessly histrionic come-on slow-jam that

the track "open[s] up a space to critique the surveillance, exchange and control of . . . black female sexuality . . among various artists, corporate entities, and men in general." Mark Anthony Neal, *Soul Babies: Black Popular Culture and the Post-Soul Aesthetic* (New York: Routledge, 2002), p. 13. See also Kelly's more recent and equally raunchy single "Ignition" off of his mea culpa recording *Chocolate Factory*.

2. *New York Times* music critic Ben Ratliff has argued that a "current crop" of African American R&B musicians tend to emphasize rediscovering "what was so good about the black music of their youth, and how it was incorporated into the wider scope of American culture." Ben Ratliff, "Out of a Rut and into a New Groove," *New York Times*, January 23, 2000, p. 4. While critics often cite D'Angelo's 1995 *Brown Sugar* LP as the earliest effort in the current "neo-soul movement," I would argue that the visual economy of this nostalgic black pop cultural trend began with the videos for Michael Jackson's "Remember the Time" (1992) and Janet Jackson's "Got 'Til It's Gone" (1997), each directed by Mark Romanek. Both clips make use of pan-African cultural metaphors as a way in which to engage issues of historical memory, cultural loss, and recuperation. A new tidal wave of nostalgia focusing on hip-hop's longevity as a two-decades-old musical art form has flourished in films such as *Brown Sugar* (2002) and in recent recordings by Common and Erykah Badu ("Love of My Life [An Ode to Hip Hop]"), the Roots *(Phrenology)*, Missy "Misdemeanor" Elliott *(Under Construction)*, and Jurassic 5 *(Power in Numbers)*.

3. Since the late 1980s, an increasing number of scholars and cultural critics have produced important work on this subject. See Trey Ellis, "The New Black Aesthetic," *Callaloo* 12, no. 1 (Winter 1989): 233–243. Greg Tate, "Cult Nats Meet Freeky Deke," *Flyboy in the Buttermilk* (New York: Fireside, 1992). Maureen Mahon, "Black Like This," *American Ethnologist* 27, no. 2 (2000): 283–311.

4. For more on Rock's autobiographical renderings of his childhood in 1970s Brooklyn, see Chris Rock, *Rock This!* (New York: Little, Brown, 1998). See also Rock's appearances on *The Larry King Show* (February 2001) and *The Oprah Winfrey Show* (February 2001). In Ellis's controversial "New Black Aesthetic" article, the band Fishbone anointed themselves "bag people" who collect, mix, and match diverse cultural forms that reflect their hybrid regional and class background. Ellis, p. 234. One could easily consider Rock to

be something of a "bag person" in regards to his free-ranging political perspectives. Black political leaders such as Al Sharpton were at once symbols of reverence and regular sources of parody on the program, alongside satirical routines lampooning the Republican Party's national convention, Anglo-American views on reparations for slavery, and the Confederate flag controversy. See Chris Rock, *Best of the Chris Rock Show, vols. I and II* (HBO Studios, 1997). Many critics have noted the wide range of views expressed in Rock's groundbreaking stand-up special *Bring the Pain,* in which the comedian swung to the right in his "Niggers vs. Black People" monologue and pulled strongly to the left with his antihomophobic "My Aunt Tom" routine. Chris Rock, *Bring the Pain* (Uni/Dreamworks, 1996).

5. The Rolling Stones, "Brown Sugar," *Sticky Fingers* (Virgin Records, 1994; original release 1971). Words and music by Mick Jagger and Keith Richards. Copyright 1971 by Gideon Music, Inc. The Ego Trip collective, a group of "outlaw" pop music critics, have asserted that "Brown Sugar" has remained "an FM radio staple . . . for decades despite the fact that its storyline celebrates a white slaveowner's sexual appetite for Black slave girls. Though some assume the song was inspired by Marsha Hunt, others believe singer Claudia Linnear is the chocolate ingenue being bigged-up." Sacha Jenkins, Elliott Wilson, Chairman Jefferson Mao, Gabriel Alvarez, and Brent Rollins, "The True Race Adventures of the Rolling Stones," *Ego Trip's Big Book of Racism* (New York: Regan Books, 2002), p. 121. See also Sheila Whitely, "Little Red Rooster v. The Honky Tonk Woman: Mick Jagger, Sexuality, Style, and Image," in Sheila Whitely, ed., *Sexing the Groove: Popular Music and Gender* (New York: Routledge, 1997), p. 78. To be sure, there's a real metaphor at work in this song too, in the sense that Mick Jagger (himself a father of African American and Latino children) and Keith Richards have made a fortune off of cannibalizing and co-opting black cultural forms.

6. Chris Rock, "Snowflake," *Bigger and Blacker* (Dreamworks Records, SKG Music, 1999). Music by Mick Jagger and Keith Richards. Lyrics by Chris Rock, Ali Le Roi, Lance Crouther, Wanda Sykes, and Paul Huston. Copyright 1999 by ABCKO Music, Inc. The track features Biz Markie's proclamation, "This is me and my man / And this is our rendition of this Rolling Stones classic / And it go like this . . . Give me any woman, just as long as she's white /

White bitches! How come you look so good? / White Bitches!! Do shit no sister would! / I sho' like some milk / Milk is NATU-RAL baby / As we continue on, I'ma tell you how much I like my white woman, baby . . . I'm not talkin bout no Reggie White / I'm not talkin bout no Barry White / White bitches!! I'm not talkin bout Snappy White / I'm talkin bout Vanna White, Bette White, and SNOW White."

7. See Henry Louis Gates, Jr., *The Signifying Monkey: A Theory of African-American Literary Criticism* (New York: Oxford University Press, 1988), p. 51. Gates defines signifying as "a trope in which are subsumed several other rhetorical tropes, including metaphor, metonymy, synecdoche, and irony (the master tropes)" (p. 52). See also Darryl Dickson-Carr, *African American Satire: The Sacredly Profane Novel* (Columbia: University of Missouri Press, 2001). In a popular-music context, signifying has a far-reaching history as well. Music critic Joe Levy recently observed of Bo Diddley's pioneering efforts in rock and roll that Diddley made deft use of "hidden humor" and that his early work consisted of "often explicitly signifying records which involve putting over a joke on someone who doesn't understand the nuances of African-American thought and speech. It makes fun of white people without them realizing it." Levy as cited in Bernard Weinraub, "Pioneer of a Beat Is Still Riffing for His Due," *New York Times,* February 16, 2003, p. A26.

8. I borrow my sense of the term *post-soul* from Mark Anthony Neal, whose usage describes "the political, social, and cultural experiences of the African American community since the end of the civil rights and Black Power movements." Neal, *Soul Babies,* p. 3.

9. The persistence of racial profiling, the racial and class exclusivity of the info-superhighway, cutbacks in affirmative action, the English-only proposition in California, the anti-immigrant legislation also in California are all evidence of the recent reactionary legislation passed in the wake of Civil Rights gains of the 1960s and '70s.

10. For nearly a century, African American scholarly studies of the dialectic between musical and literary endeavors have shaped the field, pairing black literary and musical production in order to interrogate the depth and range of critical aesthetic periods such as the Harlem Renaissance of the 1920s and the Black Arts movement of the 1960s. Langston Hughes's "weary blues" poetry, for instance, is put into dialogue with Ellington's "indigo" suites. The

insurgent bebop of Charlie Parker and Miles Davis enjoins a spir-
ited, improvisational conversation with the beat lyric and polit-
icized prose of Amiri Baraka. Critics ranging from Baraka to
Houston Baker have, in turn, offered major, influential rumina-
tions on the workings of a "black aesthetic" and a "blues ideology" in the African American literary canon. Houston Baker, *Blues,
Ideology, and African-American Literature* (Chicago: University of
Chicago, 1987). Leroi Jones [Amiri Baraka], *Blues People* (New
York: Morrow Quill, 1963).

However, little attention has been paid to the crosspollination
of aesthetic forms and content, generic strategies, and ideological
(re)visions in the literature and popular music of the post–Civil
Rights era. And in particular, the relationship between class mobility and aesthetic innovation has been greatly discounted by a
consistent critical privileging of working-class, folk culture as the
singular center of "authentic" black expressive forms. This is even
more evident in the overwhelming scholarship on hip-hop at the
expense of more extensive theoretical discussion of multiple black
subcultural music forms. More recently, and in response to the
reductiveness of this kind of critical perspective, literary scholars
such as Valerie Smith, J. Martin Favor, and Nicole King, as well
as anthropologist Mahon, have demonstrated in their scholarship the ways in which the black middle class remains an under-
theorized subject of critical interrogation. These scholars call for
a more sustained investigation of the particular ways in which, in
the aftermath of the Civil Rights movement, black cultural forms
have diversely expanded. See Valerie Smith, *Not Just Race, Not Just
Gender* (New York: Routledge, 1998). J. Martin Favor, *Authentic
Blackness* (Durham, N.C.: Duke University Press, 1999).

11. Mahon, "Black Like This," p. 284. See also Maureen Mahon, *Right
to Rock* (Durham, N.C.: Duke University Press, 2004).

12. For more on cakewalking, see Jacqui Malone, *Steppin' on the Blues*
(Urbana: University of Illinois Press, 1996); David Krasner, *Resistance, Parody, and Double-Consciousness in African American Theatre,
1895–1910* (New York: St. Martin's Press, 1997). See also my *Bodies
in Dissent: Performing Race, Gender, and Nation in the Trans-Atlantic
Imaginary* (Durham, N.C.: Duke University Press, forthcoming).
For more on the politics of cultural appropriation and imitation,
see Shane White's study of early black theater in New York City:

Shane White, *Stories of Freedom in Black New York* (Cambridge, Mass.: Harvard University Press, 2002).

13. Du Bois's canonical observation that African Americans are "gifted with a second sight," a kind of "double consciousness" in which one "ever feels his twoness,—an American, a Negro," still resonates in contemporary culture. W.E.B. Du Bois, *The Souls of Black Folk* (New York: Penguin, 1989 [1903]), p. 5. The political statement that's crucial to keep in mind here is the way in which Living Colour and other bands in the Black Rock Coalition used the forum of rock as a point of encounter with white fans to work through disturbing racial stereotypes concerning black masculinity ("Funny Vibe") or to explode the myth of equal access to suburban prosperity in the context of a real recession in the late 1980s ("Which Way to America?"). As Mahon and others have pointed out, Living Colour's music critiques inequities while participating in the genre of hard rock to express an integrated sensibility—reflecting their liminal position as largely middle-class musicians raised with a variety of cultural influences and forms.

14. Ellis, "New Black Aesthetic," p. 234.

15. Ibid., p. 233. I would add that it's important to place Fishbone in the broader cultural context of the West Coast funk-rock underground of the '80s and '90s. Other bands, such as George Clinton disciples the Red Hot Chili Peppers and San Francisco's Faith No More, relied on guerrilla-theater-turned-three-ring-circus stage antics. Nevertheless, what distinguishes Fishbone from these other acts was not only their African American identifications but also their emphasis on inserting and twisting these identifications and often placing them at the center of their live sets.

16. Fishbone, "Slow Bus Movin (Howard Beach Party)," *Truth and Soul* (Sony, 1988). Music and lyrics by Angelo Moore, Kendall Jones, Walter Kibby II, and Fish. Copyright 1988 by Music Corporation of America, Inc., and Bouillabaise Music.

17. Fishbone is not alone in this move. See Body Count's infamous debut disc, *Body Count* (Warner Bros., 1992). Although the track "Cop Killer" received the bulk of press for Ice-T's all-black, punk-metal group, other tracks such as "KKK Bitch" promote a similar use of female bodies as tools of resistance in battling white supremacy, indeed in far more hyperbolically misogynist terms.

18. Mos Def, "Rock N Roll," *Black On Both Sides* (Rawkus Records,

1999). Music and lyrics by D. Smith / L. Fernandez. Copyright 1999 by EMI Blackwood Music, Inc. / Medina Sound Music (BMI) and Psycho Les Publishing.

19. In *The White Boy Shuffle*, author Paul Beatty produces what amounts to a black feminist narrative of hip-hop masculinity that situates the protagonist, Gunnar Kaufman, in a universe of resourcefully signifying female progenitors. See Paul Beatty, *The White Boy Shuffle* (New York: Owl Books, 1996).

20. For more on racial politics and cultural appropriation, see Greg Tate, ed., *Everything But the Burden: What White People Are Taking from Black Culture* (New York: Broadway Books, 2003), p. 14.

21. Ongiri's comments were made during the "Post-Soul Satire Symposium" held at College of the Holy Cross in the winter of 2001. I'd like to thank all of the wonderful participants in that event, and organizer Bertram Ashe, Danzy Senna, Trey Ellis, Darryl-Dickson Carr, and Martin Favor, in particular, for their useful comments and feedback in the early drafting of this piece.

22. Burnt Sugar is both the name of Greg Tate's experimental alternative band project and, I would suggest, an appropriate label for those black feminist artists who radically overthrow the Stones' "Brown Sugar" racial caricatures.

9. Bits of Me Scattered Everywhere

I wish to thank Jurrien Schadron, Eleanor Ramsay, Robert Christgau, and Eric Weisbard for various assistance.

1. The Kinks, "Sitting in My Hotel," *Everybody's in Showbiz* (RCA, 1972). Words and music by Raymond Douglas Davies. Copyright 1972 by Davray Music Ltd.

2. Ray Davies, in concert, Boston 1971, attended by author.

3. In Jon Savage, *The Kinks* (London: Faber and Faber, 1984), p. 81.

4. Ray Davies, in concert, Worcester, Massachusetts, 1983, attended by author.

5. Savage, *The Kinks*, p. 124.

6. The Kinks, "Muswell Hillbilly," *Muswell Hillbillies* (RCA, 1971). Words and music by Raymond Douglas Davies. Copyright 1971 by Davray Music Ltd.

7. The Kinks, "Kentucky Moon," *Muswell Hillbillies* (Konk/Velvel CD reissue, 1998). Words and music by Raymond Douglas Davies. Copyright 1971 by Davray Music Ltd.

8. Dave Hickey, "Kinks –'Soap Opera': Rock Opera That Works," *The Village Voice*, May 19, 1975.

9. Keith Phipps, "Ray Davies," *The Onion a.v. Club*, March 28, 2002, *www.theonion.com*.

10. Richard Skanse, "The Complicated Life of Ray Davies," *Rolling-Stone.com*, March 15, 2000.

11. Thomas Pynchon, *The Crying of Lot 49* (New York: Harper and Row, 1990 [1966]) p. 33.

12. Savage, *The Kinks*, p. 136.

13. Ray Davies, *X-Ray* (London: Viking, 1994) p. 27.

14. Ibid., pp. 329–330.

15. Ibid., p. 2.

16. Ibid., p. 372.

17. Ibid., p. 11.

18. Ibid., p. 128.

19. Ibid., p. 335.

20. Ibid., p. 352.

21. Ibid., p. 294.

22. Ibid., p. 294.

23. Ibid., p. 5.

24. Ibid., p. 122.

25. Ibid., p. 370.

26. Ibid., p. 310.

27. Manny Farber, *Negative Space* (New York: Da Capo, 1998) p. 9.

28. Davies, *X-Ray*, p. 145.

29. Ibid., p. 151.

30. Ibid., p. 7.

31. Ibid., pp. 419–420.

32. Reproduced in Savage, *The Kinks*, p. 6.

33. The Kinks, "I Took My Baby Home" (Pye single, 1964). Words and music by Raymond Douglas Davies. Copyright 1964 by Kassner Music Co. Ltd.

34. Davies, *X-Ray*, p. 175.

35. Ibid., p. 284.

36. Rob Brunner, "Tom Waits Reveals His Suburban Side," *Entertainment Weekly*, April 16, 2003.

37. The Kinks, "Lola," *Lola versus Powerman and the Moneygoround: Part I* (Reprise, 1970). Words and music by Raymond Douglas Davies. Copyright 1970 by Haill & Range Songs, Inc.

38. The Kinks, "A Well-Respected Man," *The Kinks Greatest Hits*

(Reprise, 1966). Words and music by Raymond Douglas Davies. Copyright 1966 by Kassner Music Co. Ltd.

39. The Kinks, "20th Century Man," *Muswell Hillbillies* (RCA, 1971). Words and music by Raymond Douglas Davies. Copyright 1971 by Davray Music Ltd.

40. Davies, *X-Ray*, p. 311.

41. T. S. Eliot, "Andrew Marvell," in *Selected Prose of T. S. Eliot*, ed. Frank Kermode (New York: Farrar, Straus and Giroux, 1975), p. 361.

42. The Kinks, "People Take Pictures of Each Other," *Village Green Preservation Society* (Reprise, 1969). Words and music by Raymond Douglas Davies. Copyright 1969 by Noma Music, Inc. / Hi-Count Music, Inc. (BMI).

43. Dan DeLuca, "Kinks' Ray Davies Is Seizing the Moment," *Philadelphia Inquirer*, October 24, 1996.

44. The Kinks, "People Take Pictures of Each Other."

45. The Kinks, "Celluloid Heroes," *Everybody's in Showbiz* (RCA, 1972). Words and music by Raymond Douglas Davies. Copyright 1972 by Davray Music Ltd.

46. Davies, *X-Ray*, p. 49.

47. Ibid., pp. 311–312.

48. Ibid., pp. 399–400.

49. Neville Marten and Jeff Hudson, *The Kinks: Four Respected Men* (London: Sanctuary Publishing, 2001), p. 109.

50. Davies, *X-Ray*, p. 386.

51. The Kinks, *X-Norman: A Soap Opera*, Philadelphia, April 20, 1975 (bootleg recording).

52. Davies, *X-Ray*, p. 384.

53. The Kinks, *Preservation*, New York City, November 24, 1976 (bootleg recording).

54. Quoted in Savage, *The Kinks*, p. 136.

55. Ibid., p. 101.

56. Michael Edwards, *Priscilla, Elvis, and Me: In the Shadow of the King* (New York: St. Martin's Press, 1988), p. 61.

57. Ibid., pp. 85–86.

58. Ibid., p. 124.

59. Ibid., pp. 218–219.

60. Ray Davies, *Waterloo Sunset* (London: Viking, 1997), pp. 236–237.

61. Ibid., p. 236.

62. Ibid., p. 154.
63. Ibid., p. 157.
64. Ibid., p. 186.
65. Ibid., p. 237.
66. Davies, *X-Ray*, p. 259.
67. *Charley Varrick* (Universal, 1973), directed by Don Siegel.

11. All the Memories Money Can Buy

1. Charles Keil and Steve Feld, *Music Grooves: Essays and Dialogues* (Chicago: University of Chicago Press, 1994), p. 313.
2. Charles K. Wolfe, "The Birth of an Industry," in Patrick Carr, ed., *The Illustrated History of Country Music* (New York: Anchor Books, 1980), p. 35.
3. Richard A. Peterson, *Creating Country Music: Fabricating Authenticity* (Chicago: University of Chicago Press, 1997), pp. 7–8.
4. Archie Green, quoted in Loyal Jones, *Radio's "Kentucky Mountain Boy": Bradley Kincaid* (Berea, Ky.: Appalachian Center, 1980), p. 2.
5. Peterson, *Creating Country Music*, p. 37.
6. In David Evans, *Big Road Blues: Tradition and Creativity in the Folk Blues* (New York: Da Capo Press, 1987), p. 72.
7. In Nolan Porterfield, *Jimmie Rodgers: The Life and Times of America's Blue Yodeler* (Urbana: University of Illinois Press, 1979), pp. 91, 108.
8. Bill Malone, *Cowboys and Musical Mountaineers: Southern Culture and the Roots of Country Music* (Athens: University of Georgia Press, 1993), p. 43.
9. Merle Travis, "Dark as a Dungeon," *Folk Songs of the Hills* (Capitol, 1947). Words and music by Merle Travis. Copyright 1947 [backdated from 1955] by Unichappell Music and Elvis Presley Music Inc.
10. Archie Green, *Only a Miner: Studies in Recorded Coal-Mining Songs* (Urbana: University of Illinois Press, 1972), pp. 3, 299.
11. Ibid., p. 355.
12. Ibid., p. 329.
13. Evan Eisenberg, *The Recording Angel: The Experience of Music from Aristotle to Zappa* (New York: Penguin, 1988), pp. 105, 109.
14. Paul Tingen, *Miles Beyond: The Electric Explorations of Miles Davis, 1967–1991* (New York: Billboard Books, 2001), p. 61.

15. Ibid., p. 68.
16. Robert Polito, "Shadow Play: B-D-D and Back," *Tin House* 3, no. 2 (2002): 188.
17. Greg Tate, *Flyboy in the Buttermilk: Essays on Contemporary America* (New York: Simon and Schuster, 1992), p. 82.
18. Tingen, *Miles Beyond*, p. 74.
19. Chris Fujiwara, "Saved by Betrayal: The Restorations of *Touch of Evil* and *Raw Power*," *Hermenaut* 15 (2002): 109.
20. Gina Arnold, *Route 666: On the Road to Nirvana* (New York: St. Martin's Press, 1991), p. 6.

12. Authorship Meets Downpression

1. Burt Kimmelman, *The Poetics of Authorship in the Later Middle Ages: The Emergence of the Modern Literary Persona* (New York: Peter Lang, 1996), p. 120.
2. Thomas McCarthy, *Relationships of Sympathy: The Writer and the Reader in British Romanticism* (Aldershot: Scolar Press, 1997), p. 148.
3. Roland Barthes, "The Death of the Author," *Image/Music/Text* (London: Fontana Press, 1976).
4. Simon Frith, *Sound Effects: Youth, Leisure and the Politics of Rock 'n' Roll* (London: Constable, 1983), and Fred Goodman, *The Mansion on the Hill: Dylan, Young, Geffen, Springsteen and the Head-On Collision of Rock and Commerce* (New York: Vintage Books, 1998).
5. Stephen Davis, *Bob Marley: Conquering Lion of Reggae* (London: Plexus, 1994), pp. 98–108.
6. Gayatri Chakravorty Spivak, "Can the Subaltern Speak?" in *Marxism and the Interpretation of Culture*, ed. Cary Nelson and Lawrence Grossberg (London: Macmillan Education, 1988).
7. Nicholas Stolzoff, *Wake the Town and Tell the People: Dancehall Culture in Jamaica* (Durham, N.C.: Duke University Press, 2000).
8. Will Straw, "Characterizing Rock Music Culture: The Case of Heavy Metal," in *On Record: Rock, Pop and the Written Word*, ed. Simon Frith and Andrew Goodwin (London: Routledge, 1990 [1983]).
9. For an account, see Keith Negus, *Popular Music in Theory* (Cambridge: Polity Press, 1996).
10. Jason Toynbee, *Making Popular Music: Musicians, Creativity and Institutions* (London: Arnold, 2000).

11. Barthes, "The Death of the Author," p. 146.

12. Howard Becker, *Art Worlds* (Berkeley: University of California Press, 1982).

13. Verena Reckord, "Reggae, Rastafarianism and Cultural Identity," in *Reggae, Rasta, Revolution: Jamaican Music from Ska to Dub,* ed. Chris Potash (London: Books with Attitude, 1997), pp. 8–10.

14. Lloyd Bradley, *Bass Culture: When Reggae Was King* (London: Penguin), pp. 49–62.

15. Roland Alphonso, "Blackberry Brandy," Various Artists, *Trojan Ska* Box Set (Trojan, 1998).

16. The Wailers, "Simmer Down," *Bob Marley: Songs of Freedom* (Island/Tuff Gong, 1992).

17. Stolzoff, *Wake the Town and Tell the People;* Steve Barrow and Peter Dalton, *The Rough Guide to Reggae,* 2nd ed. (London: Rough Guides, 2001); Bradley, *Bass Culture.*

18. Davis, *Bob Marley,* pp. 102–3.

19. Hal Foster, "'Primitive' Scenes," *Critical Inquiry* 20, no. 1 (1993).

20. Carl Gayle, "Are You Ready for Rude and Rough Reggae?" in *Rock File 2,* ed. Charlie Gillett (St. Albans: Panther, 1974).

21. Steve Lake, "Burnin' with Marley!" *Melody Maker,* December 1, 1973, p. 17.

22. Martin Hayman, "Wailers' Simple Message," *Sounds,* June 9, 1973, p. 10.

23. Steve Lake, "Burnin' Marley," *Melody Maker,* October 20, 1973, p. 35.

24. David Milton, "Catch-A-Fire," *Melody Maker,* May 5, 1973, p. 46.

25. Sebastian Clarke, "Rastafari Rock," *New Musical Express,* May 12, 1973, p. 12.

26. Foster, "'Primitive' Scenes," p. 76.

27. Gayatri Spivak, "Subaltern Talk: Interview with the Editors," in *The Spivak Reader,* ed. Donna Landry and Gerald MacLean (New York: Routledge, 1996), p. 289.

28. Homi Bhabha, "Signs Taken for Wonders: Questions of Ambivalence and Authority under a Tree outside Delhi, May 1817," *Critical Inquiry* 12, no. 1 (1985).

29. Homi Bhabha and John Comaroff, "Speaking of Postcoloniality in the Continuous Present: A Conversation," in *Relocating Postcolonialism,* ed. David Theo Goldberg and Ato Quayson (Oxford: Blackwell Publishers, 2002), p. 34.

13. Creativity and Band Dynamics

My research and teaching in the fields of complex organization, social interaction, cultural theory, and sociology of rock music, at one point independent streams of interest, converged when I taught a series of senior seminars on rock bands as small groups. Dozens of bands were studied in terms of their patterns of social relations. These seminars, along with research spinning off from them and my interviews with musicians as a long-term rock journalist, provide the data-theory matrix out of which this reflection on band creativity has been developed. This study is part of a larger project on the full range of band dynamics (see, for example, Deena Weinstein, "Rock Bands: Collective Creativity," in *Current Research on Occupations and Professions,* vol. 8: *Creators of Culture: Occupations and Professions in Culture Industries,* ed. Muriel G. Cantor and Cheryl Zollars (Greenwich, Conn.: JAI Press, 1993), pp. 205–222; and "All Singers Are Dicks," *Popular Music and Society,* in press. The author wishes to thank Jason Toynbee and Michael Weinstein for their helpful readings of an earlier version of this chapter.

1. "Joe's Blue Plate Special Radio Show: Interview with Rancid," found at *www.joesgrille.com.*
2. Sam Blackwell, "Giving a Beating: The Wild Woman behind Kid Rock," *Southeast Missourian,* May 2, 2002.
3. "The Dolly Boy," *Woman Magazine,* October 8, 1983, n.p.
4. Mike Stax, "Wally Waller Interview," *Ugly Things* 7 (1988).
5. "Stones on Jones," *www.classicrockpage.com.*
6. "Where Are They Now," *Q Magazine* (January 1977): n.p.
7. Alex Vagelatos, "Doobie Brothers," *Whatzup: Heartland Art, Entertainment and Recreation* (2000): n.p.
8. Fred Schruers, "Tom Petty: On the Road," *Rolling Stone,* May 4, 1995, p. 50.
9. Eric Weisbard et al., "Ten Past 'Ten,'" *Spin* (August 2001): 100.
10. There is a host of analyses and descriptions in rock discourse on the centrality of the concept of authenticity. See, for example, R. Pratt, "The Politics of Authenticity in Popular Music: The Case of the Blues," *Popular Music and Society* 10 (1986): 55–78; David Sanjek, "Pleasure and Principles: Issues of Authenticity in the Analysis of Rock 'n' Roll," *Tracking: Popular Music Studies* 4 (1994): 12–21; and David Tetzlaff, "Music for Meaning: Reading the Dis-

course of Authenticity in Rock," *Journal of Communication Inquiry* 18 (December 1994): 95–117.

11. Simon Frith and Howard Horne, *Art into Pop* (London: Methuen, 1987).

12. Umberto Eco, "Innovation and Repetition: Between Modern and Post-Modern Aesthetics," *Daedalus* 114, no. 4 (Fall 1985): 161–162.

13. Deena Weinstein, "Art vs. Commerce: Deconstructing a (Useful) Romantic Illusion," in *Stars Don't Stand Still in the Sky: Music and Myth*, ed. Karen Kelly and Evelyn McDonnell (New York: New York University Press, 1999), pp. 56–69.

14. In recent decades record producers have also been royalty recipients, but their creative contributions are, except for occasional praise, left unexplored. The "What goes on in the bus, stays in the bus" dictum also seems to extend to the recording studio.

15. Christina Saraceno, "Manson Bassist Ousted," *www.RollingStone.com* (May 30, 2002).

16. One thinks of the relationships between such singular creators and bandmate sidekicks as Billy Corgan and Jimmy Chamberlin in Smashing Pumpkins, and Dave Mustaine and Dave Ellefson in Megadeth.

17. Deena Dasein, "Rob Halford: Former High Priest Turns into a Real Fighter," *Illinois Entertainer* (January 1994): 18, 29.

18. Jim Farber, "Fleetwood Mac's Bewitching Stevie Nicks Flies Solo on *Bella Donna*," *Us*, October 27, 1981, found at *www.nicksfix.com*.

19. Keith Spera, "Homemade Jams: Guest Bassists Contribute Fresh Grooves to Gov't Mule's 'Deep End,'" *New Orleans Times-Picayune*, October 25, 2002, sect. Lagniappe, p. 28.

20. Julie Slater, "Jason Newsted Cleaning Out His Recording Studio Closet," *K-Rock Radio: Music Minute* (January 2, 2003), found at *www.krockradio.com*.

21. I appreciated the ubiquity of this excuse when I ran a Google search online for the terms *creative differences* and *band:* more than 3,300 hits referenced hundreds of bands.

14. "O Secret Stars Stay Secret"

1. Television Personalities, "If I Could Write Poetry," *Mummy I'm Not Watching You* (Dreamworld, 1981); *Prime Time Television Personalities* (Nectar, 1997).

2. Philip Larkin, *Collected Poems*, ed. Anthony Thwaite (London: Faber and Faber, 1988), p. 167.

3. Paul Muldoon, *Poems 1968–1998* (New York: Farrar, Straus & Giroux, 1999), pp. 398–399.

4. Jim Elledge, ed., *Sweet Nothings: An Anthology of Rock and Roll in American Poetry* (Bloomington: Indiana University Press, 1994), p. xix.

5. In ibid., p. 207.

6. In ibid., p. 87.

7. Thomas Swiss, "Poetry and Pop," *Popular Music* 15, no. 2 (1994): 8.

8. José Ortega y Gasset, "In Search of Goethe from Within," *Partisan Review* 16, no. 12 (1949): 1184.

9. Thom Gunn, *Collected Poems* (New York: Farrar, Straus and Giroux, 1995), p. 57. Used by permission.

10. Friedrich Schiller, *On the Naïve and Sentimental in Literature*, trans. Helen Watanabe-O'Kelly (Manchester: Carcanet, 1981), pp. 35, 68.

11. In Elledge, *Sweet Nothings*, p. 43.

12. Lucie Brock-Broido, *The Master Letters* (New York: Knopf, 1995), p. 37.

13. Jeremy Reed, *Red-Haired Android* (London: Paladin, 1992), pp. 101, 95.

14. Twenty poets under forty with no more than three collections each, the New Gen poets occupied the widely noticed summer 1994 special issue of *Poetry Review;* Simon Armitage and Glyn Maxwell remain both the best known of the New Gen poets and those most strongly associated with the term. For the cartoon, see *Poetry Review*, special issue (Summer 1994): 79.

15. David Wheatley, *Thirst* (Loughrew, Ireland: Gallery, 1997), p. 16.

16. Drew Daniel, "I Wanted to Hate Slamdek," in *Slamdek A to Z: The Illustrated History of Louisville's Slamdek Record Company*, ed. K. Scott Richter (Louisville, Ky.: K Composite Media, 1996), p. 199.

17. Joshua Clover, *Madonna Anno Domini* (Baton Rouge: Louisiana State University Press, 1997), p. 1.

18. Ibid., p. 62.

19. Ibid., p. 36.

20. Jen Hofer, "do I-could-is it-among . . . ," *Kenning* 10 (2001): 10–11, p. 10; Mark Bibbins, *Sky Lounge* (St. Paul: Graywolf, 2003), p. 44; Lee Ann Brown, *Polyverse* (Los Angeles: Sun and Moon, 1997).

21. Saskia Hamilton, *As for Dream* (St. Paul: Graywolf, 2001), p. 61.

22. Rites of Spring, "For Want Of," *Rites of Spring* (Dischord, 1985).
23. Hamilton, *As For Dream*, p. 29.
24. D. A. Powell, *Tea* (Hanover, N.H.: Wesleyan University Press / University Press of New England, 1998), p. 13.
25. Ibid., p. 23.
26. Ibid., p. xiii.
27. Ange Mlinko, *Matinées* (Boston: Zoland, 1999), p. 33.
28. Ibid., p. 31.
29. Ibid., p. 52.
30. Ibid., p. 41.
31. Personal communication, February 2002.
32. Christopher Beach, *Poetic Culture: Contemporary American Poetry Between Community and Institution* (Evanston, Ill.: Northwestern University Press, 1999), p. 34.
33. Gabriel Gudding, *A Defense of Poetry* (Pittsburgh: University of Pittsburgh Press, 2002), p. 83.

16. Rapping about Rapping

1. Jimmy Spicer, "The Adventures of Super Rhymes," *Old School Classics* (Tuff City, 1989). Words and music by Jimmy Spicer. Copyright 1980 by Street Tuff Tunes (ASCAP).
2. Jay-Z, "Heart of the City (Ain't No Love)," *The Blueprint* (Roc-A-Fella/Island Def Jam, 2001). Words and music by Shawn Carter, Kanye West. Copyright 2001 by EMI Blackwood Music, Inc., Lil Lulu Publishing, and Universal Music Corp.
3. Run-DMC, "Sucker M.C.'s," *Run-DMC* (Profile/Arista, 1984). Words and music by L. Smith, J. Simmons, and D. McDaniels. Copyright 1983 by Protoons, Inc., and Rush Groove.
4. Run-DMC, "It's Tricky," *Raising Hell* (Profile, 1986). Words and music by J. Simmons, D. McDaniels, D. Reeves, and S. Brown. Copyright 1986 by Protoons, Inc., and Rush Groove.
5. Too $hort, "Rhymes," *Life Is . . . Too $hort* (Jive/RCA, 1988). Words and music by Todd Shaw. Copyright 1989 by Willesden Music, Inc., and Srand Music.
6. N.W.A, "Straight Outta Compton," *Straight Outta Compton* (Ruthless/Priority, 1988). Words and music by O'Shea Jackson, Lorenzo Patterson, Eric Wright, and Andre Young. Copyright 1989 by Ruthless Attack Muzick.

7. N.W.A, "Express Yourself," *Straight Outta Compton* (Ruthless/Priority, 1988). Words and music by O'Shea Jackson. Copyright 1990 by Ruthless Attack Muzick.

8. 2Pac, "All Eyez on Me," *All Eyez on Me* (Death Row/Interscope, 1996). Words and music by Tupac Shakur, Johnny Jackson, and Tyruss Himes. Copyright 1996 by Songs of Universal, Inc.; Joshua's Dream; BMG Songs, Inc.; Black-Hispanic Music; Zomba Entertainment, Inc.; Imperial Loco Entertainment; and Careers-BMG Music Publishing, Inc.

9. Notorious B.I.G., "Somebody's Gotta Die," *Life after Death* (Bad Boy/Arista, 1997). Words and music by C. Wallace, N. Myrick, C. Broady, S. Combs, and A. Hester. Copyright 1997 by Big Poppa Music, Justin Combs Publishing (EMI–April Music, Inc.)/Nash Mack Publishing (ASCAP), July Six Publishing (BMI), Longitude Music (BMI).

10. Juvenile, "U Understand," *Tha G-Code* (Cash Money/Universal, 1999). Words and music by Terius Grey and Byron Thomas. Copyright 1999 by Money Mack Music (BMI).

11. Missy "Misdemeanor" Elliott, "I'm Talkin,'" *Supa Dupa Fly* (The Gold Mind, Inc./Eastwest/Elektra, 1997). Words and music by Melissa "Missy" Elliott and Tim Mosley. Copyright 1997 by Mass Confusion Music and Virginia Beach Music.

12. Eminem, "8 Mile," *Music from and Inspired by the Motion Picture "8 Mile"* (Shady/Interscope, 2002). Words and music by M. Mather and L. Resto. Copyright 2002 by Eight Mile Style.

17. Bread and Butter Songs

1. Simon Frith, *Performing Rites: On the Value of Popular Music* (Cambridge: Harvard University Press, 1996), pp. 72, 275.

2. Chuck Eddy, *The Accidental Evolution of Rock 'n' Roll* (New York: Da Capo Press, 1997), p. 48.

3. Suzanne Langer, *Philosophy in a New Key,* 2nd ed. (New York: Mentor Books, 1951), pp. 208, 203.

18. Good Pop, Bad Pop

1. Or not impossible. There's much to say about the British revolution of the early twenty-first century, the "mashup": a song made by laying (generally) the instrumental track of one pop smash un-

der the vocals of another. The way in which this satisfies the fantasy of hyperconsumption, while providing an avenue of critical response to pop, serves as something like a flag, or perhaps just a headstone, for postmodernism.

2. The quotes following are from throughout the essay "On Popular Music," most recently found in Theodor Adorno, *Essays on Music* (Berkeley: University of California Press, 2002), pp. 437–469.

3. The complaints are common not just to the billions of music fans who've never read Adorno, but the thousands who have and are certain they're not snobs like Adorno, because they like jazz or something.

4. Georg Simmel, "The Metropolis and Mental Life," *On Individuality and Social Forms* (Chicago: University of Chicago Press, 1971), p. 338.

5. T. J. Clark, "Painting at Ground Level, Lecture 2: Bruegel in the Land of Cockaigne," unpublished paper provided by the author, p. 16.

19. The Carly Simon Principle

1. It's worth noting that Kurt Cobain is arguably the most painful illustration of the Carly Simon Principle, as his musical genius increased exponentially in the wake of his suicide. And unlike with Jimi Hendrix or Janis Joplin, Nirvana's legacy wasn't merely glamorized by Cobain's death—it was validated. In a genre where everyone seemed to be singing about depression and alienation, Cobain became the only grunge artist anyone believed. It's not just that Nirvana made the period's best-sounding album; Nirvana made the period's "greatest" album, and that was partially due to the retrospective assumption of the artist's sincerity. One needs to remember that, at the time of its release, some people thought *Nevermind* wasn't even as good as Teenage Fanclub's *Bandwagonesque*.

2. Some people who've read this sentence have given me confused looks and asked, "But isn't that exactly the opposite of the Carly Simon Principle?" And my response is, "Of course!" The whole thing about the CSP is not that it's logical; it's just that it's true.

3. Actually, this is not the greatest example, since Moby's album *18* pretty much tanked like a proverbial lead zeppelin, and now nobody cares about Moby or thinks he's particularly great. But it cer-

tainly seemed true on the evening I wrote this, and I've always been one to believe that if something is true once, it's kinda true forever.

20. Groove as Niche

1. Earth, Wind & Fire's video documentary *Shining Stars: The Official Story of Earth, Wind & Fire* (Eagle Vision, 2001).

2. Earth, Wind & Fire, "Reasons," *That's the Way of the World* (Columbia, 1975). Other Earth, Wind & Fire songs discussed in this essay include "Fantasy" and "Serpentine Fire," *All 'N All* (Columbia, 1977), and "September," *The Best of Earth, Wind & Fire, Vol. 1* (Columbia, 1978).

3. See Richard Middleton, *Studying Popular Music* (Milton Keynes, England: Open University Press, 1990), especially pp. 287–292.

4. John Miller Chernoff, *African Rhythm and African Sensibility: Aesthetics and Social Action in African Musical Idioms* (Chicago: University of Chicago Press, 1979). Christopher Small, *Music of the Common Tongue: Survival and Celebration in African-American Music* (Hanover, N.H.: Wesleyan University Press, 1998 [1987]). Michael B. Bakan, *Music of Death and New Creation: Experiences in the World of Balinese Gamelan Beleganjur* (Chicago: University of Chicago Press, 1999), p. 313.

5. See, for example, Paul F. Berliner, *Thinking in Jazz: The Infinite Art of Improvisation* (Chicago: University of Chicago Press, 1994), and Ingrid Monson, *Saying Something: Jazz Improvisation and Interaction* (Chicago: University of Chicago Press, 1996).

6. Thomas Turino, *Moving away from Silence: Music of the Peruvian Altiplano and the Experience of Urban Migration* (Chicago: University of Chicago Press, 1993), p. 111.

7. Anne Danielsen, "Presence and Pleasure: A Study in the Funk Grooves of James Brown and Parliament" (Ph.D. diss., University of Oslo, 2001; Hanover, N.H.: Wesleyan University Press, forthcoming).

8. Dave Marsh, in *The New Rolling Stone Record Guide,* ed. Dave Marsh and John Swenson (New York: Random House, 1983), p. 159. Patricia Romanowski and Holly George-Warren, eds., *The New Rolling Stone Encyclopedia of Rock and Roll* (New York: Fireside, 1995), p. 296.

9. Ricky Vincent, *Funk: The Music, the People, and the Rhythm of the One* (New York: St. Martin's, 1996), p. 188.

10. Or it may suggest that understanding what they did and why people cared about it is not actually the goal of much writing about music, though it is for me.

11. Peter Shapiro, "Earth, Wind & Fire," in *Rock: The Rough Guide*, ed. Jonathan Buckley and Mark Ellingham (London: Rough Guides, 1996), pp. 277–278.

12. Robert Christgau, original *Consumer Guide* note reposted on *www.robertchristgau.com*.

13. "When I talked (in *Blues People*) about surviving Africanisms in Afro-American culture, I did not take into consideration that *American culture itself* is historically partially constructed of continuing and thematic Africanisms!" Amiri Baraka, "The 'Blues Aesthetic' and the 'Black Aesthetic': Aesthetics as the Continuing Political History of a Culture," *Black Music Research Journal* 11, no. 2 (Fall 1991): 109. Paul Gilroy, *Against Race: Imagining Political Culture beyond the Color Line* (Cambridge, Mass.: Harvard University Press, 2000).

14. Maurice White, introductory liner notes for Earth, Wind & Fire, *The Eternal Dance* (Columbia/Legacy, 1992), n.p.

15. David Nathan, "The Eternal Dance of Earth, Wind & Fire," liner notes for Earth, Wind & Fire, *The Eternal Dance*.

16. Ibid.

17. Chris Heim, "Earth Wind & Fire Aglow Again," *Chicago Tribune*, February 18, 1988, sec. 2, p. 9.

18. Nathan, liner notes.

19. Maurice White, quoted in Lynn Van Matre, "Who Told Maurice White to Record 'Stand By Me'? It Was . . . a Voice," *Chicago Tribune*, December 1, 1985, sec. 13, p. 24.

20. *Shining Stars* video documentary.

21. This is the problem, as I see it, with Guy Ramsey's recent calls for white scholars to theorize their relationship to black music: it's a fine idea, but only if it is done in a way that does not reinforce simplistic binarisms. See, for example, Guthrie P. Ramsey, Jr., "Who Matters: The New and Improved White Jazz-Literati: A Review Essay," *American Music* 17, no. 1 (Spring 1999): 205–215.

22. Gilroy, *Against Race*, p. 343.

23. The progression is b-E-c#-f#, or ii-V-iii-vi.

24. The band's Web site is *www.rahowa.com/rahowa;* the genre description I quoted is their own. Rahowa's music is distributed by Resistance Records and marketed at *www.resistance.com.* The lyrics of this song begin: "Might was Right when Caesar bled Upon the stones of Rome / Might was Right when Genghis led His hordes over Danube's foam."

25. The singer bellows over a riff that starts with the eighth-note-and-two-sixteenth-notes pattern that was firmly established in the metal imagination by Iron Maiden, followed by a pause on a quarter note; three repetitions of this, all on an open E power chord, then a turnaround of quarter notes on C and A power chords—with the C chord inverted, played as a fourth rather than a fifth, so as to sound nastier. For more on such techniques, see my *Running with the Devil: Power, Gender, and Madness in Heavy Metal Music* (Hanover, N.H.: Wesleyan University Press, 1993).

26. Mitchell Morris, "Musical Virtues," in *Beyond Structural Listening: Postmodern Modes of Hearing,* ed. Andrew Dell'Antonio (Berkeley: University of California Press, forthcoming). See also Charles Taylor, *Sources of the Self: The Making of Modern Identity* (Cambridge, Mass.: Harvard University Press, 1989).

27. Christopher Small, "Why Doesn't the Whole World Love Chamber Music?" *American Music* 19, no. 3 (Fall 2001): 345.

28. This can be seen, for example, in the live performances of December 30 and 31, 1981, in Oakland, California, preserved on Earth, Wind & Fire, *In Concert* (Pioneer Artists, 2000). The punch is much stronger in these and other live performances of the time than it is on the album.

29. e-a-D-G-b-C-a-a#°-B7sus-B7.

30. This motion is especially emphatic in the *In Concert* video.

31. Richard Harrington, "Earth, Wind, & Fire Rekindles the Elements of Its Success," *Los Angeles Times,* September 12, 2001, p. F6.

32. Robin D. G. Kelley, *Freedom Dreams: The Black Radical Imagination* (Boston: Beacon Press, 2002), p. 193. Craig Werner, *A Change Is Gonna Come: Music, Race and the Soul of America* (New York: Plume, 1999), p. 178. Greg Tate, *Flyboy in the Buttermilk: Essays on Contemporary America* (New York: Simon and Schuster, 1992), p. 285.

33. Quoted on the band's Web site, *www.EarthWindAndFire.com.*

21. Unpacking Our Hard Drives

1. Simon Frith, *Sound Effects: Youth, Leisure, and the Politics of Rock 'n' Roll* (New York: Pantheon, 1981), p. 57.
2. Walter Benjamin, "Unpacking My Library: A Talk about Book Collecting," in *Illuminations: Essays and Reflections* (New York: Schocken, 1985), p. 61.
3. Ibid., p. 60.
4. Ibid., p. 67.
5. Ibid., p. 67.
6. McKenzie Wark, "The Property Question: Culture, Economy, Information," Nettime mailing list, February 12, 2002, *amsterdam.nettime.org*.
7. Benjamin, "Unpacking My Library," p. 60.

22. Lost in Music

1. Evan Eisenberg, *The Recording Angel: Music, Records and Culture from Aristotle to Zappa* (London: Picador, 1988).
2. Ian McEwan, "Solid Geometry," in *First Love, Last Rites* (New York: Vintage, 1998 [1975]).
3. Fred Vermorel and Judy Vermorel, *Starlust* (London: W. H. Allen, 1985); *Fandemonium* (London: Omnibus Press, 1990).
4. Jo-Anne Greene, "Long-Lost Punk and Folk Resurface," *Goldmine*, September 21, 2001, p. 28.
5. John Gach, "A Preliminary Inquiry into the Nature of Book Collecting," *Antiquarian Booksellers of America Association Newsletter* 10, Summer 1999.
6. Terry Zwigoff, interview with author, published as "In Between Days," *Village Voice*, July 18–24, 2001.
7. DJ Twist, interview with author, Fall 2001.
8. Jon Savage, liner notes to Saint Etienne, *Foxbase Alpha* (Heavenly, 1991).
9. Bill Drummond, quoted in Simon Reynolds, *Generation Ecstasy: Into the World of Techno and Rave Culture* (New York: Routledge, 1999 [1998]), p. 104.
10. Will Straw, "Exhausted Commodities: The Material Culture of Music," *Canadian Journal of Communication* 25, no. 1 (Winter 2000).
11. Sister Sledge, "Lost in Music" (Atlantic/Cotillion single, 1979).

Words and music by Nile Rodgers and Bernard Edwards. Copyright 1978 by Chic Music Inc.

24. More Rock, Less Talk

1. Anne Middleton Wagner, *Three Artists (Three Women)* (Berkeley: University of California Press, 1996), p. 13.

25. The Persistence of Hair

1. Reproduced verbatim, with editing indicated by brackets, from *http://members.aol.com/eyeremembru/tour2000.html*.
2. When this piece was originally presented, one could poke a little fun at Great White without sounding like an insensitive clod. In February of 2003, in West Warwick, Rhode Island, a rejuvenated Great White played a show at a club called the Station, and something went wrong with the pyrotechnics, and ninety-eight people were killed, including one of the band's guitarists. AP journalists took advantage of the occasion to trot out the old "grunge killed hair" line. There are several strands to pluck from the story of the tragic show in West Warwick, and a terrible sadness hides in almost every corner of it, but *plus ça change*, I guess—the notice in the *Washington Times* concludes: "In fact, the band mates may find themselves playing to bigger audiences. A slight uptick in Great White album sales has been noted since the Feb. 20 tragedy, according to Nielsen SoundScan." Scott Galupo, "Great White an '80s Fade-Out," *Washington Times*, February 23, 2003, p. B5.
3. Reproduced verbatim from *www.sebastianbach.com*.
4. Reproduced verbatim from *http://www.geocities.com/Paris/Cathedral/5540*. Ellipses in the original text. Used by permission.

Contributors

Daphne A. Brooks is an assistant professor of English and African American studies at Princeton University, where she teaches courses on African American literature and culture, performance studies, critical gender studies, and popular music culture. She is currently completing a book entitled *Bodies in Dissent: Performing Race, Gender, and Nation in the Trans-Atlantic Imaginary* (Durham, N.C.: Duke University Press, forthcoming). She is also developing a new project on popular music, historical memory, and cultural surrogation in the post–Civil Rights era.

Carrie Brownstein is a writer and musician from Portland, Oregon. A graduate of Evergreen State College, where she received her degree in sociolinguistics, her writing has appeared in *Index* magazine, *Time Out New York*, and the *Seattle Times*, and she is the author of *Yoshitomo Nara: Nothing Ever Happens* (Museum of Contemporary Art Cleveland / Perceval Press, 2003) and a forthcoming monograph on artist Nikki McClure. She is a guitarist, songwriter, and singer in the rock band Sleater-Kinney.

Stephen Burt teaches literature and poetry writing at Macalester College in St. Paul, Minnesota. He has published a book of poems, *Popular Music* (1999), and a critical study, *Randall Jarrell and His Age* (2003), as well as poems, literary criticism, and rock criticism in various journals, quarterlies, and zines on both sides of the Atlantic.

Robert Christgau, a senior editor at the *Village Voice,* has been a rock critic since 1967. His essays are collected in *Any Old Way You Choose It: Rock and Other Pop Music 1967–1973* (Cooper Square Press) and *Grown Up All Wrong: 75 Great Rock and Pop Artists from*

Vaudeville to Techno (Harvard University Press). Three decades of his "Consumer Guide" columns have been revised and collected in book-length versions available from Da Capo and St. Martin's Griffin, and can also be accessed at *robertchristgau.com*. In 2002 he was a senior fellow at the National Arts Journalism Program, Columbia University.

Joshua Clover, former editor at *liv tyler's sugarhigh!* and founder of the Lettrist International, writes about music, film, books, and politics for the *Village Voice* under at least four different names. He is a professor of literature at the University of California, Davis; his book on *The Matrix* will be published by the British Film Institute in early 2004.

John Darnielle was born in Bloomington, Indiana, grew up in California, and presently tends a garden in Durham, North Carolina. His self-published *Last Plane to Jakarta* welds close-reading strategies to increasingly unlikely musical texts, which isn't nearly as boring as it sounds, but what can you do? What, after all this, can you really do? Nothing, I'd wager. Darnielle is also known as "that guy from the Mountain Goats" and will someday make good on his career-long threat to perform in a clown suit.

Julian Dibbell is the author of *My Tiny Life: Crime and Passion in a Virtual World* and a visiting fellow at Stanford Law School's Center for Internet and Society. He has been writing about digital culture for more than ten years.

Sarah Dougher is a musician and educator who teaches classics and rock and roll in colleges and universities around the Pacific Northwest. She is the program manager for the Rock-n-Roll Camp for Girls in Portland, Oregon, and is working on a book about the coming-out stories of gay rockers. In addition, she is working on a song cycle based on Homer's *Odyssey*. She records for Mr. Lady Records and tours internationally.

Simon Frith is a professor of film and media at Stirling University in Scotland. His books include *The Sociology of Rock, Sound Effects, Music for Pleasure, Art into Pop,* and *Performing Rites* and, as an editor, *Facing the Music, World Music: Politics and Social Change, Music and Copyright, On Record,* and, most recently, *The Cambridge Companion to Rock and Pop.* He is a founding member and ex-chair of the International Association for the Study of Popular Music, and a founding editor of the academic journal *Popular Music.* He chairs the judges of the Mercury Music Prize.

Gary Giddins wrote the "Weather Bird" jazz column for the *Village Voice* from 1973 to 2003. His books include *Satchmo, Faces in the Crowd, Celebrating Bird, Visions of Jazz, Bing Crosby: A Pocketful of Dreams,* and *Weather Bird.*

Chuck Klosterman is the author of *Fargo Rock City: A Heavy Metal Odyssey in Rural North Dakota* and *Sex, Drugs, and Cocoa Puffs: A Low Culture Manifesto.* He is a senior writer for *Spin* magazine and has also contributed to *GQ,* the *New York Times Magazine,* and the *Washington Post.*

Geoffrey O'Brien's books include *Hardboiled America, Dream Time: Chapters from the Sixties, The Phantom Empire, The Browser's Ecstasy: A Meditation on Reading,* and *Castaways of the Image Planet: Movies, Show Business, Public Spectacle.* His poetry has been collected in four books of which the most recent is *A View of Buildings and Water.* A frequent contributor to the *New York Review of Books* and *Artforum,* he lives in Manhattan, where he is editor-in-chief of the Library of America.

Robert Polito directs the Writing Program at the New School. His books include the poetry collection *Doubles, A Reader's Guide to James Merrill's "The Changing Light at Sandover,"* and *Savage Art: A Biography of Jim Thompson,* and he has edited anthologies of noir fiction and *The Selected Poems of Kenneth Fearing* for the Library of America, and editions of Dashiell Hammett and James

M. Cain for Everyman Library. His writing has also appeared in *BOMB, Open City, Threepenny Review, Agni, Artforum, Tin House, Bookforum, Best American Poetry, Best American Movie Writing,* and *About Face,* a retrospective catalog of Manny Farber's paintings.

Ann Powers is a senior curator at Experience Music Project in Seattle. She previously worked as a pop critic for the *New York Times* and was music editor of the *Village Voice,* and has contributed to publications including *Rolling Stone, The Nation, Spin, Vibe, Slate,* and *Salon.* She is the author of *Weird Like Us: My Bohemian America,* a personal history of alternative culture in the 1980s and 1990s. With Evelyn McDonnell, she coedited the anthology *Rock She Wrote: Women Write about Rock, Pop and Rap.* She was once a Ph.D. candidate in English at U.C. Berkeley, but chose journalism over academia—for now.

Tim Quirk spent more than ten years as the singer and lyricist for the punk-pop band Too Much Joy, then politely eased his way into music journalism. He's been a regular contributor to *Raygun,* the *San Francisco Chronicle,* the *San Francisco Bay Guardian, Sassy,* and *Teen.* He's currently executive editor, music, for Real Networks and one half of the electro-pop outfit Wonderlick.

Simon Reynolds is the author of *Blissed Out: The Raptures of Rock* (Serpent's Tail, 1990), *The Sex Revolts: Gender, Rebellion and Rock 'n' Roll* (cowritten with Joy Press; Harvard University Press, 1995), and *Generation Ecstasy: Into the World of Techno and Rave Culture* (Little, Brown, 1998). A freelance contributor to the *New York Times, Village Voice, Spin,* and *The Wire,* he is currently working on a book about postpunk music from 1978 to 1984, to be published by Faber in the United Kingdom and by Viking Penguin in America. He operates the Weblog Blissblog at *http://blissout .blogspot.com* and the homepage Blissout at *http://members.aol .com/blissout/.*

David Sanjek received his Ph.D. in American literature from Washington University in 1985. He has been director of the BMI archives since 1991. In addition to his numerous articles and reviews, he is coauthor, with his late father, Russell Sanjek, of *Pennies from Heaven: The American Popular Music Business in the 20th Century* (DaCapo Press, 1996) and is completing *Always on My Mind: Music, Memory and Money* (Wesleyan University Press). He will amplify his chapter in this volume in his forthcoming book *Gimme Something Real: The Persistence of Authenticity in American Popular Music.* He is a past president of the U.S. branch of the International Association for the Study of Popular Music.

Kelefa Sanneh is a pop critic for the *New York Times.* From 1999 to 2003 he was deputy editor of *Transition* magazine, a pugnacious and funny (at least, that was the idea) journal of race and culture, where he is now a contributing editor. His writing has also appeared in the *New Yorker, Rolling Stone,* the *Village Voice,* the *Source,* and a glossy Indian "lad rag" called *Man's World.*

Luc Sante's books include *Low Life* (1991), *Evidence* (1992), and *The Factory of Facts* (1998). He is the recipient of a Whiting Writer's Award, a Guggenheim Fellowship, an Award in Literature from the American Academy of Arts and Letters, and a Grammy, for album notes, and he is a fellow of the American Academy of Arts and Sciences. He has written for many magazines, has been film critic for *Interview,* book critic for *New York,* and photography critic for the *New Republic.* He teaches at Bard College and lives in Ulster County, New York.

RJ Smith is a senior editor and media critic for *Los Angeles Magazine.* He has been a staff writer for *Spin,* and has written for the *New York Times Magazine, GQ,* and *Grand Royal.* In 1997 he was a visiting scholar at the Getty Research Institute. He is working on a book about African American Los Angeles in the 1940s.

Jason Toynbee is a lecturer at the Institute of Popular Music, University of Liverpool. He has published extensively on popular music, copyright, and creativity. His book *Making Popular Music: Musicians, Creativity and Institutions* (Arnold, 2000) deals, among other things, with the way creative musicians are granted a certain space within the market institutions they depend on. He is currently writing a book on Bob Marley and postcolonialism that highlights Marley's extraordinary status as the only global superstar from a developing country.

Gayle Wald is an associate professor of English at George Washington University and author of *Crossing the Line: Racial Passing in 20th-Century U.S. Literature and Culture* (Duke University Press, 2000). She has published articles on blue-eyed soul singers, Japanese girl pop, boy bands, and riot grrrls. Her current project is *Shout, Sister, Shout: Rosetta Tharpe, American Music, and African-American Vernacular Culture.*

Robert Walser is professor and chair of musicology at the University of California, Los Angeles. He earned doctorates in both performance and musicology and specializes in American music, especially jazz and other popular musics. He is the author of *Keeping Time: Readings in Jazz History* (Oxford, 1999) and *Running with the Devil: Power, Gender, and Madness in Heavy Metal Music* (Wesleyan, 1993). A coeditor of the Music/Culture Series published by Wesleyan University Press, he is currently president of the U.S. branch of the International Association for the Study of Popular Music.

Deena Weinstein, playing both sides of the street—rock criticism and cultural studies—supplements academic analyses of popular culture with experiences garnered from her career as a rock critic. She has written numerous scholarly articles, book chapters, and books, including *Heavy Metal: The Music and Its Culture.* She has also published scores of features, interviews, and album reviews. As professor of sociology at DePaul University,

Weinstein teaches courses in the sociology of rock music and rock criticism. Beyond cultural studies, she has done scholarly work on the interface between modernist and postmodernist critical theory, and on opposition to organizational authority.

Eric Weisbard is a senior program manager in the Education Department at Experience Music Project, where he organizes the annual Pop Conference, edits book projects, works on radio programs, and curates exhibits, including "Disco: A Decade of Saturday Nights." Before coming to EMP, he pursued a Ph.D. in history at U.C. Berkeley, then dropped out to become a senior editor at *Spin*, edit the *Spin Alternative Record Guide* (1995), serve as music editor at the *Village Voice*, and write for numerous publications.

Douglas Wolk writes about music and comic books for the *Village Voice, Spin, Rolling Stone, Publishers Weekly*, and elsewhere. He is the author of *Live at the Apollo* (Continuum Books, forthcoming), runs the tiny record label Dark Beloved Cloud, plays bass in a couple of new wave bands, and lives in Portland, Oregon.

Acknowledgments

Experience Music Project is a great place to work because the beliefs that underpin this book—that popular music is a serious intellectual subject, but that pursuing that subject ought to be a blast—are taken as a given. Director and CEO Bob Santelli, himself from both a university and a scribe background, dreamed of doing a pop studies conference from his arrival at EMP and never wavered in his support. Dan Cavicchi, my predecessor in EMP's education department, took the initial steps in organizing the event and then became an enthusiastic collaborator as the focus shifted, the "academic" yin to my "journalistic" yang.

The EMP staff's pride in running the Pop Conference each year has made a difficult organizational task almost seem easy. In particular, Shannon O'Hara has coordinated many of the conference details, creating a structure where none existed and making all the participants feel unusually welcome. Financial support for the Pop Conference, and for this book, came from The Allen Foundation for Music, which constantly enriches the cultural life of the Pacific Northwest. Thanks, too, to EMP's collaborators in the grant: Shannon Dudley and the other faculty and students at the University of Washington School of Music, and Tom Mara and his team at community radio station KEXP.

Our program committee the first year included Harris Berger, Jonathan Bernard, Rob Bowman, Dan, Robert Christgau, Andre Millard, Robert Polito, Patricia Shehan Campbell, and Carol Vernalis. Polito and Christgau, in particular, reached out to many writers, convincing people with little sense of EMP to take a chance on a fledgling gathering. It wasn't always easy for the committee, sifting through proposals that represented such a vast range of attitudes toward good writing. But the spirit that prevailed, of finding common ground and enjoying the differences for what they were, was an early hint that we were on the right track.

The conference itself, which involved about a hundred presenters and thirty-plus panels, fed on the giddiness of the participants and inspired EMP to make the event an annual affair. Thanks to all who took part: the quality and energy of the talks impressed even those who'd attended with barely veiled skepticism. Unfortunately, the demands of keeping this book at a readable length has precluded the inclusion of much superb work.

Lindsay Waters of Harvard University Press got on the plane at the last minute, attended the conference, and raved that what we were doing was just what academia needed to be hearing. Throughout the process of crafting this book, he's been a terrific co-conspirator. Sarah Lazin agented the project as a labor of love. The writers were wonderfully patient as we sorted out our intent for the manuscript: no simple task. In many cases, they've been my sounding board, the editor's editor. But none more so than Ann Powers, my wife, fellow EMP employee, and biggest inspiration in what it means to write from both the head and the heart.

Eric Weisbard

Index